The Scholarship & Financial Aid Solution

How to Go to College for Next to Nothing with Short Cuts, Tricks, and Tips from Start to Finish

By Debra Lipphardt

THE SCHOLARSHIP & FINANICAL AID HANDBOOK: HOW TO GO TO COLLEGE FOR NEXT TO NOTHING WITH SHORT CUTS, TRICKS, AND TIPS FROM START TO FINISH

Copyright © 2007 by Atlantic Publishing Group, Inc.
1405 SW 6th Ave. • Ocala, Florida 34471 • 800-814-1132 • 352-622-1875–Fax
Web site: www.atlantic-pub.com • E-mail: sales@atlantic-pub.com
SAN Number: 268-1250

ISBN-13: 978-1-60138-261-0   ISBN-10: 1-60138-261-8

Library of Congress Cataloging-in-Publication Data

Lipphardt, Debra, 1954-
  The scholarship & financial aid solution : how to go to college for
next to nothing with short cuts, tricks, and tips from start to finish /
by Debra Lipphardt.
      p. cm.
  Includes bibliographical references and index.
  ISBN-13: 978-1-60138-261-0 (alk. paper)
  ISBN-10: 1-60138-261-8 (alk. paper)
  1. Scholarships--United States--Handbooks, manuals, etc. 2. Student
aid--United States--Handbooks, manuals, etc. I. Title. II. Title:
Scholarship and financial aid solution.

  LB2338.L57 2008
  378.3'4--dc22
                          200800013

Printed on Recycled Paper

INTERIOR LAYOUT DESIGN: Vickie Taylor • vtaylor@atlantic-pub.com

Printed in the United States

"The world of scholarships is huge, and the possibilities to excel are endless. Mrs. Lipphardt knows all the tips and secrets to success. She is, without a doubt, The Scholarship Queen, which gives her the experience to write this book."

Katherine Stewart
Vanguard High School
Class of 2007

"What Debra Lipphardt excels most in and finds sublime happiness in is scholarship counseling. One thing is for sure: Her knowledge on this topic is vast and incomparable to any other. She has received awards, honors, and numerous distinctions in this area, which shows her proficiency. Her work has allowed countless students to attend college, when before it was unimaginable. I hope everyone across the nation can take advantage of the knowledge she shares in her book."

Cheri Cox
Vanguard High School
Class of 2004
Florida State University, Sports Management and
Business

"A much needed resource for students and parents! Good information given with a hands-on understanding!"

Deb Chappell Bond
Educational Consultant & College Admissions
Guidance Counselor
Ocala, Florida

We recently lost our beloved pet "Bear," who was not only our best and dearest friend but also the "Vice President of Sunshine" here at Atlantic Publishing. He did not receive a salary but worked tirelessly 24 hours a day to please his parents. Bear was a rescue dog that turned around and showered myself, my wife Sherri, his grandparents Jean, Bob and Nancy and every person and animal he met (maybe not rabbits) with friendship and love. He made a lot of people smile every day.

We wanted you to know that a portion of the profits of this book will be donated to The Humane Society of the United States.

–Douglas & Sherri Brown

THE HUMANE SOCIETY OF THE UNITED STATES ©

The human-animal bond is as old as human history. We cherish our animal companions for their unconditional affection and acceptance. We feel a thrill when we glimpse wild creatures in their natural habitat or in our own backyard.

Unfortunately, the human-animal bond has at times been weakened. Humans have exploited some animal species to the point of extinction.

The Humane Society of the United States makes a difference in the lives of animals here at home and worldwide. The HSUS is dedicated to creating a world where our relationship with animals is guided by compassion. We seek a truly humane society in which animals are respected for their intrinsic value, and where the human-animal bond is strong.

Want to help animals? We have plenty of suggestions. Adopt a pet from a local shelter, join The Humane Society and be a part of our work to help companion animals and wildlife. You will be funding our educational, legislative, investigative and outreach projects in the U.S. and across the globe.

Or perhaps you'd like to make a memorial donation in honor of a pet, friend or relative? You can through our Kindred Spirits program. And if you'd like to contribute in a more structured way, our Planned Giving Office has suggestions about estate planning, annuities, and even gifts of stock that avoid capital gains taxes.

Maybe you have land that you would like to preserve as a lasting habitat for wildlife. Our Wildlife Land Trust can help you. Perhaps the land you want to share is a backyard—that's enough. Our Urban Wildlife Sanctuary Program will show you how to create a habitat for your wild neighbors.

So you see, it's easy to help animals. And The HSUS is here to help.

The Humane Society of the United States
2100 L Street NW
Washington, DC 20037
202-452-1100
www.hsus.org

DEDICATION

I would like to dedicate this book first to all of the hundreds and hundreds of students who have touched my life. Getting to know you and watch you grow into young adults is something that will be with me forever. Whether I had the opportunity to assist you in scholarships, careers, colleges, or just to talk to you, all of you will always have a special place in my heart. If it was not for you, this book would never have been written. And to those of you who had such faith in me during the past two years, thanks so much for your belief in me.

And to my family — my husband Jim and my wonderful children Jessica and Michael — I just want to thank you three for putting up with all my late nights of working on scholarships and this book and for all your love and understanding. And thanks to my mom, Joanne, and my sister, Mary Lou, who have always encouraged my writing and my dreams. And to my Aunt Lois for always asking how it was going, along with all my walks and talks with Jeanine, and to all the rest of my very good friends, young and old, who all believed in me and my desire to write this book.

And lastly, Dad, thank you for teaching me to face life's challenges with unwavering determination; "to dream the impossible dream and to reach the unreachable star."

Thanks to all of you — I love you!

TABLE OF CONTENTS

INTRODUCTION

I have always enjoyed writing short stories and have entertained the thought of writing a novel one day. But my idea of writing always leaned toward fairy tales and suspense. So what is my first attempt at an actual book? A non-fiction book about scholarships – a big surprise to me! I have always read that, when writing, you should write about something you are familiar with and something you enjoy. Well, I love working with scholarships, have done a lot of research, and I have given countless lectures and workshops on them. When deciding to finally start my great American novel, I sat down and started this book. So much for fairy tales, but the endings are both happily ever after.

I am writing this book not only for the students, but also as a guide for parents and other school personnel to assist them in aiding the students with scholarships. This comes from me – first, as a mom with a 21- and 25-year-old, (one still a college student and the other a college graduate) and also as a College and Career Center Specialist/Scholarship Coordinator.

My awareness of scholarships started while I was working in the guidance office in a local high school. A few scholarship applications and advertisements would come in the mail and they intrigued me. No one had ever talked about scholarships with me when I was in high school, so my curiosity and questions began. How much could students actually benefit from these scholarships? Were they easy to obtain? How do the students apply?

There seemed to be quite a variety of requirements, each application different from the other. I began to investigate the different scholarships and applications that came in, looking anywhere possible to find even more. Much to my surprise, there were a lot more out there than I could ever imagine. As my position changed to College and Career Center Specialist, I was able to add Scholarship Coordinator to my title and work even more with the students in this capacity. I more or less created this position on my own, as my actual job did not include the working with scholarships to the extent that I do. Much of the work is done on my own time at home – time that I give freely because I love doing it.

After finding so many different scholarships, I then started looking for eligible students to apply, matching them up with each type of scholarship, and encouraging them to apply. Many times I would – and still do – encourage, beg, or nag the students to apply, whichever one works. When they actually started winning money for college through scholarships, I was excited, and from then on I started looking for even more scholarships on my own.

I discovered that there were scholarship opportunities

everywhere. I found them in stores, heard about them on the radio, and read about them in the newspaper and at the public library. I found free Web site searches and started doing searches, under different names, genders, races, and college majors. Many times I felt as if I had inherited multiple personalities with the variety of searches I did. I also found plenty of searches that will charge a fee to search for you, which needs to be avoided, but this will be further explained in Chapter 12 on scams.

As the Scholarship Coordinator, I have had a yearly scholarship workshop for the past five years. I have lectured at various clubs, churches, parent workshops, and organizations locally, and have been interviewed several times by local radio stations. I have received various awards, including County School Employee of the Year – twice – local club awards, and several Veterans of Foreign Wars (VFW) awards through my work.

I have worked with students and scholarships for the past 11 years, and our high school, one of six in the county, has won the most awards each year, with the exception of one year when we were in a very close race for first place. In fact, my school and seniors did so well the past two years that we won 47 awards at the County Awards Night in 2006, with the second place school winning 15. In 2007 we won 49 awards, with the second place school winning 17 awards! The seniors at our school have averaged over two million dollars worth of scholarship money each year. The past five years they have averaged close to three million dollars per year. This consists of all the different scholarships, including athletics and the Florida Bright Futures scholarships.

The joy and thrill I felt whenever any of my students would come in and tell me they had received a scholarship was, and still is, one of my greatest pleasures. I have had numerous students come up to me, years after graduation, thanking me for all my assistance and for helping make it possible for them to go to college and make a better life for themselves. Their thanks makes it all worthwhile.

My own children also benefited from what I have learned. In the beginning, when I first discovered the wonderful world of scholarships, they were only in elementary and middle school. At that time, I had not even thought of how all this would affect them. Little did I know that my work would pay off when it was their turn to apply for scholarships.

My daughter won enough money to pay for tuition and books for her first two years and still had money left over to go toward years three and four. My son, four years later, was also able to put money in the bank for his first two years of college. I had to keep after them to apply for just about any application they were eligible for, and they did. They both were in the top 20 percent of their class, with average ACT scores, more than 100 hours of community service, and more involvement in sports than in clubs. Many other students they competed against had even higher grades, test scores, and more community service, yet my son and my daughter still won, sometimes just because of their answer to the essay question.

I cannot guarantee that everyone will win a scholarship, but I have found out that just about everyone has a chance. The odds are higher, of course, if you have above average grades, extracurricular activities, and volunteer hours, as you will have more applications available to you.

One of my most moving experiences involved a young student with a slightly less than average grade point average. He came from an extremely impoverished background, living in a harsh and very disadvantaged neighborhood. This young man had a great personality, and we talked often about his outlook on life and dreams for his future. There was only one problem: There was very little money to help him achieve his goals. There was a women's club that gave out scholarships each year, but these were for females only. I worked with the head of the scholarship committee, and one day she approached me and said they would like to give a scholarship that year to a male student instead of the usual female. She asked if I had any suggestions. I told her about the young man I had come to know and what a great person he was. I felt that giving him a scholarship could make a world of difference. Not only did they award him a $2,000 scholarship, but because he was doing so well, they renewed it the following year. Two years later I ran into him, and he was working his way through college with the help of his scholarships. He greeted me with delight, and as I introduced him to my mother and sister, he sat down and started to talk to them about me. He told them that, without the aid of the scholarship money, he would have never left his neighborhood. That money made all the difference in the world to him. Furthering his education, and my faith in him, helped him get where he was. I know that he probably could have made something of himself without me because he is such a great person, but he made me feel that, perhaps, I had helped to make a difference in his life. That feeling was one of the most rewarding experiences in my life. His enthusiasm made me want to help even more students win scholarships and achieve their dreams. Hopefully, this book will assist you and others in winning money for college, too.

Chapter 1

SCHOLARSHIP INTRODUCTION

The majority of scholarships are available to students during their senior year of high school. Unfortunately, too many adults expect students to take on the responsibility and do it all themselves. Even the most mature seniors I have met still manage to catch that age-old disease of "senioritis." Many seniors realize, when it is too late, that slowing down can be hazardous to their financial status in college. It is a very confusing time in their lives; they are on the verge of growing up, but they still do not understand the true meaning of being an adult. They are only beginning the journey to adulthood. They still not only need some guidance, but also the nagging from their parents and other adults. You can help them with scholarships by urging your students to keep looking for ones they are eligible for and to turn them in on time. It does not hurt to help with ideas, perhaps even type up an essay or two that they have written, and proofread the work for grammatical errors. Your support will help them go a lot further. The parents, and even some teachers, need to remember that they are still children and still need direction.

Many seniors and many of their parents do not realize the very real cost of college. I have had many students tell me that their college is all paid for, either through the Florida Bright Futures scholarships (which is a program Florida has for its students who will be attending a Florida college or university) or through the International Baccalaureate Program. The Florida Bright Futures helps students get between 75 and 100 percent of their tuition paid for if they attend a public college in Florida. They have to meet certain criteria, such as grades, classes taken, and ACT or SAT scores, and then they qualify. The International Baccalaureate (IB) students can earn a full tuition scholarship in Florida with their IB diploma. Everyone should check with their guidance counselors to see if their own state has something similar (see Chapter 10).

These programs, however, only provide tuition for up to four years, and in the case of IB students, until they earn a Bachelor's degree. If they are planning on going for their Master's or graduate degree, the tuition is no longer covered. The point is that it is not a full ride; it is for tuition only. The most expensive cost of college is room and board. When you have to pay for your room and board, books, and other fees besides tuition, this is where it really gets costly.

The cost of a college education, like everything else, keeps escalating. Unfortunately, tuition for a public university or college is only a small portion of the total costs. Room and board can triple the amount of tuition. Right now, a public college (if you are a resident of that state) averages around $3,500 per year, books average between $500 to $1,000 per year, and room and board averages around $8,000 or more per year.

College is expensive, but it is still possible through many different avenues. There are scholarships – local, state, and national – and there are state and federal grants. There are also federal loans with a low interest rate. But loans should be used as a last resort only. Free money that you do not have to pay back is the best way to go.

There are so many different types of scholarships. They are possible to obtain with research and determination. The main ingredient to winning scholarships is "apply and apply, again and again." Do not give up. It is not a guarantee that everyone will win a scholarship, but you will definitely lose out if you do not even try. Not one student can walk away from my room without at least two or three different applications, no matter what their grades are or what their outside school involvement is.

In the following chapters, I will discuss scholarship requirements, where to find them, and how to fill out applications. I will also go over a résumé you can use with the applications, tips on essays and letters of recommendations, and shortcuts in filling out the applications. Throughout this book, I will repeat some of the information in different ways and more in depth. I cannot help but believe that the more you hear or read something, the more attention you will pay to it. Also, while this book was written for students, as well as parents or other concerned adults, but when it gets down to the actual process of the scholarship application, the student must do the follow up work and the actual applying.

Chapter 2

DIFFERENT TYPES OF GENERAL SCHOLARSHIPS & DEFINITIONS

There are so many different scholarships, and each has different requirements. The most common ones are based on a combination of academics, awards and honors, SAT and/or ACT test scores, extracurricular activities, and community service. Then there are the scholarships that are based only on community service or those that are awarded just for an essay written by the student. There are also ones based on the major the student has chosen, and then there are those that are based on financial need.

When an application states that it is for a specific requirement only, such as volunteer, academic, leadership, or extracurricular, you must have experience in whichever subject they are looking for to be eligible. But many times the scholarships are general and will overlook the fact that one area is lacking if you spend most of your time with another one. For example, you may have only a few hours volunteer work because you are involved in sports, or you may work. This is taken into consideration on many scholarships because it still shows student involvement.

The same goes for the work experience question. You may have many community service hours and have a lot of other extracurricular involvement and not have time to have a job. The main thing many scholarships are looking for is some type of outside involvement, beyond the regular school day.

Before going any further, I will explain and define the most common requirements in more detail. Then, later in the book (Chapters 5 and 6), you can use this information to help you fill out the scholarship applications.

ACADEMICS

Academics include your overall grade point average (GPA) during your high school years, generally ninth through twelfth grades, and your test scores, generally the SAT and/or the ACT.

If a student has strong grades for all four years, this is excellent. Many times it takes a year or two for the student to realize how important grades are to their future. However, this "growing up process" can also be taken into consideration, if the student improves drastically during the last two or three years. They can write an explanation about their attitude and why it has changed or their views on the importance of grades in some of the required essays.

There are also more difficult obstacles that many students have to overcome, such as a learning impairment, divorce, or a death in the family. These are some of the tribulations that can definitely affect a student's grades, and this is the time for you, the student, to let the scholarship committee know of these obstacles, not for pity, but to see how you overcame and dealt with these problems.

Your SAT and/or ACT scores will also fall under academics. You can take one or both of these college prep tests, and these scores will be on your transcripts.

A very common requirement for most applications is the need for an official transcript to prove your grades and test scores. You usually get these from your guidance office. They will include all your high school classes and grades, your test scores, and sometimes your activities and service hours. They will come in a sealed envelope. If you open it, the transcript will no longer be official. If the application does not require an official transcript, they usually have a place for your guidance counselor to sign for verification of your grades and test scores.

AWARDS AND HONORS

Awards and Honors vary. Some applications will ask for any awards or honors, while others will ask for Academic Awards and Honors, and Non-Academic Awards and Honors.

Academic Awards would include the type of classes you have taken, whether it is Honors or Advanced Placement (AP) classes, the International Baccalaureate Program, or even a class that may pertain to your major (such as teacher assisting classes for those going into education or health classes for those planning on going into the medical field).

Other academic awards include class rank or whether the student is graduating with Honors, High Honors, or Highest Honors (refer to Chapter 4, under Education). You can list this as "will graduate with Honors," or if you are close but unsure, you can list it as, "plan to graduate with Honors." Even if the student's grades are average, but below a 3.0, and they have been on the honor roll a few times, they can list "honor roll" as one of their academic awards. If the student took Honors or AP classes, they can write that as "Various Honors and/or AP classes." There will be more detail on this in Chapters 4 and 5.

Being a member of the National Honors Society is also an academic award. Even though it is also membership in an organization, it needs to go under awards, as the student has to be invited to be a member because of his or her academic (and, in some schools, discipline) history. We have a math club, Mu Alpha Theta, at our school that would need to be listed as an academic award, as you must get an invitation to become a member. If you were invited to be in one of these academic honors clubs and declined, you may still list it, but only as a nominee. Just remember that being a nominee is not as strong as being a member.

You should include any type of positions you may have been selected for as a result of your grades. Students need to keep track of any type of award they receive in high school, including class awards (Math, Science, English, and so on) and any they may have received in the mail, such as National Honor Roll and even Who's Who Among American High School Students. The last two are not always considered as one of the top awards, but it is still an award, as some teacher had to take the time to send in the student's name and address to honor that student.

My son was nominated to participate in the National Defense Intelligence Agency Forum. It would have been a wonderful experience, but it cost around $2,000 to go. However, he still put it under academic awards and honors on his applications because someone thought enough of him to nominate him.

Non-Academic Awards would include being a captain of a team, an officer of a club, being on the varsity team, and any other awards the student may have received from a sport, club, or even from an organization he or she volunteered for. Being an officer, a captain, or even on the varsity team, also leads into another skill that scholarships ask about: leadership.

LEADERSHIP

Leadership skills are not asked for on all scholarship applications, yet you will see it several times. You need to really think about this, as leadership can be demonstrated in many different ways.

Our city has a Leadership Youth Board that the student has to first be nominated for, and then they have to be interviewed to be selected. They also have to have a certain GPA and no discipline record. This position would go under leadership, unless there is no space for leadership, in which case it would go under the academic awards.

Being an officer of a club, a captain on a team, on a varsity team, or a member of student council or government all are obvious leadership positions, but there are other types as well. You might have worked on a committee to plan something, helped coach a younger team, tutored someone, or even taken care of younger children. In many of these situations your leadership skill is setting an example for others. You could have helped organize something in one of your classes or just taken the lead in something that helped make a difference, even a small one. All these are qualities of leadership. So think hard; you may have used some leadership skills that you did not even realize you were using at the time.

TEST SCORES

SAT and/or ACT scores are a very common question on the majority of scholarship applications. There is a CPT test in Florida that can be taken in place of the SAT or ACT but only for community colleges. Many students prefer to take this rather than the SAT or ACT, as is seems easier and is less expensive, but I have yet to see it included as one of the questions on any scholarship application. I always urge the students to start taking the SAT or ACT, not only for college entrance and the Florida Bright Futures, but for scholarship applications as well.

These tests can be costly, as most students need to take them more than once. For those with low incomes, there are waivers that can be used (usually one per year). You need to visit your guidance counselor to see if you qualify.

You do not have to have the highest scores to win the scholarships, as many other factors are considered. It does show that you are serious about going on to college. However, if the scholarship is based mainly on academics or if you are applying for any national academic type of scholarship, the higher the score, the better chance you will have to win.

The main difference between the two tests is that the SAT is divided into Math and Verbal, while the ACT is divided into Math, Reading, Verbal, and Science. The common factor is that they both now have a written essay included. I always encourage my students to take both of these college prep tests because it is a good idea to see which one you did better on, as most students tend to score higher on one. Then, if you need to retake it for higher scores, you can concentrate on the one you did the best on. Many times students who test well on math tend to do better on the SAT. Some students, though, will score high on both tests.

Another difference is if you answer a question incorrectly on the SAT, it counts **more against you** than leaving it blank. However, an incorrect answer on the ACT is the **same** as a blank answer.

EXTRACURRICULAR ACTIVITIES

Extracurricular Activities include a variety of different things. They show dedication and commitment to an organization of some type and involvement beyond the required school courses and hours. They also show that you most likely will grow up to be a productive and caring member of your community. Extracurricular activities include clubs – in your school or in your community –sports – also inside and outside of school – being a member of your student government or a class representative, or if you participate in a church youth group or choir. I would even include lessons, such as music, dancing, and acting, as well as any competitions you might take part in, such as Motocross racing or gymnastics. All these are types of commitments.

You could even count belonging to the school band or being in the ROTC as an extracurricular activity, as both of these have many hours of participation outside the classroom. Many students belong to concert bands outside their school, which also counts as extracurricular and volunteering. You should always list the number of years you belonged and any positions or offices you may have held (this refers back to leadership). Include any type of awards you may have received as part of that club or sport, unless you listed that award somewhere else on the application. Repetition is not a good thing on applications, unless it stresses an important point about something. All this will be discussed again in Chapters 4 and 5.

There are usually service clubs or academic clubs in most schools that students can join. There are some clubs, though, that not just everyone can join. Many clubs have a "cap," meaning there is only a certain number that can be members. You can always start your own club with a new set of bylaws, which include what it requires to be a member (founding a club such as this would also be an example of leadership skills).

A wonderful example of this is a club that I sponsor at my school. There was a need for a club that anyone could join so that they could have the experience and be able to do some community service. Five girls got together and came up with some simple bylaws for a club that would not exclude anyone. You have to have at least a 2.0 GPA, attend one of two meetings a month, commit to two hours of community service per month, and there would be no cap. The club, called the Pink Ladies Service Club (from John Travolta's movie, *Grease*), was created with over 150 members. We started out helping with all the concession stands at home games, but now are involved in many community activities. It is now the largest and most active club at our school and is recognized by the community as a full-fledged service club. This club has taught many of the students leadership skills as well. We even give out our own scholarships to senior members, and many of them have won several other scholarships due to their participation and community service with our club.

We have also had other students start small clubs at our school with something that interests them, such as an Environment Club (cleaning up the community), a Cancer Aid Club, an Alzheimer's Club, and a Chemistry Club. Take something that you want to become involved in, talk to some friends, and then go to your student activity director or the principal to get started.

The main thing to remember is that an extracurricular activity is any type of organization you belong to and that you are an active participant. You do not need to be the leader to be a good member. Most organizations are also a good way to become involved in community service.

COMMUNITY (OR VOLUNTEER) SERVICE

Community (or Volunteer) Service involves helping a nonprofit organization or needy individuals and you do not get paid for it. Family does not count, and I also have had to tell several students that "community service" given to them from a judge is not voluntary; therefore, it does not count toward volunteer hours.

There are numerous ways to get your volunteer hours. There are so many different places that need your help, and you can pick and choose the one that is right for you. For example, if you feel that you want to go into the medical field, you should volunteer at a hospital or clinic. Even if you volunteer at a doctor's, veterinarian's, or dentist's office, (which are for-profit organizations) list it, as most scholarship committees will still take it into consideration, and it also shows that you are serious about that career choice.

Church is also a great type of community service. You could be part of the choir, usher, help with the lights, or maybe teach Sunday school. All this helping at your church counts for community service hours, but attending church and listening to the sermon does not.

Often students have more of these hours than they realize. The second year that I became involved in scholarships, I approached a young man who was not only ranked fifth in his class, but had extremely high test scores (he only missed one question on his SATs), yet he had never applied for any scholarships. I was talking to him one day, discussing his academics, and asked him why he had never picked up any scholarship applications. He told me that he did not belong to any clubs and had never participated in any sports, so he felt he was ineligible. When I asked what he did in his spare time, he told me that all his free time was spent at church, and he even had a sidewalk Sunday school that went to several of the poorer parts of our town every Sunday. I got excited when I learned this and told him that his church involvement was a great type of community service. He then shared with me that he had never thought of it that way, that it was just his way of giving what he had learned to others, and was a natural part of his life, not volunteer work. His way of thinking was very unselfish, but fortunately scholarship committees do think of helping your church as a type of volunteer service. He started applying for scholarships, and when our county had their annual awards night, he won so many that they jokingly wanted to rename that night after him.

There are so many worthwhile places to give your time, and you really get back so much more than just volunteer hours. Most students will share with me the great feeling they get when they help others. To know that you can make a difference somehow, even if it is only a small dent, can give you a wonderful feeling. I have met so many amazing students that do fantastic things, and it really helps me know that our future is in good hands. Volunteering is an excellent life learning experience for all.

Whether you help a Girl Scout or Boy Scout troop, the Explorers, Habitat for Humanity, the Humane Society, an environmental group, a local school, a museum, the Salvation Army, the American Cancer Society, any similar health organizations, or even entertain for the benefit of something, there are so many avenues for you to venture into. This is also a good time to experiment with your career choices. Many students have found a path to follow through volunteering. I tell my students that, if you find somewhere to volunteer that interests you, you will only want to do more, and it becomes a normal part of your life.

You also need to include any hours you spend helping out your clubs or any other organization you belong to. This would include preparing for the meetings or practicing for the play or presentation. Another good example of volunteering that you may include is being an officer of a club. The student can log the hours of organization time under the club name, but separately from the required hours, as many scholarships want to see hours beyond what was required by the organization. A student who is an officer was elected; it is not a required position.

When listing your volunteer hours on any scholarship application, list the required hours (for example, two hours monthly and the number of years), but under that, list the hours you spent planning, organizing, and delegating as an officer. You would not believe the number of hours it takes to organize just one project. You can also list different projects you may have worked on, especially if they required a lot of hours, separately and not under the club, unless it was a requirement of the club.

There are many scholarships that are interested only in the volunteer work a student has done. These usually do not ask for grades or for extracurricular activities or financial status. This kind of scholarship is great for those so involved in community service that they do not have time for much else. They usually have you write an essay on the volunteering and what effects it had on whoever you helped or on yourself. Grades do not play a factor in most of these.

Then there are the scholarships that, though they are based mainly on community service, they also take into some consideration the grades and extracurricular activities. When there are students who are close (competition-wise) in community service, the grades or other activities may be what influences the final decision.

It is extremely important to keep track of all your hours you spend with whatever community service you do. In our school, you turn in your hours (signed by someone you worked for) to our Student Activity Director, and she puts it into the computer so that it is documented on your transcripts. Just make sure that you keep some type of log to document all your hours and what it was for. Remember that you need to count planning time (such as putting together a project or even Sunday school plans for a class), time spent traveling to and from the volunteer destination, and the actual hours you are there helping. All these hours count. Keep track of all your hours and the years you did them. There are a select few scholarships that want your hours during a certain time period. Another reason to list the number of years is, if you have hundreds of hours, such as 350, it sounds more feasible that it was done over two or three years, instead of during just one year.

Refer to Chapter 4 on Résumés, for more examples on Academics, Awards and Honors (Academic and Non-Academic) Extracurricular Activities, and Volunteer Experience.

ESSAYS

There are also many scholarships that are based on

essays. Almost all scholarship applications have an essay question. As a senior, these essays are mainly ones from your thoughts and from your heart, not research essays. The most common one is: What are your education and career goals? This can be anywhere from 100 to 500 words, depending on the application. I have also seen several on the importance of helping others. I have also seen "Service Above Self," "How Can One Person Make a Difference," and "Why is Volunteering Important?" All these are basically the same essay, just reworded a little bit. Another common essay that I have been seeing more lately is one on a person who has made an impact on your life, another one that is based on your opinion more than anything.

There are also many scholarships with an essay question being the only criteria. These are the types that anyone can apply for. They do not require a certain GPA, community service, or extracurricular activities. They are based solely on the essay itself. Some may involve a little research, but many are just common sense essays. They may be on the career the student is planning or why education is important. There have been essays on how a realtor helps his community, how fire sprinklers help, or on someone who has impacted your life. These are for the students that have lower GPAs or even the ones who have to work and have no time for community service or extracurricular activities.

Remember that most students do not like to write essays, especially the ones that require extra work. If you are required to read a book or do research for the essay, you know that this cuts the competition way down.

You need to remember, on most essays, to write from the

heart, but for more information on how to write an essay, see Chapter 7.

FINANCIAL NEED

There are scholarships based solely on financial need. Some just want to know the family's income, but unlike the Pell Grant from the FAFSA (see Chapter 10), many will ask about extenuating circumstances, which vary from family to family. It could be a change in one of the parents' jobs, your parents might have recently separated or divorced, maybe there have been some extra medical bills, or maybe a grandparent recently moved in with you, but they all fall under unusual financial circumstances or financial need with circumstances. Sometimes the school costs and types of education (two years versus six or more and public schools versus private schools) will count toward the need. There are also those applications that look at financial need, but it only counts as a small percentage in the overall picture. For example, if the student has high credentials in other areas, such as volunteer service and grades, this may outweigh the financial need criteria. I have seen students that did not really have as much financial need as others win because they had higher points in all other areas.

There is also the Free Application for Federal Student Aid (FAFSA) for students going to college, based only on family and the student's income (this is discussed more in Chapter 10).

MINORITY SCHOLARSHIPS

Minority scholarships vary. Some are for African Americans

only, some for Native Indians, Asians, and Hispanics. The most commonly seen minority scholarships are for African Americans first and then Hispanics. However, Asians are becoming included more as the years pass. There are also several for Native Americans, but most of those are given out by the actual Indian tribe, and you usually have to have a Tribal Card to apply. You can go online to find your tribe's official site and contact them about becoming a member.

Most of these scholarships can be found online, but many of the local ones come from different organizations or even ones for certain majors. We have several African American sororities in our town that offer scholarships for females and a local NAACP that offers them also. We have an American Spanish Club that has scholarships for Hispanic students only. Our community college even has one for the African American student with the highest GPA from each high school in our county, and one for African American males who will be majoring in education. There are also many universities that offer minority scholarships.

Several of the scholarship applications that require a particular major also offer them specifically for a minority student, as they need more minority employees in that career field. There are even some for females of any race, listed as a minority. It is best to have your race on your official transcripts, as it is more proof of your heritage.

SCHOLARSHIPS BASED ON MAJORS

There are scholarships based on the student's planned major. The word "planned" is used because it is understood that many students will change their majors while in college, some even before they start, but everyone needs to have a "planned major." Remember that the most common essay during the senior year is education and career goals. So even if the student is not completely sure of a major, they must have one that at least interests them, so they can write with feeling about it.

One important thing I feel I need to point out, relating to your major and saving money, is that the earlier a student can find a major, the sooner they can start taking classes toward that major. You can actually start taking some classes toward your major during your first two years of college in place of electives. But changing your major gets more critical and costly the further along you are in your schooling. If you do a complete change during your junior or senior year of college, you will most likely have to backtrack and take other classes, and this could add another year or two to your degree. That is where it gets more costly. So try to explore all your options before your junior year in college, through research, interning, or volunteering in the different fields that interest you.

> *"[Mrs. Lipphardt] helped me win almost all my scholarships, and she pushed me to do more when I got discouraged. Although no one in my family has attended college, it is an honor to have met Debra Lipphardt because she has shown me that there is hope for everyone."*

> **Brianna Tanner**
> **Vanguard High School**
> **Class of 2007**

Some of the scholarships that require a certain major are from a company or organization that specializes in that particular field and may even be a foot in the door for the winners. Many of these have an awards ceremony of some type to meet the recipient of their scholarship. But most of them will never even see the student again, so they do not keep track of the student once they have awarded them the scholarship. However, there are a few that are renewable while the student is in college, as long as the major stays the same. Using your major can come in handy in another way also, which I will discuss in Chapter 3.

UNUSUAL SCHOLARSHIPS

Last but not least there are the "unusual" scholarships that everyone talks about. Unfortunately, no one knows the exact name of them or how to find them. A good example of this is the scholarship for left-handed people. I have had so many students and parents ask me about a left-handed scholarship. A college representative even brought it up during a presentation, but no one, not even the representative, could tell me where they heard it from or the name of it so that I could search for it; they just knew it existed. I looked all over for this on the Internet and in scholarship books and still could not find it. In fact, on all the different scholarship search programs I used, I never even came across a question asking which hand you used. Finally, after much research, I found it at the public library. Unfortunately, the scholarship was for a particular college in Pennsylvania only, meaning you first had to attend that school to qualify. So yes, there are probably many unusual scholarships out there, but these are most likely under very special circumstances only. There are also many organizations that have their own unusual scholarships, such as the Florida Peanut Producers, for which you have to have had a peanut business to apply. Perhaps there is a left-handed club out there somewhere that also may have a scholarship, but for the most part, the odd ones are very special circumstances only.

SCHOLARSHIP FOLDER

Starting in ninth grade, keep a folder that is all about you. Keep track of anything that remotely seems important and keep it updated throughout all four years of high school.

A very important thing to remember is to start keeping track of all your involvement, beginning freshman year. Keep a list or copy of all your awards, academic and non-academic, all your extracurricular activities, and all your volunteer work and hours. Also, keep any well-written essays because you never know when you may be able to use them or even a part of them for a scholarship application down the road. This is the same folder in which you should keep copies of all your scholarship (and college) applications and all your letters of recommendation. Any copies of recent report cards and an extra copy of official transcripts can go in here, too.

Lastly, you must apply and apply, again and again. If you are in doubt about eligibility, call a contact number, which is usually on the application. I have even seen some where a scholarship from a music singing club had no applicants, so they accepted instrument players. If you are close, it may be acceptable. You never know unless you ask. Apply for as many as you possibly can, whenever you can.

Here is a list of items that I suggest you keep in your folder:

- Any essays that are well written and ALL of them that are personal

- All community service hours, starting in ninth grade

- Keep track of any clubs, organizations, sports, and school involvement or committees that you participate (d) in

- Grades (honor roll), Honors classes, and so on, and a list of classes taken

- ANY special awards – academics and non-academics – such as sports and volunteer work or any you may have received in the mail

- Letters of recommendation

- Copies of any completed applications, scholarship or college

- Yearly academic history, such as final report cards or a print out from your guidance counselor and an extra copy of an official transcript, just in case you cannot get one for any "last minute" applications

Chapter 3

WHERE TO LOOK FOR SCHOLARSHIPS

YOUR HIGH SCHOOL

The first and easiest place to look is in your own school. If you do not have a scholarship coordinator at your school, go to your guidance counselor. Many applications or information regarding the scholarship applications are sent directly to the guidance office, especially the local ones. When I refer to local scholarships, this does not mean going to a local college, but it means that the scholarship itself is given out locally, usually to students from high schools in the county. Regrettably, most guidance counselors do not have the time needed to work with scholarships, as there are so many other types of paperwork they must do. Offer to go and make your own copy if there is only one and keep checking with them so they learn your name and know you are really interested. Unfortunately, if your school does not receive this information, you will need to track it down yourself. Try going to your local school board and see what they can tell you. There is usually a department that has received scholarship information, such as Guidance and Testing or School Activities. Also read your local newspapers, as I have seen many local scholarships advertised in that way.

LOCAL ORGANIZATIONS

Local organizations love to assist schools and the students. There are so many different ones in your immediate area that give to the community in different ways, one of which is scholarships. Some good examples would be any local clubs in your community, such as the GFWC Women's Club, the Elks Club, Lions Club, Rotary Club, Exchange Club, Daughters of the American Republic, or any civic club in your area. Also check with your nearest VFW posts, as they always have different scholarship contests, and your local American Legion will also have various scholarships available. Look up organizations in your phone book and start calling around.

Many of these organizations also have scholarships for the members' children. You might not ever find out unless you ask.

BUSINESSES/STORES/CHURCHES

Many companies provide scholarships for students who will be majoring in their field, such as engineering, medical, or even various pharmacies. Some of them even want the students to come back and work for them after they graduate. Many also provide scholarships for their employees' children or even for their own employees, such as Wal-Mart and Target. Not only are they giving help to their own employees, but they are also giving back to the community.

I have also found scholarships in different stores such as Wal-Mart, Target, Best Buy, Sears, JCPenney, and even Burger King and Kentucky Fried Chicken. These were all for local students (one or two per store), and some of them even move up to a national level. Stores that have scholarships given out countywide usually have ones for their employees also. Whether it is at your parents' work or your own, ask the manager or owner about scholarships for employees. If they do not know anything about scholarships, get a phone number and the name of someone high up in the corporation. Keep asking until you get a definite answer.

Churches are another good place to check (as long as you are an active member) for scholarships, and many also have low rate loans for members. Ask the minister or even contact the main chapter of the church.

WEB SITES

One of the best resources is the Internet. There are many scholarship searches that require you to fill out a questionnaire or personal profile, and then they will find scholarships to match your profile. Some excellent ones are Fastweb.com, Scholarship.com, and Salliemae.com. You can also do a search for more scholarships and scholarship search sites to find even more. Just make sure that you NEVER pay someone to do a search for you. There are too many free ones out there. I had one student pay $40 for a search, and she brought me the results. Most of them I already had through my free searches. There were only about five of them that I had never heard of, and two of these no longer existed. Once again, many of these are one time only and are no longer available.

Something to remember on any type of search is that there will always be scholarships that come up that you are not eligible for. My daughter was majoring in education and her search turned up one for education majors who were Jewish. The one common factor (education) pulled the scholarship up. I have also seen a profile that states that the student will be a freshman in college and a resident of a certain state, but then they are matched with a scholarship for graduate students only or for students who are a resident of a completely different state. It can take just one factor to match you up with a scholarship that is not even close. So when you do a search, carefully read all the eligibility rules before applying or sending for it. You will save yourself a lot of time. Remember also to look at the deadline. Sometimes scholarships will be discontinued or are simply no longer available.

The one downfall of Web site results is that almost all these scholarships are national scholarships. Remember that the competition is much harder, and you are competing against many more students. Yes, it is possible to win a national scholarship, but you need to have a strong background in whatever they require to compete. My son applied for a national athletic/academic scholarship online, which we thought he would have a fairly good chance at, as he played sports full time for four years and excelled in one or two of them. Then we found out that 76,000 other students also applied for that same scholarship. I have found that many more students seem to apply when the Internet is involved.

You can also do manual searches yourself either at your local or school library, which will usually have scholarship books in their research section. The only problem with these is that many are no longer available, depending on how recently the books were published. I have seen scholarships that seem to last forever, and then there are those that only have money for one or two years. I have also seen some end one year and then return again the following year. Just make sure that one of the first things you do, after reading the eligibility requirements, is to check the deadline.

Another important factor is, if you need to write and request an application, to make sure you send a self-addressed, stamped envelope. This just makes it easier for them to send the application to you.

FINANCIAL AID OFFICE

Another excellent source is the college that you have been accepted by. Call the college financial aid office and get a list of scholarships and application deadlines. Many colleges also have scholarships within the programs you are majoring in.

Do not give up after your freshman year if you do not receive any. Try every year you are there. One of my former students told me that, though there are fewer to apply for, it seems that less students compete, and he has won quite a few since being in college.

Another student of mine went in to visit the financial aid department on a weekly basis, after school had already started. On her third or fourth visit, she was rewarded for her persistence. They gave her a $1,000 scholarship that someone else received, but never attended the school to get it. Do not give up!

Do not forget to call your state's financial aid office about any scholarships or grants they may have for state residents (see Chapter 10).

Chapter 4

RÉSUMÉS — MY MULTI-FUNCTIONAL RÉSUMÉ

During their senior year, my students make a professional résumé. There are four ways they can be used. They can use them for college applications, scholarship applications, letters of recommendation, and to get a job. Once they have a résumé, it can be a key tool for shortcuts on filling out scholarship applications. I will go over how to use them for this in Chapter 6, but this chapter is how to create one in the first place.

Your basic résumé can be done on most office programs, such as Microsoft Word, using their résumé builder or templates. Some scholarship applications even ask for a résumé only, instead of questions. After creating a résumé, it is beneficial to take that same format and type it up in a blank document, with the same headings, because the majority of the applications will have questions asked in a variety of ways and orders. My cut, paste, cut, tape, and copy method is used for these types of applications and seems to work best when it is not on a program's template. It is more user-friendly. Again, refer to Chapter 6 for more information on my shortcut methods.

At the end of this chapter, I will show you a sample résumé and take that same information and set it up to use for my shortcut method.

Your basic résumé starts with the header, being your name and address/telephone information. Then you have your objective.

OBJECTIVE

The "Objective" is the top subject. This can vary, depending on what you are using the résumé for. A scholarship résumé's objective could read the same as the college résumé one. You can use something like, "Planning to major in (insert major)." Or you may just leave the objective off.

WORK EXPERIENCE

The next subject is "Work Experience." There are many scholarships that consider the fact that the student works, and because of this, he or she may not have time to participate in as many extracurricular or volunteer activities. Others just like to see that the student is already trying to help themselves or their families.

Work experience should be listed from the present job to the past. You should have the starting date, the ending date (or "present" if still there), the name of the company, your job title, and a brief description of what you do. Leave out the first person pronouns to make it briefer. Also keep in mind examples that might show leadership skills, such as being in charge of either a certain job or even of other employees.

Obviously if you left a job under a bad situation, one that you do not want to list as a reference, or if you only stayed a short time, do not list it. Believe it or not, one of my students was fired for theft (but not arrested) and claimed that he was wrongly accused so he still wanted to list that job. Thankfully, I talked him out of it, as you cannot defend yourself in a résumé. If the topic were to come up in an interview, that would be the time to discuss what really happened.

EDUCATION (OR ACADEMICS ON SCHOLARSHIP APPLICATIONS)

"Education" is the next subject. Scholarships are only interested in your high school years. Begin with the name of your school and your projected graduation date. Then list all your academic honors. You can start with your graduation status (if it is a good one). Our students graduate with Honors with a 3.0 to 3.49, 3.50 to 4.0 is High Honors, and 4.0 and above is Highest Honors. A student with a 3.5 could list, "Graduating with High Honors," or if you hope to have a 3.5 by the time you graduate but do not at this time, you could list it as "Plan to graduate with High Honors." If your GPA is not quite that high but you have been on the honor roll a few times, you could just list it as "Honor Roll," and even that sounds good. Of course, if your GPA is low, leave it out. Also, list the overall types of classes you have taken if they are Honors, Advanced Placement, or International Baccalaureate classes, as these are all harder classes than the normal ones, which will also be taken into consideration. Do not list each one separately; instead, for example, you might put "Various Honors and AP classes – 4 years" or "All Honors classes – 4 years."

"I personally, with the help and guidance of Mrs. Lipphardt's wide range of knowledge, obtained over $21,000 in scholarship money to assist me in furthering my education."

Danielle Borth
Vanguard High School
Class of 2007

Next, list any academic type organizations you may belong to. These are the types of clubs for which you need to meet certain grade criteria to be invited to join, such as the National Honor Society. This is where the academic math club, Mu Alpha Theta, would also be listed. If the club invited you to join, but you did not, you could list it as "National Honor Society – nominee." Always list the number of years of membership. If you have belonged only one year, you can omit the years. You would also put down, under the organization, any offices you held or any awards you may have won.

List any other academic type awards you may have received. Some examples would be Math Award, Student of the Year Award, National Honor Roll, and even Who's Who Among American High School Students. Just remember that, if you did not send in the paperwork, you are only a nominee. If you were selected more than once and returned the paper work each time, you would put "Multiple Honoree." Another thing to remember is to list the most important awards first, with any "nominee" only awards last, as they are still awards, but not as strong as being an actual member or participant.

You should also list any vocational type classes you took for two or more years, especially if they pertain to your major. This shows the scholarship committee that you are serious about this career choice and more likely to put their money to good use. Examples of these classes would be: teacher assisting, art, drafting, cabinet making, business classes, auto mechanics, criminal justice, health occupations, or even extra academic classes, such as sciences, if you are planning on going into that field.

Band and ROTC are always good classes to list, if taken for at least two years, as these classes usually require extra hours, and they show a commitment on your part. If your education is lengthy and your extracurricular is short, you could always list these two under that instead. When in doubt where something should go, look at the subject area that has the least amount of information and put it there.

Also remember to list any summer school like activities that you may have done, such as summer classes at a college for credits.

EXTRACURRICULAR ACTIVITIES

"Extracurricular Activities" is the next subject. This can be done in one of two ways. You can list clubs (or any organization) that you belong to, along with sports, or, if you have a long history in sports, "Sports" can be its own subject. Once again, this time frame starts with high school.

Always put down the number of years you have participated in any given activity. If you are an officer, captain of a team, or on a varsity team, list that, too. You would add any awards you may have received in whatever organization you are writing about. For sports, this includes that piece of paper or certificate you may have received for the Most Valuable Player, Most Improved Player, and the like. And, if your team and you won any championships, this would go here, too. Once again, remember that being an officer, captain, or on a varsity team, are all types of non-academic awards, as well as leadership skills.

It is always best to list the activity that you have the most participation in first, then continue until the smallest amount or least time of membership is the last one. If you are putting clubs and sports together under extracurricular, keep the list of clubs together, then go on to sports. Put whichever you have the most experience in, clubs or sports, first.

Let us say you listed clubs first. You need to remember to put down your school involved ones, and then you can list the community (or outside school) ones.

It has to be something that you participate in on a regular basis to be extracurricular. Student Council or Student Government are great organizations to belong to, and while they are not really considered a club, they are very active organizations. Do not, however, list anything twice on your résumé or scholarship application. Keep National Honor

Society under education or, in a scholarship application, under academic awards, and do not list it again under extracurricular activities.

Sports can be done a little differently. Always put the school team first, but if you were involved with the same sport but in perhaps a city league, list the school sport, then the same sport outside school before going on to a completely different sport. See my résumé sample under sports.

Think long and hard about the different types of organizations you may have belonged to. Include church membership, church youth groups or choir, any clubs, any sports, Explorers, 4-H, Girl Scouts or Boy Scouts, and even any types of lessons you may have taken or are taking (music, dance, acting). You should also list any camps or conventions you have attended for that particular sport, club, or organization. All these show an involvement in something that you have done or are doing on your own time. Scholarship committees love to see that a student is involved in something outside the classroom.

If you are no longer involved in one of the clubs or sports, put it down anyway. Yes, the longer the involvement the better, but on the other hand, a little is better than none. However, you must belong for a full school year (unless membership started half way through) to count it. If you quit in the middle of a season or school year, you cannot count it.

VOLUNTEER SERVICE

The next subject on the résumé is "Volunteer Service," also

called community service or involvement. Some students volunteer at their school, others in the community, and many even go on mission trips to other states or countries with their churches. Wherever you volunteer, whatever you do, keep track of it. Some scholarships prefer it when you volunteer for a nonprofit organization, but many will still look at any type of volunteering you have done. As you really do not know what they are looking for, unless they specify it, make sure you include everything.

You need to look really hard at all the times you may have given some of your time to help someone or an organization and count up all those hours. You can also include any planning you may have had to do, such a preparing to teach a Sunday school class or getting your club or a school dance together. Also include the time it took you to travel to the volunteer site. It is all part of your free time that you gave to help someone or something.

As in extracurricular activities, list the service that you have the most hours in first. If it is an incredible amount of hours (over 50) tell briefly what the service was.

You need to remember to put down the hours spent, next to the activity. You may have "Band performance for nursing homes," but if you do not put down hours, it would look like you only did it once or twice.

There are two ways to list your hours. You can either put total hours or put how many hours weekly or monthly and how many years you have done it. Just remember that, if you list your hours the second way, weekly or monthly, you need to also have the number of weeks, months, or years you were involved. If you only put three hours weekly but forget the years, it sounds like you might have just done it once or twice or that you just started doing it. Or if you put the number of years without the hours, it once again sounds like you only did it once or twice.

However, there are many types of volunteer work you may have only spent a few hours on. Anything less than five hours total, I would list without the hours or group it together with similar activities. Perhaps you volunteered at an elementary school's carnival, their open house, and tutored students there, and your hours were only two or three at a time. Then add them all up and put them under "Assist local elementary school with various events." If you volunteered just a few hours at a large variety of functions, with none of them similar, you could add up all those hours and put them under "Various Community Service Activities."

But if it really was an isolated incident that could not be added up with anything else, such as a club requires the new members to visit a nursing home two different times only, I would then list this as, "Nursing Home Visits," and leave it at that.

Any planning, organizing time, or even leading meetings also counts as part of your service hours, just as the travel time to get there does, too. You can list things such as tutoring students for free or helping an elderly neighbor, even though it is not an organization.

I would also include performances you do not get paid for, such as a play, singing, or even instrumental events. Our school's band members have to perform at the football games, which cannot be counted as volunteer service as it is a part of their grade, but when they march in the Christmas parade or perform at graduation, they can count those hours. You can also count helping a teacher in their classroom or just helping the school clean up, inside or out. You can count working at concession stands, keeping score for any sport, or even recording statistics for a sport.

But, once again, if you have performed community service as a requirement from the judge or court, this is not the kind you can include on a scholarship or college application.

There are many clubs that require so many hours of service per month from their members to remain in the club. My club requires two hours monthly, but my officers and many of my members spend much more time than that. This is where you would list the other hours under the project you were involved in and the hours that were spent on this particular project. Some students and most officers go far beyond the required hours. When listing this on an application or résumé, they should name the club, then so many hours per month (write the required hours only), and how many years they have done this. Then they need to list all the extra hours under something different. For example, the student may have spent 20 hours on one particular project in one month, but the club only required two hours of service that month. So list the 18 extra hours under the name of the project they were involved in. Many scholarship committees want to see more than just the "required" hours, and as these hours were not a requirement, they can be listed separately.

Fundraisers are another kind of service. Tell what you are raising the money for, if it is a worthwhile cause, such as Red Cross for hurricane victims or money for scholarships. You do not always receive hours for fundraisers at some schools, but it is still worth mentioning, as it still shows a commitment on your part.

You also need to include any awards or special recognition you may have received for the volunteer work under the activity. List this under the volunteer activity itself. It is also a type of non-academic award, which I will give more examples of in Chapter 6.

Once again, you need to keep track of anything you do, starting your freshman year, and also keep all this in your folder. The four years you are in high school may seem short, but I find that many of my students have a difficult time remembering everything they did two or three years ago.

SKILLS

Last but not least, on a résumé, you list your "Skills." But you will only list skills when you use the résumé for job applications, so if you are sending the résumé to a college or scholarship competition, you need to leave off skills.

I have made up a sample résumé for you on the next page. But you will then need to refer to Chapter 6 to see how I took this résumé and set up the parts for my quick and easy way to fill out multitudes of applications.

	1234 NE 8th Terrace Ocala, FL 34479 Phone: (352) 611-1222
Mark J. Lane	
Objective:	Planning to major in Architecture
Work Experience:	06/03-present Painter's Paradise Ocala, FL Painter's Apprentice - two separate businesses • Prep and paint interiors and exteriors and pressure clean 06/01-08/03 Publix Supermarkets Ocala, FL Customer Service • Assist customers, bag groceries, and store maintenance
Education	Graduation 05/07 Vanguard High School Ocala, FL Will graduate with High Honors National Honors Society - 2 years • Historian Florida's Top 20 Scholars Who's Who Among American High School Students - multiple Nominated to Nat'l Youth Leadership Forum
Extracurricular Activities	VHS Football Team - 4 years • Varsity - 2 years • Super Knight Award - 2 years • Summer Work-Out Camp - 4 years VHS Varsity Wrestling Team - 2 years • Captain - 1 year • 2006 Marion County Champion • 2006 Wrestling Regional Finalist / 2006 USA Wrestling - 2005 VHS Basketball Team - 2 years Student Government Representative - 2 years Interact Service Club - 2 years Anchor Service Club - Elected Sweetheart

1234 NE 8th Terrace
Ocala, FL 34479
Phone: (352) 611-1222

Mark J. Lane

Volunteer Experience	Vanguard High School Volunteer - 3 years - 110+ hours • Assisted office personnel with school start and ending
	Anchor Service Club T-Bird - 1.5 years - 4 hours monthly (not required)
	Bible School Aide - 20 hours
	Warm-up Ocala Campaign for Homeless and Needy - 20 hours
	Various sports fundraisers and field clean-ups
Skills	Quick learner and reliable
	Work Well With Others

Chapter 5

BASICS ON
FILLING OUT
APPLICATIONS

Neatness is extremely important when filling out an application of any kind. There are even some scholarships that have a preliminary elimination process, and a sloppy application can be tossed out for that reason alone. Try to always type your application, whether you use a computer or a typewriter. If there is no possible way to use either of these, print or write very carefully in your best handwriting. When you make a mistake, if possible, start over. If it is not possible to start fresh, use a small amount of white-out only. Presentation says a lot about you. Making your application neat makes more people want to read it more thoroughly.

While being neat is important, so is correct grammar, punctuation, and spelling. There are many times when it is hard to choose the winner because the scholarship committee finds many well-qualified applications. Using proper grammar and spelling could make the difference. I have met some people that will not even consider looking at an application if the grammar is bad or if there are misspelled words. You should first proofread it yourself for any mistakes and then have your parents and/or an English teacher proofread it for you. It never hurts to ask for help.

Another important aspect is that you must read all the directions. If the application asks for black ink, do not use a pencil or blue ink. Some require typing only, and I have even seen some that require you to hand write your answers for the essay. One mistake can disqualify you. When you take the time to do something this important, do it right.

Read all the questions carefully. Many applications have similar questions, but not exactly the same answers. Examples of these similar questions are used in my cut and paste method in Chapter 6. Make sure you understand any essay questions and give the answer that is asked for. Do not stray from the subject. More details on writing essays can be found in Chapter 7.

Look over and make sure that any extra attachments are included, such as letters of recommendation or official transcripts. I have come across some that want a transcript and also a copy of your most recent report card. Even though those grades should be on your transcripts, send both if required. There are even some that want any attachments stapled in a certain place or require you to put your name on the application in a certain way. Then there are those that ask for no attachments. Do not attach anything when this is a requirement.

Do not leave any questions blank. I had a student several years back who was highly qualified for one particular scholarship that was worth $20,000. When he found out that one of his friends, who was a lot less qualified than he, was a semi-finalist and he was not, we all wondered why. I called the organization and found out that even though this application was for seniors only and even though he had a senior guidance counselor's signature, he left one question unanswered, one of the easiest questions on the application: *What grade are you in?* But because this was an application on which you colored in the circles, the computer threw him out because he skipped that question. If you do leave a question blank, you might need to practice your proofreading skills.

Deadlines are extremely important. Never send in the application late. This is just another way to get it thrown out. Unless I see the actual word, "postmark," I assume the deadline date is when they want to receive the application. I mail my students' applications from the school at least a full week ahead of time. I have mailed two different items at the same time, to the same city, and one got there the next day and the other took five days to reach its destination. After doing all that work, what a waste to have it disqualified just because it did not get there in time. If you are not clear on the deadline, see if there is a phone number to call and to ask for more specific instructions.

Many scholarship applications are now available online, and they sometimes can only be done this way. For these be sure to be early in case you have computer or Internet problems. You can always go to your public library or even your school library if your computer messes up, that is, if you are not too late to begin with. Be sure to read the Internet instructions carefully as well. Many will request that you do part of the application online, but will still tell you to send hard copies of specific items by mail. The deadlines might even differ.

I have come across many local scholarships that have extended their deadlines. It just depends on how many applications they have received. I have even had a couple of students have extenuating circumstances and bring their applications in late to me because of a family emergency. I called the committee, and they let the students drop them off or mail them late. It never hurts to ask; just do not plan on them letting you be late.

There are also times when a student is running close to the deadline and they have a couple of other options. They can mail it priority mail, which is relatively inexpensive and will usually get it there in one or two days, or they can overnight it, but this is much more costly. With many of the local ones, as long as there is a physical address, the student can then drop it off themselves. It is always a good idea to call first to make sure they know someone is coming.

Another important thing to remember, if possible, is to know your judges. Of course, there are many applications that this is impossible to do for, but think of all the ones you can pretty much figure out. The VFW has an essay contest every year, and obviously the members are the judges. They are older, patriotic people who have serviced their country. Appeal to that side of them. If a company is giving out a scholarship for a major in their area of practice, focus on the type of company it is. Many clubs have scholarships. Check to see what they focus on, if it is community service, and what type of service it is. Many times you can relate your essay to the type of organization. For example, if a church is giving out a scholarship, you need to relate all and any of your participations and service to the church.

Then when you think you are done, double-check everything one last time. Be sure to make a copy of every application you submit in case they have an interview or just in case you can use some of it again on a different scholarship application.

One of my students called me in a panic because she received a call requesting an interview. She was not sure which application it was for, as the name of the scholarship was in remembrance of a former member, not the name of the organization. Luckily, I remembered (I was at home, without the application to refer to) the name of the organization, which was the Lions Club. She found her application copy and was able to prepare for some of the questions. And as it happened, even though the essay question was more about her college major, her volunteer work was with a young blind girl, teaching her how to cheerlead with other girls her own age. This experience was very moving for her, and she enjoyed helping the little girl feel like the other girls. She then read up on the Lions Club before the interview and learned that the Lions Club helped the blind, and if possible, she planned on somehow bringing it up in the interview. This is another example of knowing your judges, which I will go over again in Chapter 7.

You need to be careful of other things in your essay or even your answers when you apply. I had three students who applied for over 15 scholarships each and did not win any of them. One of them had written in every career goal essay that she wanted to be a lawyer. We later found out that her sealed letter of recommendation from her guidance counselor (which she used for almost every application) said what a great doctor she would make. This was a definite instance of miscommunication. Another student had an abnormally large number of volunteer hours with his church, as his father was the pastor, but he had not logged any of these hours anywhere, so they were not confirmed on his transcripts and the amount of hours was hard to believe. The third student did not bring any of her applications to me until toward the end. She told me that she filled them out exactly as I had told her to. I finally convinced her to bring me one toward the end of the year and found out that she not only needed proofreading on her essays, but when she made an error, she simply drew a line through it. After working with her on her last few applications she did win one small scholarship. Hopefully, after reading this book you should be able to avoid mistakes like these.

Chapter 6

Short Cuts —
Simple Tips on
Making It
Easier For You

A typed (or computer generated) application always looks better than a hand written one. They not only come across neater and more professional, but they are usually easier to read. My shortcut method makes it so you can provide a nicely printed application, but you do not have to retype your answers each time you have a different application to do.

My daughter filled out a few scholarship applications before her senior year, but when her senior year arrived, she started filling them out in earnest. She applied for over 25 different scholarships. We found a way to fill them out in a speedy, almost assembly line-like manner using my shortcut method.

The majority of scholarships have many of the same questions, sometimes just asked in different ways. I came up with a simple way for her to use her resources and take shortcuts. She did seven different scholarships this way in one night.

The first thing you need to do is have your résumé ready.

Then, as I previously mentioned in Chapter 4, retype your résumé without the use of the template. I find it best to go to the résumé and transfer the information to a blank document. Using the data directly from the résumé is possible, but when you need to cut, copy, and paste from the résumé, the template is not user-friendly. You can do it, but it needs a lot of repairs.

The simplest way is to start off on the blank document with your work experience, but using briefer information than you would on a normal résumé. Most questions on the applications that ask about work experience mainly want to know where you worked, how long you have been there, and sometimes how many hours you work per week. List them as you did on the résumé, present to past.

Your next section will be the education part. You can set this up like the résumé, putting all your awards and honors in this part. I call this "Academic Awards." List them starting with the most impressive ones, as they are ones seen first. Then keep on setting it up in the same order as the résumé, with your extracurricular and/or sports and your volunteer service.

Now that it is all retyped, be sure to save it on the hard drive, and to be extra safe, as this can be a lot of work, save it to two discs and even a flash drive as well. Yes this might be overly cautious, but I have seen lightning strike computers and computer crashes, and I have also copied to a bad disc. It was brand new, but still did not work. Something this important needs to be saved. Now that everything is typed, the hard part is over. This is where my shortcut method comes into play.

Most scholarship applications ask basically the same questions – they just change the wording or the order in which they are asked.

Some applications want academic awards separate from non-academic awards, while others will ask for ALL awards. Some will ask for school extracurricular activities and community extracurricular, while others will just lump extracurricular together in one question. Community service (volunteer hours) is usually the same. I have, however, seen a few where they ask for community volunteer service and church activities separately. When an application asks for school and community activities and does not mention volunteer, this is where you would put your volunteer service under either school or community activities. You would put anything you did that would be school-related (clubs, helping at other schools or your own) under the school activities and anything outside school, (church, Habitat for Humanity) with the community activities. Just make sure that the volunteering goes under some sort of category, even if you have to bring it up in your essay.

Here are some examples.

ACADEMIC HONORS

This would be all your academic honors, such as how you will be graduating – Honors, High Honors, or even Honor Roll, National Honor Society, or any other academic organizations you belong to. It also includes any academic awards you may have received, such as Math Award, English Award, and any Honors, Advanced Placement, dual enrollment or International Baccalaureate classes you have taken.

NON-ACADEMIC AWARDS

This would include extracurricular and volunteer awards, such as being an officer in a club (include any officer positions here, even if it was an academic club), a student government representative, a captain of a team, being on the varsity team, a Best Player award, or even an award from somewhere or someone that you volunteered for.

Or the application could include all the above by asking for academic and non-academic awards and honors in one question. Then you would list all awards and honors from each category, both academic and non-academic. You would just cut and paste to put them together.

If the application does not specifically ask for awards, make sure you still list them in their own category (i.e., captain or varsity with the sport and officer with the organization).

Some applications also separate activities in how they phrase the question. Here are some examples.

LIST ALL YOUR SCHOOL ACTIVITIES.

This would include school-based clubs, sports, and any other school activities, including volunteering if there is not a separate question for that.

LIST ALL YOUR COMMUNITY ACTIVITIES.

This would be clubs or sports not related to your school and also community service, unless there is a question just for volunteer service.

The very first thing you do after getting all your information together is to go to your blank document and type the name of the scholarship you are working on. Then type up each question as a heading. At the end of this chapter, I will use the résumé from Chapter 5 and then retype it for you, as you would do to get ready. Then, I will highlight some of the examples I just went over. I will also show you some sample questions, and you can see where I actually put each answer.

After the "retype" of your résumé is ready, the cut and paste method comes in. You have an application that asks for awards and honors as one question. You name the scholarship, type "Awards and Honors," and cut and paste all your awards from each category together.

You answer each question like that and then print it. After printing, you again cut, but this time with scissors. Place the cut-out answers, lined up neatly, on the application and use a small piece of tape to secure it. Do that for all the questions. Then you simply make a xeroxed copy of the taped up application, and you no longer see the tape. Sometimes you will need to make your print smaller to fit the section, or you can cut your list in half and tape it side by side.

Another possibility would be to simply print out the original form that you made for that application, write the questions word for word, and attach the entire paper to the application. Do not forget to print out "see attached" by each question. Just remember that some applications do not want any attachments, so read the directions carefully. And if you do attach a page, make sure you use the same format and order that the application has. You most likely will still have to cut and paste on the computer copy to it get it right. DO NOT print out the information in just any order (I cannot stress this enough); you must make sure your information is in the exact same order as the application questions are.

Of course, if you have a scanner with the correct program, you can skip all the above and just scan the application and type in the answers. You can just cut and paste your information onto the application. Most students I assist do not have a scanner, and my method still cuts down on a lot of work.

All of this saves you from typing the same information over and over again, especially when you may have several scholarships due at the same time.

Now the application is almost finished except for the first part, which usually is just basic data – name, address, school you are attending, and any colleges you want to attend. This can just be typed with a normal old-fashioned typewriter or you can hand print the information, or even very carefully type, print, hand cut, tape, and copy as you did the answers.

Now onto the essay questions that usually come with most applications. When you answer any essay, save it in the same place under that particular scholarship. You may have to have an interview, and you want to be sure to remember during that interview what you wrote in your essay for that particular scholarship (refer to Chapter 9 for more on interviews).

You will find that you can reuse many of the essays, add on or subtract from them, or even just reword them somewhat to use them more than once. I will go into more detail on this in Chapter 7, which is on essays.

Sample Résumé (to refer to for your transfer to a blank document)

	1234 NE 8th Terrace Ocala, FL 34479 Phone: (352) 611-1222
	Mark J. Lane
Objective:	Planning to major in Architecture
Work Experience:	06/03-present Painter's Paradise Ocala, FL Painter's Apprentice - two separate businesses • Prep and paint interiors and exteriors and pressure clean 06/01-08/03 Publix Supermarkets Ocala, FL Customer Service • Assist customers, bag groceries, and store maintenance
Education	Graduation 05/07 Vanguard High School Ocala, FL Will graduate with High Honors National Honors Society - 2 years • Historian Florida's Top 20 Scholars Who's Who Among American High School Students - multiple Nominated to Nat'l Youth Leadership Forum
Extracurricular Activities	VHS Football Team - 4 years • Varsity - 2 years • Super Knight Award - 2 years • Summer Work-Out Camp - 4 years VHS Varsity Wrestling Team - 2 years • Captain - 1 year • 2006 Marion County Champion • 2006 Wrestling Regional Finalist / 2006 USA Wrestling - 2005

	1234 NE 8th Terrace Ocala, FL 34479 Phone: (352) 611-1222
Mark J. Lane	
	VHS Basketball Team - 2 years
	Student Government Representative - 2 years
	Interact Service Club - 2 years
	Anchor Service Club - Elected Sweetheart
Volunteer Experience	Vanguard High School Volunteer - 3 years - 110+ hours • Assisted office personnel with school start and ending
	Anchor Service Club T-Bird - 1.5 years - 4 hours monthly (not required)
	Bible School Aide - 20 hours
	Warm-up Ocala Campaign for Homeless and Needy - 20 hours
	Various sports fundraisers and field clean-ups
Skills	Quick learner and is reliable
	Work Well With Others

Type up similar to the résumé, using a blank document.

Work Experience:

06/06-Present   Painters Paradise - Apprentice

06/04-08/06   Publix Supermarket - Customer Service

Academics:

Will graduate with High Honors

National Honors Society - 2 years

- Historian

Florida's Top 20 Scholars

Varsity Scholar Letter

Who's Who Among American High School Students - multiple

Nominated to National Youth Leadership Forum

Extracurricular Activities:

VHS Football Team - 4 years

- Varsity - 2 years

- Super Knight Award

- Summer work outs - 4 years

VHS Wrestling Team - 2 years

- Captain Wrestling Team

- 2006 Marion County Champion

- 2006 Wrestling Regional Finalist

USA Wrestling Team

VHS Baseball Team - 2 years

Student Government Representative (elected)

Interact Service Club - 2 years

Anchor Sweetheart - 2 years (elected)

Volunteer (Community) Service

Vanguard High School Volunteer - 3 years - 110+ hours

- Assisted various office personnel with school start and ending

Anchor Service Club Sweetheart - 2 years - 4 hours monthly (not required)

Bible School Aide - 20 hours

Warm-up Ocala Campaign for the homeless and needy - 20 hours

Various sports fundraisers and field clean-ups

Now for the differences and how you would cut and paste.

THE MARK MM SCHOLARSHIP

1. List all your awards - both Academic and Non-Academic.

(This is where you will cut and paste all award-type answers – as I did below.)

Awards: Academic and Non-Academic

Will graduate with High Honors

National Honors Society - 2 years

Historian of National Honor Society

Florida's Top 20 Scholars

Varsity Scholar Letter

Who's Who Among American High School Students - multiple

Nominated to Nat'l Youth Leadership Forum

Varsity Football Team - 2 years

Super Knight Award

Varsity Wrestling Team - 2 years

Captain Wrestling Team

2006 Marion County Wrestling Champion

2006 Wrestling Regional Finalist

Student Government Representative (elected)

Anchor Sweetheart - 2 years (elected)

OR the question could be: **List all your Academic Awards**, then the next question would be **List all your Non-Academic Awards**. You would simply cut and paste the exact order that is used above. Below is an example.

Academic Awards:

Will graduate with High Honors

National Honors Society - 2 years

Florida's Top 20 Scholars

Varsity Scholar Letter

Who's Who Among American High School Students - multiple

Nominated to Nat'l Youth Leadership Forum

Non-Academic Awards:

Varsity Football Team - 2 years

Super Knight Award

Varsity Wrestling Team - 2 years

Captain Wrestling Team

2006 Marion County Wrestling Champion

2006 Wrestling Regional Finalist

Historian of National Honors Society

Student Government Representative (elected)

Anchor Sweetheart - 2 years (elected)

Do not leave out anything you did, no matter how insignificant, if there is room to put it down. For example, under academic activities, let us say there is only room for five items, and the application does not want any attachments. You could put "Historian" next to National Honors and remove the activity you were only nominated for. And if you had to leave out one more item, leave out the "Who's Who."

Example :

List five Academic Awards:

Will graduate with High Honors

National Honors Society - 2 years - Historian

Florida's Top 20 Scholars

Varsity Scholar Letter

Who's Who Among American High School Students - multiple

Or the question could be: **List your Awards: Academic and Non-Academic Award**. However, they only leave five spaces; they do not mention a limit on the number to use, but they do not want attachments.

So you would want to use at least ten things, using abbreviations and sometimes more than one item (if related) spaced together, so that you can use as much as possible. Below is what it will look like after you copy, paste, print, scissor cut, tape, and copy.

Will graduate with High Honors

Varsity Wrestling Team - 2 yrs - Captain

National Honors Society - 2 yrs - Historian

'06 County Wrestling Champ

Florida's Top 20 Scholars

'06 Wrestling Regional Finalist

Varsity Scholar Letter

Student Government Rep. - elected

Varsity Football Team - 2 yrs - Super Knight Award

Anchor Sweetheart - 2 yrs -elected

OR the questions could go like this: **List all Academic Awards and Honors,** then **List all Extracurricular Activities:** But there is no "Volunteer" question, so you include that with the rest of the extracurricular activities. You also incorporate the non-academic awards you received under the activities with sports or clubs.

Academic Awards

(Also included is "Historian," as there is no separate question for non-academic awards, but it still needs to listed be somewhere.)

Will graduate with High Honors

National Honors Society - 2 years

   • Historian

Florida's Top 20 Scholars

Varsity Scholar Letter

Who's Who Among American High School Students - multiple

Nominated to Nat'l Youth Leadership Forum

Extracurricular Activities

(Remember we are including non-academic awards as well as volunteering even though they were not specified.)

VHS Football Team - 4 years

- Varsity Team - 2 years

- Summer Work Outs - 4 years

- Super Knight Award

VHS Wrestling Team - 2 years

- Captain

- 2006 Marion County Wrestling Champion

- 2006 Wrestling Regional Finalist

USA Wrestling Team

VHS Baseball Team - 2 years

Student Government Representative (elected)

Interact Service Club - 2 years

Anchor Sweetheart (elected) - 2 yrs. - 4 hrs. monthly community service

Vanguard High School Volunteer - 3 years - 110+ hours

Assisted various office personnel with school start and ending

Anchor Service Club T-Bird - 1.5 years - 4 hrs. monthly (not required)

Bible School Aide - 20 hours

Warm-up Ocala Campaign for homeless and needy - 20 hours

Various sports fundraisers and field clean-ups

Then there is the question:

List All Leadership Skills or Examples

This is where you would put being an officer of a club, a captain of a team, being on the varsity team of a sport, and being a member of the student government.

Example:

Leadership Skills

Historian of the National Honors Society (an officer 'leads' the members)

Varsity Football Team - 2 years (varsity team 'leads' JV and freshman teams)

Varsity Wrestling Team - 2 years

Captain – Wrestling Team (captain 'leads' the team by setting examples)

Super Knight Award (an award for 'leading' the team in training)

Student Government Representative (elected) (you are leading the school)

Bible School Aide (you are 'leading' children)

There are so many different questions, yet they all result in using basically all your information, just in a different order. There is a way to include almost everything, and it does not take that much time when you have all your data typed up and ready to use.

After answering all the questions, type up the essay, title it, print it, cut it out with scissors, tape it to the application, and then copy the entire page (unless you can attach a separate page with the essay).

You would be surprised how much time this saves. Now perhaps you can see how my daughter did seven different applications in about one and a half hours time.

Chapter 7

ESSAY WRITING

Neatness, correct grammar, punctuation, and spelling should all go without saying, but I have read many essays that had great content, but a dreadful use of words or many misspelled ones. Some of these have not only been written by intelligent students, but by some teachers as well (as in the letters of recommendations - see Chapter 8). Remember that not everyone is a writer. You may need some help with putting your thoughts into proper order. Do not have someone write it for you, but have someone who can offer advice. Some of the strongest essays I have read are from the student's heart and soul. You should always have someone proofread your work, if at all possible. You can ask an English teacher, (or any teacher, but English teachers tend to watch for those grammatical errors), a guidance counselor, your parent, or even a friend. Spell check is great, but it does not catch all the errors. You may type in the wrong word, but if it is spelled correctly, it will not show up.

Read all the directions carefully before you even start. Do not go over the maximum words allowed or, as some applications may require, under the minimum allowed. Turning in an essay that is either too short or too long can automatically disqualify you. Many applications ask for typed (or computer generated) essays, double-spaced, and some even stipulate a certain font or font size. There are even a few that want the essay handwritten in a certain color of ink. If the directions do not say how to write it, remember a simple font, typed, and double-spaced is always best. It is much easier for the judges to read these, especially if they have a great number to go over. If you have to use your own handwriting, black ink is also easier to read. You can use print or cursive, whichever is your neatest.

You need to make sure you clearly understand the essay topic or question. The opening sentence should grab the attention of the reader, making them want to read more. Do not get off the subject. You need to follow the main idea throughout the entire essay. Start out with an introduction that shows that you know the objective of the essay, following with examples or explanations. Examples from your own experiences tend to make the essay more personal. Whenever a student can write about obstacles they themselves have overcome, such as divorce, death, poverty, or even a type of disability, it shows strength and determination. Always finish with a strong conclusion that supports the main idea, something that can bring out a powerful emotion in the judges.

This leads to what I always stress to my students, which is to always consider who the judges will be. For example, if you know that the judges are from the VFW, you know that your audience is of the older generation and that they hold patriotism highly. If your judges are all females (such as an all women's club), then by all means, if you are a male, do not sound too domineering or chauvinistic, and if you are a female, show your strengths in being a young woman. If your application is from an educational panel, then you usually need to tie in the importance of education somewhere in your essay. Just as if the scholarship is from a certain business, you need to find out what type of business and use that to strengthen your essay, leaning toward their commitments. Your audience could also be an organization that is concerned with community service. Find out what their concerns are and write about it if possible, or, if you cannot tie in that type of service, at least write about a similar kind of volunteer work or experience. Another piece of advice is to not go into religion or politics too deeply. There are so many different views on these two topics, and you do not want to insult someone whose beliefs may differ from yours.

Fortunately, the large majority of scholarships for seniors have similar essay styles. The most popular essay is, "What are your educational and career goals?" You need to research the type of education needed for your chosen career, the number of years of education needed, and what you will need financially to get there. Many of you will change your career goal before you complete your degree, but for now, write about the one that you believe you want and the one about which you can write the most passionately. You need to also express why you have chosen that particular career choice. The main difference in this type of essay, from application to application, is the number of words required. I suggest you write one that is approximately 500 words ahead of time, and then you can either shorten it or add on to it, depending on the particular word count requested. When shortening it, keep the most important parts and use contractions when possible. When lengthening it, write more about your dreams and desires, and, if you still need more words, you can write about an experience that led you to that choice of careers or even an interview with someone who is in that field.

As most scholarships are awarded only once, the majority of the committees are not going to follow you to school to see if you majored in the field you wrote about. You should be truthful and write about the major you are planning on. It always makes a better essay, and you can write with more feeling this way. You should also keep writing about the same major the entire year, as many local scholarships have some of the same people on different scholarship committees.

Some of you might even change your mind about your career during your senior year, but for the local scholarships especially, you need to focus on one particular career. One of my former students wanted to major in telecommunications with a possible backup career in nursing. For one application she wrote of her desires to be in the telecommunications industry, and for another scholarship application she wrote about nursing for a career. She won the first one from a local television company, and the second scholarship committee loved her essay on nursing, but there was a problem. One of the judges on the scholarship panel had been on both committees. The judge called her and asked what was going on, and she explained about her double major. They let her keep the first scholarship, but could not award her the second, as our county has an annual Scholarship Recognition Night, and it would have been awkward to award one student for two scholarships based on two different majors. If she had written about wanting to have a double major on both applications, she would have had a better chance to win them both, as her essays were excellent.

This case is also serves as another example but in a completely different way. This same student had less than a 3.0 GPA with very few service hours, yet she was still the chosen winner for the scholarships because of the content of her essay. This proves that an essay can weigh the odds in your favor.

There are a select few that will ask you to sign a paper saying that, if you change your major, you will have to pay them back, but I have only seen two different ones in all the years I have been working with scholarships. There are also the few that are renewable, meaning that you can reapply each year for them, or some even automatically renew if you keep up your grade point average

Many times the local scholarship applications will add on to the basic education and career goal question by asking how you will use your choice to come back and better your community. As none of you really know where you might end up after college, answer as if you will return. Think of how you could use your career to make your home town a better place to live. Remember that there really is "no place like home" – you just do not realize it yet.

Another popular essay topic is community service and why it is important. Again the main difference is the length of the essay. A common number of words is 500. You can shorten it using the methods discussed above. On shorter ones, keep only the strongest points, and on the longer ones, tell why you did it and how it made a difference. On the longer essays, this is a great time to use personal examples and to relate how it made it difference in someone else's life as well as your own.

Keep a copy of all your essays, and then you can simply edit and re-edit most of them in a very short amount of time. You should even keep the essays you might have previously written in school, as some scholarships may have an unusual essay question and you may be able to refer back to them for help.

Make sure that you write with sincerity and heart. Do not be afraid to tell of any problems you had to overcome or of any learning experiences you had that helped you become the person you are today.

Chapter 8

LETTERS OF RECOMMENDATION

L etters of recommendation are an extremely important part of a scholarship application. You need to be prepared and have these letters ready, as I have seen many students unable to turn in an application just because they did not have their letters. You have to depend on someone else to help you with this part. Many students put it off until the last minute, and the person they ask may not have the time to write one or, if they do it in a hurry, it may not be the best one they could have written. One of the first rules is to always ask for the letter with plenty of notice. Two weeks is perfect, with a gentle reminder in the second week. One week ahead of time is not bad timing, but two is more courteous.

The second rule would be choosing the best recommender to write the letter. When you ask someone to write one for you, there are a couple of easy guidelines to remember. First, make sure you ask an adult who is not related to you and who likes you. This may seem odd, but I have actually seen two different students ask a teacher they had some previous problems with for a letter of recommendation.

Fortunately, I was able to read these letters and send the student out for a different recommendation. One of these was on the rude side, and the other was just plain cold. Never ask someone to write you a letter unless you know they like and respect you. Teachers should be honest and professional with students. If they do not think a student is worthy of a letter, but the student asks them for one, they should either let them know that they do not have the time or that they honestly cannot write a good letter of recommendation for them. Teachers should also send students to someone else who might be willing to write a letter. However, not all adults can act professionally. The best people to ask are the ones who have worked closely with you; therefore, they know you better than the others and can usually write a more sincere letter.

Then there are the people that really like you, but just cannot write. Some people just do not have the talent to give you a well-written letter. I have seen a few of these, too. It is always best to get more letters than you need, so you can pick the best ones to send.

The third rule is to give the person who is writing the letter a copy of your résumé. They may know you in their classroom or even volunteering with their organization, but more than likely they do not know all the different things you are involved in. The résumé fills in the blanks for them and aids them in writing a better letter. It is also a good idea to sit down and talk with them if possible. Tell them even more about yourself, and most important, let them know a few things about the scholarship application and what they are looking for. For instance, if it is one for someone majoring in education, talk about your desire to teach and any qualifications or dreams you may have for that career.

The fourth rule would be to make copies of your letters. Provide a disc and ask the person writing the letter to make a copy of it on the disc. This way you can ask for a new letter with a fresh signature and new date every time you need it. The copy helps if the person is unavailable and it is addressed in general (Dear Scholarship Committee). Then you can just send in the copied letter. Some people like to address the letter to "such and such scholarship committee," but if they ask you, just have them address it to "Dear Scholarship Committee," so that it can be used for any application.

Lastly, make sure that you proofread the letter yourself. I have found incorrect information, and one time the student's name was even misspelled. We are all human, and we can all make mistakes.

Generally, you will need at least two letters from two different teachers (or members of your schools' staff), one from an administrator (this includes your principal, assistant principal, and/or your guidance counselor), and one from someone in the community. Some scholarship applications want a letter from the person in the community to be someone you did volunteer work for, and some just want a letter from someone outside your school. If you can get one from the person you volunteered for, you have covered both bases. You can also ask an employer, your minister, or even a family doctor. And if you can find none of these, there are always your neighbors or even a friend of the family.

These letters can also be used for college and job applications with just a little bit of revising by the writer.

Just make sure you have them on hand, as I have seen some local scholarships sent to the school at the last minute, giving the students a week to meet the deadline. Many students could not apply simply because they were not prepared and did not have any letters, and no one could write one for them on such short notice. This was a huge advantage for those students who were prepared.

Always remember to thank the person that wrote the letter for you, and when you have used the last letter, it is a good idea for you to write them a short thank you note. If it is one of those last minute letters, though, one where they wrote one for you with little or no notice, send them a thank you letter right away. It takes a lot of time and thought to write a good letter for someone, and sometimes that letter can help sway the scholarship panel's decision.

Chapter 9

INTERVIEWS

Some scholarship committees have interviews to actually meet the semi-finalists. This interview could be the determining factor in who will be awarded the scholarship.

As in any interview, you need to remember to be yourself as much as possible. First impressions are extremely important. Have confidence in yourself, as your application has already gotten you this far.

Dress in business attire. Males should wear dress pants with a collared shirt that is tucked in. Dress shoes should also be worn. Avoid T-shirts and baggy pants. The females should either wear a decent length dress or skirt or dress pants with a nice top. Girls should avoid mini skirts and low cut tops. Everyone needs to avoid wearing jeans.

When entering a room, stand tall and walk up to the judge or judges with a smile on your face, looking directly into their eyes. Then you can shake each judge's hand firmly as you say hello and introduce yourself.

You should wait to be asked to be seated. Try not to cross your legs because this leaves you vulnerable to that nervous leg bounce. Never cross your arms or put your hands in your pockets during an interview, as this can seem disrespectful or defiant. Remember also to never look at a clock or your watch during an interview.

When asked a question, pause shortly to think about your answer. Your answers should be brief, but do not limit them to a simple yes or no. Taking a short pause before answering shows that you are seriously thinking about the questions. At the same time, do not make your answers too lengthy either. Saying too much can sound like you are rambling on. When you leave the interview, thank them for their time, and if appropriate, shake their hands again, with a smile.

BEFORE THE INTERVIEW

You will need to look over your copy of the scholarship application before you go, in case they ask any questions of you that were on the original application. You should also read your essay if there was one. This is another good time to look up who the organization is. You never know when doing so may come in handy.

Here are some basic questions that are often asked during many types of interviews. This might help prepare you a little for your own interview. I have given a few suggestions on how to answer each one, but that is all they are – suggestions.

What are your career goals? Remember what you have been writing about in your career goal essays.

Why did you choose this career? Only you can answer this one.

Do you think you will make a difference with this career choice? Once again, you are the one to answer this question, but if all else fails say something about helping people or helping the environment, which usually goes with most careers.

What are your education goals? (Once again, your career and education essay.)

Where do you see yourself five years from now? Ten years from now? Be honest but brief. Also be realistic, as you will be much more mature than you are now. Five years from now, some of you may still be in school, while others will just be beginning your career, and if that is the case, think where you would like to work. Pick the best as this is just a question. Ten years from now, think about family and settling down. You can also think of advancement in your career path.

How can you help your community after you begin your career? Act like you will be coming back home to work – you never know – and think what you can do to help improve your community wherever you are. You might be able to volunteer your time by relating it to whatever your career is or volunteering in other areas, just so it is something you would enjoy so that you can talk about it with enthusiasm.

Name someone who has had an impact on your life and tell us how they impacted it. This needs to be someone you admire and look up to. You can use a relative or even a "hero" who you do not know but have always thought highly of. Have specific reasons why you look up to them. Someone may have done something to make you a better person, but someone could have also set such a wonderful example that you want to be like them, even if you do not know them.

Tell us an experience that impacted your life and how it did. If you have any obstacles that you have had to face, this is the time to tell about them. If you cannot think of any, think about a time that you had to use teamwork, sharing, helping others, or even an experience with an animal – just so that it is something that had a positive effect on you. It can be toward your grades, what type of person you want to be, or even something that helped you make a decision about your career choice.

What is your best quality? What is your worst quality? What do your friends like about you? What would your parents or teachers say? What do you like about yourself? As far as the worse quality – what is there that you would like to change?

If you could change one thing in education, your community, the world, or your life, what would it be and how would you change it? Make sure that it is a change you can give a realistic solution to. It does not have to be something major, like saving the world, but something you can answer with passion, something that you really care about. It can be as simple as wanting to help the needy, which you can do by volunteering. It only takes one person to get something started.

Why should you be a recipient of this scholarship? Here is where you can tell how hard you have worked to be where you are today – your grades, your volunteering, your sport, your club. Do not say, "I should be the recipient;" instead say something like, "I would be honored to be the recipient of your scholarship because I have..." It could even be because of your desire to further your education or pursue your dream career.

Why do you need this scholarship? Some of you will be able to say that without help it will be difficult to attend college, or you could even say that you want to pay for your education yourself and be independent of your parents, and this scholarship would go a long ways in helping you with your future.

What is the most important quality you look for in a friend? (Be honest; this is an easy question.)

Describe yourself in one (or two or three) word. Make it positive! It could be reliable, humorous, caring, loving, outgoing, responsible, reliable, trustworthy, friendly, loyal, dependable, witty; there are so many positive words. Think about this question ahead of time.

I have seen or heard of all these questions being asked during scholarship interviews. They are all a little different, but if you think about some or all these questions ahead of time, you will be prepared to go in with confidence. No one can give you any set answers. Mine are only suggestions to get you to use your imagination. Just remember to be positive at all times and to think back to your résumé for many of the questions. If you go over the sample questions with another adult that you look up to and one that knows you, perhaps someone that you asked for a letter or your parents, have them ask the questions and listen to your answers. Then they can give you a critique of your responses. Go to more than one person if you are not confident about their reactions.

This will be a fantastic experience for you even if you do not win. Most of us go through many types of interviews for colleges, job interviews, and even meeting your friends' parents. Interviews can pave the way for you throughout your life.

Chapter 10

STATE GRANTS AND THE FAFSA

Every state has different types of state grants, scholarships, and loans, and the Free Application for Federal Student Aid (FAFSA) also gets into different types of grants and loans. I would still like to share some of the things I have learned about these programs that may benefit you, no matter what state you live in.

The FAFSA, which is for every state, is a financial need application only, but still needs to be done yearly no matter what your income is. It is based on you and your parents' income from the previous year. The main factor taken into consideration by the FAFSA are the numbers of immediate family members attending college for that year. They do not care about all the normal bills everyone has to pay. The report from the FAFSA is sent to the colleges of your choice, then the college's financial aid office actually determines the amount you will receive, and whether it will be a grant (you do not pay back) or a low interest rate loan, subsidized (interest starts after graduation) or unsubsidized (interest is paid while in college) that you pay back after graduation.

If you have had a change that has affected the actual year the student will be attending versus the previous year that you are actually going by on the application, the college's financial aid office will usually work with you and readjust the amount of grants or loans you will receive. For example, the student will be attending college in the Fall of 2007, and the application is filled out using 2006 tax forms. If your income for 2007 drops by a good amount, perhaps because of divorce, a death, a huge hospital bill, or new financial care for an elderly relative, contact the college's financial aid office and let them know. They may ask for something in writing, but many times they will be able to help you out. It never hurts to ask.

I have also come across many students who basically are supporting themselves through high school, and this can present a problem. In one young man's situation, his father kicked him out and refused to give him any income information. The college that he applied to made him use his mother's income, even though she lived in another state and sent him no support money; he had only talked to her twice in the past four years. The college refused to help him, but luckily his mother sent him her information, and she had a low income so he received some financial aid. Another young man's mother recently passed away, and his biological father had never played any role in his up bringing. I talked to the financial aid office, and they asked for some of the teachers and coaches at our school to write a letter verifying this, and then they would work with him to finance his education. Each college is different, just as each circumstance is. I also had a young girl who was living with another family, paying them rent, and paying the rest of her bills. She had no adult to support her. When

I called the financial aid office, luckily, they decided to work with her and have her claim independent status. Not every college will do that. If a college will not work with a student with any of these problems, perhaps the student needs to contact a different college that will help them.

There is also the work-study program through the FAFSA. Work study involves working at the college in one of its many departments, and, although it is available at many colleges, it is not offered at all of them. The financial aid department in each college decides the amount of work study awards they will provide and who can receive them. This amount is determined by financial need, but priority does not necessarily go to those who have exceptional financial need. It is a still a good idea to say yes, even if the student already has a good job at the time. My daughter marked no, because she loved her part-time job, but later she wanted to work at the college's daycare center. She was unable to even apply because she marked no. You never know what job may come up at the college. It does not require you to work there even if you do answer yes.

"With the help of Mrs. Lipphardt, I was able to win scholarships and learn to think outside the box to accomplish my goals. I would have never been able to afford out-of-state tuition at New York University if it had not been for scholarship workshops and aid I received from Mrs. Lipphardt."

Sarah Tona
Vanguard High School
Class of 2007
New York University

The Pell and Perkins Grants are given to those in financial need. Many of us cannot afford to send our children away to college, but if your income is middle class (sometimes even lower middle class), you may qualify for the loans, but most likely not for the grants. The grants are for low income families. However, one girl came across a problem with the Pell Grant. She won a scholarship, and as most of them are sent directly to the college, the money she had won went to take the place of part of her Pell Grant. For example, say her grant was for $1,500 per semester, and she received a $500 scholarship. Instead of adding that $500 to her $1,500 grant, they took the money and somehow put it back into the Pell Grant, so that she still only got the original $1,500, not $2,000 as she thought. She was fortunate that the scholarship committee decided to give her cash instead. Scholarship winnings do not usually affect the state grants, however.

Another reason to fill out the FAFSA is that many times a scholarship or college will see the fact that you did not receive federal aid. This could be a determining factor in them awarding you a scholarship. They see that you did not receive any federal help, but they also see that most of us still need extra money to go to college.

You need to fill out the Federal Application for Free Student Aid as soon as possible, especially if you are eligible for financial need. You can apply in January of the year you will be attending college. Each school gets so much money from the government, and you need to try and get it just in case they run out. One financial aid officer told me the applications that come to them first usually receive larger amounts of money.

Every guidance office in high school and the financial aid office at the colleges should have the FAFSA application for you. You can also apply online. You need to be careful when you apply online and make sure you are on the correct Web site. More than one student has come to me and asked if they have to pay the $79 fee that is being charged to them on the Web site. Of course, I tell them no. Do not pay anything, as the key word in the FAFSA is FREE. They have gone to the wrong Web site. Make sure you go to **www.FAFSA.ed.gov** – NOT .com. I have been told that the .com Web site, the one that charges you, is not illegal. They still send in your information as a third party, but it sounds pretty illegal to me.

State grants, as I said before, vary, and they can change from year to year, if the money is not there. They work differently from the federal grants. Some are based on financial need, but many on entirely different things. My daughter received a grant for education, The Chappie James, which is no longer in effect. It was sent to the college, then they reimbursed her anything over her tuition. This was used for books, and then put into a special college savings account for future college needs. This grant was not based at all on income, but you must still fill out the FAFSA to be eligible to receive some state grants, no matter what they are based on.

Our Florida students apply for state grants when they apply for the Florida Bright Future Scholarships. This is a wonderful program that pays between 75 and 100 percent tuition to a Florida public college. It is based on classes taken during high school, GPA, and ACT or SAT scores.

If you live in Florida, the parent and the student need to visit their guidance counselor to see if they qualify, or what they need to do to qualify. It is guaranteed as long as you meet the criteria, and there are three different ways in which you can do that. If you do qualify for the Florida Bright Futures, or even think that you will, you need to apply online early (usually starting in December). It automatically makes you eligible for the other state grants at the same time.

The student still has to maintain a certain grade point average during their college years for it to continue. It can also be used towards Florida private colleges or vocational schools, but they only get the public tuition amount. Just last year there was a change for one of the Bright Futures 75 percent scholarships. When a student attends a Florida public community college, the 75 percent changes to 100 percent for the two years at that school, then returns back to 75 percent if they transfer to a four-year college or university.

The Florida Bright Futures Scholarships is a fantastic program, and I could probably write an entire chapter on it, but as this book, I hope, is read outside Florida, I will just urge all of you to talk to your counselor to see where you stand. If the counselor is vague, call the state financial aid office (usually a toll free number). No matter what state you live in, find out about your state grants and any special programs your state may have, like the Florida Bright Futures.

I do not want to go into loans in any depth, as this book is about scholarships. Loans are to be used as a last resort only. One very important factor about loans, though, is, depending on your family's income, you can be awarded a subsidized and an unsubsidized loan at the same time. This would be a total of four different loans during the course of one year. They each count as separate loans and are considered separate loans per semester also. Later, after your graduate, if you had both types of loans each year, you could end up with 16 different loans. Unless you are able to consolidate them all into one loan, it will hurt your credit to have so many different loans. Keep your loans to the minimum, as I have known people who were still paying off their school loans ten to fifteen years or more later. One of my friends, in fact, almost was unable to purchase a house because of her student loans.

Chapter 11

How Do I Get The Money & Where Does It Go?

O nce you have been awarded a scholarship, how do you actually get it? And what if you still are not sure what college you will be attending when you find out that you have won a scholarship? As in everything else, it depends on the scholarship and the committee and on how they disburse the money to you.

Do not worry about the college choice, as most scholarships will want you to notify them of your decision, usually with proof of acceptance. If you are still undecided at the end of the school year, simply call or write and say that you are still making your final decision and that you will let them know as soon as you make your choice.

Most scholarships are sent directly to the college's financial aid office. Many times the money gets there before you even schedule your classes, so that when you do schedule, the money is there for your use when paying class fees. Some scholarships will be sent to your address, but the check is made out to the college. Then it is your responsibility to get it to the financial aid office as soon as you can. Call first to see if it should be sent to any one individual's attention, and then call again to make sure they received it. Then there are the easy ones to take care of; those are the scholarships that are sent to you, and the check is made out in your name. If this is the case, I strongly urge you to put the money in a separate account, just for college expenses.

Here are some examples on how it is generally done. Let us say that you have received two scholarships for $500 each and both are sent directly to the college. You sign up for classes and the cost is $600, which should all be covered. But some colleges take the money and divide each scholarship amount into two semesters. This means that you would end up with $500 in your account for the fall semester and $500 in your account for the spring semester. If this is the case, you will owe the college $100 for your classes in the fall (or first) semester. Or if your scholarship amount is over the tuition and fees, they will either apply it to your dormitory account or simply send you a check for the amount overpaid.

Then there are the scholarships that award you savings bonds. One in particular that is given out to our students does not mature to the full amount until 30 years later. That is a long time to wait, especially when you are young. You do have the choice of cashing it in before that time but with a loss. This particular one could be turned in for half the amount of the savings bond after one year's wait. But even that is better than nothing, and a year later that money will come in handy.

One of the most important things to remember is to make

sure you know exactly how much money you have coming to you. Keep a record of all awards and even the loans, just to make sure you receive all the money that should be coming to you. Colleges can make mistakes because, once again, the human factor comes into play. Make a copy of any checks sent to you, before you deposit it so you have proof of what was sent to you.

When my daughter won several different scholarships, one was for $1,000 for the college of her choice. They divided it up into two semesters. When I asked what would happen to the second half of the scholarship ($500) if she changed colleges in the spring semester, I was told that they would simply send the remainder back to the donor. If she did change colleges, she would have to call the scholarship committee and ask them to resend the $500 to another college. This is a hassle, but what can you do? You need to make sure that you follow up on this money, though, as in my daughter's case, this $1,000 scholarship was for the college of her choice. That money was hers, no matter where she attended college.

Now let us look at another example. Let us say that you were awarded one $1,000 scholarship and two $500 scholarships, a total of $2,000, and your bill for one semester is $600. Depending on the college, they may send you a refund of $1,400 or, if they divided it up into two semesters, the refund would be for $400, and the remaining $1,000 will go into your account for the following term. After signing up for and paying for your second term, you should then get the remainder of that amount sent to you.

Unfortunately, at most colleges, you cannot use the money in your college account to pay for your books until it is sent to you. The book store is usually a separate business from the college, and as the refund usually takes a few weeks to get, you will have to pay for the books up front and reimburse yourself when you receive the scholarship refund.

You need to keep track of all scholarships you receive. As I stated before, mistakes happen. During my daughter's first year of college, she had more than enough scholarships to pay for her classes. Even with the college dividing up her scholarship money into two semesters, they still owed her quite a bit just from the first semester.

In Florida, where we have the Florida Bright Futures, she received 75 percent of her tuition. This money is sent to the college, but the college does not always apply it toward the students' fees upon registration. The student has to pay up front for their first semester, and then the college will send them a check for 75 or 100 percent of their tuition, but not until after the drop period. Jessica's first semester had already been paid for by her other scholarships. After paying she still had over $1,000 in extra money and the college sent her that amount. After receiving the check she did not really pay attention to the fact that she never received her Bright Futures money. However, I kept track of all her scholarships and how much was spent and how much she was reimbursed. When the drop period was over and several students that I knew had already received their Bright Futures money, I called the college financial aid office. They told me that she had never returned the letter to the state program telling them which college she was going to attend. I then called the state financial aid office in Tallahassee, explaining the problem to them. They informed me, that not only had they received the letter from Jessica naming her college, but the money was already at the college, sent in her name. The next day I went directly to the senior guidance counselor, who called the college and told them that they had exactly one week to get the check in the mail to Jessica. And lo and behold, she got it in less than a week. The whole point to this story is that some students' money seems to fall through the cracks, and sadly enough, if someone is not paying attention, it will stay there.

Another good example was when my son won his scholarships. Four years after Jessica's problems, her brother started college, and midway through his first semester the problems started. Michael had also received the Bright Futures 75 percent scholarship and other scholarships as well. Some of the checks were sent directly to him (after he had sent them proof of enrollment) and some to the college. About two months into the first semester, the college sent him notice that the scholarships had been awarded through their offices. He was sent four different letters. There were two separate letters for two different scholarships. The first set was for $200 for the fall and a second letter from the same scholarship for $200 for the spring semester. The second set of letters was from another scholarship for $300 for the fall semester and another $300 for the spring. He had already paid in full and even received reimbursement for the fall semester, so he should have had a $500 check sent to him in the mail. Instead they sent him a check for $206 – an odd number, seeing how neither scholarship was for that exact amount. Two months had passed and he still had not received anything else, so we called the financial aid department and were told that he still had a balance of $294 for the fall semester. We were also told that he should be getting a check in the mail within the next two weeks. Four weeks later we called again, and once again we were told that he would receive a check within a week. He did get a check, but it was only for ten dollars. When we called again, we were told that this was a refund for a ticket that he had paid. He deserved the ticket (incorrect parking place), so why would they refund him the money? Again, none of this answered the questions we were asking.

Then they told us they only had a copy of two letters he should have gotten, not four. We had to tell them that we had four letters, and we would bring them in or fax the letters to them. Lo and behold, they found all his scholarship money, but the problems did not stop there.

I had carefully calculated what his fees and tuition were going to be, how much money he had in scholarships, and what they had reimbursed him. I was relieved when the check they sent him for his second semester was for everything (except the Bright Futures), including the money they had owed him from the fall semester. I kept a close eye on the dates when the Bright Futures money should be coming out for the second semester.

I gave them six weeks, and then once again, called the financial aid office. They told me that they automatically apply the Bright Futures when students enroll for their second semester, and that he had already been sent a check. I told them that the amount did not include the Bright Futures, only the scholarship money that had been in his account previously. The person then told me, as she was looking at his records, that he was paid in full. I then went over in detail the amount of each scholarship that he got, his tuition and fees, the reimbursement checks that he had received from them, and the amount that they STILL owed him. I had to do this twice, and then she finally seemed to listen and told me that she would have to turn this over to her supervisor. The next day a check was cut and he got his 75 percent shortly after.

So how many students out there do not get their money? I am afraid that this might be a rather scary answer. As far as either of my children was concerned, the college had sent them both a rather large reimbursement, and they just assumed that the college had paid them in full. Needless to say, I was pretty upset that I had to call and demand, in both of my children's cases, that the college return all their money. I even called the same counselor that had helped me with Jessica and told her of Michael's injustice. She wanted me to put it all in writing to give to the Dean's wife, as she works at our school. I did this, but was told that the turnover in that office was extremely high and that there was little they could do to sort this out. I felt that it was my duty to do this for all the other students and their parents, so I repeatedly tell all students to be sure and keep a close eye on their money and the financial aid office. You have to pay attention to every little amount that should be coming back to you. Many students and parents do not realize exactly how to do this or that there is a need for double checking the amount. It is really not that difficult as long as you keep records of all the amounts awarded, how much is paid for tuition and fees, and then the amount that is reimbursed.

You also need to keep careful watch over money sent to you from loans. If the college says they sent you a check for $2,000 and you only received $1,000, the only real way to prove this is for you to have made a copy of the check before depositing it or cashing it. The same goes for scholarship reimbursements. Keep a copy of the check; you never know when you may have to prove what was sent to you.

I just came across another problem this year with one of my seniors from the previous year. He filled out the FAFSA and answered yes to the question about needing loans just in case he would need it (which is usually a good way to answer the question). He then proceeded to get more than enough money from scholarships and he did not need any loans. He did not fill out any more forms to get one, as most colleges require you to fill out additional forms and choose your lenders. One day he was checking his account and it showed that a certain bank (one of the lenders) had over $900 in loans for him for each of the two semesters. He called and was told that money was there for him "just in case," but it showed up as a loan. He was able to get them to remove it, as he never borrowed any money from them, but what might have happened if he had never checked his account? He was told that if he had not called, it might have shown up as a loan by the time he graduated. So be sure to keep track of anything that has to do with your money.

But that is not the only thing you need to stay on top of. Some scholarships will specify when they will send the money. If this is the case, make sure you call the financial aid office before the college tuition is due and then you will not have to pay out of your own pocket first. You always need to make sure you have already sent the scholarship committee your college information and proof of enrollment whether they require it or not. Even if the scholarship organization has not given you a timeline for when they will send the scholarship money, you still need to send them your proof of enrollment and wait three to four weeks before you call the college's financial aid office to see if they have received the money yet. If they have not received it, wait another week or two, and call again. If the college still has not gotten the money, you may have to call the scholarship committee yourself to find out when they will be sending it. Be sure to remain polite, even if you are getting frustrated.

I have actually seen a case in which a local club gave out scholarships, and between sending the award letter and the money, they had an officer change, and the money never got sent until the student called to remind them. Another student had me call to ask what had happened to the money from one of her scholarships, and I was told that they had lost her address, and they were glad

I had contacted them. So keep a copy of all letters of confirmation of scholarships, just as you have kept a copy of all applications. You never know when you may need it for proof or just for a contact name and address or phone number.

When you receive a scholarship, a thank you note is a must. You can send it right away or after the money has been sent, but please do not forget to send a letter. It is the least you can do when someone has been generous enough to help you finance your education. You never know when a scholarship (especially local ones) may renew itself, and that thank you letter might just keep your name in someone's mind. I will also remind you again that you should take the time to write thank you letters to anyone who wrote you a letter of recommendation. Not only do letters of recommendation take time and effort to write, but they can play a huge role in helping a committee choose their winner.

> *"Financing college would have been a very stressful experience for me without the help of Mrs. Debra Lipphardt. Coming from a single-parent family, the costs of college would have drained all savings and emergency funds in our family accounts within the first year. However, Mrs. Lipphardt's various techniques and strategies for getting national, as well as local, scholarships worked phenomenally. With her expert methods I was able to collect over $34,000 in scholarships for four years that helped me complete my major senior year goal: going to college for a complete year without being a financial*

burden on my mom. In addition, she has helped me communicate with the Office of Financial Aid as well as places to look and people to talk to for scholarships at the college level."

Michael Jones
Vanguard High School
Class of 2006
Florida State University

Chapter 12

SCAMS

You need to be aware of scholarship scams. They come in many forms. There are so many free scholarship searches (see the last page of this chapter for some Web sites), and you can always go to the public library and use their scholarship books to search for even more. You should never have to pay for a search. You apply for scholarships to get money, not to spend the money first. I have seen a couple of searches that charged between $40 and $50, and they actually did do a search for the student. Most of the addresses they sent to the student were for national scholarships, none for local ones, and many of the scholarships no longer existed. I compared my list of scholarships to that list; I had over 80 percent of them, and it did not cost me anything to compile my list.

Be wary of any scholarship application that requests money to apply. Contests, mainly the artistic type, sometimes do ask for an entrance fee. Many of these are legit; just do not spend too much money on any of them. I have seen some basic, non-artistic applications ask for as much as $20. Do not waste your money.

One of the worst types of scams, though, is the one where you will receive an official looking letter, inviting you to participate in a scholarship information workshop. They usually hold these in a conference room at a reputable hotel. They talk about helping you apply to a variety of colleges and scholarships, making the entire process easier for you.

First of all, you do not need to pay anyone to help you with your college applications. There is an application fee that goes to the college, and that is more than enough to have to pay. Go to your guidance counselor if you need help on the applications. You can also go to an English teacher for help with the essay, if one is required, or you can go online and search for examples of college essays.

Then there is the catch: "Pay us, and we promise that you will receive a scholarship." No one can promise that you will win a scholarship. There was one such company that came to our town, and one young man and his mother paid $1,000 for them to help him with scholarships. They "guaranteed" that he would get some money, even telling them that he would receive at least $2,000 minimum. The first mailing he received from this company was a preview of what he would be getting from the Free Application for Federal Student Aid (FAFSA).

Notice the word "free." The FAFSA is just that – a free application. It just so happened that this young man's mother was living on a very low income, and the only way she was able to pay for this "help" was from a small inheritance she had just gotten. Anyone could predict that he would receive grants from Federal Aid because of his mother's income. Another month or two went by, and he received a nice package from this company. It was in a binder, and each page was in plastic sheet protectors. What the holders contained, though, was a joke. They had simply detailed everything he should receive from the FAFSA in grants and student loans. They had not sent him one scholarship application.

I got their phone number and called them myself. I let them know that we knew what they sent was a waste, as we knew that the college would be sending the same information for free, just not in such nice wrapping. I then asked them about scholarship applications, and they just kind of stuttered and tried to talk about what they had already done for him, which was nothing. I sent him to an attorney, but unfortunately he never came back to let me know what happened, so I assumed that he was unable to get anything from this except a lesson. I never got to see a copy of the contract his mother signed, but I always wondered if the fine print said something about guaranteeing money for him, but not where it was coming from. Even I could have guaranteed that he would get something from the government. But there are no guarantees on winning scholarships.

The saddest thing about all this was that I had all these applications that he could have applied for, and they would not have cost him anything, just his time. Instead, his mother paid money that she could not afford and could have put toward paying for his education.

Every year, our students receive these letters, asking them to attend a workshop, and every year I get calls from parents asking my advice. I tell them to attend if they want but NOT to pay ANY money. Most of them throw away the letters, but the few that decide to attend, hoping they can get free money, find out that the price is steep. Each time they come to our area, they come under a different name and usually rent out various places. One even had their meeting at one of our popular public universities. The letter made it sound like they were part of the college, but did not come right out and say it. There was no college logo on the letterhead either. I contacted the college and was told that whoever this company was, they were not affiliated with their college and that they were only renting a room from them. These "scam" companies always seem to rent a room at reputable places. It makes them seem more real.

Just remember this: NEVER PAY for what you can get for free.

Here are just a few phrases to watch out for in the world of scholarship scams:

- We can guarantee you financial aid, or you will get your money back." Are they talking about loans by any chance? Anyone can go to the bank for those.

- "You can't get this information anywhere else or from anyone else." Except perhaps at your school or surfing on the Internet.

- "You must have a credit card OR bank account number in order to apply for this scholarship." I have yet to see ANY scholarship application that requires either of these.

- "We'll do all of the work for you." Something for nothing? No one but you can do this.

- "This scholarship will cost you some money." Maybe on Wall Street, but not for scholarships.

- "You are a semi-finalist (or finalist), or you have been selected." The only problem is you never applied for this in the first place. When it seems too good to be true, it usually is.

So please do not pay anyone to help you get a scholarship; do the work yourself and save your money for a better purpose. It all goes back to what my father used to tell me: You do not get something for nothing; life just is not that easy.

A FEW SCHOLARSHIP WEB SITES TO TRY

- **www.fastweb.com**

- **www.salliemae.com**

- **www.students.gov**

- **www.scholarships.com**

- **www.fastaid.com**

- **www.collegenet.com**

- **www.finaid.org**

- **www.collegeboard.com**

- **www.collegeanswer.com**

Chapter 13

MY METHODS

There are a variety of ways to get scholarship information and applications to the students. My method, I am sure, is one of many.

I first start out with the all the local scholarships that come in to the guidance office or that go directly to the senior guidance counselor. Many counselors at the other schools simply file these and have them for the students to go through on their own time. I retrieve them, advertise, make copies, and then file them. I also send out over 300 letters of requests for applications each year. And as I said earlier, I go on scholarship searches as different types of students to get even more applications.

Once again, the main thing to remember is that even though these students are seniors, they are still just students needing extra guidance to help them along. I have tried to make it easier for them. I read each scholarship application I receive, then type up a bulletin, simplifying the whole process for them. If it is an application that can only be done online, I print out copies of whatever information I can in place of the application, just so the students have a little extra help. Whether it is online only or a hard copy of the application, I type them up in my bulletin using the same method. I start out with the title (which is what they are filed by in my scholarship files), with the next line being the grade level the scholarship is for. I also code each one for the different grade levels with colored check marks on the left side of the description. I use pink for the freshman, yellow for sophomores, and blue for juniors. Seniors need to read all of them, as most of the scholarships pertain to them. This makes it easier for the underclassman to glance through and find the few that I have for them.

After the grade level, I put the most basic requirement for each scholarship. Some may be as simple as "Seniors: Who will be attending college in the Fall," "Who will be majoring in Education" (or Music, Communications, Engineering, and so on), "For Females Only," "Minority Students Only," "Students with Community Service," "Leadership Skills." This makes it much easier for the students to glance at them and see if they are eligible or not right away. Sometimes they have to read a little further to the next part, which is Requirements. This can include a minimum GPA, numbers of letters of recommendation, transcripts, and any essay information. The student can read this bulletin and decide if this scholarship is for them or not, without having to read the entire application, which can take much more time.

I then give the amount and the number of scholarships offered, with the deadline being the final part. Whenever there is a deadline, as I said before, if I do not see the words "postmark," I assume that the deadline is when they want to receive the application. It is always better to be early, as late applications are rarely accepted. I mail them myself if the students get them to me by my deadline. I mail them one week early to be sure they get them on time. It never hurts to send the application in early.

I also type up a deadline list for all the scholarships in the order they are due. This seems to help the students get them in order better than on their own. The student can then take a piece of paper and write the titles and deadlines of the ones they want to do. Many times I try to go over the list with them, as they always seem to miss some that pertain to them. I also date each bulletin, so if the student comes in on a regular basis, they do not have to reread each bulletin.

I try to always have the applications on hand, by asking the students to let me know when the file is down to the last application. Then I can find the master and request more copies.

I have a book in which I have the students enter their name, their major, and the college they plan to attend, so when I have specific scholarships, I can then call them down to my classroom to get the application.

"As a senior English teacher, I know directly how dedicated Debra Lipphardt is in providing all seniors with information about scholarships, publicizing the scholarships, conducting workshops and classroom visits, or calling students in individually if she knew that a scholarship fit that student. The lengths she goes to in order to seek out new sources of money to benefit our students is amazing. Her knowledge

and experience have helped so many. Her efforts on behalf of Vanguard's students have been extremely successful. So many students have won scholarships."

Brenda Dilley, Reading Coach; formerly English IV teacher Vanguard High School

I try to always be available to answer questions or help the confused find what they need or need to know. And when I have my students for classes, I always mention scholarships, and the older they get, the more in depth I get with the information they will need.

My job consists of so many different variables, from helping students search for careers or colleges, to sponsoring my club, to coordinating graduation, to being on a variety of committees. But assisting students with scholarships is by far my most favorite thing to do and one of the most rewarding parts of my life.

I have written this book to help you, the student, your parents, and even other school personnel, to better understand scholarships, how to find them, and the best way to apply for them. Hopefully many of you will get more than just words of wisdom from this book, but will get money to help you through college and reach your dreams.

A simple overall review of this book:

- Keep your grades up; do not give up on them.

- Join organizations that interest you so that you will become more involved.

- Get volunteer hours. Not only does this open up more scholarship opportunities, but allows you to help others in need.

- Have your résumé ready for scholarship applications.

- Have your letters of recommendation ready.

- Read ALL directions.

- Write your essays with heart.

- Have someone proofread your work.

- Look for all the applications you are eligible for.

- Be neat and complete the entire application.

- Be on time.

Apply, apply, and apply for as many scholarships as possible.

- Do not give up!

STATE AID SOURCES

ALABAMA

Alabama Commission on Higher
Education
Suite 205
3465 Norman Bridge Road
Montgomery, Alabama 36105-2310
(334) 281-1998
State Department of Education
Gordon Persons Office Building
50 North Ripley Street
Montgomery, Alabama 36130-3901
(205) 242-8082

ALASKA

Alaska Commission on Postsecondary
Education
3030 Vintage Boulevard
Juneau, Alaska 99801-7109
(907) 465-2967
State Department of Education
Goldbelt Place
801 West 10th Street, Suite 200
Juneau, Alaska 99801-1894
(907) 465-8715

ARIZONA

Arizona Commission for Postsecondary
Education
2020 North Central Ave., Suite 275
Phoenix, Arizona 85004-4503
(602) 229-2531
State Department of Education
1535 West Jefferson
Phoenix, Arizona 85007
(602) 542-2147

ARKANSAS

Arkansas Department of Higher
Education
114 East Capitol
Little Rock, Arkansas 72201-3818
(501) 324-9300
Arkansas Department of Education
4 State Capitol Mall, Room 304A
Little Rock, Arkansas 72201-1071
(501) 682-4474

CALIFORNIA

California Student Aid Commission
Mailing address:
P.O. Box 419026
Rancho Cordova, CA 95741-9026
Street Address:
California Student Aid Commission

3300 Zinfandel Drive
Rancho Cordova, CA 95670
Customer Service (916) 526-7590
California Department of Education
721 Capitol Mall
Sacramento, California 95814
(916) 657-2451

COLORADO

Colorado Commission on Higher
Education
Colorado Heritage Center
1300 Broadway, 2nd Floor
Denver, Colorado 80203
(303) 866-2723
State Department of Education
201 East Colfax Avenue
Denver, Colorado 80203-1705
(303) 866-6779

CONNECTICUT

Connecticut Department of Higher
Education
61 Woodland Street
Hartford, Connecticut 06105-2391
(203) 566-3910
Connecticut Department of Education
165 Capitol Avenue
P.O. Box 2219
Hartford, Connecticut 06106-1630

DELAWARE

Delaware Higher Education Commission
Carvel State Office Building, Fourth Floor
820 North French Street
Wilmington, Delaware 19801
(302) 577-3240
Delaware Department of Education
Townsend Building #279
Federal and Lockerman Streets
P.O. Box 1402

Dover, Delaware 19903-1402
(302) 739-4583

DISTRICT OF COLUMBIA

Department of Human Services
Office of Postsecondary Education,
Research and Assistance
2100 Martin Luther King, Jr., Avenue, SE
Suite 401
Washington, DC 20020
(202) 727-3685
District of Columbia Public Schools
Division of Student Services
4501 Lee Street, N.E.
Washington, DC 20019
(202) 724-4934

FLORIDA

Florida Department of Education
Office of Student Financial Assistance
1344 Florida Education Center
325 West Gaines Street
Tallahassee, Florida 32399-0400
(904) 487-0649

GEORGIA

Georgia Student Finance Commission
State Loans and Grants Division
Suite 245
2082 East Exchange Place
Tucker, Georgia 30084
(404) 414-3000
State Department of Education
2054 Twin Towers East, 205 Butler Street
Atlanta, Georgia 30334-5040
(404) 656-5812

HAWAII

Hawaii State Postsecondary Education
Commission
2444 Dole Street, Room 202

Honolulu, Hawaii 96822-2394
(808) 956-8213
Hawaii Department of Education
2530 10th Avenue, Room A12
Honolulu, Hawaii 96816
(808) 733-9103

IDAHO
Idaho Board of Education
P.O. Box 83720
Boise, Idaho 83720-0037
(208) 334-2270
State Department of Education
650 West State Street
Boise, Idaho 83720
(208) 334-2113

ILLINOIS
Illinois Student Assistance Commission
1755 Lake Cook Road
Deerfield, Illinois 60015-5209
(708) 948-8500

INDIANA
State Student Assistance Commission of
Indiana
Suite 500, 150 West Market Street
Indianapolis, Indiana 46204-2811
(317) 232-2350
Indiana Department of Education
Room 229 - State House
Center for Schools Improvement
and Performance
Indianapolis, Indiana 46204-2798
(317) 232-2305

IOWA
Iowa College Student Aid Commission
914 Grand Avenue, Suite 201
Des Moines, Iowa 50309-2824
(800) 383-4222

Iowa Department of Education

KANSAS
Kansas Board of Regents
700 S.W. Harrison, Suite 1410
Topeka, Kansas 66603-3760
(913) 296-3517
State Department of Education
Kansas State Education Building
120 East Tenth Street
Topeka, Kansas 66612-1103
(913) 296-4876

KENTUCKY
Kentucky Higher Education Assistance
Authority
Suite 102, 1050 U.S. 127 South
Frankfort, Kentucky 40601-4323
(800) 928-8926
State Department of Education
500 Mero Street
1919 Capital Plaza Tower
Frankfort, Kentucky 40601
(502) 564-3421

LOUISIANA
Louisiana Student Financial Assistance
Commission
Office of Student Financial Assistance
P.O. Box 91202
Baton Rouge, Louisiana 70821-9202
(800) 259-5626
State Department of Education
P.O. Box 94064
626 North 4th Street, 12th Floor
Baton Rouge, Louisiana 70804-9064
(504) 342-2098

MAINE
Finance Authority of Maine
P.O. Box 949

Augusta, Maine 04333-0949
(207) 287-3263
Maine Department of Education
23 State House Station
Augusta, ME 04333-0023
Voice: (207) 287-5800
TDD/TTY for Hearing-Impaired: (207)
287-2550
Fax: (207) 287-5900

MARYLAND

Maryland Higher Education Commission
Jeffrey Building, 16 Francis Street
Annapolis, Maryland 21401-1781
(410) 974-2971
Maryland State Department of Education
200 West Baltimore Street
Baltimore, Maryland 21201-2595
(410) 767-0480

MASSACHUSETTS

Massachusetts Board of Higher
Education
330 Stuart Street
Boston, Massachusetts 02116
(617) 727-9420
State Department of Education
350 Main Street
Malden, Massachusetts 02148-5023
(617) 388-3300
Massachusetts Higher Education
Information Center
666 Boylston St.
Boston, Massachusetts 20116
(617) 536-0200 x4719

MICHIGAN

Michigan Higher Education Assistance
Authority
Office of Scholarships and Grants
P.O. Box 30462

Lansing, Michigan 48909-7962
(517) 373-3394
Michigan Department of Education
608 West Allegan Street
Hannah Building
Lansing, Michigan 48909
(517) 373-3324

MINNESOTA

Minnesota Higher Education Services
Office
Suite 400, Capitol Square Bldg.
550 Cedar Street
St. Paul, Minnesota 55101-2292
(800) 657-3866
Department of Children, Families, and
Learning
712 Capitol Square Building
550 Cedar Street
St. Paul, Minnesota 55101
(612) 296-6104

MISSISSIPPI

Mississippi Postsecondary Education
Financial Assistance Board
3825 Ridgewood Road
Jackson, Mississippi 39211-6453
(601) 982-6663
State Department of Education
P.O. Box 771
Jackson, Mississippi 39205-0771
(601) 359-3768

MISSOURI

Missouri Coordinating Board for Higher
Education
3515 Amazonas Drive
Jefferson City, Missouri 65109-5717
(314) 751-2361
Missouri State Department of Elementary
and

Secondary Education
P.O. Box 480
205 Jefferson Street, Sixth Floor
Jefferson City, Missouri 65102-0480
(314) 751-2931

MONTANA
Montana University System
2500 Broadway
Helena, Montana 59620-3103
(406) 444-6570
State Office of Public Instruction
State Capitol, Room 106
Helena, Montana 59620
(406) 444-4422

NEBRASKA
Coordinating Commission for
Postsecondary Education
P.O. Box 95005
Lincoln, Nebraska 68509-5005
(402) 471-2847
Nebraska Department of Education
P.O. Box 94987
301 Centennial Mall South
Lincoln, Nebraska 68509-4987
(402) 471-2784

NEVADA
Nevada Department of Education
400 West King Street
Capitol Complex
Carson City, Nevada 89710
(702) 687-5915

NEW HAMPSHIRE
New Hampshire Postsecondary
Education Commission
2 Industrial Park Drive
Concord, New Hampshire 03301-8512
(603) 271-2555

State Department of Education
State Office Park South
101 Pleasant Street
Concord, New Hampshire 03301
(603) 271-2632

NEW JERSEY
State of New Jersey
Office of Student Financial Assistance
4 Quakerbridge Plaza, CN 540
Trenton, New Jersey 08625
(800) 792-8670
State Department of Education
225 West State Street
Trenton, New Jersey 08625-0500
(609) 984-6409

NEW MEXICO
New Mexico Commission on Higher
Education
1068 Cerrillos Road
Santa Fe, New Mexico 87501-4925
(505) 827-7383
State Department of Education
Education Building
300 Don Gaspar
Santa Fe, New Mexico 87501-2786
(505) 827-6648

NEW YORK
New York State Higher Education
Services Corporation
One Commerce Plaza
Albany, New York 12255
(518) 474-5642
State Education Department
111 Education Building
Washington Avenue
Albany, New York 12234
(518) 474-5705

NORTH CAROLINA
North Carolina State Education
Assistance Authority
P.O. Box 2688
Chapel Hill, North Carolina 27515-2688
(919) 821-4771
State Department of Public Instruction
Education Building
Division of Teacher Education
116 West Edenton Street
Raleigh, North Carolina 27603-1712
(919) 733-0701

NORTH DAKOTA
North Dakota University System
North Dakota Student Financial
Assistance Program
600 East Boulevard Avenue
Bismarck, North Dakota 58505-0230
(701) 224-4114
State Department of Public Instruction
State Capitol Building, 11th Floor
600 East Boulevard Avenue
Bismarck, North Dakota 58505-0164
(701) 224-2271

OHIO
Ohio Board of Regents
P.O. Box 182452
309 South Fourth Street
Columbus, Ohio 43218-2452
1-888-833-1133
State Department of Education
65 South Front Street, Room 1005
Columbus, Ohio 43266-0308
(614) 466-2761

OKLAHOMA
Oklahoma State Regents for Higher
Education
Oklahoma Guaranteed Student Loan

Program
P.O. Box 3000
Oklahoma City, OK 73101-3000
(405) 858-4300
1-800-247-0420
State Department of Education
Oliver Hodge Memorial Education
Building
2500 North Lincoln Boulevard
Oklahoma City, Oklahoma 73105-4599
(405) 521-4122

OREGON
Oregon State Scholarship Commission
Suite 100, 1500 Valley River Drive
Eugene, Oregon 97401-2130
(503) 687-7400
Oregon State System of Higher
Education
700 Pringle Parkway, S.E.
Salem, Oregon 97310-0290
(503) 378-5585
Oregon Department of Education
255 Capitol Street NE
Salem, OR 97310-0203

PENNSYLVANIA
Pennsylvania Higher Education
Assistance Agency
1200 North Seventh Street
Harrisburg, Pennsylvania 17102-1444
(800) 692-7435
P.O. Box 8114
Harrisburg, Pennsylvania 17105-8114
(717) 720-2075

RHODE ISLAND
Rhode Island Board of Governors for
Higher Education &
Rhode Island Office of Higher Education
301 Promenade Street

Providence, Rhode Island, 02908-5720
Voice: (401) 277-6560
Fax: (401) 277-6111
E-Mail: RIBOG@uriacc.uri.edu
Rhode Island Higher Education
Assistance Authority
560 Jefferson Boulevard
Warwick, Rhode Island 02886
(800) 922-9855
State Department of Education
22 Hayes Street
Providence, Rhode Island 02908
(401) 277-3126

SOUTH CAROLINA

South Carolina Higher Education Tuition
Grants Commission
1310 Lady Street, Suite 811
P.O. Box 12159
Columbia, South Carolina 29201
(803) 734-1200
State Department of Education
803-a Rutledge Building
1429 Senate Street
Columbia, South Carolina 29201
(803) 734-8364

SOUTH DAKOTA

Department of Education and Cultural
Affairs
Office of the Secretary
700 Governors Drive
Pierre, South Dakota 57501-2291
(605) 773-3134
South Dakota Board of Regents

TENNESSEE

Tennessee Higher Education Commission
404 James Robertson Parkway
Suite 1900
Nashville, Tennessee 37243-0820
(615) 741-3605

State Department of Education
100 Cordell Hull Building
Nashville, Tennessee 37219-5335
(615)741-1346 or (800) 342-1663 (TN
residents only)

TEXAS

Texas Higher Education Coordinating
Board
P.O. Box 12788, Capitol Station
Austin, Texas 78711
(800) 242-3062

UTAH

Utah State Board of Regents
Utah System of Higher Education
355 West North Temple
#3 Triad Center, Suite 550
Salt Lake City, Utah 84180-1205
(801) 321-7205
Utah State Office of Education
250 East 500 South
Salt Lake City, Utah 84111
(801) 538-7779

VERMONT

Vermont Student Assistance Corporation
Champlain Mill
P.O. Box 2000
Winooski, Vermont 05404-2601
(800) 642-3177
Vermont Department of Education
120 State Street
Montpelier, VT 05620-2501
Voice: (802) 828-3147
Fax: (802) 828-3140

VIRGINIA

State Council of Higher Education for
Virginia
James Monroe Building
101 North Fourteenth Street

Richmond, Virginia 23219
(804) 786-1690
State Department of Education
P.O. Box 2120
James Monroe Building
14th and Franklin Streets
Richmond, Virginia 23216-2120
(804) 225-2072

WASHINGTON
Washington State Higher Education
Coordinating Board
P.O. Box 43430, 917 Lakeridge Way, S.W.
Olympia, Washington 98504-3430
(206) 753-7850
State Department of Public Instruction
Old Capitol Building, P.O. Box FG 11
Olympia, Washington, 98504-3211
(206) 753-2858

WEST VIRGINIA
State Department of Education
1900 Washington Street
Building B, Room 358
Charleston, West Virginia 25305
(304) 588-2691
State College & University Systems of
West Virginia Central Office
1018 Kanawha Boulevard East, Suite 700
Charleston, West Virginia 25301-2827
(304) 558-4016

WISCONSIN
Higher Educational Aids Board
P.O. Box 7885
Madison, Wisconsin 53707-7885
(608) 267-2206
State Department of Public Instruction
125 South Wester Street
P.O. Box 7841

Madison, Wisconsin 53707-7814
(608) 266-2364

WYOMING
Wyoming State Department of Education
Hathaway Building
2300 Capitol Avenue, 2nd Floor
Cheyenne, Wyoming 82002-0050
(307) 777-6265
Wyoming Community College
Commission
2020 Carey Avenue, 8th Floor
Cheyenne, Wyoming 82002
(307) 777-7763
PUERTO RICO
Council on Higher Education
Box 23305 - UPR Station
Rio Piedras, Puerto Rico 00931
(809) 758-3350
Department of Education
P.O. Box 759
Hato Rey, Puerto Rico 00919
(809) 753-2200

U.S. DEPARTMENT OF EDUCATION
SSIG Program
Office of Postsecondary Education
Student Financial Assistance Programs
Pell and State Grant Section
U.S. Department of Education
ROB #3, Room 3045
600 Independence Avenue, S.W.
Washington, DC 20202-5447
(202) 708-4607

AUTHOR
BIOGRAPHY

Debra Lipphardt

I am the Career and College Center Specialist and Scholarship Coordinator for a local high school in our county. I actually created the position of Scholarship Coordinator because I found the results of winning scholarships so fascinating. I am the only one in the county out of six other schools with this title of Scholarship Coordinator, mainly because most of the work I do on scholarships is on my own time at home. Our students have won the most awards for the past 10 out of 11 years over the other six schools in our district since I began working with scholarships, averaging over 2.7 million dollars in scholarships per year (in fact for the last five years they have averaged over 3.1 million). During the past three years our school has been ahead of the second place school by over 20 awards, and the year that we placed second, we were only behind by four awards.

I have given countless lectures and workshops, three to four weekly private meetings with parents and students, and have been interviewed on several local radio stations concerning scholarships. I have also received several awards for my work with scholarships as well. I received the County School Employee of the Year in 2000 and 2004, the first person to ever receive this honor twice and Vanguard High School's Employee of the Year twice. I have been honored by being the District Teacher of the Year for the VFW in 2000, 2004, the post winner for 2007, and currently selected as the District winner for 2008, and was a Semi-Finalist for the Junior League's Three Who Care Award in 2007. I am also in Who's Who Among America's Teachers (multiple times), Cambridge Who's Who Among Professional and Executive Women-2007/2008(-Honors Edition) Emerald's Who's Who for Executives and Professionals-2007, Biltmore Who's Who of Professional and Executive Women-2007, Princeton Premier Business Leaders and Professionals-2007, and Madison Who's Who Among Executives and Professionals-2007/2008.

I have always loved writing and telling stories to my children so I thought that my first attempt at a novel would be fairly tales. Instead, one day I sat down and started to write about scholarships, a subject that I love working with and have researched and implemented with accomplishment, a total hands on approach to winning scholarships.

After being asked by a multitude of other schools' counselors and personnel on how my students have been so accomplished at obtaining scholarships, I decided to share this secret of achievement by writing it down and putting it into a book. I believe that with my hands on approach, that this book will be able to assist a multitude of students and parents in finding, applying, and winning scholarships to make college more than just a dream.

INTENDED MARKET

I wrote this book not only for the students, but also as a guide for parents and other school personnel to help them in aiding the students with scholarships. This comes from me- first, as a mom with a 21 and 25-year-old, (one still a college student and the other a college graduate) and also as a College and Career Center Specialist/Scholarship Coordinator.

No one had ever talked about scholarships to me when I was in high school, so when I first discovered scholarships my curiosity and questions began. How much could students actually benefit from these scholarships? Where do they find them and how do they go about applying?

I feel that I have learned so many different things about scholarships and people; students, parents, and guidance counselors from other schools are always calling or e-mailing me with countless questions. My principal (three in fact) have reminded me that I work for their school, and any assistance to others outside our district must be on my own time, and that I should charge a high consultation fee.

That is when I decided that by writing a book about scholarships I could reach so many different students who have no one to turn to for advice. College is so expensive, and cost should not be the reason that the future generation does not attend. The joy and thrill that I feel whenever any of my students come in and tell me that they have received a scholarship, was and still is, one of my greatest pleasures in my job and life, and I wanted to share this with a wider audience.

I have read other books on scholarships and my book is different from all of those that I have found so far. In fact after a visit to Barnes and Nobles and Books a Million, in search of scholarship books, I was saddened at their lack of books in this area, but also excited, as I really believe they could benefit by adding my book to their stores. My book covers the many different types of scholarships, how to find them (no matter where you live), what the basic requirements are, and most importantly how to fill out the applications. I write about essays, letters of recommendation, the judges, and have a very simple short cut method that makes applying to a vast number of different scholarships quick and simple.

I also cover what to do when you win a scholarship and many other various bits of information. My book includes real life examples of success and failures, making the reading more enjoyable than a research type of book would be.

Tools for Decision Making

A Practical Guide for Local Government

David N. Ammons

CQ PRESS

A Division of Congressional Quarterly Inc.
Washington, D.C.

CQ Press
A Division of Congressional Quarterly Inc.
1255 22nd Street, N.W., Suite 400
Washington, D.C. 20037

(202) 822-1475; (800) 638-1710

www.cqpress.com

⊚ The paper used in this publication meets the minimum
requirements of the American National Standard for Information
Sciences—Permanence of Paper for Printed Library Materials,
ANSI Z39.48-1992.

Printed and bound in the United States of America

05 04 03 02 01   5 4 3 2 1

Library of Congress Cataloging-in-Publication Data

Ammons, David N.
   Tools for decision making : a practical guide for local government/
David N. Ammons.
      p. cm.
   Includes bibliographical references and index.
   ISBN 1-56802-641-2
   1. Local government—Decision making.   2. Public administration—Decision
making.   I. Title.
   JS78 .A49 2002
   352.3'7214—dc21

                                                              2001006183

To my parents,
Margaret and Ernest Ammons

Contents

Tables

Figures

Preface

Tools for Decision Making is a guide to practical techniques of analysis for local government. It features analytic methods selected for their relevance to everyday problems encountered in cities and counties—and in only slightly different form, at other levels of government as well. Most of the techniques described in this volume can be mastered quickly and easily. Several are among the simplest that the fields of industrial engineering, policy analysis, and management science have to offer. None requires advanced mathematical skills—at least, not in the form presented here. Nor do most even require a computer, although software suggestions, spreadsheet tips, and helpful Web sites are offered for computer-savvy readers.

Many books that address this topic are of questionable value to readers in search of handy techniques that can be put to immediate use on the job. They focus on impressive techniques that are difficult to grasp without extensive formal training or a major commitment to self-directed study. Spare time for developing new skills, however, is a commodity in short supply for the busy practitioner who seeks timely solutions to pressing problems.

Some books miss the mark for their readers because they scattershoot the target by providing a broad overview rather than practical methods. They may theorize about decision making or perhaps extol the virtues of a rational approach, but then confine their description of analytic methods to only two or three rarely used techniques selected for their simplicity, not their usefulness.

Tools for Decision Making is different. Techniques that are abstract, impractical, or that demand advanced mathematical skills are not included. Instead the reader will find easy-to-understand, easy-to-apply, practical techniques of analysis especially suited to local government. Each is offered as a simple tool for the busy public official who favors data-based decision making over intuition.

This is the second edition of a book that was popular with students and local government practitioners alike for more than a decade under the title *Administrative Analysis for Local Government*. Students liked the book's practical orientation and choice of useful analytic techniques that could be applied in other courses and used on the job. They particularly valued the entertaining scenarios that illuminated the techniques and demonstrated their relevance. Practitioners praised the same things, appreciating especially the succinct and easy-to-grasp manner in which the techniques were introduced. The second edition has a new title, but it retains the same proven elements.

The book is arranged in seven parts. Parts I and VII offer introductory and concluding comments, respectively, on the role of analysis in local government. Parts II–VI focus on analytic techniques, arranged generally from the simplest to the more complex. Each chapter poses a problem in the form of a hypothetical local government scenario, describes a technique of analysis, and demonstrates the use of that technique. Like its predecessor, the second edition was written with practitioners and students of public administration and local government in mind. For the classroom market, this book will be a useful addition in public administration courses on research or analytic methods, statistics, policy analysis, budgeting, financial management, urban management, urban service delivery, and productivity improvement.

The first edition of this book was published by the Carl Vinson Institute of Government at the University of Georgia when I was a faculty member there. Initial drafts of several eventual chapters were developed as instructional material for a series of management seminars conducted with department heads and other administrative officials of Glynn County, Georgia. Graduate students Richard Huddleston, Roderick C. Lee, and James A. Russell assisted me ably in that endeavor. Our task, as initially conceived, was to collect a set of already published materials on handy techniques for analyzing practical day-to-day problems. Our discovery of a gap between methods textbooks oriented toward academic research, on the one hand, and the analytic needs of practicing administrators, on the other—a gap that our Glynn County drafts filled—led to the book.

The second edition builds on the first by strengthening or replacing some of the original chapters, adding new chapters on topics such as benchmarking and the analysis of survey data, and providing additional analytic examples and tips for spreadsheet and other computer applications for readers so inclined. Now at the University of North Carolina at Chapel Hill, I have been assisted on the second edition by graduate student Andy Williams and by Carla Pizzarella, a colleague at the Institute of Government. In addition, my daughter Paige prepared some of the graphs that appear in the book and developed most of the boxes that explain how to use spreadsheet programs to perform calculations called for by various analytic techniques. I am thankful for their help.

Several scholars offered insights along the way: Maureen Berner, William Rivenbark, Jack Vogt, and Philip Young, University of North Carolina at Chapel Hill; Ross Clayton, University of Southern California; Charles Coe, North Carolina State University; James DeAngelis, University of Pittsburgh; Robert England, Oklahoma State University; David Folz, University of Tennessee; Michelle Piskulich, Oakland University; David Schultz, Hamline University; and Sherman Wyman, University of Texas-Arlington. All graciously consented to review and offer suggestions for improving various chapters. The book has benefited wherever their advice was taken. Any errors that may remain are, of course, my responsibility.

The University of North Carolina's Institute of Government is fortunate to have an excellent staff providing support services for its projects, including this one. The assistance of Mark Dowell, Patt Dower, Nate Edgerly, and Elaine Welch was first-rate. Their role in this project is gratefully acknowledged.

David N. Ammons
Chapel Hill, North Carolina

Applying Analytic Techniques

Analytic Technique	Chapter	Use	Responding to Questions Like These . . .
Benchmarking	25	Detect performance gaps and identify, through comparison with top performers, ways to close the gaps	How does the pet adoption rate at the animal shelter compare with standards or with the rates of top shelters? What conditions or operating practices account for superior results in top shelters and which of these are adaptable for local use? Is the tonnage of refuse collected by the average sanitation worker comparable to performance statistics elsewhere? Would comparison with top departments and private collectors yield important lessons regarding equipment and route configurations?
Central tendency statistics	2	Identify the norm, typical, or average case	What's the typical police salary in this city? How many refuse complaints are received daily?
Chi-square statistic	23	Detect and report statistically significant relationships between nominal variables	Do the residents of various neighborhoods feel about the same regarding the quality of police services they are receiving? Are employees who participate in the tuition reimbursement program more likely than non-participants to remain with the county government at least five years?
Compounding	10, 13	Calculate the cumulative effect of interest on an investment	If the city invests $50,000 annually for the next five years at 6 percent interest as a strategy for funding a special project, how much money will be available?
"Constant dollar" calculations	12	"Factor-out" the effects of inflation when examining changes in revenues or expenditures	Controlling for inflation, have expenditures increased or decreased for various services? By how much?

Term		Description	Example
Correlation	24	See the extent to which increases in one variable tend to be accompanied by increases (or decreases) in another variable	How closely does the pattern of lifeguards on duty coincide with the number of swimmers at the pool? How closely does the demand pattern at the customer service desk correlate with the number of clerks on duty?
Cost-effectiveness analysis	16	Analyze the cost differences among a set of options that will provide equivalent benefits or analyze the different benefits among options having equivalent costs	Considering several alternatives for maintaining landscaped medians at a specified level of quality, which option offers the best value? Given a specified level of resources for combating the loss of books from the library's inventory, which of three options is most likely to solve the problem?
Demand analysis	3	Identify patterns of demand for a given service	What are the consumption patterns for water or electricity? When does consumption typically begin to subside? What strategies might help shave the demand peaks? What are the demand patterns for other local government services?
Depreciation	11	Calculate annualized costs for equipment and other capital items	How much of the unit cost of the service we provide is attributable to the cost of the equipment we use? How do our capital costs compare to those of other organizations doing similar work?
Discounting	13	Consider the present value of resources that will be received in the future	If the city offers an industrial recruitment incentive with a projected long-term payout, is it a good deal for general taxpayers?
Floating average	19	Smooth short-term fluctuations in performance statistics by reporting averages over longer periods of time	The city could report monthly fire incident and fire loss statistics or it could report the monthly average for the last twelve or twenty-four months. Which option would be better?

(continued)

Applying Analytic Techniques *(Continued)*

Analytic Technique	Chapter	Use	Responding to Questions Like These . . .
Future value	10, 13	See what today's resources, if invested, will be worth in tomorrow's dollars	If the city invests $70,000 annually for the next four years at 7 percent interest as a strategy for funding a special project, how much money will be available?
"Go-Away Costs"	15	Compare the cost of contract services to a corresponding reduction of in-house expenditures if a local government chooses to no longer produce the service itself (excludes from consideration any overhead and other costs that will continue despite a contracting decision)	How much will the local government save, if anything, by contracting refuse collection services? Custodial services? Street maintenance? Data processing? Other services?
Identifying full costs of a program	14	Incorporate into total costs not only direct costs but also indirect and other costs that often fail to be included in the reporting of program or activity expenditures	What does it cost to repair a pothole? To respond to a fire alarm? To what extent are the full costs of the building inspection program recovered by fees?
Investment calculations	10	Calculate yields from simple or compound interest; calculate interest rates; calculate yields from a series of even, annual investments (annuity)	How well are the county's investment strategies working? Can sufficient resources be accumulated from systematic set-asides to meet our capital program needs?
Job travel mapping	5	Detect inefficient travel patterns to enhance work scheduling and routing; improve office design	Have the work schedules of building inspectors been planned in a manner that minimizes inefficient or crisscrossing travel patterns and uncoordinated sequencing of stops? What about the schedules of code enforcement officials, case workers, health inspectors, street patching crews, parks maintenance crews?

Lease-buy analysis	18	Calculate the financial advantage or disadvantage of purchasing an item rather than leasing it	Would the county be ahead financially to buy its sedans and pickups or to lease them? What about leasing other equipment?
Life-cycle costing	17	Consider all costs associated with an item over its useful life when deciding whether to purchase it, rather than purchase price alone	Should the county convert its gasoline-powered fleet to an alternate fuel? Which pumper should the fire department and fleet maintenance recommend? What are the life-cycle ramifications of purchasing smaller-capacity, gasoline-powered refuse collection trucks rather than larger, diesel trucks?
Measures of dispersion	2	Identify how tightly clustered a set of cases is	How widely spread are property values in this community? Is there much variation in calls for police service from one night to another?
Opportunity costs	13	Help sort out choices among possible resource uses by comparing the benefits of one choice to the opportunities forgone by failing to select another option	Would a multimillion-dollar expenditure for a general aviation airport be a wise investment for the community? Would the development of an industrial park be a better choice?
Performance measurement	8	Gauge the quantity, quality, efficiency, and effectiveness of performance by a work unit, department, or program	How well is the parks maintenance function being performed? Is the quality satisfactory? What about the level of efficiency? Does the performance compare favorably with relevant benchmarks? Has the department reported its performance to the city council and to the citizenry?
Performance standards	9	Judge the adequacy of current services or the proficiency of current performance	How does local performance compare with published standards for grounds maintenance, custodial service, or vehicle repair?

(continued)

Applying Analytic Techniques *(Continued)*

Analytic Technique	Chapter	Use	Responding to Questions Like These . . .
PERT/CPM charts	4	Plan, coordinate, and monitor the steps required to complete a project	When Roger retires next year, will anyone around here know how to conduct a local election? Now that we have voter approval for a new civic center, let's see if we can move smoothly through the planning and construction stages. Does anyone have any idea what steps we need to follow?
Present value	13	See what a future accumulation of resources would be worth in today's dollars	If the city offers an industrial recruitment incentive with a projected long-term payout, is it a good deal for general taxpayers?
Process flow charts	6	Identify and analyze each step of a regularly performed process in an effort to eliminate unnecessary steps, reduce delay, and streamline procedures	Why can't we recruit and hire new employees more quickly? Why does approval of permit applications take so long? Why can't account clerks process more transactions per day? Why does it take so long to dispatch emergency calls?
Rating systems	22	Increase the likelihood that decisions reflect pre-established priorities	How can the city sort out its various objectives to select the best site for a new general aviation airport? Which proposed capital projects should be given top priority? Which administrative applicant is the best choice, considering the various criteria?
Regression	25	Describe the relationship between two or more variables[a] or perhaps predict changes in one variable based on the actual or projected behavior of other variables	How much is the level of participation in the city's recreation programs influenced by demographic factors as opposed to things like scheduling and participation fees? Given current economic factors and the community's demographics, what rate of tax delinquencies may we forecast? What level of general fund revenue should we project?

Revenue loss analysis	21	Estimate revenue losses attributable to procedural inefficiencies	Some city departments promptly deposit daily receipts and others are slower. How much revenue is the city losing because of delays?
Sampling, randomization	2	Learn about a larger population by studying a carefully selected subset	Are citizens generally satisfied with recreation services? What do they think about the city's traffic engineering efforts? Do the citizens support the local efforts to find a site for a local airport? How much of an account clerk's workday is devoted to handling calls (work sampling)? What is the transaction error rate (audit sampling)?
Sensitivity analysis	16, 18	Test a given analytic result's sensitivity to various assumptions embedded in the analysis by repeating the analysis using different assumptions	How much would the analytic result differ if the analyst had assumed a higher or lower rate of interest? A longer or shorter useful life for the equipment? A larger or smaller cost-of-living increase for employee wages?
Staffing factor calculation	20	Calculate the staffing required to provide coverage of essential positions in an extended-hour operation	The swimming pool will be open 72 hours per week this summer. How many lifeguards should the recreation department hire to be certain that it has a qualified person on each of the three lifeguard towers whenever the pool is open?
Work distribution analysis	7	Identify the time devoted by each member of a work unit to various tasks performed by the unit as a means of checking the alignment of priorities and resource allocations, qualifications and tasks, degree of specialization, and backup capabilities	Is this work unit directing sufficient time of skilled employees to top-priority tasks? Is the degree of specialization appropriate? When absences occur, can we still cover all tasks? Are employee skills and tasks suitably matched?

[a]Classically, all variables in a regression analysis would be continuous, but, practically, the independent variables can be of other types as well.

Part I
Introduction

Many local government issues are debated and decided without the benefit of systematic analysis. The choices made in such instances often suffer from the absence of an analytic ingredient because someone mistakenly believes that all analytic techniques are highly sophisticated and difficult to learn and apply.

This volume describes a variety of practical analytic techniques that are directly applicable to local government problems. Each is presented in the context of a fictitious scenario in a hypothetical community. The techniques are easy to learn, but simply understanding the mechanics of a particular technique is rarely sufficient to ensure effective administrative analysis. Other factors, such as the following, are also important:

- knowledge of when to apply a given analytic technique
- skill in presenting analytic information
- awareness of the political environment in which decisions are made
- sensitivity to the concerns of public employees and decision makers
- a realistic perception of the place of analysis in a government setting

When appropriate techniques are chosen carefully, applied properly, and presented effectively, well-reasoned analysis can play a role—sometimes a very important role—in local government decision making.

1

The Role of Analysis
in Local Government

Too often, important decisions in local government are made without the benefit of careful analysis. Conclusions are drawn and choices are made in the absence of systematic assessments of alternatives and probable consequences, and often even without an assessment of service needs.

Decision making in local government sometimes involves matters as crucial to a community's well-being as the development of long-term strategies for economic development or as seemingly mundane as revising refuse collection routes. Whether crucial or mundane, a local government decision is much more than simply the logical product of careful analysis. Good analysis does not automatically influence decisions; in fact, the recommendations in carefully prepared analytic reports often are rejected.

Few, if any, local government officials, elected or appointed, are willing to let the numbers derived from analysts' calculations make their decisions for them. Each brings to office a point of view, an inclination to judge problems and programs from a perspective developed over a lifetime, and perhaps a vision of where the community is or should be going. Most have advisers whose judgment is particularly influential. And then there is politics—the struggle to influence the use of resources and the distribution of public benefits, the quest for control.

Personal views and politics play powerful roles in local government decision making, as they should. Democratic principles require nothing less. Too often, however, the perceived dominance of personal and political factors is used as an alibi to excuse the absence of analysis in the decision-making process.

There is room in local government decision making for carefully conceived, accurately reported analysis—not as a pat decision-making formula but simply as one of several influences. Frequently, the findings of a careful study will bolster the confidence of persons already inclined to favor a position supported by that research or spur to action persons already interested in an issue but undecided on a stance. Systematic analysis occasionally will reverse a person's prior misconceptions—but not always. The analytically supported "right" answer is not always the one chosen, and that may discourage an analyst or a manager who has devoted time and effort to the task. But only the most naive of analysts and analytically oriented managers would believe the fruits of their labor would sway every decision. For that matter, the same could be said about an operative whose stock-in-trade is political influence rather than systematic analysis. Few of the latter would abandon their efforts because of an occasional setback; why should the former?

ANALYTIC HERITAGE

Many of the tools for decision making in local government are drawn from management science, industrial engineering, and, to a lesser degree, policy analysis. The first two fields, more than the third, focus on operational details. They offer a greater variety of techniques less tied to statistics or to models requiring advanced training. Nevertheless, all three fields contribute in some manner to a variety of analytic techniques—even to some of the simplest and most practical.

Systematic analysis of operational details is most aptly traced to industrial engineering and management science. Frederick Taylor, considered "the father of industrial engineering," was a prominent figure not only in the history of that field but also in the development of public administration. Taylor contributed much to management thought, including advocacy of methods study, time study, standardization of tools, and the use of task systems featuring bonuses for exceeding performance standards. His work influenced public as well as private management. Taylor's notions of "scientific management" and especially his dispassionate attitude toward workers— though perhaps less condescending than sometimes depicted—remain controversial. The controversy, however, need not overshadow his contribution.[1]

Taylor believed that the systematic analysis of a job would permit the development of an ideal procedure for performing that job, the design of ideal tools for carrying it out, and the identification of personal characteristics desired in persons selected to perform the work. Optimum performance could be secured by careful selection, precise training, and an incentive system that rewards overachievers. His theories were supported by abundant evidence of his own success in the application of scientific management principles in industrial settings. Techniques for work analysis, equipment and facility design, and the development of streamlined procedures drawn from Taylor's prescriptions and those of his successors continue to provide an analytic basis for management decisions.

Additionally, techniques designed to enhance rational decision making in the use of resources can make an important contribution in local government. Sloppy analyses that fail to identify relevant cost components of program options or fail to adjust or otherwise account for inflation, if relevant, may misinform rather than illuminate. Simple calculations can help decision makers avoid that pitfall.

---

[1]See, for example, Hindy Lauer Schachter, *Frederick Taylor and the Public Administration Community: A Reevaluation* (Albany: State University of New York Press, 1989). A brief account of Taylor's contributions is available from *Encyclopaedia Britannica* online at http://www.britannica.com/eb/article?eu=73317.

RESISTANCE TO ANALYSIS

Increased use of analytic techniques will not be welcomed by everyone at city hall or the county courthouse. Systematic analysis of problems and options will threaten the status quo. Accordingly, resistance may be anticipated from the following quarters:

- persons benefiting from current policies
- persons benefiting from current operational inefficiencies
- persons who fear new technologies or new operational methods
- persons who feel incapable of applying or understanding the results of analytic techniques
- persons who dominate the decision-making process through charisma or brokering abilities and prefer not to have that dominance threatened by the introduction of a new element in the process

Local government decisions are sometimes made on the strength of "feel," intuition, self-proclaimed skill as a "keen judge of character," or experience gained from "more than twenty years in this job." Where these decisions have seemed to be satisfactory, resistance to a new frame of reference emphasizing the importance of empirical evidence and systematic analysis should not be surprising.

Analysts and managers who are insensitive to the reasons for resistance or who are tactless or impatient with persons who adapt slowly to the introduction of analytic processes are unlikely to experience the degree of success that might otherwise be possible. The effective analyst is usually much more than a good "numbers cruncher." Often, effectiveness is also related to the analyst's ability to interact with and gain the cooperation of officials and employees in the program under review and to transform the analysis into a report that conveys the analyst's message in a manner and format both meaningful and satisfactory to the audience.

INTERACTION WITH PROGRAM OFFICIALS AND EMPLOYEES

Analysis can be threatening to people employed in or responsible for an operation under review. An analyst from the mayor's or manager's office who just drops in on a department and begins an analysis of operations will almost inevitably be viewed with suspicion and resentment. A far better approach might begin with a meeting involving the mayor or manager, the affected department head, and the analyst.[2] The purpose and general procedures of the analysis could be described at that meeting, and, if applicable, reassurances to reduce the level of anxiety could be offered. The mayor or manager might explain, for example, that the department's contributions and those of the department head are highly valued, if that statement is true, and that the analysis will simply explore the possibility of enhancing or refining those contributions.

---

[2]In some cases, the manager will perform the analysis personally, and no additional analyst will be involved.

Ideally, the department head and departmental personnel can be offered a role in the analysis. At minimum, their cooperation or acquiescence should be enlisted. Where departmental resistance is evident, efforts should be made to adopt a research design that is especially sensitive to managerial concerns and has as little adverse impact on day-to-day operations as possible—even if that means modest losses in detail and precision. Where the response is warmer and more cooperative, major research design concessions are less likely to be necessary; modest inconveniences and minor disruptions to normal operations that often accompany thorough analytic projects will be regarded as reasonable to achieve the accuracy that all parties, including departmental officials, desire.

Subsequent meetings of a similar nature should include the manager or analyst, the department head, and affected departmental employees. Once again, the purpose and procedures of analysis should be described and reassurances, as appropriate, given. Employees should be encouraged to offer suggestions throughout the process.

Employees may react positively or negatively to the prospect of analysis of their work. On the positive side, workers may be pleased that their work is regarded as important by management and flattered by the attention an analyst is giving to what the workers do and how they do it. In what researchers call the Hawthorne effect, workers might respond to this attention by improving performance.[3] Although the organization undoubtedly will appreciate performance gains, the analyst is left to sort out the effects attributable to the experimental treatment (that is, the subject of the study) and those attributable to the Hawthorne effect. This task is made simpler when the analyst considers the possibility of the Hawthorne effect from the outset and takes appropriate steps in research design to guard against it or to quantify its impact.[4]

On the negative side, employees may become anxious about job security or may dig in their heels behind civil service rules or union protection. Managers should address honestly any possibility that the analysis may result in revised work procedures or reduced levels of employment. Those who are able to promise that any employment reduction will be achieved through normal attrition or reassignment rather than by layoffs can often gain important benefits in employee morale and cooperation.

---

[3]The Hawthorne effect got its name from a series of experiments at the Hawthorne Plant of Western Electric in 1924. In a controlled experiment involving plant lighting, worker productivity improved even among members of the control group who received no improved illumination at their workstations. This gain was attributed to the attention lavished on the workers by the experimenters. See F. J. Roethlisberger, *Management and Morale* (Cambridge: Harvard University Press, 1941). For contrary views on the findings and relevance of the Hawthorne studies, see H. M. Parsons, "What Caused the Hawthorne Effect?" *Administration and Society*, 10 (November 1978): 259–283, and Richard H. Franke and James D. Kaul, "The Hawthorne Experiments: First Statistical Interpretation," *American Sociological Review*, 43 (October 1978): 623–643.

[4]An example of a measure taken to gauge and adjust for the Hawthorne effect in medical research is the use of placebos—for example, sugar pills having no medicinal value that may nevertheless induce improved conditions in the control group of an experiment. To be judged effective, the actual test medication must produce gains greater than those experienced by patients taking the placebo.

When restrictive civil service rules and union agreements inhibit production, they can also render a department vulnerable to the threat of privatization. In such cases, resistance to the analysis of operations can be especially harmful. Workers and their unions must be persuaded that finding ways to improve departmental performance will be in everyone's best interest.

Ideally, the analysis will proceed openly and cooperatively, with program personnel reviewing and offering insights on the analyst's preliminary findings. Difficult circumstances occasionally preclude the level of openness most conducive to good administrative analysis. When that happens, the likelihood of errors in observation or interpretation is increased, and the analytic product often suffers. Even in the most trying circumstances, the analysis should be conducted with integrity and courtesy. When the analysis has been completed and the recommendations are firm, program personnel should receive a briefing prior to the release of the formal report, if possible.

Various aspects of the analytic process—observing, measuring, questioning, and perhaps recommending change from the status quo—are understandably threatening to employees. Program or operational criticisms will almost inevitably be taken personally, even when they are not intended to be. Courtesy, sensitivity, and common sense should govern the analyst's actions throughout the process.

PRESENTATION OF FINDINGS

The interpersonal dimension of administrative analysis is relevant to more than just relations with program personnel. Effective analysts also pay attention to their relationship with the recipients of analytically based recommendations. The intended consumers of the analytic product—local government decision makers—can be "turned off" by a technical report that describes the results of highly sophisticated analysis in terminology more suited to a gallery of statisticians than to themselves. Analysts who are more intent on improving local government operations and policies than on demonstrating methodological prowess are attentive to the need for understanding and acceptance at both ends of the process—among program personnel and decision makers. They will report their analysis in an accurate and comprehensible manner that, ideally, captures the interest of decision makers.

The presentation of research findings should be as clear and concise a reflection of the analysis as possible. Important documentation, including a brief description of research methods, should be included. Less important material should be summarized or excluded. Few decision makers appreciate the tendency of some analysts to dump all information they collect into the report. Vital information should be included in the body of the report, important supporting information should be placed in an appendix, and superfluous information should be banished altogether. Attaching a one-page executive summary to the front of the report is often a good idea.

The use of graphics to demonstrate major points is a helpful and, through computer assistance, increasingly practical method of presentation. The adage that a picture is worth a thousand words applies to charts and graphs as well. A clearer and more lasting impression might be produced by incorporating pie charts showing how resources are allocated, bar charts demonstrating the growth of sales tax revenue relative to property tax revenue, or line graphs showing trends in intergovernmental revenues over time, for example, than would a narrative alone. Graphics should be used judiciously, however, highlighting only particularly important points or findings.

THE ROLE OF ANALYSIS

Doing everything right—developing a good analytic design, conducting careful analysis, interacting effectively with program personnel, and preparing a solid report—still does not guarantee success. Would-be analysts who hope to dominate the decision-making process on the strength of their work will almost inevitably be disappointed. Analysis should be an important component of the decision-making process; it may occasionally even dominate. Often, however, it will be nothing more than a counterbalance to irrational arguments that, despite evidence to the contrary, continue to be given credence.

Analysts must remember that people—not numbers—make an organization go. A wealth of behavioral science research tells us that the human factor, the power of motivation, the importance of morale, the pride of personal responsibility, and the thrill of achievement are factors that must not be overlooked. Human response—from the lowest level of the organization to the highest—cannot be factored out. Compassion, compromise, tradition, and emotion all have a place in public decision making, as they should. But systematic analysis should have a place as well. Decision makers can weigh the various elements and make their choices accordingly—perhaps sometimes ignoring, while ideally never being ignorant of, analytically based recommendations.

FOCUS OF THIS BOOK

Government managers whose own backgrounds and whose staff members' backgrounds do not include extensive training in formal policy analysis or industrial engineering but who nevertheless wish to upgrade the analysis performed in their organization will find help in this book. The techniques presented are practical and easy to learn and apply. Neither advanced mathematical skill nor access to computers is necessary, although available computer programs can make simple techniques even simpler. None of the techniques requires extensive study or imposes time-consuming conditions that would be impractical for quick application. With this volume, an enterprising manager could simply point to a given chapter and tell an administrative assistant, "I want you to do this kind of analysis" to evaluate a proposal or an existing program.

This book is not a comprehensive compendium of the "best" techniques of policy analysis, management science, and industrial engineering. Although the methods described are among the most useful for the analysis of local government problems, many other excellent techniques have been omitted simply because they require more specialized skills or more extensive study time than most busy managers or administrative assistants have or are willing to invest. Local governments would benefit from the application of more sophisticated techniques, several of which are identified in the appendix to this chapter. They may find, however, that the most reasonable avenue to highly sophisticated analysis is through the addition of staff members with advanced analytic skills or through the use of specialized consultants for such purposes.

The format of this book is designed to emphasize practical application of the analytic techniques selected. It is also designed to minimize the dread many readers feel for methods textbooks.

Analytic techniques are clustered within Parts II through VI of this book, based on various similarities. For example, analyses dependent on graphic techniques are clustered in Part II. Techniques used for work analysis are grouped in Part III. Generally, the simplest techniques are introduced first.

Beginning with Chapter 3, each analytic technique is presented and applied in the context of a brief, hypothetical case describing a common local government problem in a fictitious community. As in real life, analysis of these hypothetical problems rarely dictates a solution, but often the analytic process illuminates the strengths and weaknesses of various options.

SUGGESTED FOR FURTHER INFORMATION

Aft, Lawrence S. *Work Measurement and Methods Improvement.* New York: John Wiley & Sons, 2000.

Barnes, Ralph M. *Motion and Time Study: Design and Measurement of Work.* New York: John Wiley & Sons, 1980.

Berman, Evan M. *Productivity in Public and Nonprofit Organizations: Strategies and Techniques.* Thousand Oaks, Calif.: Sage Publications, 1998.

Bingham, Richard D., and Marcus E. Ethridge, eds. *Reaching Decisions in Public Policy and Administration: Methods and Applications.* New York: Longman, 1982.

Groves, Sanford M., and Maureen Godsey Valente. *Evaluating Financial Condition: A Handbook for Local Government,* 2d ed. Washington, D.C.: International City/County Management Association, 1994.

Koehler, Jerry W., and Joseph M. Pankowski. *Continual Improvement in Government: Tools and Methods.* Delray Beach, Fla.: St. Lucie Press, 1996.

McKenna, Christopher K. *Quantitative Methods for Public Decision Making.* New York: McGraw-Hill, 1980.

Meier, Kenneth J., and Jeffrey L. Brudney. *Applied Statistics for Public Administration,.* 4th ed. Fort Worth, Texas: Harcourt Brace, 1997.

Mundel, Marvin E. *Motion and Time Study: Improving Productivity.* Englewood Cliffs, N.J.: Prentice-Hall, 1985.

Nyhan, Ronald C., and Lawrence L. Martin. "Assessing the Performance of Municipal Police Services Using Data Envelopment Analysis: An Exploratory Study," *State and Local Government Review* 31, no. 1 (Winter 1999): 18–30.

———. "Comparative Performance Measurement: A Primer on Data Envelopment Analysis," *Public Productivity and Management Review,* 22, no. 3 (March 1999): 348–364.

Summers, Michael R. *Analyzing Operations in Business: Issues, Tools, and Techniques.* Westport, Conn.: Quorum Books, 1998.

Weimer, David L., and Aidan R. Vining. *Policy Analysis: Concepts and Practice,* 2d ed. Englewood Cliffs, N.J.: Prentice Hall, 1992.

Welch, Susan, and John Comer. *Quantitative Methods for Public Administration: Techniques and Applications.* Chicago: Dorsey, 1988.

White, Michael J., Ross Clayton, Robert Myrtle, Gilbert Siegel, and Aaron Rose. *Managing Public Systems: Analytic Techniques for Public Administration.* Lanham, Md.: University Press of America, 1985.

Wholey, Joseph S., Harry P. Hatry, and Kathryn E. Newcomer, eds. *Handbook of Practical Program Evaluation.* San Francisco: Jossey-Bass, 1994.

Simple Techniques[5]

Adjusting Multiyear Revenue/Expenditure Comparisons for Inflation—through the use of an appropriate index, the conversion of dollars from different time periods into a uniform value or "constant dollars" for fiscal trend analysis (Chapter 12)

Annualizing Capital Costs—techniques, such as straight-line depreciation, to account for capital costs over the full life of an item rather than entirely at the time of acquisition (Chapter 11)

Demand Analysis—the tabulation and comparison of demand patterns (for example, service requests by time of day, day of the week, or geographically) and resource allocation patterns (for example, budgeted funds or employees available to provide services—by time of day, day of the week, or geographically) (Chapter 3)

Descriptive Statistics—the use of simple descriptive statistics (for example, mean, median, range) to draw conclusions about a subject (Chapter 2)

Estimating Potential Gains through Timely Invoicing—a technique using a sample of a jurisdiction's transactions to project revenue losses from late invoices (Chapter 21)

Floating Averages (also called moving averages)—the use of multiperiod averages (for example, three- or five-year averages) to smooth otherwise erratic single-period figures (Chapter 19)

Interest Rates and Yields—basic investment calculations (Chapter 10)

Job-Travel Plot—the tracing of work area travel patterns of people, documents, or material, typically to detect procedural, deployment, scheduling or work station location problems (Chapter 5)

Life-Cycle Costing—the identification of total costs of owning an item through its useful life, including acquisition, operation, and maintenance, usually for the purposes of comparing alternatives (Chapter 17)

Performance Standards Analysis—the comparison of actual performance with engineered performance standards or standards established by records of performance in the past (Chapter 9)

Process Flow Charting—a technique for documenting and categorizing the steps in a routine procedure for purposes of identifying inefficiencies and designing improvements (Chapter 6)

---

[5]Several of the techniques labeled as "simple" or "intermediate" are actually fairly complex techniques presented here in simplified form with only minimal loss of precision or utility.

Program Evaluation Review Technique/Critical Path Method—the identification of all elements in a project, the sequencing and coordination of those elements to minimize project delays, and the estimation of time required for project components and the project as a whole (Chapter 4)

Staffing Factor Calculation—a technique for estimating the number of personnel needed for extended-hour or uninterruptable services (Chapter 20)

Work-Distribution Analysis—a technique for analyzing the allocation of personnel to the various tasks associated with an operation (Chapter 7)

Intermediate Techniques

Cost-Effectiveness Analysis—a shortcut—and more limited—version of cost-benefit analysis, a more complex technique for identifying, quantifying, and comparing the intended and unintended, direct and indirect costs and benefits of a program, project, or decision (Chapter 16)

Full Cost Identification—the systematic incorporation of direct and indirect costs of a program for purposes of disclosure, comparison, or subsequent analysis (Chapter 14)

"Go Away Costs"—the tabulation of costs associated with in-house operations that would be eliminated by a decision to contract for services, omitting from the tabulation all costs that would continue regardless of the decision (Chapter 15)

Inferential Statistics—the use of statistics from a sample to make inferences about a larger set or population or to make predictions (Chapters 23, 24, 25)

Lease/Buy Analysis—a technique for comparing the relative advantages of buying versus leasing equipment (Chapter 18)

Opportunity Costs, Discounting, Compounding, Future Value, and Present Value—mathematical calculations that permit the comparison of one option for the use of funds (for example, investment in a particular project or program) with the opportunity forgone for a different (perhaps hypothetical) investment (Chapter 13)

Performance Measurement—the use of indicators of service quality, efficiency, and effectiveness to gauge departmental, program, or work unit performance (Chapter 8)

Sensitivity Analysis—a process for predicting the effects of adopting different parameters or assumptions for a given problem (Chapters 16 and 18)

Systematic Choices Based on Weighted Criteria—the development and use of clearly articulated criteria for making systematic choices that emphasize these criteria (Chapter 22)

Advanced Techniques[6]

Data Envelopment Analysis—a special application of linear programming that makes simultaneous comparisons of data elements to rank order the performance of multiple service providers

Modeling—the representation of relevant factors of a decision situation, often through the use of a computer, for purpose of analysis

---

[6]More extensive descriptions of advanced techniques may be found in the suggested readings in this chapter.

Motion and Time Studies—the systematic analysis of the processes in a work activity, the design of preferred work methods, and the determination of the amount of time required to perform the activity

Optimum Facility Siting—the identification, often via computer model, of ideal sites for public facilities, given various physical criteria, service objectives, and community preferences

Optimum Routing—the identification, often via computer model, of ideal routes (such as for sanitation collection, meter reading), given various constraints (for example, terrain, distance between units) and the objectives of equalized workloads and a fair day's work; additionally, the identification of ideal routes for emergency vehicles, given points of departure and destination

Queuing Model—a technique for predicting the consequences of various service delivery alternatives on waiting time

Simulation—any of several techniques that may be used to imitate a real decision system or situation, thereby offering opportunities for experimentation

2

A Few Basics

Although few local government managers and administrative assistants consider themselves to be expert statisticians or "world-class" analysts, through daily exposure most are familiar with many of the basics of analysis and could easily draw on that familiarity to examine systematically many of the problems and opportunities they confront. Having the ability to apply even the simplest methods has become increasingly useful as the public becomes more accustomed to receiving information derived from the application of analytical techniques.

No one can escape the daily barrage of facts and figures that represent one form of analysis or another. Unemployment and inflation rates, school dropout rates, Dow-Jones averages, Nielsen ratings, Gallup polls, election night projections, even the label on the side of the cereal box stating how much of the recommended daily allowance of various vitamins and minerals is in a single serving—all of these expose us to the analyst's stock-in-trade and serve as a subtle primer for understanding and applying basic analytic techniques.

Local government analysts are not likely to be asked to track the stock market, to gauge the popularity of television programs, or to analyze the ingredients of food items. But the regular reporting of these and other products of analysis warms all of us—including the potential analyst—to the use of numbers and charts to make important points. Perhaps without knowing it, seeing how the media and advertisers use these techniques makes people more analytically creative, more willing to try simple analysis, and more receptive to the analysis of others.

Simple exposure to the presentation of facts and figures in the popular media, sometimes accompanied by a sentence or two about the methods used to arrive at them, cannot replace advanced training as a means of preparing local government analysts, but it does provide a starting point. From that common point, every manager and administrative assistant is at least capable of improving the quality of written and oral reports by including the simplest of descriptive statistics—for example, relevant percentages, trend lines, averages, and perhaps more detailed information from a sample of the whole. Incorporating information of this type should not be difficult; after all, administrators have seen similar uses of data over and over again.

Nevertheless, a word of caution is in order. While it is true that many administrators fail to recognize the analytic capability they already possess, it is also true that others make unfortunate mistakes because they assume they know more than they actually do about even the simplest aspects of analysis. For example, a manager who uses the arithmetic mean to describe the "typical case" in a group has selected the most popular statistic for that purpose but not necessarily the best. Similarly, the manager who proudly reports results from what he calls a "random sample" may be embarrassed when a more methodologically sophisticated critic informs him that "random" does not mean "haphazard." Devoting a little time to the basics to supplement the foundation already acquired through exposure to the popular media is a wise investment.

In this chapter, two basic topics important to practical analysis are examined. First, the most elementary of descriptive statistics, those measuring central tendency and dispersion, are addressed. Second, procedures for obtaining representative samples are explored.

CENTRAL TENDENCY AND DISPERSION

"How many cases of arson do you have in this town in an average year?"

That question seems simple enough. Just add all the cases over a period of years, divide by the number of years, and the result is the yearly average—technically referred to as the *arithmetic mean.* Although the mean is the most commonly used measure of central tendency, two other measures—the median and mode—may be as informative or even preferable in some circumstances.

Suppose, for example, that the town of Sparksville is a quiet community that has rarely experienced more than two cases of arson in a year. In 1998, however, an uncharacteristic rash of arsons occurred, leading to the arrests of three youths. Calculating the yearly mean for the five-year period from 1997 through 2001 yields an average of 2.6 arsons per year (Table 2-1). While mathematically accurate, that figure surpasses the actual number of arsons in every year except 1998, when ten of the period's thirteen cases occurred. If the questioner was really interested in knowing the number of arsons in a typical year in Sparksville, the median or mode would probably be a measure preferable to the mean.

Table 2-1 Incidents of Arson in the Town of Sparksville: Measures of Central Tendency

Year[a]	Incidents of Arson	
1998	10	
1999	2	
2001	1	← Median
1997	0	⎫
2000	0	⎭ ← Mode
Five-year total	13	
	13/5 = 2.6	← Mean

[a] The years have been arranged in descending order of arsons rather than chronologically in order to demonstrate how the median value is found.

From the Electronic Toolkit ●————————————————————————————

Box 2-1 Entering Data in a Spreadsheet

Some readers will prefer to perform the various calculations prescribed in this book by computer rather than by hand or pocket calculator. For those readers, the boxes labeled "From the Electronic Toolkit" provide instructions or helpful hints.

Many administrators and prospective administrators who use computers in their work or studies are acquainted with spreadsheet programs. Because Microsoft Excel is among the more popular of these programs, the instructions found in this and many subsequent boxes will help readers apply analytic techniques using that spreadsheet program.

This box is an introduction. The first step is to enter some data that can later be analyzed or depicted in the form of a graph.

To open Excel, either double click on the Excel icon on the Office tool bar appearing on your computer screen or select the Excel option from the Programs choice on the Start menu. A grid should appear, full of empty rows and columns.

To insert the data in the grid, click on a cell and simply type the information. Consider each column to be a variable (for example, population, number of arrests, or number of business licenses issued) and each row to be an observation. Each cell may be identified by its column letter and row number. For example, the first cell is in column A, row 1; therefore, it is named cell A1. The entry in cell A1 might be a city's population, while A2 through A100 might be the populations of other cities in the state. Or the entries in A1 through A12 might be the number of arrests made by a police department in each month of the year, or the number of business licenses issued per month.

The data from a given cell can be included in a calculation by inserting the cell's name in a formula. Formulas are entered in the same way that data are inserted in the grid. Type the formula directly into a cell. In order to indicate to the computer that a formula is being entered, rather than simply more data, the user must place an equal sign (=) before formulas. An alternative method for writing a formula would be to select the command from the Function choice on the Insert menu.

When applied using Excel, many of the tools and techniques described in this and subsequent chapters will call for the use of the Data Analysis Option. For instructions on installing the Data Analysis Option, if it is not already available on the user's computer, see Appendix E.

The mode is the number appearing most frequently in an array of numbers. In this case, zero appears twice, so the mode is "0." It could be argued that in a typical year in Sparksville there are no incidents of arson.

The median value for an ordered array of numbers is the midscore of the distribution—that is, there are as many scores in the array with values higher than the median as there are scores with lower values. In the case of Sparksville, the median is "1"—for there exist two years with higher numbers of arson and two years with a lower number. It could be argued that one arson per year is most representative of reality in Sparksville.

The choice of a particular measure of central tendency should be made carefully, for each has strengths and weaknesses as a representation of the central value of a set of numbers. The most popular measure of central tendency, the mean, is perhaps the best understood by most audiences and is also the measure called for most often in statistical formulas. Nevertheless, it is more vulnerable than the median or the mode to the distorting effect of extreme outliers—values far greater or far smaller than most of the others in the group.[1] For example, including the salary of a highly paid supervisor could substantially inflate the mean salary of an otherwise low-paid unit and leave the impression that the workers are relatively well paid. The median salary of the work unit would be less influenced by outliers and would probably be a more appropriate choice as the measure of central tendency in that case. The decision to include or exclude the salary of the supervisor would shift the midscore of an ordered array of salaries only slightly.

Unlike measures of central tendency, measures of dispersion indicate how tightly clustered or spread out a set of numbers is. A statistic known as the *standard deviation* performs that function by indicating with a single measure how much the individual numbers in a set differ from the mean value of that set. A standard deviation of zero would indicate the ultimate in tight clusters: all values in such a set would be exactly the same, so none would deviate at all from the group mean; larger standard deviations would indicate greater spread.

Although the formula for calculating the standard deviation may look rather complicated to persons unaccustomed to mathematical symbols, the computation is actually quite simple.[2] Much to the dismay of statisticians, who correctly point out the necessity of the standard deviation calculation for many useful analytic techniques, few audiences for practical analysis performed in local governments today insist on a measure of dispersion as precise as the standard deviation or the application of the more sophisticated techniques that call for it. For most purposes, simply reporting the range from the lowest to the highest number in the array is deemed sufficient. A slightly more sophisticated approach omits the outliers at the extreme ends of the distribution by dropping the upper and lower quartiles (that is, the top 25 percent and

---

[1] In statistics terminology, a distribution of observations is said to be "skewed" when there are more extreme cases in one direction than the other. These outliers have a greater influence on the mean of the distribution than on the median.

[2] The standard deviation may be calculated by first finding the mean of the numbers involved, squaring the difference between each number and the mean, adding those squared values together, dividing by the number of values in the set, and finding the square root of that quotient. For readers familiar with mathematical symbols and formulas, the standard deviation is as follows:

$$s = \sqrt{\frac{\sum_{i=1}^{N}(x_i - \bar{x})^2}{N}}$$

From the Electronic Toolkit ●———————————————————————————

Box 2-2 Finding the Mean, Median, and Mode

Using Microsoft Excel, the mean, median, and mode of a set of numbers can be found without calculations or manual sorting of the data. First, enter the data in column A or another column of your choice. (For directions on opening Excel and entering data refer to Box 2-1.) To find the **mean** of the data, use the AVERAGE function. Suppose the data were entered beginning in cell A1 and down to cell A8. To find the mean, enter "=AVERAGE(A1:A8)" in the next cell or any cell of your choice. (An alternative to typing this instruction would be to use Function choice (**fx**) from the Insert menu. The (**fx**) symbol also appears on the standard toolbar. This feature will list the available functions, including "average.") After pressing enter, the mean will appear. To find the **median** of the data, use the MEDIAN function. Enter "=MEDIAN(A1:A8)" in any cell and the computer will determine the median of the data entered from cell A1 to cell A8. To find the **mode** of the data, use the MODE function. Enter "=MODE(A1:A8)" into any cell and the computer will report the mode of the data.

Suppose the data were entered somewhere else on the spreadsheet. Simply change the input to fit the addresses of the data. For example, if the data of interest were entered in cells C14 to C23, simply change the formulas to "=AVERAGE(C14:C23)" or "=MEDIAN(C14:C23)" or "=MODE(C14:C23)."

To find mean, median, and mode simultaneously, use the Data Analysis option from the Tools menu. (For instructions on installing the Data Analysis Option, if not already available, see Appendix E.) Select Descriptive Statistics from the choices provided by the Data Analysis pop-up box. In the Input box enter the range of the data; for example, "$C$14:$C$23" designates cells C14 through C23. (These cells may also be designated by highlighting them using the mouse.) In the Output options box, check the box beside Summary Statistics. Click "OK" and a new sheet will appear with a chart containing the mean, median, and mode, as well as other statistics, including the standard deviation.

the bottom 25 percent of the distribution) and reporting the range of the second and third quartiles only. This "interquartile range" extends from the 25th percentile to the 75th percentile and represents the heart of the distribution.

The full range and interquartile range of a distribution may be depicted simply in a graph called a "box-and-whiskers" plot (Figure 2-1). This graph shows the highest, median, and lowest values in the distribution and highlights the interquartile range.

SAMPLING

For many types of analyses, examining every relevant case would be impractical. Carefully examining a representative sample of the complete set is a more practical alternative.

Sampling is a common analytic technique. The Nielsen people do not contact all television viewers. The Gallup and Roper polls rely on samples. The Dow-Jones aver-

Figure 2-1 Box-and-Whiskers Plot

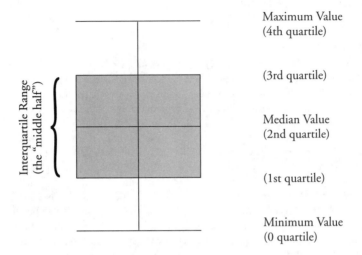

ages are based on a relatively small selection of stocks. The Associated Press polls that produce football and basketball rankings reflect the views of the sportswriters who are polled. They do not represent the opinions of sports fans in general and may even differ somewhat from the views of most sportswriters.

The purpose of a sample is to help an analyst or researcher draw conclusions about a larger group without examining every element in that group. The key to the usefulness of a sample is how well it represents the larger group. Interviewing a sample of people drawn from a conviction list of traffic offenders may produce an interesting set of opinions on the local law enforcement and justice systems. If drawn with care, that sample and the views expressed might well represent the larger group of traffic offenders. It would be inappropriate, however, to misrepresent the findings as reflecting the views of the general citizenry or even of the people who have come into contact in one way or another with the local police and courts. The method used in selecting a sample can dramatically affect the representativeness of that sample and the appropriateness of inferences to a larger group based on analysis of sample data.

The intended inference determines whether it would be wise or unwise to draw a sample from a particular source. For instance, it would be wise to draw a sample from a conviction list if the purpose is to make inferences about that group; it would be unwise if the purpose is to make inferences beyond that group. For much the same reason, public hearings are often poor devices for making inferences about the general public because such hearings rarely draw a representative cross-section of the citizenry. Instead, they tend to attract disproportionate numbers of local activists, persons most directly affected by the topic being discussed, and others with "axes to grind."

In most cases, the ideal sampling method is random sampling—but it is not always feasible. For a truly random sample, all potential observations or interviewees in the

Box 2-3 Finding the Standard Deviation
and the Interquartile Range

Once the data from a sample are entered, software like Microsoft Excel can easily compute the standard deviation and interquartile range of the sample. (For directions on opening Excel and entering data refer to Box 2-1.) To find the **standard deviation** using Excel, use the STDEV function. If the data of interest appear in cell A1 through cell A8, enter "=STDEV(A1:A8)" in any cell and the output that appears in that cell will indicate the standard deviation. (An alternate method for finding standard deviation is described in Box 2-2.)

Finding the **interquartile range** is simple, too. Just use the QUARTILE function to find the first quartile and third quartile. These are the boundaries of the interquartile range. To find the first quartile for a set of data displayed in cells A1 through A8, enter "=QUARTILE (A1:A8,1)" in a cell of your choice and for the third quartile enter "=QUARTILE(A1:A8,3)" in another cell. (An alternative to typing this instruction would be to use Function choice (**fx**) from the Insert menu. The symbol for this choice (fx) also appears on the toolbar.) To find the width of the interquartile range, subtract the smaller quartile number from the larger. (If you displayed the first quartile result in cell A9 and the third quartile result in cell A10, then "=A10–A9" can be entered in a different cell to display the width of the interquartile range.)

relevant "universe" have an equal chance of being selected for the sample. That way the chances of a biased sample are reduced. A random sample of police incidents, for example, could be drawn by writing each incident number on a separate slip of paper, mixing the slips thoroughly, and blindly (that is, randomly) drawing the cases for examination. As a simple alternative, a random sample could be drawn using a random numbers table.

Suppose, for example, that a sample of 400 cases is to be drawn from a total population of 6,450 cases. If the researcher is lucky, each of the cases already has been assigned a four-digit case number; if not, the researcher could assign each a number from 0001 through 6450. Then, through the use of a table of random numbers (Table 2-2), a random sample can be selected.

To avoid biasing the sample selection process, even the beginning point for drawing numbers from the table should be determined at random. Dozens of strategies are available for picking a starting place, but perhaps the simplest is to blindly place a pointed object on the page and begin at the spot indicated. Once the entry point to the table is selected, the numbers can be read left-to-right, right-to-left, within columns, across columns, downward, or upward. In the example only the numbers from 0001 through 6450 can be used; therefore, numbers outside that range are simply discarded. Each random number falling within the range identifies a case that is added to the sample until the desired sample size is reached.

When random sampling is impractical, systematic sampling and stratified sampling are among the reasonable alternatives. Systematic (interval) sampling is very

Table 2-2 Using a Random Digits Table

10097	32533	76520	13586	34673	54876	80959	09117	39292	74945
37542	04805	64894	74296	24805	24037	20636	10402	00822	91665
08422	68953	19645	09303	23209	02560	15953	64	35080	33606
99019	02529	09376	70715	38311	31165	88	74397	04436	27659
12807	99970	80157	36147	64032	36653		16877	12171	76833
66065	74717	34072	76850	36697	0	65813	39885	11199	29170
31060	10805	45571	82406	35	42614	86799	07439	23403	09732
85269	77602	02051	65692	5	74818	73053	85247	18623	88579
63573	32135	05325	47	90553	57548	28468	28709	83491	25624
73796	45753	03529	8	35808	34282	60935	20344	35273	88435
98520	1776	05	68607	22109	40558	60970	93433	50500	73998
11805	05	39808	27732	50725	68248	29405	24201	52775	67851
83452	634	06288	98083	13746	70078	18475	40610	68711	77817
88685	40200	86507	58401	36766	67951	90364	76493	29609	11062
99594	67348	87517	64969	91826	08928	93785	61368	23478	34113
65481	17674	17468	50950	58047	76974	73039	57186	40218	16544
80124	35635	17727	08015	45318	22374	21115	78253	14385	53763
74350	99817	77402	77214	43236	00210	45521	64237	96286	02655
69916	26803	66252	29148	36936	87203	76621	13990	94400	56418
09893	20505	14225	68514	46427	56788	96297	78822	54382	14598
91499	14523	68479	27686	46162	83554	94750	89923	37089	20048
80336	94598	26940	36858	70297	34135	53140	33340	42050	82341
44104	81949	85157	47954	32979	26575	57600	40881	22222	06413
12550	73742	11100	02040	12860	74697	96644	89439	28707	25815
63606	49329	16505	34484	40219	52563	43651	77082	07207	31790

Source: The random numbers shown in this table are excerpted from The RAND Corporation, *A Million Random Digits with 100,000 Normal Deviates* (Glencoe, Ill.: The Free Press, 1955). Copyright © 1955 by The RAND Corporation. Reprinted by permission of The RAND Corporation. A more extensive set of random numbers is found in the appendix.

Instructions: Suppose the "population" from which a random sample is to be drawn consists of cases numbered 0000 through 6449. A random sample can be drawn by entering the table blindly and reading four-digit numbers systematically, rejecting all numbers that lie outside the 0000-6449 range. In this example, a pencil blindly laid on the table points to the starting point. A left-to-right reading system would produce the following numbers: 5402, 0086, 5075, 8401 (rejected), 3676, etc. A stacked, downward reading system would produce the following numbers: 5402, 4673, 1176, 4356, 0998, etc. A downward, single-column reading system would produce the following numbers: 5414, 0639, 6406, 3060, 9717 (rejected), etc. Other reading systems might consist of right-to-left, upward, or any other systematic strategy; however, the reading system should be decided prior to entry to the table.

From the Electronic Toolkit ●─────────────────────────────

Box 2-4 Creating a Random Numbers List

Lists of random numbers also may be generated by computer. This can be especially helpful to researchers conducting telephone surveys who are intent on eliminating the threat unlisted numbers pose to true randomization in more manual systems. See, for example, Research Randomizer (*www.randomizer.org*), a Web site that generates random numbers in the range specified by the researcher. If the researcher wishes to draw fifty numbers from a particular telephone exchange (that is, the first three digits in the seven-digit telephone number) within a community, the specified range can run from the smallest possible number beginning with those three digits (that is, XXX0000) and end with the largest possible number (that is, XXX9999). The same procedure would be followed for each telephone exchange in proportion to the number of units in the various exchanges. If the survey involves only residents, the researcher may choose to specify more random numbers than are actually needed, retaining the first calls completed to the desired number of residents in the telephone exchange and dropping numbers found to be unassigned or assigned to businesses.

Some software programs will not only generate random telephone numbers but also will perform a variety of other survey-processing functions. These more elaborate programs are referred to as Computer-Assisted Telephone Interviewing (CATI) systems. See, for example, StatPac for Windows survey and analysis software (*www.statpac.com*); the Computer-Assisted Survey Execution System (CASES), developed by the University of California at Berkeley (http://otl.berkeley.edu/ UCB89056.html); and the Fully Integrated Control System (FICS), developed by the Research Triangle Institute (*www.rti.org*).

common—probably because it is simple and can be done more quickly than most other acceptable alternatives. A systematic sample is drawn by taking each case following a predetermined interval (for example, every tenth case). The appropriate sampling interval may be calculated simply by dividing the total population by the desired sample size. If the total population is 1,000 and the desired sample size is 200, the sampling interval would be 5 (based on the simple calculation: $1,000 \div 200 = 5$). The starting point would be selected randomly from the first five cases in a list of the total population. Thereafter, every fifth case would be added to the sample. The use of systematic sampling represents a tradeoff: although it is often easier and more practical to draw a systematic sample than a true random sample, a systematic sample is likely to be a somewhat less accurate representation of the population from which it was drawn.

Stratified sampling requires some knowledge of important population characteristics—for example, percentage of African Americans in a predominantly white community or, perhaps, percentage of management employees in a workforce that is predominantly laborers. If the researcher is worried that the sampling process may over- or underrepresent a minority stratum (for example, African Americans in a community survey, management in an employee survey), the technique of stratified sampling can be used to ensure appropriate representation. One approach is to identify relevant strata within the total population and randomly sample each stratum, drawing a sample size that is proportionate to the relationship between the stratum population and the total population. Another approach would involve drawing fairly large samples from each stratum, the calculation of stratum statistics, and their consolidation on a weighted basis.[3]

Random samples, systematic samples, and stratified samples are common sampling techniques that produce useful research results. Audit procedures normally incorporate one or more of these methods in the sampling of transactions. Another prime example is the use of sampling techniques for properly conducted citizen surveys.

Unfortunately, it is as easy to cite poor examples of sampling for the analysis of local government problems as it is to cite good examples. Local officials who base judgments on "public opinion" as expressed in a mail-in newspaper poll or the "overwhelming two-to-one margin of support" among the twelve people who called their council members or the city manager to voice their opinions on an issue are mistakenly bestowing representativeness on an unrepresentative sample.

Local officials should not assume that a technique is reliable simply because they have seen it applied elsewhere. For example, phone-in and Internet polls regularly conducted on television sports programs are not necessarily representative of the total public, all sports fans, or even all sports fans who happen to be watching that program. They represent only that portion of the viewing audience that wants to voice opinions, has access to a telephone or computer, and is willing to invest a little effort and perhaps incur some expense.

The size of the sample is another important factor to be considered. Although a large sample is generally preferable to a small one, randomly drawn samples need not be huge.[4] For example, sample sizes for citywide citizen surveys commonly range from 300 to 700 households even in fairly large cities.[5] Table 2-3 shows the relationship between sample size and levels of precision for citizen surveys. (See Table 21-1 for recommended sample sizes for sampling invoices.)

---

[3]If, for example, a particular stratum represents only 2 percent of the total population, normal sampling might result in only 10 or 12 members of that stratum being selected—too few to permit meaningful inferences. Therefore, the analyst might choose to draw a larger sample of representatives from this stratum to permit more reliable analysis. However, when these observations are combined with those from other elements of the total population, each stratum's influence should be weighted according to its proper proportion of the whole, so as not to be overrepresented and thereby distort the general findings.

[4]Increasing the size of a sample tends to increase its accuracy in representing the population from which it was drawn; however, the accuracy increases with the square root of the sample size. In other words, a sample must be quadrupled to double its accuracy. See Russell Langley, *Practical Statistics Simply Explained* (New York: Dover Publications, 1970), 45.

[5]Harry P. Hatry, Louis H. Blair, Donald M. Fisk, John M. Greiner, John R. Hall Jr., and Philip S. Schaenman, *How Effective Are Your Community Services? Procedures for Measuring Their Quality,* 2d ed. (Washington, D.C.: Urban Institute and International City/County Management Association, 1992), 173–184.

Table 2-3 Relationship between Sample Size and Precision in a Simple Random Sample Poll: 95 Percent Confidence Level

It the percentage of respondents giving the same answer to a question is	and the sample size is . . .					
	50	100	200	400	500	1,000
	then there is a 95 out of 100 chance that the percent of the total population that would respond the same way would fall within these ranges . . . [a]					
10	0.7 – 19.3	3.6 – 16.4	5.6 – 14.4	6.9 – 13.1	7.3 – 12.7	8.1 – 11.9
20	7.9 – 32.1	11.7 – 28.3	14.2 – 25.8	16.0 – 24.0	16.4 – 23.6	17.5 – 22.5
30	16.3 – 43.7	20.5 – 39.5	23.4 – 36.6	25.4 – 34.6	25.9 – 34.1	27.1 – 32.9
40	25.4 – 54.6	29.9 – 50.1	33.0 – 47.0	35.1 – 44.9	35.6 – 44.4	36.9 – 43.1
50	35.1 – 64.9	39.7 – 60.3	42.8 – 57.2	45.0 – 55.0	45.5 – 54.5	46.9 – 53.1
60	45.4 – 74.6	49.9 – 70.1	53.0 – 67.0	55.1 – 64.9	55.6 – 64.4	56.9 – 63.1
70	56.3 – 83.7	60.5 – 79.5	63.4 – 76.6	65.4 – 74.6	65.9 – 74.1	67.1 – 72.9
80	67.9 – 92.1	71.7 – 88.3	74.2 – 85.8	76.0 – 84.0	76.4 – 83.6	77.5 – 82.5
90	80.7 – 99.3	83.6 – 96.4	85.6 – 94.4	86.9 – 93.1	87.3 – 92.7	88.1 – 91.9

Source: Adapted from Harry P. Hatry, John E. Marcotte, Therese van Houten, and Carol H. Weiss, *Customer Surveys for Agency Managers* (Washington, D.C.: Urban Institute Press, 1998), 69, and Carol H. Weiss and Harry Hatry, *An Introduction to Sample Surveys for Government Managers* (Washington, D.C.: Urban Institute, 1971).

[a]More precisely, if an infinite number of samples of indicated size were taken, 95 percent would contain the true value of the total population in the given confidence ranges.

Box 2-5 Drawing Random Samples by Spreadsheet

To draw a **random sample** from a "population" of numbers, first create a list of the numbers that constitutes the entire population. To do this, enter the smallest number of the population set in the first cell, then enter the next larger number in the next cell. (For directions on opening Excel and entering data refer to Box 2-1.) Click on the first cell and move the mouse to drag the curser down to highlight both of the cells. With the two cells highlighted, position the mouse on the lower, right-hand corner of the lower block until a thin, black cross appears. When the cross appears, click and drag the mouse down to the desired boundary of the list, including the largest number in the population set. Then, the numbers will appear in order. For example, if the desired pool of numbers extends from 0001 to 6450, enter "1" in cell A1 and "2" in cell A2. Then after dragging the mouse down to cell A6450, a list from 1 to 6450 will appear.

After creating the population list, select the Data Analysis option from the Tools menu. Select Sampling from the choices provided by the Data Analysis pop-up box. In the Sampling pop-up box, enter the range of the list created above in the Input box. In the example above, the user would enter "$A$1: $A$6450" as the range in the Input box. Still in the Sampling pop-up box, the default for the Sampling Method is the Random choice. Leave this highlighted and enter the size of the needed random sample in the Number of Samples box. Click "OK" and a random sample of the desired size will appear.

If your spreadsheet contains a column of names—perhaps utility customers, property owners, or members of neighborhood associations—a similar procedure may be used to draw a random sample from that list.

A sample is expected to approximate the population—the more accurate the approximation, the better. The only way to get absolute precision is to survey the entire population, but that is rarely practical. Surveying a sample is a more practical alternative, but settling for a sample instead of the whole introduces a degree of imprecision that is expressed in terms such as *margin of error, confidence interval,* and *level of confidence.* When a survey showing 61 percent of the respondents satisfied with police services has a margin of error of ± 5 percent, the pollster is declaring that the corresponding percentage for population as a whole is projected to be somewhere between 56 and 66 percent. This range is the confidence interval.

Level of confidence refers to the pollster's degree of certainty that the sample reflects the parameters of the full population. A confidence level of 95 percent, as reflected in Table 2-3, asserts that drawing random samples of a given size would reflect population parameters to the specified degree 95 out of 100 times. The pollster might declare, for example, 95 percent confidence that the opposition to a bond proposal is between 25.4 and 34.6 percent, based on negative responses from 30 per-

Box 2-6 Other Applications of Measures of Central Tendency, Measures of Dispersion, and Sampling

Practically every analysis, it seems, calls for a measure of central tendency. How many inspections does an electrical inspector complete in a week? What is the fire department's "control time" for working fires? How quickly does the public works department respond to pothole complaints? Each of these calls for a measure of central tendency. But which one—mean, median, or mode? The most common choice is the mean, but that is not always the best choice.

Measures of dispersion offer important information regarding many aspects of community condition as well as local government performance. The range, interquartile range, or standard deviation of household incomes or housing values is much more revealing information than the mean family income or median house price alone. Similarly, measures of dispersion can provide reassurances of consistent quality and timeliness of local government services. If the county reports that the average property appraisal is within five percent of market value, can we be confident that most appraisals are within fifteen percent? If the police department reports an average emergency response time of five minutes, should we assume that most responses are between three and seven minutes? If the average sick leave usage rate among municipal employees is five days per employee per year, should we assume that the city has few, if any, problems with sick leave abuse? Measures of dispersion will tell us.

Carefully drawn samples can serve a variety of research needs. The most obvious application is citizen surveys conducted to gauge satisfaction with services or perceptions regarding local issues. Other applications include user surveys focusing on clients of a particular service, audit or evaluation studies drawing conclusions from a sample of transactions or cases, and job studies that rely on observations at random times rather than continuous observation.

cent of a 400-person sample. (This result is shown at the intersection of the "400" column and "30%" row of Table 2-3.) Formulas showing the relationship between sample size, confidence levels, and confidence intervals more precisely may be found in many statistics and survey research texts.[6]

BUILDING ON THE BASE

Most managers and administrative assistants have been exposed more often than they probably realize to the products of analysis. By building on that base through the development of practical analytic skills, they can improve the quality and persuasiveness of their recommendations. The chapters that follow describe a variety of analytic techniques that will help them in that endeavor.

---

[6]For example, see David H. Folz, *Survey Research for Public Administration* (Thousand Oaks, Calif.: Sage Publications, 1996), 46–54.

SUGGESTED FOR FURTHER INFORMATION

Blalock, Hubert M., Jr. *Social Statistics.* New York: McGraw-Hill, 1979.

Folz, David H. *Survey Research for Public Administration.* Thousand Oaks, Calif.: Sage Publications, 1996.

Hatry, Harry P., Louis H. Blair, Donald M. Fisk, John M. Greiner, John R. Hall Jr., and Philip S. Schaenman. *How Effective Are Your Community Services? Procedures for Measuring Their Quality,* 2d ed. Washington, D.C.: Urban Institute and International City/County Management Association, 1992.

Malan, Roland M., James R. Fountain Jr., Donald S. Arrowsmith, and Robert L. Lockridge II. *Performance Auditing in Local Government.* Chicago: Government Finance Officers Association, 1984.

Meier, Kenneth J., and Jeffrey L. Brudney. *Applied Statistics for Public Administration,* 4th ed. Fort Worth, Texas: Harcourt Brace, 1997.

O'Sullivan, Elizabethann, and Gary R. Rassel. *Research Methods for Public Administrators,* 3rd ed. New York: Longman, 1999.

Webb, Kenneth, and Harry P. Hatry. *Obtaining Citizen Feedback: The Application of Citizen Surveys to Local Governments.* Washington, D.C.: Urban Institute, 1973.

Welch, Susan, and John Comer. *Quantitative Methods for Public Administration: Techniques and Applications.* Chicago: Dorsey, 1988.

Part II
Graphic Techniques for Planning, Monitoring, and Evaluating

Some techniques of administrative analysis are more visual than computational. They help the analyst or manager to *see* the problem or opportunity and may inspire an appropriate strategy. Relationships that escape detection when compiled in tabular form as rows and columns of numbers may suddenly become clear when presented graphically. Similarly, individual steps in a complicated process are less easily overlooked in a graphic display that makes an omitted or inappropriate step seem almost as glaring as the missing piece in an otherwise complete jigsaw puzzle.

3.

Demand Analysis

All organizations—public or private—are vulnerable to bureaucratic rigidity. They may become enmeshed in unnecessary or unnecessarily precise rules of operation, hamstrung by intentional or unintentional emphasis on employee rather than client convenience, or simply enslaved by force of habit: "We've always done it this way!"

Progressive organizations attempt to get the best possible return for their investment of resources. Even long-standing programs and practices in such organizations are subject to refinement or total revision. Sometimes such changes simply involve a better matching of resources and service demands—that is, marshaling necessary resources, including personnel, and having those resources available and functioning when they are needed most.

SCENARIO: NEWBERN, OHIO

The employment practices of the city of Newbern, Ohio, conform to the standard pattern adopted by most other local governments with regard to hours of operation and manpower scheduling.[1] Most employees work full-time, forty-hour schedules from Monday through Friday. Notable exceptions are found in the public safety operations, where police officers and firefighters maintain schedules that differ sharply from the norm.

Except for administrative personnel, the employees of the Newbern Fire Department are assigned to one of three shifts. Each shift begins at 8:00 A.M. one morning, ends at 8:00 A.M. the next morning, and does not begin again until forty-eight hours later. This is commonly called a twenty-four-hour-on/forty-eight-hour-off schedule. For example, the firefighters on Platoon A may report for duty at 8:00 A.M. Tuesday, complete their tour at 8:00 A.M. Wednesday, and report for duty again at 8:00 A.M. the following Friday. The shift beginning at 8:00 A.M. Wednesday is covered by Platoon B, and the shift beginning at 8:00 A.M. Thursday is covered by Platoon C. Fire fighters in Newbern are assigned to one of four fire stations located in roughly equivalent quadrants of the city.

---

[1]The various cities, counties, and local government officials depicted in the scenarios of this volume are fictitious.

Standard police shifts in Newbern are eight hours in length. The morning shift runs from 7:00 A.M. to 3:00 P.M.; the evening shift, from 3:00 P.M. to 11:00 P.M.; and the midnight shift, from 11:00 P.M. to 7:00 A.M. All police officers operate from the single police station located in downtown Newbern.

Most offices of the municipal government are located in Newbern's city hall. A few, however, were relocated to an office building several blocks away because of crowded conditions in city hall. Almost all clerical and administrative employees report to work at 8:00 A.M., have an hour off for lunch at or near midday, and conclude their workday at 5:00 P.M.

A CASE OF UNDERSTAFFING?

For a couple of years, the city manager of Newbern has been convinced that the city government is understaffed. Several department heads have requested additional employees, citing numerous instances in which the current staff has been overwhelmed by a crushing workload. Several of those instances have been corroborated by telephone calls to the city manager from citizens angry about service delays or long lines at city hall. The police chief and fire chief are both pressing for additional personnel to bring their numbers a little nearer to those recommended by their professional associations for cities the size of Newbern.

Last year the city manager rejected most requests for increased personnel. It was an election year, and he knew the city council would be especially resistant to recommendations that would require a tax increase. For the most part, department heads were encouraged to try to get by with current staffing levels. This year, however, when the city manager's budget recommendations included moderately increased staffing levels—an increase that he felt was more than a year overdue—he was startled to have them all rejected by the city council.

Frustrated by the rejections and intent on getting the facts that might either suggest a solution to the problem or convince the city council of the need for additional employees, the city manager instructed an administrative assistant to collect data on the increasing workload in several city departments. After discussing workload problems with department heads and observing office and field operations, the administrative assistant suggested to the city manager that workload fluctuations might be a key aspect of the problem. While it was true that the departments were occasionally swamped by the workload, other periods seemed fairly light. Together, the city manager and administrative assistant decided to undertake a simple form of demand analysis. The results caused them to modify their thoughts regarding the solution to the problem.

DEMAND ANALYSIS

In its simplest form, demand analysis is nothing more than a fairly detailed examination of workload patterns. Typically, the examination incorporates graphs that depict work volume and show how it varies over time or from one geographic location to another. Although line graphs and bar graphs (that is, histograms) are most common, simple frequency tabulations may also serve the analyst's purpose. Incoming workload may be recorded by month in order to detect seasonal fluctuations, by day of the month, by day of the week, by time of day, or by geographic location.

Demand analysis has several important uses, including the following:

- *Resource deployment.* Once the pattern of demand is identified, the need for revised deployment may be clarified. Ideally, the deployment pattern for personnel and other resources will match the demand pattern.
- *Geographic considerations.* Careful consideration of facility location and strategies for service delivery can sometimes increase benefits to service recipients at little additional cost or even at a savings to the service provider.
- *Adjustment of demand.* In some instances, the service provider can influence changes in the demand pattern. The adjustment of fees for services (to discourage overconsumption) and the staggering of expiration dates for permits (to flatten the demand curve) are two examples.

FINDINGS

The administrative assistant and city manager of Newbern found that their demand analysis challenged several of their initial assumptions regarding the need for more employees. For example, plotting calls for police service by hour of the day revealed a remarkable swing in the number of calls (Figure 3-1). Calls were consistently heaviest from 2:00 P.M. to 1:00 A.M. and lightest from 3:00 A.M. to 7:00 A.M. This fluctuation revealed the inappropriateness of Newbern's "constant manning" approach to deployment, whereby each shift had the same number of police officers assigned. The addition of just one police officer to the streets around the clock under the constant manning strategy, as previously proposed by the city manager, would require the employment of five new officers.[2] The city manager decided, instead, to recommend establishing a fourth shift beginning at 2:00 P.M. and ending at 10:00 P.M. (Figure 3-2). This special shift would be staffed not by new officers but by twelve current officers—four drawn from each of the three primary shifts. In this manner, on-duty strength would be reduced during off-peak times and increased during peak periods at no additional personnel cost to the city.

Fire Department

A similar pattern was found regarding the incidence of fire alarms. Most fires occurred in the evening hours from 5:00 P.M. to 10:00 P.M. Initially, a strategy similar to that taken for police deployment seemed applicable to the fire department. However, because the fire company strength in Newbern is only three firefighters per engine, a reassignment that would reduce the response strength to two firefighters for

---

[2]Each additional police officer would provide coverage for forty hours per week, minus any time taken by that officer for vacation, sick leave, and other forms of absence. Because of such absences and because the police patrol function is a seven-days-a-week activity, considerably more than three employees are needed to cover one position around the clock, seven days a week. See Chapter 20.

Figure 3-1 Average Number of Calls for Police Service, by Hour of the Day

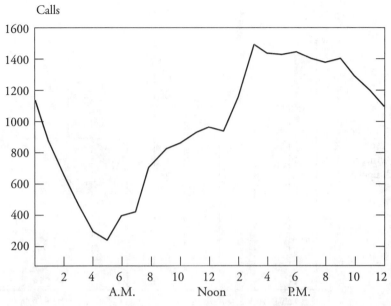

Source: John S. Thomas, "Operations Management: Planning, Scheduling, and Control," in *Productivity Improvement Handbook for State and Local Government,* ed. George J. Washnis (New York: John Wiley & Sons, 1980), 176. Copyright © 1980 by the National Academy of Public Administration. Reprinted by permission of John Wiley & Sons, Inc.
Note: Based on statistics from the police department of Kettering, Ohio.

some off-peak alarms seemed inadvisable. Instead, the city manager would direct his strategy toward the possibility of hiring two or three new firefighters who would work eight-hour shifts five days a week, covering the evening hours when fire incidence was historically highest. They would be assigned to stations with the heaviest demands.

The number of firefighters proposed for the special shift was subsequently increased to four by a creative coalition of the fire chief and recreation director. The peak period for recreation activity in Newbern occurs weekday afternoons during the "after-school program" from 3:30 P.M. to 5:00 P.M. The recreation director finds it difficult to hire responsible supervisors for such short periods of time and has consistently been turned down in her requests for an appropriation for full-time or more substantial part-time help. Consequently, the recreation director suggested that the two departments join forces: they would request authorizations for four new employees who would serve as recreation supervisors from 3:00 P.M. to 5:00 P.M. and as firefighters from 5:00 P.M. until 11:00 P.M. The fire chief agreed to give it a try.[3]

---

[3]Fire departments tend to be strongly influenced by traditional practices; however, some have been creative in the assignment of nontraditional functions to qualified firefighters, often reporting favorable results.

Figure 3-2 Plan for Revised Deployment of Newbern's Patrol Officers

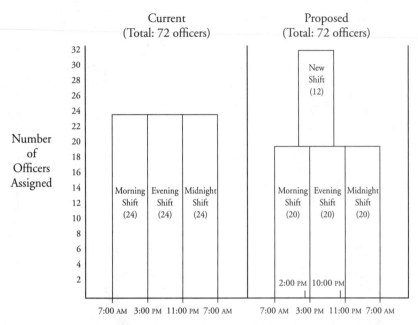

Note: This figure depicts the number of officers assigned to each shift, not the number on duty at a given time. Because of the need to provide two days off per week, plus vacation time, holidays, and occasional absences for illness and other reasons, the number of on-duty officers at any given time will be less. See Chapter 20.

Customer Service Center

Other mismatches in demands and resource allocations were discovered in office operations. Three years earlier, a customer service center had been established as a convenience to persons paying utility bills, purchasing plastic garbage bags, or pursuing other matters requiring permits or fees. Most of those functions had been concentrated in that single location. Four finance department clerks were assigned to cover the center's counter, as needed, in addition to their other bookkeeping duties. The demand analysis revealed that counter activity is light most mornings until about 11:30 A.M. and becomes light again after about 1:30 P.M. For two hours at midday, however, counter business is often heavy. The traditional scheduling of lunch breaks for the four employees makes an already difficult situation even more burdensome and contributes to complaints of long lines and slow service. With two of the four clerks taking their lunch hour beginning at 11:30 A.M. and the other two leaving for lunch at 12:30 P.M., only two employees are on duty during the peak counter demand period.

Following discussions about the problem, the finance director proposed that the office move gradually—through attrition in order to avoid layoffs or forced reassignments—to a staff of two full-time and four half-time clerks. The authorized

From the Electronic Toolkit ●

Box 3-1 Creating Line Graphs and Bar Graphs

No doubt, many readers have already discovered that spreadsheet programs, such as Microsoft Excel, simplify the creation of line graphs and bar graphs and make them look professional. To make a **graph** using Excel, begin by entering the data in columns. (For directions on opening Excel and entering data refer to Box 2-1.) Then, highlight the data ("select" the data, in Excel parlance) and either click the graph icon on the tool bar or choose the Chart option from the Insert menu. Choose the type and subtype of graph that are appropriate for the data. The most useful graph types will probably be the Column, Bar, Pie, and Line options. After choosing, click "Next" to proceed.

In the second step, make sure that the correct data are used and are used correctly. For example, if the data of interest are entered in A1 through B12 (meaning both columns A and B are filled to row 12), the graph should use the data in A1 through B12. The graph might have two bars for every entry. (An example would be if every month has one bar for the number of arrests of the police department and another bar for the number of crimes reported per month. In this example, the graph would have two bars for every month.) The two bars must be labeled so that the information that each bar describes is evident. To insert names for the separate data in the legend, click on the Series tab at the top of the box for step 2 and type a name into the blank box for each series. Click "Next" to proceed.

In the third step, choose the options best for the graph. Here, the user can enter the title of the graph and the titles for the x and y axes. Also, the user can play with the visual aspects of the graph, such as the number of gridlines or the appearance of the data labels. Click "Next" to proceed to the last box.

In the last step, choose whether the graph should be displayed on its own or as part of the spreadsheet. Usually, choosing to put the graph in the spreadsheet is a better option because it can be more easily modified in the spreadsheet. To put the graph in the spreadsheet, highlight the "As an object in:" option. Click "Finish" to complete the graph and it will be displayed. If changes in the features of the graph need to be made, highlight the chart and use the Chart menu to make changes or left-click on the area that needs to be changed. For example, if the scale of an axis needs to be altered, then left-click on that axis and a menu will appear. Highlight Format Axis and a box will appear that will allow changes to be made. Many parts of the graph can be changed in this manner.

strength of 4.0 person-years would not be affected, because two full-time and four half-time employees still equal 4.0 person-years. Two of the part-time clerks would work from 9:30 A.M. to 1:30 P.M., and the other two would work from 11:30 A.M. to 3:30 P.M. The four part-time clerks would be assigned primary counter duty, thereby allowing the two full-time clerks to work on bookkeeping assignments without interruption unless absences forced them to cover counter duty temporarily. Because all four part-time clerks would be on duty during the 11:30 A.M. to 1:30 P.M. time period, counter strength would be doubled during peak periods at no additional cost. In fact, the city of Newbern incurs few fringe benefit expenses for part-time employees, so total costs actually would be reduced.

Human Resources Department

Demand analysis uncovered a similar problem in the human resources (HR) department. Although the department is small, consisting of the director, one technician, and a secretary, it was among the units relocated to an office annex when city hall became overcrowded. In conducting demand analysis for the HR operation, the administrative assistant not only relied on departmental records but also spent several lunch hours over a four-week period in the lobby outside the HR office and kept a log of job applicant traffic. He discovered that a substantial volume of job seekers arrives during the noon hour when all three staff members are away at lunch. This discovery not only prompted concern from a public relations standpoint but also raised the question of whether the city might be losing some of the best potential applicants. It seemed reasonable to assume that persons already employed elsewhere but wishing to improve their status would be likely to explore alternate opportunities during the noon hour. Unemployed persons could come anytime.

When shown the demand statistics, the HR director was surprised by the volume of noontime traffic. He immediately expressed interest in improving the situation, although he preferred that his own time and that of the technician be left as free as possible for technical and administrative duties more demanding than receiving applications. Three options seemed most reasonable: (1) employment opportunities could be posted at the service center at city hall and applications received at that location; (2) a "mini-service center" could be established at the office annex at least during the noon hour for services handled at that location, with staffing provided on a rotating basis by departments located there; or (3) the secretary and HR technician could take staggered lunches to assure service for job applicants during the noon hour.

Business License Issuances

Focusing attention on still another office operation—demand analysis of business license issuances and renewals—revealed an unbalanced workload (Figure 3-3). Most business licenses expire in November or July, creating a workload burden during those months. By staggering expiration dates throughout the year, the burden could be spread more evenly, allowing prompt action on renewal applications, causing less interference with other office duties, and eliminating the need for overtime.

The results of demand analysis in the departments examined encouraged the city manager to request subsequent analyses for other departments and activities. Specifically, he wanted demand analyses completed for the civic center, the swimming pool, parks maintenance, and equipment repair activities. Demand variations at the civic center and swimming pool by season, day of the week, and time of day could suggest changes in the hours of operation of those facilities, as well as modified staffing levels and deployment patterns. Seasonal variation in the parks maintenance activities could suggest revised strategies for the use of seasonal help; the deferral of some activities, such as minor construction, to the off-season in order to level out the workload; and perhaps merger or coordination with public works crews for the use of parks maintenance employees for snow removal and other off-season activities.

Figure 3-3 Demand Profile for Business Licenses and Permits

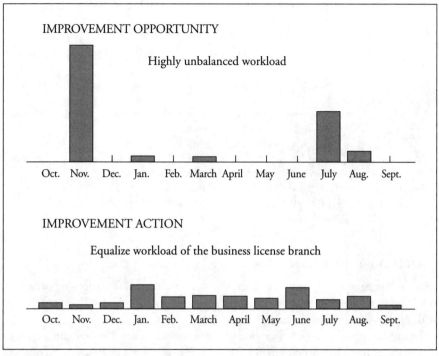

Source: John S. Thomas, "Operations Management: Planning, Scheduling, and Control," in *Productivity Improvement Handbook for State and Local Government,* ed. George J. Washnis (New York: John Wiley & Sons, 1980), 176. Copyright © 1980 by the National Academy of Public Administration. Reprinted by permission of John Wiley & Sons, Inc.
Note: Based on information for business licenses and permits in the District of Columbia.

Analysis of the demand for equipment repair could reveal the introduction of high volumes of workload in late afternoons near the close of the normal work shift for most departments. Vehicles brought in for repair or preventive maintenance might be unavailable for use the following day and perhaps longer, not because maintenance actually requires twenty-four hours or more but because the demand is initiated at a time when most mechanics are leaving work for the day. Such findings might justify establishing a second shift for equipment maintenance. Although a second shift could be staffed by adding mechanics, it could also be established without expanding employment by reassigning current mechanics or assigning new employees following attrition among current mechanics. Perhaps without increasing the total number of mechanics, the productivity of the equipment maintenance function could be improved by better matching the availability of mechanics with the time that vehicles are most available for repair or preventive maintenance.

Box 3-2 Other Applications of Demand Analysis

Logical candidates for demand analysis include the following:

- a swimming pool that is open and staffed at 9:00 A.M. but draws few swimmers before 10:30 A.M.
- a library that consistently experiences difficulty closing at the announced time because many patrons are still in the building
- a parks maintenance department that has the same staffing year-round—that is, an equal number of full-time equivalent employees summer and winter
- a streets department that has the same staffing year-round
- suppliers of water, gas, and electricity that encounter wide variations in demand, as they seek to design strategies to level out peak demand times or seasons
- service calls—emergency and otherwise—in a given department, as a step toward developing personnel deployment strategies that efficiently match call-for-service patterns

UTILITY OF DEMAND ANALYSIS

Simple demand analysis requires careful observation and tabulation but little else. If adequate records are already on hand, it is an especially simple form of analysis with great potential usefulness.

Many local government operations have been established under the apparent assumption that a balanced demand for services exists. That assumption frequently is incorrect. A service agency may be staffed from 8:00 A.M. to 5:00 P.M., Monday through Friday, in a pattern totally at odds with client preferences for evening and weekend service. Under such circumstances, demand analysis might reveal peak demand at or near the close of normal working hours.

Prime candidates for demand analysis would include operations whose clients frequently incur long waiting periods for services; operations that may have grown somewhat lax or indifferent to their clients' demands, whether those clients are internal to the organization (that is, other local government departments) or external; operations that stress symmetry and administrative convenience over functionality and productivity; operations that place a premium on employee rather than client preferences; and operations that simply have not recently compared patterns of demand and resource allocation and wish to assure themselves of a proper match.

SUGGESTED FOR FURTHER INFORMATION

King, Norman R. "Manage Demand, Not Supply." *Governing* 9, no. 12 (September 1996): 13.
Thomas, John S. "Operations Management: Planning, Scheduling, and Control." In *Productivity Improvement Handbook for State and Local Government,* edited by George J. Washnis, 171–203. New York: John Wiley & Sons, 1980.

4

Program Evaluation Review Technique/Critical Path Method

Perhaps it would stretch a point to contend that good employees who have performed a particular task thousands of times could do it while asleep, while wearing a blindfold, or with one hand tied behind their back. It would not stretch a point, however, to argue that the sequence of steps has been so ingrained through repetition that adhering to the proper order is almost instinctive. But not all local government functions are so routine. Some, like the preparations for an election or for the ceremonial lighting of the municipal Christmas tree, may occur only once a year. Others, like the construction of a civic center or the merging of city and county health departments, may happen only once in a lifetime. Such projects could hardly be labeled routine. They often are complicated and require careful planning, coordination, and meticulous attention to detail throughout implementation.

Even the most complicated, nonroutine functions can be untangled and demystified by careful identification and sequencing of the individual components of those functions. Most administrators do just that sort of project planning hundreds of times during their careers, but they usually do it only in their heads—rarely if ever plotting their mental plan in detail on paper. Occasionally, however, charting the elements in sequence and on paper proves helpful.

Over the years two techniques of network analysis have demonstrated their value for project planning and monitoring. They are the Program Evaluation Review Technique (PERT) and the Critical Path Method (CPM). In simplified form, the basic concepts underlying PERT and CPM can be mastered easily.

SCENARIO: HERRMANVILLE, TENNESSEE

During budget time the past two years, two or three members of the city council in Herrmanville, Tennessee, had become increasingly inquisitive about travel expenses for staff conferences and training. Phil Alford, Herrmanville's budget director, was convinced that something fairly drastic was about to happen. "Curiosity may have prompted their questions the first year," he said in a meeting with Randall

Robinson, the city's human resources director, "but it was more than curiosity last year and you can be pretty sure they are coming after us if they bring it up again this year. We'd better get our information together on this and talk it over with the city manager."

Alford and Robinson introduced their discussion with the city manager by presenting a chart showing the city's total annual expenditures for conferences and training sessions attended by management employees. The chart showed that expenditures for registration, travel, lodging, and meals had grown dramatically over the past several years into a substantial figure. "The word on the street," reported Alford, "is that Councilman Tolliver has been doing his own arithmetic on this subject and may try to make political points at the budget hearings this spring by contending that travel expenses have been excessive."

It pleased the budget director to be able to present sensitive information that the city manager had not already heard; it made him seem well connected and politically astute. He was relieved that he did not have to reveal his source (his barber, who also cuts Councilman Tolliver's hair).

PLANNING AND COORDINATING A NEW PROGRAM

"I've been thinking for quite some time about the advantages of bringing several management development courses to city hall," said Robinson, "rather than sending department heads and their assistants to programs scattered around the country. Phil and I have been discussing this possibility over the last several days, and we think it might be the perfect time to reduce travel expenses and convert a portion of those resources to an in-house management development program. We would need some lead time to develop the program, but we think it could be successful."

"I'm interested in this," the city manager responded, "and not just for the potential savings. I've had reservations, myself, about the value of some of these conferences, based on what appear to be sketchy agendas and superficial topics. Whenever I've raised questions about a particular agenda, I've been told that the conference's greatest value was in making contacts with other attendees, anyway. I know that's true to a degree, but I'm not sure that the value of making new contacts or renewing old acquaintances reaches what we are having to pay for it. Prepare a proposal on your idea and let me take a look at it. Remember, I'll need it before our budget presentation on May 14 for next fiscal year's appropriation."

The two men left the city manager's office and returned to the human resources department, ready to begin developing their ideas more fully. After discussing the broad framework of their management development proposal, they decided to use a simple network analysis technique to design the details of the plan. The approach they selected borrows elements from two network analysis stalwarts: PERT and CPM.

Box 4-1 Gantt Charts

A device much simpler than PERT/CPM charts for project scheduling and monitoring was developed by Henry L. Gantt in 1918. The Gantt chart simply lists major tasks down the left column and displays time frames for each task on a scaled time line to the right. A task requiring considerable time for completion is allotted a lengthy bar, while one requiring little time receives a shorter bar. Overlapping bars depict tasks that may be performed simultaneously.

A Gantt chart for a typical local government budget calendar is shown on page 40. Note that the efforts of the city council to establish local priorities and those of the city staff to forecast revenues occur concurrently. The development of a proposed Capital Improvement Program begins prior to the completion of the first two tasks and continues beyond the projected time of their completion.

More sophisticated Gantt charts often depict the status of the various tasks. For instance, the bar for each task could be shaded to depict the percentage of a given task that has been completed—for example, a task that is half completed would be depicted by a bar that is one-half solid and one-half patterned.

Gantt charts are simpler than PERT/CPM charts, but they are well suited for monitoring many types of projects and remain popular with many executives. On the other hand, Gantt charts fall short of PERT/CPM charts in some important respects. They are less able to depict dependency relationships among the tasks and less useful as a device for focusing the attention of the project monitor on the set of tasks most crucial to keeping the project on schedule (that is, the critical path in PERT/CPM charts).

(Box continues on next page)

PERT AND CPM

PERT and CPM are remarkably similar project planning and monitoring techniques that were developed in the mid-1950s.[1] They are so similar, in fact, that their labels often are used interchangeably or combined as PERT/CPM.

PERT/CPM charts provide project managers with a simple technique for planning a project, including the proper sequencing and scheduling of project elements, and then monitoring its progress. The technique forces the project manager to think through many of the details of the project before they are actually confronted in implementation, thereby reducing the likelihood that an element will be overlooked and cause the project to be delayed until that element can be completed. PERT/CPM

---

[1]PERT was developed by the U.S. Navy's Office of Special Projects and the management consulting firm of Booz, Allen, and Hamilton to boost project management success as the United States rushed to construct the Polaris nuclear submarine missile system during the cold war arms race with the Soviet Union. CPM was developed independently by the DuPont Company and Remington RAND Corporation as a scheduling technique for the construction and maintenance of chemical plants.

Box 4-1 (continued)

Budget Preparation Timeline

Schedule	December	January	February	March	April	May	June
City council establishes priorities	▨						
Staff develops revenue forecast	▨	▨					
Staff develops proposed Capital Improvement Program (CIP)		▨	▨				
Departments prepare requested operating budgets		▨	▨				
Departmental budget hearings			▨				
City manager reviews budget requests and prepares preliminary budget				▨			
Departmental appeals				▨			
City manager prepares recommended budget					▨		
City manager presents recommended budget to City Council					▨		
City council holds work sessions on budget						▨	
Public hearings						▨	▨
Budget and CIP are amended/finalized for adoption							▨

Note: This chart was prepared in a Microsoft Excel spreadsheet. Special software for preparing Gantt charts is also available from other sources. See, for example, SmartDraw 5 at www.smartdraw.com.

Figure 4-1 Hypothetical PERT/CPM Chart

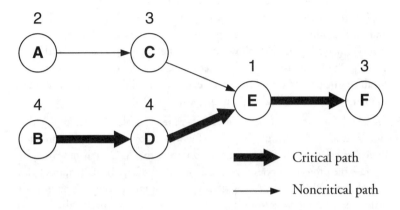

charts are also valuable tools to local government managers attempting to report the status of a project to a supervisor, the city council, the media, or interested citizens. The chart shows the sequencing and interrelationship of program activities, the progress made to date, the activities being undertaken currently, and the activities still to be tackled.

In its simplest form, a PERT/CPM chart consists of a series of circles or nodes depicting events or activities in a project, linked by arrows showing which activities lead to others. In the hypothetical PERT/CPM chart shown in Figure 4-1, the project begins with activities A and B and ends with event F. Activities A, B, C, D, and E must be completed in order to make event F possible. The numbers adjacent to the nodes indicate units of time—perhaps hours, days, or weeks—required to complete each activity or event. In this example, two units of time, say 2 days, will be required to complete activity A and 3 days will be required for activity C, both of which must precede activity E. If these were the only prerequisite events for activity E, then activity E could commence in 5 days; however, activities B and D, requiring 4 days apiece, must also be completed before activity E can begin. Therefore, it will take 9 days for completion of element E (8 days for prerequisite activities and 1 day for activity E, itself), not 6, and 12 days for completion of the project (4 + 4 + 1 + 3), rather than 9.

Several important features of PERT/CPM charts are demonstrated by this example:

1. The most important path for planning and monitoring progress of a project is the *longest* path from start to finish. That is the path that provides the project manager with an estimate of the time needed to complete the project. If the project manager can find ways to reduce the time required in that path, the project will be completed earlier. Alternatively, if unexpected delays are encountered in that path, the project may miss its deadline. For these reasons, the longest path is called the *critical path*.

2. The importance of considering, at the outset, all elements that are necessary for completion of a project, is demonstrated by the chart. If the project manager had proceeded from A to C and on to activity E before considering the need for activities B and D, the project would have been delayed several days. Similarly, if the project manager had adopted the philosophy of taking "one step at a time" rather than proceeding simultaneously with sequences A–C and B–D, the amount of time required for the entire project would have been extended. PERT/CPM charts help to identify elements that can be tackled simultaneously.

3. *Slack* and *float* are terms that denote extra time available in noncritical paths. This is time that an activity could be delayed without slowing the overall project. In the hypothetical PERT/CPM chart, for example, the A–C path has 3 days of slack because the project cannot move to E in less than 8 days (B–D requires 8 days). The availability of slack in the A–C path suggests that monitoring this path is not as crucial as monitoring progress in the B–D path. It may also suggest that the wise project manager will search for ways to reallocate some of the slack resources (for example, funds or personnel) from the A–C path to the B–D path, if such a reallocation would help to ensure meeting the projected schedule or, better still, would allow the time requirement for B–D to be reduced to less than 8 days.[2]

PLANNING THE MANAGEMENT DEVELOPMENT PROGRAM

As Herrmanville's budget director and human resources director began listing the many elements associated with conducting a management development program, they were a bit overwhelmed. After just an hour or two, their list had grown to twenty-five elements. They arranged the list in roughly sequential order (see Table 4-1) and realized that they might have a problem meeting the most crucial deadline: their proposal must be prepared prior to the city manager's budget presentation to the city council on May 14.

Careful consideration of time requirements for each element and the identification of elements that could be handled simultaneously convinced Alford and Robinson that they could, in fact, meet the May 14 deadline (see Figure 4-2).[3]

---

[2]A word of caution is in order here. Project managers should be careful not to allow their zeal for diverting slack resources to the critical path or their neglect of noncritical paths to come back to haunt them. If the project manager directing the project in Figure 4-1 shaves a few days from the B–D path's time requirement but unintentionally allows the A–C path's time requirement to expand to 8 days, no time whatsoever will have been saved by the project overall.

[3]Realistic estimates of time requirements for the various steps are crucial to PERT/CPM charting. Occasionally, time lines are rigid, as when a project requires a public hearing and state law stipulates publication of a notice fifteen days prior to the hearing. At other times, staff records and the informed judgment of persons who have dealt with similar projects in the past offer the best basis for projecting time requirements. In their classic form, PERT charts often incorporate three time estimates for each activity or event: optimistic, most likely, and pessimistic.

Table 4-1 Elements Associated with Herrmanville's Proposed Management Development Program

Activity	Description	Immediate predecessor	Completion time (workdays)
A	Identify management development needs	—	10
B	Identify a suitable facility (considering, for example, price, availability)	—	5
C	Design a general plan for evaluation of the program	—	10
D	Identify the best-qualified instructors	A	5
E	Prepare budget proposal	B,C,D	3
F	Final preparations and budget presentation (May 14)	E	5
G	Budget adoption (June 18)	F	25
H	Decide on date/time for conference (avoid conflicts)	G	3
I	Develop detailed evaluation plan	C	20
J	Line up instructors	H	10
K	Secure facility	H	5
L	Determine room assignments and configurations	J,K	2
M	Make meal/refreshment arrangements	K	3
N	Make travel arrangements for instructors	J	10
O	Arrange for audiovisual equipment	J	7
P	Prepare program	L	8
Q	Prepare evaluation materials	I	10
R	Distribute program/publicize conference	P	15
S	Conduct registration of participants	R	10.4
T	Establish evaluation benchmark: pretest of participants to see what they know about subject	Q,S	0.1
U	Conduct sessions	M,N,O,T	1.5
V	Conduct primary evaluation: Opinions of participants and posttest to see what they learned	U	1
W	Conduct secondary evaluation: Are lessons being used on the job?	U	15

(continued)

Table 4-1 *(Continued)*

Activity	Description	Immediate predecessor	Completion time (workdays)
X	Conduct final evaluation:		
	Impact of lessons on the job	U	30
Y	Assess results and decide whether to		
	conduct another conference	V,W,X	3

Notes: Each element in the process may itself have several subelements that must be considered carefully to arrive at reasonable estimates of time requirements. Consider, for example, elements B and K in the above list. Identifying a suitable facility for purposes of developing a budget would first require the program planner to decide on at least the approximate type, number, and sizes of rooms needed, followed by calls to determine availability and cost. At a subsequent stage, actually securing a facility would require visual inspection of the most promising facility options, selection of the preferred facility, reservation, and confirmation. Thus 5 workdays apiece have been allotted to elements B and K in the PERT/CPM chart shown in Figure 4-2.

Allowances must also be made for unavoidable delays. Although the actual adoption of a budget (element G) will occur in a matter of hours during the council meeting on June 18, that meeting will occur 25 workdays after the budget presentation on May 14 (element F). Because of the required time interval between budget presentation and adoption, the completion time for element G is, in effect, 25 workdays.

Although five major elements would have to be completed prior to budget presentation, their PERT/CPM chart indicated a critical path of 23 workdays—or just less than 5 weeks—to budget presentation. They could make the May 14 deadline!

Projections of the time requirements for implementing the proposal, once approved, indicated a critical path of 48.5 workdays from budget approval on June 18 to the actual management development sessions toward the end of August. Alford and Robinson plan to conduct a detailed evaluation of the development program's effectiveness rather than what they derisively call "one of those pseudo-evaluations that really only tells you if the audience was entertained." Their more elaborate evaluation plans extend the time line 33 workdays beyond the conclusion of the sessions.

Upon receiving the PERT/CPM chart for the management development program, the city manager immediately spotted an advantage supplemental to the persuasiveness of the underlying budgetary argument, which is that it makes more sense to bring a few expert instructors to Herrmanville than to send department heads to points scattered across the country. The supplemental advantage gained by taking such a systematic approach to planning is the usefulness of the PERT/CPM chart as a tool for selling the proposal. The chart presents a rather complex project in a relatively simple diagram that demonstrates the proposal has been well thought out.

UTILITY OF PERT/CPM CHARTS

Many textbooks may be guilty of overstating the utility of PERT or CPM charts by implying that they are heavily used management tools. In fact, many local government managers have enjoyed successful careers without ever drawing a PERT or

Figure 4-2 Planning and Monitoring Preparations for an In-House Management Development Program

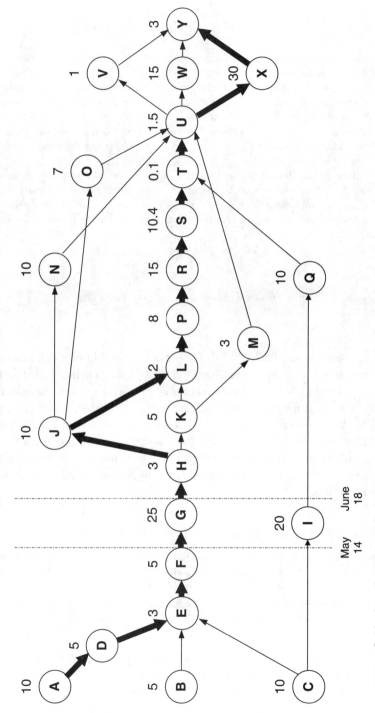

Critical path: 131 work days.

Notes: See Table 4-1 for a description of the project elements. This chart was prepared using the drawing toolbar in Microsoft Word. Special software for developing charts is also available from other sources. See, for example, SmartDraw 5 at www.smartdraw.com.

Box 4-2 Having Difficulty Estimating Time Requirements?

Sometimes it is fairly easy to estimate the amount of time required for a given activity in a PERT/CPM chart. Sometimes it is not.

If assigning times to PERT/CPM activities is problematic, check the organization's records to see if the activity was performed in the past and how long it took. If such records are unavailable or if the activity is a first-time event in your organization, perhaps contacts in other organizations can share their experience. Electronic listserves connecting occupational counterparts by their e-mail addresses often can serve this function. In some cases, the "best guess" of field experts will be the best available option.

When estimating the duration of activities for which there is little history or experience, consider adopting the approach often used in the development of PERT charts. Get three estimates: the most optimistic estimate, the most pessimistic estimate, and the estimate of the most likely amount of time required for the activity. Then use the following formula for estimated activity duration, T_e:

$$T_e = \frac{a + 4m + b}{6}$$

where:

a = most optimistic time; b = most pessimistic time; m = most likely time

CPM chart. Nevertheless, PERT/CPM charts can be useful in particular circumstances—especially, for example, when a complicated project is being tackled for the first time, when a manager wants reassurance that a project supervisor has planned adequately, when a projected completion date seems too distant, when a "mental PERT/CPM chart" of a critical process is about to exit city hall with a retiring official, or when an audience is otherwise unlikely to grasp the interrelationships among project elements or the complexity of an overall task. Even those successful managers who have never in their careers drawn such charts might have found the technique helpful in such cases.

SUGGESTED FOR FURTHER INFORMATION

Clayton, Ross. "Techniques of Network Analysis for Managers." In *Managing Public Systems: Analytic Techniques for Public Administration,* by Michael J. White, Ross Clayton, Robert Myrtle, Gilbert Siegel, and Aaron Rose, 86–107. Lanham, Md.: University Press of America, 1985.

Eppen, G. D., F. J. Gould, C. P. Schmidt, Jeffrey H. Moore, and Larry R. Weatherford. *Introductory Management Science,* 5th ed. Upper Saddle River, N.J.: Prentice Hall, 1998.

Groebner, David F., and Patrick W. Shannon. *Management Science.* New York: Macmillan/ Dellen, 1992.

Gupta, Dipak K. *Decisions by the Numbers: An Introduction to Quantitative Techniques for Public Policy Analysis and Management.* Englewood Cliffs, N.J.: Prentice Hall, 1994.

Lock, Dennis. *Project Management,* 6th ed. Brookfield, Vt.: Gower, 1996.

From the Electronic Toolkit ●──

Box 4-3 Drawing Gantt Charts and PERT/CPM Charts

Special software is available for drawing Gantt and PERT/CPM charts. See, for example, SmartDraw 5 at *www.smartdraw.com*. Simple versions of these charts, such as those presented in this chapter, may also be developed using products such as Microsoft Excel (Gantt charts) or the drawing toolbar in Microsoft Word (PERT/CPM charts).

Box 4-4 Other Applications of
Gantt Charts and PERT/CPM Charts

Logical candidates for PERT/CPM charts include the following:

- the annual budget process
- the process for the city's upcoming "Vision 2020" strategic planning effort
- the steps in preparing for and conducting local elections
- the steps involved in completing a two-year project, supported by outside grants
- a major construction or renovation project
- coordination of plans for the local Founders' Day celebration.

McGowan, Robert P., and Dennis P. Wittmer. "Five Great Issues in Decision Making." In *Handbook of Public Administration,* 2d ed., edited by Jack Rabin, W. Bartley Hildreth, and Gerald J. Miller, 293–319. New York: Marcel Dekker, 1998.

Summers, Michael R. *Analyzing Operations in Business: Issues, Tools, and Techniques.* Westport, Conn.: Quorum Books, 1998.

Taylor, Bernard W., III. *Introduction to Management Science,* 6th ed. Upper Saddle River, N.J.: Prentice Hall, 1999.

Taylor, James. *A Survival Guide for Project Managers.* New York: AMACOM, 1998.

Thomas, John S. "Operations Management: Planning, Scheduling, and Control." In *Productivity Improvement Handbook for State and Local Government,* edited by George J. Washnis, 171–203. New York: John Wiley & Sons, 1980.

5.

Plotting Job Travel to Diagnose Scheduling Problems

Just as salespersons find it advantageous to cluster their visits to customers in the Northeast one week, the Midwest another week, and the Pacific Coast region another, local governments may also reap benefits by carefully considering the scheduling of work crews across their jurisdiction and even the "travel patterns" of office employees within city hall. The same principles apply; only the scale is different. For the most part, time spent in transit is time lost from actual production.

MAPPING "TRAVEL PATTERNS"

The mapping of work area travel patterns requires nothing more than a pencil; a map of the service area or, in the case of office workers, a sketch of the office building; and accurate work activity records or a willingness to record work area travel as it occurs. Travel patterns for field operations often may be reconstructed and mapped from existing departmental records, such as completed work orders and daily activity reports. Work "travel" within city hall is less likely to be routinely recorded, and mapping normally requires the maintenance of a log by employees in the office under review or observation of work patterns by an analyst.

A variation of the mapping technique is the development of a daily trip frequency chart of office activity. Such a chart simply records trip frequency from one workstation to another.

SCENARIO: ROCKWOOD, KENTUCKY

The city manager of Rockwood, Kentucky, had long suspected that a great deal of time could be saved through better scheduling of work. One day he asked an administrative intern to test his theory by plotting the work sequence of a variety of city activities—some in the office and some in the field.

HEALTH CARE VISITATION

The field activity that the intern focused on first was home visitation by nurses in the public health department.[1] The availability of home visitation records made

---

[1] This health care visitation scenario is adapted from David N. Ammons, "Analysis of the Nursing Services Section of the Oak Ridge Health Services Department," City of Oak Ridge, Tennessee, February 1981.

the intern's task simple. Several copies of the map of Rockwood were used in the analysis, one for each week of the period under review. On each map, the intern recorded the approximate location of each home visit for two nurses during a given week, using symbols that distinguished between the nurses and also between days of the week (see Figure 5-1). The result was a series of maps showing wide dispersion of home visits by each nurse. Although some clustering of home visits within a close geographic area occurred, more commonly the nurses traveled from one end of town to the other, often crossing each other's path.

Based on her findings, the intern recommended that the city be divided into two geographic districts and that each nurse be assigned responsibility for home health care visits in one of the two zones. She further recommended that home visits be scheduled in more tightly clustered daily batches in order to decrease travel time and increase actual visit time or time for other duties.

PHOTOCOPIER TRAFFIC

In city hall itself, the city manager had noticed an almost constant stream of traffic to and from the single photocopying machine located in the building. Several department managers insisted that a second machine was needed—and he was aware that they could be right—but he suspected that the constant traffic, in some measure, reflected poor work scheduling (perhaps even intentionally poor work scheduling!). A few office workers seemed to enjoy the opportunity to visit with coworkers along their sometimes circuitous routes to and from the copy machine. The city manager asked the intern to explore that possibility.

The intern tackled the assignment in two stages. The first stage simply involved placing a pad of paper at the copy machine with instructions for users of the machine to record the date, department or office, and number of copies made. After a few days, the intern was able to review the log for volume of use and trip frequency by the various work units.

The second stage of the analysis involved a more detailed examination of activity patterns in the office that used the copy machine the most. The more detailed review was undertaken for two reasons: first, if a second copy machine was needed, perhaps that office would be the logical place for it; second, if scheduling or location problems did exist in the office, it made more sense to examine the office's activities as a whole rather than only its photocopying activities.

The intern identified the major workstations associated with the office, constructed a grid featuring those workstations, and observed and tallied travel frequencies, adding a mark to the appropriate cell each time a person from one workstation traveled to another (see Figure 5-2). She noted that both clerks in the office frequently used the copy machine and that the secretary visited the filing cabinets more often than did either of the clerks. Based on the tabulation and conversations with the persons working in the office, the intern developed a proximity chart identifying which workstations needed to be situated near one another (see Figure 5-3).

Figure 5-1 Home Health Care Visits by Public Health Nurses

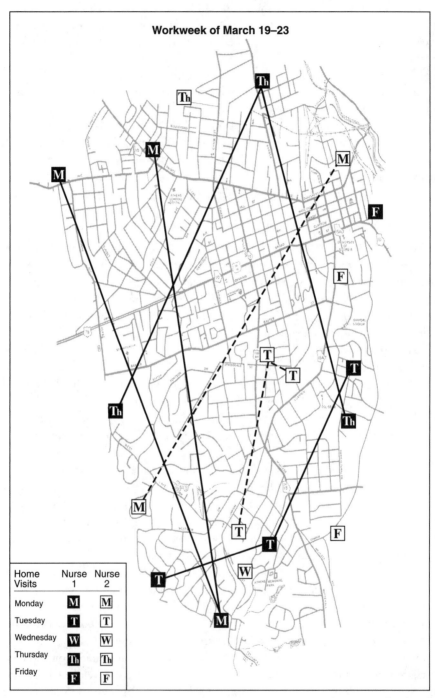

Workweek of March 19–23

Home Visits	Nurse 1	Nurse 2
Monday	M	M
Tuesday	T	T
Wednesday	W	W
Thursday	Th	Th
Friday	F	F

(continued)

Figure 5-1 *(Continued)*

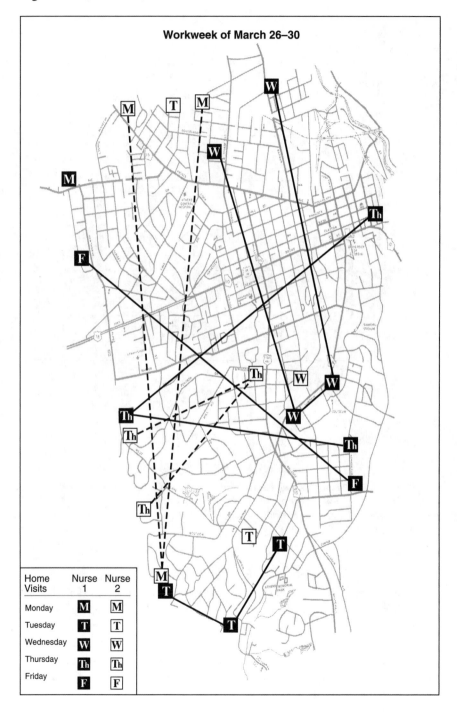

Workweek of March 26–30

Home Visits	Nurse 1	Nurse 2
Monday	M	M
Tuesday	T	T
Wednesday	W	W
Thursday	Th	Th
Friday	F	F

Figure 5-2 Tally Sheet Showing Daily Trip Frequencies within the Office

From \ To (Workstation)	1	2	3	4	5	6
1		卌 卌 III	III	卌 卌 卌	卌 卌 卌 / 卌	II
2	卌 卌 卌 / 卌 卌 IIII		卌 IIII	II	卌 卌 卌 / 卌 卌 II	卌
3	卌 卌 I	卌 II		卌 卌 卌 / 卌 III	卌	卌 卌 卌 / 卌 卌 卌
4	IIII	卌 卌	卌 卌 II		III	卌 卌 卌 / 卌 卌 卌 / 卌 IIII
5	卌 卌 卌 / 卌 卌 卌 / II	卌 卌 卌 / IIII	卌 II	II		
6	II	卌	卌 卌 卌 / 卌 卌 III	卌 卌 卌 / 卌 卌 II		

Workstation	Description
1	Manager's desk
2	Secretary's desk
3	Clerk A's desk
4	Clerk B's desk
5	File
6	Copy machine

Source: Patricia Haynes, "Industrial Engineering Techniques," in *Productivity Improvement Handbook for State and Local Government,* ed. George J. Washnis (New York: John Wiley & Sons, 1980), 213. Copyright © 1980 by the National Academy of Public Administration. Reprinted by permission of John Wiley & Sons, Inc.

The intern showed the city manager the results of her investigation. They discussed the apparent advantages of locating a copy machine nearby, based on the heavy usage pattern of that office. The city manager, however, felt that before either purchasing a second photocopying machine or creating any inconvenience for other users through relocating the current machine nearer this heavy-use office, he wanted the analysis reopened for a third stage. "Before we do anything," he told the intern, "I want you to see whether or not all those trips are necessary. Why couldn't they stack up their copying needs for three or four trips per day?"

Figure 5-3 Proximity Chart

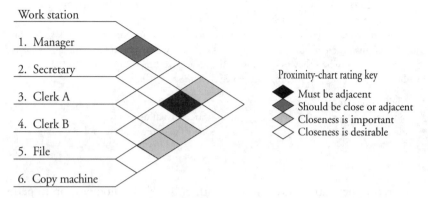

Source: Patricia Haynes, "Industrial Engineering Techniques," in *Productivity Improvement Handbook for State and Local Government,* ed. George J. Washnis (New York: John Wiley & Sons, 1980), 212. Copyright © 1980 by the National Academy of Public Administration. Reprinted by permission of John Wiley & Sons, Inc.

POSTSCRIPT

The application of a particular analytic technique will sometimes yield findings that provide ample justification for a final recommendation. At other times, only preliminary recommendations and a resolve to investigate further, perhaps using other methods, will result. The Rockwood case provides an example of each.

Sufficient justification was gathered through the mapping exercise to establish new guidelines for assigning caseloads to public health nurses and for scheduling home health visits. Combined travel time for public health nurses was reduced by 200 hours despite a slight increase in caseload and home visitations during the first year under the new guidelines. That time became available for clinic work.

The intern was disappointed that she had not been able to present as convincing a case on the office photocopier assignment. She had to agree with the city manager, however, that in this case applying the mapping technique had answered a few questions but had raised others. She was determined that when she returned to the city manager with a subsequent recommendation on that issue, it would be solid and well documented.

Using a technique called process flow charting (see Chapter 6), the intern carefully recorded all the steps in the major functions involving clerk A and clerk B—the two employees who, according to the mapping exercise, used the photocopy machine most frequently. Careful analysis confirmed the city manager's suspicions; most individual trips to the copier could be delayed and more efficiently handled in a batch process. A new procedure was proposed whereby clerk A and clerk B would alternate on hourly trips to the copier to handle all the copying needs for both desks. Each clerk would go to the copy machine four times per day.

Box 5-1 Other Applications of Job Travel Mapping

Time lost to excessive travel due to poorly sequenced jobs or uncoordinated work scheduling can be a serious problem. Job travel mapping is a simple way to reveal or highlight the degree of such problems, when they exist. Among the local government operations sometimes vulnerable to sequencing and scheduling problems are the following:

- building inspectors
- health inspectors
- code enforcement officials

- case workers
- street-patching crews
- parks maintenance crews

The recommendation was approved with only a slight modification to permit more frequent trips to the copy machine as required by rush jobs. Even so, trips to the copy machine dropped from a combined daily average of 69 to an average of only 11 trips per day—an 84 percent reduction. (Neither clerk spoke to the intern for three days following implementation, however!)

Similar studies were planned for two other offices. Proposals to purchase an additional copy machine were put on hold.

UTILITY OF JOB TRAVEL MAPPING

For most jobs, travel time is time lost from productive purposes. Sometimes large amounts of travel time are unavoidable. At other times, however, mapping job travel can help identify alternative procedures or revised work site arrangements that can minimize avoidable travel time. Analysts may be surprised to discover the amount of time street patching crews, parks maintenance crews, building inspectors, and health inspectors spend in transit—time that might be reduced by more efficient planning of job sequences. They may also be surprised by the amount of productive time that is lost through the travel habits of office workers.

SUGGESTED FOR FURTHER INFORMATION

Haynes, Patricia. "Industrial Engineering Techniques." In *Productivity Improvement Handbook for State and Local Government,* edited by George J. Washnis, 204–236. New York: John Wiley & Sons, 1980.

Hicks, Philip E. "Production Systems Design." In *Introduction to Industrial Engineering and Management Science,* 61–104. New York: McGraw-Hill, 1977.

Morley, Elaine. "Improving Productivity through Work Redesign." In *A Practitioner's Guide to Public Sector Productivity Improvement,* 89–117. New York: Van Nostrand Reinhold Co., 1986.

Part III
Work Flow and Work Measurement

Whether or not they are intended to be permanent, operational practices established informally or to meet a specific temporary need often become locked in place. Procedures that were simply the personal preferences of an early operator become the expected pattern for all successors.

New responsibilities undertaken by a work unit are not always blended carefully into current procedures or assigned to particular employee positions as part of some logical strategy. Instead, the new task often is added to the duties of an individual who is thought to be qualified to do it, who has the time for it, or who has not received a new assignment as recently as other coworkers.

Employees may come and go, but procedures and workload distributions—even when poorly devised—often remain. Managers may be so accustomed to their operation as they inherited it or as it has evolved that they fail to see procedural inefficiencies or the misallocation of work duties; they simply assume that their work units are functioning appropriately.

Techniques of work-flow analysis and work measurement can help managers see their operations more objectively. Process flow charting helps by isolating steps in a routine procedure; work-distribution analysis examines the allocation of human resources to the tasks of a work unit; and the use of performance standards enables the manager to gauge more clearly whether the performance of the work unit measures up.

Process Flow Charts

Administrators occasionally assume incorrectly that persons who have performed a particular function for many years and understand its intricate details will naturally devise and adhere to the best procedures for carrying it out. Decisions regarding operational steps are left to the operators themselves or to line supervisors. Other administrators, priding themselves as "hands-on managers," may immerse themselves in the details of a process but never really examine those details systematically with an eye toward streamlining procedures or eliminating unnecessary steps. Opportunities for improvement can be missed either way.

SCENARIO: PROCEDURAL PROBLEMS IN TARA COUNTY, GEORGIA

Department heads and supervisors in Tara County, Georgia, have been increasingly frustrated by the time-consuming procedures required to secure supplies and materials for their operations. County administrator Charlotte O'Hara has parried the complaints of one department head after another with reminders of the importance of a centralized purchasing system for securing competitive bids and volume discounts. Today, however, Clarence "Red" Butler, the county's public works director, stormed into her office and began explaining how current procedures are hurting his department's productivity.

"I'm not opposed to centralized purchasing," Butler said, "but when I have to adjust crew assignments because I don't have materials I should have received days ago, we're not getting full advantage of our scheduling efforts. It seems to take forever to get our requisitions processed and a purchase order out to a supplier."

After discussing the problem at some length, O'Hara decided that it was time to take a closer look at requisition procedures. She summoned purchasing agent Stanley Wilkes to her office and asked him to consult with the public works director and prepare a detailed evaluation of current procedures to see if some improvements could be devised. The two men decided to begin their analysis by developing a process flow chart for the requisition-to-purchase-order process.

PROCESS FLOW CHART

Process flow charting is a simple technique for documenting the steps in a routine procedure. By recording in sequence and categorizing each step of the process, inefficiencies are often exposed and opportunities for improvement identified. Although process flow charting and Program Evaluation Review Technique/Critical Path Method (PERT/CPM) charting (see Chapter 4) both emphasize identification and sequencing of the steps in a process, they differ in format as well as in their degree of detail and application. Process flow charts typically break the steps in a process into finer detail than PERT/CPM charts. A PERT/CPM chart, for instance, might specify "secure needed supplies" as an activity in a larger project, while process flow charting would identify each step in the supply acquisition process. With their greater degree of operational detail, process flow charts are most suitable for analyzing repetitive operations; PERT/CPM charts are more useful for planning and monitoring nonroutine projects.

Little specialized knowledge is necessary for rudimentary process flow charting. Other than familiarity with a set of five symbols that help to categorize elements of the process (see Figure 6-1), the primary requisite for process flow charting is the ability to conduct careful observation. The successful *use* of flow charts also requires perceptiveness and thorough consideration of alternate procedures and strategies.

Using a special form, commonly called a *process chart* or an *operation chart,* the analyst records the steps involved in the current process and categorizes each step by chart symbol (see Figure 6-2). The steps are then analyzed in an effort to eliminate unnecessary or duplicative operations and inspections, reduce transportation and delay components, and generally streamline the process. A perceptive analyst will question the purpose of each step in a given process, the sequencing of steps, the assignment of duties, and the possible existence of cheaper, faster, or more reliable alternatives. A new process flow chart is prepared for the proposed procedures, thereby providing a simple means of comparing the present and proposed methods and highlighting the advantages of the latter.

Figure 6-1 Process Flow Chart Symbols

Symbol	Name	Definition
O	Operation	An item is acted upon, changed, or processed.
⇨	Transportation	An object is moved from one place to another.
☐	Inspection	An object is examined to be sure quantity and/or quality is satisfactory.
D	Delay	The process is interrupted as the item awaits the next step.
▽	Storage	The item is put away for an extended length of time.

Figure 6-2 Process Flow Chart

PROCESS CHART			

Present Method ☐
Proposed Method ☐
SUBJECT CHARTED _____ DATE _____
_____ CHART BY _____
_____ CHART NO. _____
DEPARTMENT _____ SHEET NO. _ OF _

DIST. IN FEET	TIME IN MINS.	CHART SYMBOLS	PROCESS DESCRIPTION
		○ ⇨ ☐ D ▽	
		○ ⇨ ☐ D ▽	
		○ ⇨ ☐ D ▽	
		○ ⇨ ☐ D ▽	
		○ ⇨ ☐ D ▽	
		○ ⇨ ☐ D ▽	
		○ ⇨ ☐ D ▽	
		○ ⇨ ☐ D ▽	
		○ ⇨ ☐ D ▽	
		○ ⇨ ☐ D ▽	
		○ ⇨ ☐ D ▽	
		○ ⇨ ☐ D ▽	
		○ ⇨ ☐ D ▽	
		○ ⇨ ☐ D ▽	
		○ ⇨ ☐ D ▽	
		○ ⇨ ☐ D ▽	
		○ ⇨ ☐ D ▽	
		○ ⇨ ☐ D ▽	
		○ ⇨ ☐ D ▽	
		○ ⇨ ☐ D ▽	
		○ ⇨ ☐ D ▽	
		○ ⇨ ☐ D ▽	
		○ ⇨ ☐ D ▽	
		○ ⇨ ☐ D ▽	
		○ ⇨ ☐ D ▽	
			Total

Source: Adapted from Patricia Haynes, "Industrial Engineering Techniques," in *Productivity Improvement Handbook for State and Local Government,* ed. George J. Washnis (New York: John Wiley & Sons, 1980), 211. Copyright © 1980 by the National Academy of Public Administration. Reprinted by permission of John Wiley & Sons, Inc.

A STREAMLINED APPROACH

Examination by the purchasing agent and public works director revealed that the requisition-to-purchase-order process was more tedious, time-consuming, and laborious than necessary (see Figure 6-3). Requisitions prepared by a supervisor were carried by a messenger to a secretary for typing. The typed requisition was returned to the supervisor for review and signature before being routed to the purchasing agent. If approved by the purchasing agent, the form was routed to a typist who drew information from the requisition and prepared a purchase order. Numerous delays were found throughout the process, as the document awaited routing, typing, review, and approval.

The public works director suggested a revised procedure that, with a few modifications by the purchasing agent, met the objectives of both parties. The new approach (see Figure 6-4) would computerize the requisition process. Under this plan, a supervisor could initiate the process by keying the requisition onto a template in the computer. The requisition would be routed electronically to the supervisor's department head for approval. If rejected, the department head would be prompted by the computer to provide a reason for rejection and that reason would be transmitted to the requesting supervisor. If approved by the department head, the requisition would be routed electronically to the purchasing office. Following review in the purchasing office, approved requisitions would be posted automatically and assigned a purchase order number.[1]

The proposed procedure reduces delays and saves secretarial time for other duties without adding work for the supervisor. In fact, it reduces the chances for error introduced by the current procedure's requirements for retyping information on various forms and eliminates the need for the supervisor and purchasing agent to review that retyping. By using the computer to convey "paperwork" electronically, *physical* transportation distances, which totaled 105 feet in the current procedure, were eliminated.

Comparison of the two charts showed that the new procedure would eliminate one operation, two transportation steps, and six delays. All parties agreed that the revision looked promising. As a precaution, however, they decided to initiate the revised procedure as a six-month pilot project involving only purchases from the public works department. If successful after that period, they would consider recommending adoption countywide.

UTILITY OF PROCESS FLOW CHARTS

Many local government operations have grown incrementally beyond their initial stage. New procedures have been tacked repeatedly onto old procedures. For example, instead of modifying the original form to cover the new features introduced from

---

[1]Some purchases, because of their nature or magnitude, might require approval from the chief executive or from the governing body prior to signature by the purchasing agent.

Figure 6-3 Process Flow Chart—Present Method

PROCESS CHART			

Present Method ☒
Proposed Method ☐
SUBJECT CHARTED Requisition for small tools   DATE _____
Chart begins at supervisor's desk and ends at typist's desk in   CHART BY **HR/CH**
purchasing department.   CHART NO. **R 136**
DEPARTMENT _____ SHEET NO. 1 OF 1

DIST. IN FEET	TIME IN MINS.	CHART SYMBOLS	PROCESS DESCRIPTION
		○⇨□ D ▽	Requisition written by supervisor (one copy)
		○ ⇨ □D ▽	On supervisor's desk (awaiting messenger)
65		○ ⇨□ D ▽	By messenger to superintendent's secretary
		○ ⇨ □D ▽	On secretary's desk (awaiting typing)
		○⇨□ D ▽	Requisition typed (original requisition copied)
15		○⇨□ D ▽	By secretary to superintendent
		○ ⇨ □D ▽	On superintendent's desk (awaiting approval)
		○ ⇨ □ D ▽	Examined and approved by superintendent
		○ ⇨ □D ▽	On superintendent's desk (awaiting messenger)
20		○⇨□ D ▽	To purchasing department
		○ ⇨ □D ▽	On purchasing agent's desk (awaiting approval)
		○ ⇨ □ D ▽	Examined and approved
		○ ⇨ □D ▽	On purchasing agent's desk (awaiting messenger)
5		○⇨□ D ▽	To typist's desk
		○ ⇨ □D ▽	On typist's desk (awaiting typing of purchase order)
		○⇨□ D ▽	Purchase order typed
		○ ⇨ □D ▽	On typist's desk (awaiting transfer to main office)
		○ ⇨ □ D ▽	
		○ ⇨ □ D ▽	
		○ ⇨ □ D ▽	
		○ ⇨ □ D ▽	
		○ ⇨ □ D ▽	
		○ ⇨ □ D ▽	
		○ ⇨ □ D ▽	
105		3 4 2 8	Total

Source: Adapted from Patricia Haynes, "Industrial Engineering Techniques," in *Productivity Improvement Handbook for State and Local Government,* ed. George J. Washnis (New York: John Wiley & Sons, 1980), 211. Copyright © 1980 by the National Academy of Public Administration. Reprinted by permission of John Wiley & Sons, Inc.

Figure 6-4 Process Flow Chart—Proposed Method

PROCESS CHART			

Present Method ☐
Proposed Method ☒
SUBJECT CHARTED Requisition for small tools _____ DATE _____
Chart begins at supervisor's desk and ends at purchasing _____ CHART BY **HR/CH**
department with assignment of Purchase Order number. _____ CHART NO. **R 136**
DEPARTMENT _____ SHEET NO. 1 OF 1

DIST. IN FEET	TIME IN MINS.	CHART SYMBOLS	PROCESS DESCRIPTION
		○⇨☐D▽	Requisition entered in computer by supervisor
0		○⇨☐D▽	Requisition conveyed electronically to dept. head
		○⇨☐D▽	On department head's computer (awaiting review)
		○⇨☐D▽	Dept. head approves (or rejects) requisition
0		○⇨☐D▽	Approved req. conveyed electronically to purch. office
		○⇨☐D▽	On purchasing agent's computer (awaiting review)
		○⇨☐D▽	Examined and approved by purchasing agent
		○⇨☐D▽	Req. posted automatically and assigned P.O. #
		○⇨☐D▽	
		○⇨☐D▽	
		○⇨☐D▽	
		○⇨☐D▽	
		○⇨☐D▽	
		○⇨☐D▽	
		○⇨☐D▽	
		○⇨☐D▽	
		○⇨☐D▽	
		○⇨☐D▽	
		○⇨☐D▽	
		○⇨☐D▽	
		○⇨☐D▽	
		○⇨☐D▽	
		○⇨☐D▽	
0		2 2 2 2	Total

	SUMMARY		
	PRESENT METHOD	PROSPOSED METHOD	DIFFER-ENCE
Operations ○	3	2	1
Transportation ⇨	4	2	2
Inspections ☐	2	2	0
Delays D	8	2	6
Distance traveled in feet	105	0	105

Source: author.

Box 6-1 Other Applications of Process Flow Charts

Every local government process is a candidate for flow charting. For example, a promising candidate for flow charting and process improvement could have been found in 2000 in the emergency dispatch operation of Kansas City, Missouri. Medical emergencies in that community often involved two and sometimes three agencies, with communication procedures that sometimes produced unfortunate delays. Upon receiving an emergency call, the call taker at the 911 dispatch center would first decide whether a police response was necessary in addition to response by medical personnel. If so, the call taker would enter information into the police computer-aided dispatch (CAD) system to initiate a police response and would then call the ambulance provider. The ambulance provider's dispatchers would then enter the information into their own CAD system and determine whether a "first response" by the fire department was also needed. If so, the call information would be transmitted electronically to a terminal in the fire department and then manually entered into the fire CAD. Ironically, the designated "first responder" could be the last to get the word.

Noting that information about a single call in such cases would be entered manually into three different CAD systems, the city auditor concluded that system changes were in order, including upgraded technology that could link the three separate systems and allow more efficient data transfer and quicker dispatching.[1]

Process flow charting can help sort out problems and contribute to operational improvements. It is a technique that is especially suitable whenever:

- a current process is confusing, erratic, or redundant
- technology or coordination could allow sequential steps to be handled simultaneously
- current processes are plagued by delays

---

[1] City of Kansas City Auditor's Office, *Performance Audit: Emergency Medical Services System* (Kansas City, Mo.: City Auditor's Office, January 2000), 14.

year to year for a given transaction, a supplemental form may have been added to the required paperwork each time. Information stored in computers may duplicate rather than replace information stored in file cabinets. Old practices may be preserved unnecessarily.

Furthermore, in changing old procedures, managers may not have fully considered the effects of those changes on associated operations. It is also possible that current processes may have been poorly designed. Process flow charts provide a systematic means of identifying cumbersome or unnecessary practices and designing streamlined procedures.

SUGGESTED FOR FURTHER INFORMATION

Aft, Lawrence S. *Work Measurement and Methods Improvement.* New York: John Wiley & Sons, 2000, 33–104.

Haynes, Patricia. "Industrial Engineering Techniques." In *Productivity Improvement Handbook for State and Local Government,* edited by George J. Washnis, 204–236. New York: John Wiley & Sons, 1980.

Hicks, Philip E. "Production Systems Design." In *Introduction to Industrial Engineering and Management Science,* 61–104. New York: McGraw-Hill, 1977.

Morley, Elaine. "Improving Productivity through Work Redesign." In *A Practitioner's Guide to Public Sector Productivity Improvement,* 89–117. New York: Van Nostrand Reinhold Co., 1986.

Siegel, Gilbert B. "Seeing the Problem Systematically: Flowcharting." In *Managing Public Systems: Analytic Techniques for Public Administration,* edited by Michael J. White, Ross Clayton, Robert Myrtle, Gilbert Siegel, and Aaron Rose, 47–85. Lanham, Md.: University Press of America, 1985.

Summers, Michael R. *Analyzing Operations in Business: Issues, Tools, and Techniques.* Westport, Conn.: Quorum Books, 1998.

7

Work Distribution Analysis

Sometimes, problems in local government operations are less the result of procedural shortcomings than symptoms of inappropriate work priorities, a mismatch of job and employee skills, misunderstanding of objectives, improper training, or poor employee deployment strategies.

SCENARIO: WEBER, PENNSYLVANIA

The mayor of Weber, Pennsylvania, was enjoying his regular Saturday morning game of golf with three longtime friends and golfing buddies. By the third hole, the usual banter had begun to die down, and the mayor's thoughts began to drift back to city business.

"Sam, you're an officer with one of the biggest auto parts dealers in the region," the mayor remarked. "I used to see your company's name on our bid sheets all the time, but I don't any more. Why have you stopped competing for the city's business?"

"Simple. We weren't winning any bids," Sam replied. "Call it 'sour grapes' if you want, but it seemed to our people that your buyers drew up specifications that favored one or two of our competitors and never gave consideration to any factor other than purchase price. We think our parts are better than anything our competitors offer. They last longer and work better—and we can document that claim. We have a better warranty. But it never seemed that those factors were given any consideration in the comparison of bids."

"Why haven't you said anything about this earlier, Sam?"

"I didn't want you to think I was trying to get some special consideration because of our friendship. Besides, these are just the opinions of some of our sales people. I haven't looked into it, personally."

"Well, you can bet that I will!" remarked the mayor.

Back in the office on Monday morning, the mayor summoned an administrative aide. He reported his friend's comments and asked if the aide had heard similar criticisms.

"No, nothing like that. I've heard occasional gripes about equipment downtime and mechanics blaming it on inability to get parts, but that's all I've heard."

The mayor asked the aide to investigate the situation and to let him know what he found.

OVERLY RESTRICTIVE SPECIFICATIONS?

The aide knew that when the mayor asked for an investigation of a problem, he expected more than a report of the comments of persons connected with the operation in question. He wanted facts and figures.

The aide began his investigation with a visit to the parts manager. He described the allegations regarding bid specifications drawn to favor particular vendors. The parts manager reacted angrily, but his comments failed to deflect the criticism.

"Look, we just try to get the best parts we can. If we've had good luck with a part in the past, why shouldn't the specifications reflect the features of that part? If other manufacturers want our business, let them make a product just like it."

The aide did not argue with the parts manager, but he knew that there was another side to that issue. Overly restrictive specifications might eliminate inferior products, but they may also eliminate good products that will perform the intended function as well as or better than the previously preferred product. A preemptive narrowing of the field may reduce the competitiveness of subsequent bids.

The aide suspected that there might be substance to the comments made by the mayor's golfing buddy. He decided to proceed in two directions. To determine the nature and magnitude of the problem, he collected a sample of two dozen bid specifications for major parts orders that he could review for restrictiveness.[1] To determine how much attention was being given to the preparation of specifications and the comparison of vendor bids, and by whom, he decided to prepare a work-distribution analysis. That analysis would also give him an opportunity to explore the criticism he had heard personally regarding equipment downtime for lack of needed parts.

Review of the sample of bid specifications confirmed the allegations. Almost half unnecessarily restricted competition by specifying intricate design features rather than performance capabilities and characteristics.

"Sure, this approach simplifies the job," the aide muttered to a colleague. "They don't have to develop a set of specifications. They just use their favorite manufacturer's specs. And comparing bids is a snap! But our objectives should be product and price—not how easy it is to come up with specs!"

WORK-DISTRIBUTION ANALYSIS

The aide was convinced that proper training or reorientation was needed for persons involved in the specification and bid comparison process. Furthermore, he wanted to assure himself that sufficient emphasis was being placed on that process—both in allocating the proper amount of time and in assigning appropriate employees to that task—to achieve output quality in keeping with its importance.

---

[1] The aide decided that drawing a systematic sample would be satisfactory and most practical in this instance (see Chapter 2). Upon his request, a list was prepared showing all parts orders during the previous twelve months that exceeded $5,000. The list had 245 entries, so he randomly selected a parts order from among the first 10 entries, marked that order and every tenth entry thereafter for a total of 24, and requested bid specifications from those orders for detailed examination.

With the assistance of the parts manager, the aide constructed a work-distribution chart for the vehicle maintenance parts room (Table 7-1). Such a chart can be developed for any operation or department without much difficulty, especially if guided initially by a person well acquainted with all the major processes or tasks involved in that operation or department.

Although variation is possible, most work-distribution charts follow a similar format: major processes or tasks are identified in the left-hand column, all employees are identified by title across the top row, and the number of hours devoted by each employee to each task in a given period (for example, one week) is reported at the intersection of the appropriate row and column.

The employees in the parts room were asked to record all their activities for one week, noting how much time was devoted to each of the task categories identified previously with the assistance of the parts manager. One week later, parts person 1 reported that he had spent 5 hours comparing vendor prices, 5 hours selecting vendors and placing orders, 25 hours distributing parts to mechanics, 4 hours updating computer records, and 1 hour ordering new parts. Those figures, plus the numbers reported by the other nine employees, are recorded in Table 7-1. Each employee column is totaled and shows a full accounting for a forty-hour workweek. In addition, rows are totaled to show "total staff hours" devoted to each task. Finally, the overall percentage allocation for each task is displayed in a column labeled "% Total."

Work-distribution charts frequently reveal shortcomings in work assignments that lie hidden until subjected to systematic analysis. Patricia Haynes notes five fairly common shortcomings:

- Work priorities may be misdirected or lacking altogether, as when too much time is spent on relatively unimportant tasks rather than on work associated with the principal objective.
- In government, overqualified personnel tend to be assigned to jobs that lesser skilled employees could perform, or employees are assigned to do work for which they lack the proper training.
- When employees are assigned to several unrelated tasks, problems can arise because more errors tend to occur when people are interrupted frequently or when they must switch to another, unrelated activity.
- Employees assigned too few tasks may become bored, lose interest, and perform poorly. Moreover, it may be difficult to find satisfactory substitutes when those employees are on vacation or sick leave.
- Assigning the same task to a number of employees can lead to problems, since individual styles differ and tend to result in inconsistencies in work procedures. This breeds excessive cross-checking of work assignments and, unless guidelines and quality controls are enforced, leads to inconsistent results.[2]

[2]Patricia Haynes, "Industrial Engineering Techniques," in *Productivity Improvement Handbook for State and Local Government,* ed. George J. Washnis (New York: John Wiley & Sons, 1980), 208. Copyright ©1980 by the National Academy of Public Administration. Reprinted by permission of John Wiley & Sons, Inc.

Table 7-1 Work-Distribution Chart, Vehicle Maintenance Parts Room, City of Weber

Process/Task Description	Total staff hours	% Total	Parts manager	Assigned Staff Hours								
				Parts person 1	Parts person 2	Parts person 3	Parts person 4	Stores clerk 1	Stores clerk 2	Stores clerk 3	Buyer 1	Buyer 2
New vehicle parts purchases												
Reviews orders, specifications	38	10	10								10	18
Compares vendor prices	49	12		5	3						25	16
Selects vendor, places order	22	6		5	2	4					5	6
New vehicle parts distribution												
Receives and stocks parts	69	17			5			23	34	7		
Distributes parts to mechanics	97	24		25	30	31				11		
Tire control												
Receives and stocks tires	12	3						5	4	3		
Distributes tires to mechanics	7	2						3		4		
Discards old tires	6	2						2	2	2		
Inventory maintenance												
Updates computer records	23	6	5	4		4		7		3		
Orders new parts	13	3	10	1		1				1		
Rebuilt parts control												
Recieves and stocks parts	12	3					12					
Distributes parts	28	7					28					
Administration and miscellaneous	9	2	5							4		
Supervision	15	4	10							5		
Total staff hours per week	400	101[a]	40	40	40	40	40	40	40	40	40	40

Source: Adapted from Patrick Manion, "Work Measurement in Local Governments," *Management Information Service Report*, vol. 6, no. 10 (International City Management Association, Washington, D.C., 1974), 3; reprinted in Patricia Haynes, "Industrial Engineering Techniques," in *Productivity Improvement Handbook for State and Local Government*, ed. George J. Washnis (New York: John Wiley & Sons, 1980), 207. Used by permission of the International City/County Management Association.

[a]Column does not sum to 100 percent due to rounding.

FINDINGS

The work-distribution chart did not hand the administrative aide any solutions on a silver platter, but it did identify some areas for more detailed investigation. For example, is the reviewing of orders and specifications important enough to justify more than 10 percent of the total time? Why does the parts manager have no role in the comparison of vendor bids? And why does he devote 15 hours (almost 40 percent of his time) to updating computer records and ordering new parts? Could those functions be handled by the stores clerks and buyers, respectively, allowing the parts manager to devote more attention to supervision, reviewing orders and specifications, and comparing vendor bids?

The work-distribution chart also sheds light on the intermittent difficulties encountered by mechanics in their attempts to obtain parts from the maintenance parts room. Most of the problems have occurred when one particular employee, parts person 4, is absent from work. Unfortunately, that seems to be happening more and more frequently, with increasing instances of the employee calling in sick. A review of the work-distribution chart reveals that parts person 4 devotes all his time to receiving, stocking, and distributing rebuilt parts and that no other employee is engaged in those functions. Two questions seem worth exploring. First, why is not at least one other employee involved in this activity to provide backup capability in case of absences? Second, has the specialization of parts person 4 led first to boredom and then to recurring "sickness"?

The aide also noted that six employees are involved in purchasing parts. Have all those employees been adequately trained to perform that function—that is, are they all fully qualified? To ensure adequate skills for this function should a third buyer be hired, or should one of the parts person positions be converted to a buyer position?

RESULTS

The aide discussed his findings with the parts manager. Although the manager was defensive at first, he eventually softened his stance and agreed that increased efforts should be made to avoid unnecessarily restrictive specifications and that he should become more involved personally in the preparation of specifications and the comparison of vendor bids. He was especially intrigued by the aide's thoughts regarding work-distribution strategies and agreed to explore revised work assignments as a possible remedy to some of the problems being encountered in the maintenance parts room.[3]

The aide was encouraged by the parts manager's response and reported his findings and recommendations for less restrictive specifications and revised work distribution to the mayor. The mayor was pleased with the thoroughness of the aide's work and was particularly impressed with the work-distribution chart.

---

[3]In some cases, civil service regulations or union rules may restrict managerial discretion regarding work reassignments. Even in such cases where negotiation is required, systematic analysis of operations can still play an important role. Careful analysis that identifies crucial factors restricting performance will help management establish its negotiation priorities and will help document the basis for its position.

From the Electronic Toolkit

Box 7-1 Creating Work-Distribution Charts

Administrators may prefer to use Microsoft Excel in the creation of **work-distribution charts** because the computer will do all the calculations, and, after the chart is prepared once, it can easily be used as a template and reused when other data are plugged in. To begin, enter the labels for each column and row. (For directions on opening Excel and entering data see Box 2-1.)

Using Table 7-1 as an example, the label "Process/Task Description" would be entered in cell A1. The tasks ("New vehicle parts purchases" and so on) would be entered from A2 through A20. To make the column wider so that the entire title can be read, move the cursor up to the line between column A and column B. Wait for the cursor to change into a black line with arrows on both sides of it. When that shape appears, click and hold it down, moving the mouse to drag the side of the column to a more appropriate width. Another way to alter the width of the column is to use the Width choice from the Column option of the Format menu.

After entering the data labels, use other columns to enter the actual data or the actual observations. At the end of each column, all the observations may be added together. To do this calculation, use the SUM function. To find the sum of the first column of numerical data, enter "=SUM(B2:B20)" and the total will be calculated. (An alternative to typing this instruction would be to use Function choice **fx** from the Insert menu. The **fx** symbol also appears on the toolbar.) If you wish to calculate totals for every column, you could enter this command manually for each of the columns or you could use a simpler method. With the shortcut method, simply highlight the cell that contains the command, then move the cursor to the lower, right-hand corner of the cell and wait for it to change into a black cross. Click and hold it down while dragging the mouse across the chart until reaching the last column of data. This action will copy the command to all the affected cells and also change all the addresses to the appropriate cell names. If a similar chart needs to be made for another set of data, simply change the data and the results of the calculations will change as well.

"I want to talk to the parts manager myself before deciding on this," the mayor said, "but I want you to know that I am inclined to accept your recommendations. This is very good work."

UTILITY OF WORK-DISTRIBUTION ANALYSIS

Work-distribution analysis offers a useful method for examining the application of human resources in an organization and detecting possible problems. In local government applications, for example, it could reveal instances where police officers are devoting inordinate amounts of time to duties that could be handled by civilian clerks, library aides are attempting to perform librarian duties for which they are ill prepared, and parks maintenance employees are spending more time on equipment repairs than on mowing. Analysis of this type could prove beneficial for virtually every local government operation.

Box 7-2 Other Applications of Work-Distribution Analysis

In addition to its value as a means of checking the alignment of work priorities, tasks, and staff skills, work-distribution analysis is also a useful device for organizations attempting to implement **activity-based costing** or embarking on other efforts to identify the full costs of various operations (see Chapter 14). Such efforts depend on a reasonable level of precision in identifying the amount of time and other resources devoted to each activity or service. Work-distribution analysis can be helpful in that regard.

SUGGESTED FOR FURTHER INFORMATION

Brimson, James A., and John Antos. *Activity-Based Management for Service Industries, Government Entities, and Nonprofit Organizations.* New York: John Wiley & Sons, 1994.

Haynes, Patricia. "Industrial Engineering Techniques." In *Productivity Improvement Handbook for State and Local Government,* edited by George J. Washnis, 204–236. New York: John Wiley & Sons, 1980.

Manion, Patrick. "Work Measurement in Local Governments." *Management Information Service Report* 6, no. 10 (Washington, D.C.: International City Management Association, 1974).

Morley, Elaine. "Improving Productivity through Work Redesign." In *A Practitioner's Guide to Public Sector Productivity Improvement,* 89–117. New York: Van Nostrand Reinhold Co., 1986.

8

Performance Measurement and Monitoring

Performance measurement is a fundamental building block for performance management and evaluation. A set of performance measures typically provides information about how much service was provided by a given program or department. If it is a *good* set of measures, it also provides vital information about the efficiency with which these services were provided, the quality of the services, and the effect that the services had on their recipients or on the community in general.

Many cities and counties cite accountability as their chief objective in performance measurement. First and foremost they want to document their level of service in reports to the governing body and the citizenry. As important as accountability is, local governments that are determined to get the greatest value from their performance measurement system want even more. These governments use performance measures not only for accountability but also to monitor and improve services. They measure more than just workload or "outputs" (for example, applications processed, cases filed, or tons of asphalt laid). They also measure efficiency (for example, cost per unit of service or lane-miles swept per operator hour) and effectiveness or "outcomes" (for example, percentage of refuse collection routes completed on-schedule or percentage of fires confined to the room of origin). They set performance targets and establish systems of regular performance feedback to department heads, supervisors, and employees.

SCENARIO: CREW PERFORMANCE TRACKING IN MINEOLA, MISSOURI[1]

"I just handled another inquiry from an out-of-state caller who heard about our system for tracking the performance of water system maintenance crews," Peg Waugh

---

[1]Like other cities and counties depicted in scenarios in this volume, Mineola, Missouri, is a fictitious community. The performance tracking system in Mineola, however, is based on a system developed in the Canadian city of Winnipeg, Manitoba, as described in Stanley Y. Siu, "Performance Chart Increases Crew Productivity," *Journal of the American Water Works Association* 84, no. 2 (1992).

announced to her boss, Sean Kobesky, director of Mineola's water department. Peg is Kobesky's administrative assistant and has received a steady stream of such calls. "This was an official from a city in New Jersey, who was impressed with our tracking system and amazed by the motivating force it has on work crews. He said that their crews are not very task-oriented and seem more interested in avoiding work than in completing it. I guess I am so used to this system I would probably take it for granted without calls like that."

"It's interesting that you should bring up our performance tracking system," Sean replied. "I have just been thinking about it, myself. I would like to take some steps to strengthen it. Don't get me wrong; I think it's a good system, too, but I would like to make it even better if we can. I'd like for you to take a hard look at it over the next few days and see what suggestions you can make."

Peg left Sean's office thinking she had been given a futile assignment. "We have a good system now. I cannot imagine what we need to do to improve it," she thought. "Why do we want to mess with something that has been so successful?"

SEEKING TO MAKE A GOOD MEASUREMENT SYSTEM EVEN BETTER

Peg knew the history of Mineola's performance tracking system well. She should, having recounted that history to many callers! The system was established in 1995 and is based on a set of standard "work points" assigned to the common tasks performed by water system maintenance crews (see Table 8-1). A task that typically requires a large crew and lots of time to complete (that is, a high number of labor hours) is awarded more work points than a task requiring few workers and little time (that is, fewer labor hours). Some tasks are valued at four times the work-point level of other tasks. Although some aspects of the point system are a bit subjective, work records from prior years provided a reasonably solid basis for assigning points and minor adjustments have been made from time to time.

Box 8-1 Performance Reports

Most cities and counties that collect performance measures report many of these measures in their annual budget documents. Some—including Albuquerque, N.M.; Ann Arbor, Mich.; Bellevue, Wash.; Boston, Mass.; Chapel Hill, N.C.; Charlotte, N.C.; Cincinnati, Ohio; Corpus Christi, Tex.; DeKalb County, Ga.; Long Beach, Calif.; New York City, N.Y.; Philadelphia, Pa.; Portland, Ore.; Raleigh, N.C.; Scottsdale, Ariz.; Sunnyvale, Calif.; Winnipeg, Manitoba; Winston-Salem, N.C.; and others—produce quarterly or annual performance reports that focus primarily on performance measures. Sample pages from the annual performance reports of Bellevue and Long Beach follow.

(Box continues on next page)

Box 8-1 *(Continued)*

Exhibit 8-A Sample Page from the City of Bellevue's Performance Report

Fire Department
ANNUAL SCORECARD OF PERFORMANCE MEASURES

Key Performance Measures	1997 Actual	1998 Target	1998 Actual	1998 Target met or exceeded
Program: Fire Suppression and Rescue/ Emergency Medical Services (EMS)				
Effectiveness				
1. Percent of fires confined to room of origin	86%	85%	89%	✓
2. Cardiac arrest survival rate	40%	38%	33%	
3a. Average response time to fire suppression calls from receipt of call to arrival (minutes)	6.0	6.0	6.0	✓
3b. Average response time to EMS calls from receipt of call to arrival (minutes)	5.8	5.8	5.8	✓
4a. % of fire suppression response time 6 minutes or less	65%	65%	64%	
4b. % of EMS response time 4 minutes or less	21%	21%	22%	✓
Workload				
5a. Number of fire services requests/ unit responses generated	3,832/ 8,726	3,900/ 8,800	3,957/ 8,829	
5b. Number of EMS service requests/ unit responses generated	11,153/ 17,475	11,500/ 18,000	11,728/ 18,889	
6. Number of annual fire company fire inspections	5,400	4,900	4,637	
7. Number of annual fire company training hours	8,551	8,700	7,844	
Program: Fire Prevention				
Effectiveness				
8. Fire loss in inspected buildings ($000)	$418	$400	$638	
Program: Emergency Preparedness				
Effectiveness				
9. Emergency preparedness response hands-on-skilled training programs	2	20	5	
Workload				
10. Emergency preparedness audiences reached—general education	4,465	3,900	3,779	

Source: City of Bellevue, Wash., *1998 Performance Measures*, 25.

Exhibit 8-B Sample Page from the City of Long Beach's Performance Report

Planning and Building Expenditures and Staffing Data

	City population	Budgeted staffing	12 month adopted budget	Total budget per capita
FY 92–93	442,106	106.1	$9,373,116	$21.20
FY 93–94	437,816	105.0	$9,456,483	$21.60
FY 94–95	436,776	94.5	$9,222,278	$21.11
FY 95–96	433,218	90.5	$9,112,950	$21.04
FY 96–97	425,807	91.5	$9,025,944	$21.20

Performance Measures and Benchmarks:
What are they and why are they important?

Performance Measures highlight important service accomplishments. Benchmarks are an average of the same service and performance accomplishments in similar cities; they are for comparison purposes only and, because of local differences, may not always be an appropriate target to strive for. The comparison cities for planning and building are Lubbock, El Paso, Phoenix, and Portland. Data used are the most comprehensive and recent available.

Average Number of Inspections Per Inspector

Average annual number of inspections conducted per staff inspector.

Approximately 60,000 inspections are conducted each year. This measure reflects the city's effort to be responsive to the needs of developers and home and business owners when building inspections are necessary. It is important to the public that these inspections are done in a timely manner.

(continued)

Exhibit 8-B *(Continued)*

Average Plan Check Turnaround Time

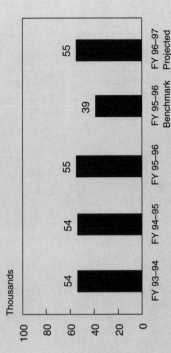

Average time necessary to process a set of construction plans from the date of first submittal to the date a permit is received.

Approximately 3,000 construction plans are checked annually for code compliance. Timeliness is an important consideration for customers; however, budget cuts have reduced staff. The reduction in staff has increased the turnaround time.

Number of Code Enforcement Investigations Performed

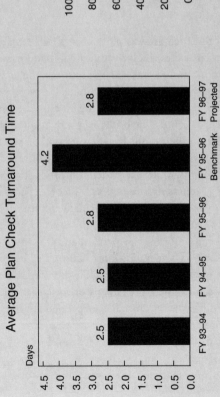

Total annual number of code enforcement investigations conducted after a complaint has been received.

Investigations are conducted for substandard buildings, lack of property maintenance, weed abatement, zoning compliance, and other regulatory issues. Maintaining building safety and neighborhood zoning code standards is important in maintaining the quality of life within each neighborhood.

Source: City of Long Beach, Calif., *Hitting the Mark: City Services and Performance, Fiscal Year 1996–97,* 31.

Table 8-1 Maintenance Tasks and Work Points

Water Task Number	Description	Work Points
110	Excavated repair to service boxes	25
112	Service excavation and repair (more than 2 inches)	70
113	Service excavation and repair (2 inches or less)	62
122	Service renewal (2 inches or less)	82
129	Planned valve installation	80
130	Excavated valve replacement	84
133	All excavated valve box repairs	53
142	Excavated hydrant repairs	62
143	Planned hydrant installation	100
144	Hydrant replacement	100
149	Water main repair (pavement)	84
150	Water main repair (grassy area)	69
157	Water main mini-renewals	*

Source: Based on the system used by the city of Winnipeg, Manitoba, as reported in Stanley Y. Siu, "Performance Chart Increases Crew Productivity," published in *Journal AWWA*, vol. 84, no. 2 (February 1992), by the American Water Works Association.

* Work points for task 157 are calculated by multiplying by 2 the length in feet of the renewed water main.

Each workday, the performance of each crew is plotted on a performance chart (see Figure 8-1). Although charts such as these look complicated, they are really quite simple. Each chart covers a two-week period, and each column of the chart represents a single day. The person filling out the chart simply totals the work points for the tasks completed by the crew in a given day, divides the sum by the total labor hours available to the crew that day, and enters the result as "production units" at the bottom of the chart and as a point on the graph. If a crew earns 153 work points based on the tasks completed during a given day and has 32 work hours available to it that day (4 crew members times 8 hours), it is awarded 4.8 production units for that day (153 divided by 32). The system is so simple that Mineola officials estimate it requires only about two minutes per crew per day to calculate and record the daily results.

Some in Mineola say that the beauty of the crew performance chart system is its simplicity. Others say it is its valuable management information. Peg is convinced, however, that the key feature of the system is the feedback it provides to the crews, themselves. These charts are rarely sent to the city manager or the city council—and on those rare occasions, only in summary form for all crews. Their routine destination is the wall of the crew room, right next to the performance charts for all the other crews. This way each crew can see its daily results, and everyone else can, too!

Although most crews do not particularly care whether they are the top-performing group, no crew likes to bring up the rear with the lowest number of production

Figure 8-1 Crew Performance Chart

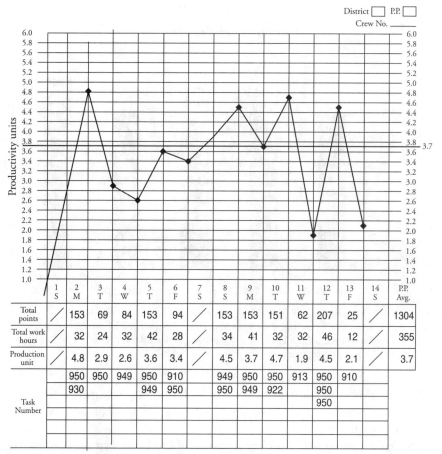

	1 S	2 M	3 T	4 W	5 T	6 F	7 S	8 S	9 M	10 T	11 W	12 T	13 F	14 S	P.P. Avg.
Total points	/	153	69	84	153	94	/	153	153	151	62	207	25	/	1304
Total work hours	/	32	24	32	42	28	/	34	41	32	32	46	12	/	355
Production unit	/	4.8	2.9	2.6	3.6	3.4	/	4.5	3.7	4.7	1.9	4.5	2.1	/	3.7
		950	950	949	950	910		949	950	950	913	950	910		
		930			949	950		950	949	922		950			
Task Number												950			

Source: Based on the system used by the city of Winnipeg, Manitoba, as reported in Stanley Y. Siu, "Performance Chart Increases Crew Productivity," published in *Journal AWWA*, vol. 84, no. 2 (February 1992), by the American Water Works Association.

units. Having observed the comings and goings of water crews over the past few years, Peg has noticed an interesting reaction to this performance feedback. When a dip on the performance chart is attributable to bad weather, every crew's performance drops and none reacts one way or another. On other occasions, however, a low performance day usually draws a reaction from the crew, often directed toward the work scheduler. Peg has observed more than one crew chief angrily confronting the work scheduler, saying, "What's the idea of sending us from a job on one side of Mineola to a job on the other side and back again. You're killing our performance with travel time and making us look bad!" Or, "If you are only going to give us 69 points of work

Figure 8-2 Average Production Units of District Crews

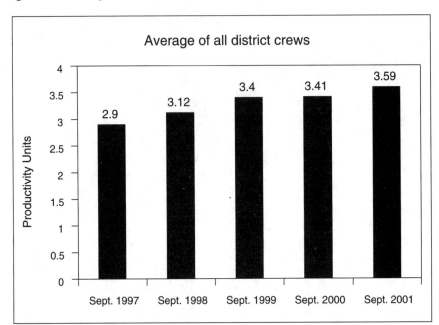

Source: Based on the system used by the city of Winnipeg, Manitoba, as reported in Stanley Y. Siu, "Performance Chart Increases Crew Productivity," published in *Journal AWWA*, vol. 84, no. 2 (February 1992), by the American Water Works Association.

to do, don't send us out with such a big crew!" It is clear in such instances that a feedback system designed to appeal to the personal and professional pride of crew members is having an impact.

Has the system improved performance overall? Peg has recited the favorable statistics repeatedly. Average productivity units for all district crews have risen steadily over the years (see Figure 8-2). When the water department examined the performance of selected tasks in more conventional terms, it found that the number of work hours required for a given service or repair usually had declined (see Figure 8-3).

"It's a good system," Peg thought. "Sean wants me to suggest improvements and I don't want to return empty-handed, but I'm stumped. What's missing from this system?"

KEY ELEMENTS OF AN ADVANCED PERFORMANCE MEASUREMENT SYSTEM

A quick perusal of the literature on performance measurement did two things for Peg. First, it reassured her that the system in Mineola had far more pluses than minuses. Second, it helped her spot what appeared to be the system's single deficiency, a weakness that could be remedied easily.

Figure 8-3 Average Labor Hours Required to Repair a Water Main Break

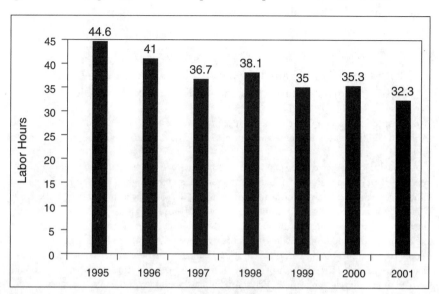

Source: Based on the system used by the city of Winnipeg, Manitoba, as reported in Stanley Y. Siu, "Performance Chart Increases Crew Productivity," published in *Journal AWWA*, vol. 84, no. 2 (February 1992), by the American Water Works Association.

It was clear that the crew performance system did not suffer from two of the most common shortcomings in local government performance measurement—failure to advance beyond workload measures and failure to use the measures for operating decisions. While many performance measurement systems rely exclusively on workload or output measures, the Mineola system did not simply count the number of repairs or tasks completed. Instead, it linked tasks with resources in a meaningful way to provide more sophisticated and more meaningful measures. Furthermore, the measures were being used in important ways in Mineola—not the least of which was to provide meaningful feedback to employees on a daily basis. In many cities and counties, performance measurement is done annually, strictly to meet the demands of the budget office or the manager's office rather than to serve the operating needs of the department. In Mineola, the measurement system's primary use is at the department level.

The deficiency in the crew performance chart system, Peg now realized, was that in stepping beyond raw workload counts it moved only in the direction of efficiency measurement rather than toward both efficiency *and* effectiveness measurement. The fundamental measures in Mineola's system focused on efficiency—that is, they related output (various maintenance tasks completed) to resources consumed in the form of work hours. The system ignores the quality or effectiveness of repairs. Without measures addressing effectiveness, Peg cannot rule out the possibility that the quality of repairs might be declining along with work hours.

Box 8-2 Evaluating Service Effectiveness from Performance Records: A Fire Inspection Example

A fire inspection program that works as it is intended reduces the likelihood of fire in the inspected buildings. Recently inspected facilities should be less vulnerable than those inspected long ago.

Although a computerized version of the system described below would no doubt be a welcome relief from the tedium of a manual process, the system's logic is clear and the steps are simple (see exhibit). Each month, the analyst enters the number of months since the latest inspection for each of the major buildings in town. If a building was inspected that month, the entry for that building is 0. If a fire occurs in any of the buildings, a box is drawn around the entry for that building, showing that a fire occurred "X" months following an inspection. If only large numbers are boxed, the analyst may conclude that the inspections are effective—that is, fire hazards in recently inspected buildings have been spotted, eliminated, and have not had time to develop anew. The analyst might question, however, the infrequency of inspections. If small numbers are boxed, the analyst might question the quality or effectiveness of the inspections.

Exhibit 8-A Example of Estimating Fire Inspection Effectiveness

Suppose there are only ten buildings subject to inspection in the community. Their inspection histories for a year might look like the chart below.

Building number	Jan.	Feb.	March	April	May	June	July	Aug.	Sept.	Oct.	Nov.	Dec.
				Number of months since last inspection								
1	8	9[a]	10	0[b]	1	2	3	4	5	6	7	8
2	3	4	5	6	7	8	0	1	2	3	4	5
3	2	3	4	5	6	7	8	9	10	11	12	13
4	6	0	1	2	3	4	5	6	0	1	2	0[b]
5	5	6	7	0	1	2	3	4	5	6	7	0
6	10	11	12	0	1	2	3	4	5	6	7	8
7	9	0	1	2	3	4	5	6	7	8	0	1
8	1	2	3	4	5	6	0	1	2	3	4	5
9	7	8	9	10	11	12	13	14	15	0	1	2
10	3	4	0	1	2	3	4	0	1	2	3	4

[a]A boxed entry indicates that building had a fire in that month. For example, Building 1 had a fire in February, and at that time Building 1 had not been inspected for nine months.

[b]A "0" entry means that the building was inspected in that month. Note that the inspection frequency varies considerably among the ten buildings, and in some cases (such as Building 4) the inspection frequency varies for the same building.

(continued)

Exhibit 8-A *(Continued)*

Summary Analysis

Number of months since last inspection	Number of entries showing that this many months had elapsed since last inspection	Number of fires in buildings that had gone this many months since last inspection	Incidence of fire in buildings that had gone this many months since last inspection
0–2	40	0	0 = 0/40
3–5	37	0	0 = 0/37
6–8	24	1	.05 = 1/24
9–11	11	2	.18 = 2/11
12–15	7	3	.43 = 3/7
All entries	120	6	.05 = 6/120

Source: Harry P. Hatry, Louis H. Blair, Donald M. Fisk, John M. Greiner, John R. Hall Jr., and Philip S. Schaenman, *How Effective Are Your Community Services? Procedures for Measuring Their Quality,* 2d ed. (Washington, D.C.: Urban Institute and ICMA, 1992), 99.

Note: The fire incidence ratios shown in the last column indicate that a considerable increase in fire incidence occurs when buildings have gone without inspections for a long time. Of all fires, for example, 83 percent (5 of the 6) occur in buildings that have gone at least nine months without an inspection, but buildings are in that position only 15 percent of the time (18 of the 120 entries). In practice, the exact fire incidence likelihood numbers will not be known because data on all months will be collected for only a random sample of buildings in the program; however, the percentage increases in the ratios computed will be the same as the percentage increases in the underlying fire incidence values. Also in practice, some adjustments have to be made to reflect the possibility that, when a fire and an inspection in the same building occur in the same month, the fire may have preceded the inspection and thus not have been affected by it.

BACK IN THE DIRECTOR'S OFFICE

"We can improve the performance chart system by adding some measures that address the quality or effectiveness of the work being performed," Peg blurted out as she walked through the doorway of Kobesky's office.

Box 8-3 Other Applications of Performance Measurement

As demonstrated in this chapter, performance measurement can enhance accountability (for example, performance reports for department heads, managers, elected officials, and citizens) and can provide valuable feedback to supervisors and employees. Every department of local government can benefit in both ways.

In addition, a well-developed set of performance measures provides information regarding service quantity, quality, equity, effectiveness, and efficiency that can improve a local government's planning and budgeting processes. Such measures are also fundamental elements of program evaluations and performance contracts. Furthermore, local governments that wish to improve operations by means of the process known as *benchmarking* will quickly discover that performance measurement is an essential ingredient in that endeavor as well.

"Excellent suggestion!"

"Perhaps we could do it by building a quality component into the production units," Peg continued, "but I am inclined to keep it simple by merely supplementing the current system with a few measures of service quality or effectiveness. I hope we discover that the quality of our work is improving or at least remaining constant, even as we improve efficiency. That is something we need to know."

SUGGESTED FOR FURTHER INFORMATION

Ammons, David N. *Municipal Benchmarks: Assessing Local Performance and Establishing Community Standards,* 2d ed. Thousand Oaks, Calif.: Sage Publications, 2001.

———, ed. *Accountability for Performance: Measurement and Monitoring in Local Government.* Washington, D.C.: ICMA, 1995.

Broom, Cheryle, Marilyn Jackson, Vera Vogelsang Coombs, and Jody Harris. *Performance Measurement: Concepts and Techniques.* Washington, D.C.: American Society for Public Administration, 1998.

Hatry, Harry P. *Performance Measurement: Getting Results.* Washington, D.C.: Urban Institute, 1999.

Hatry, Harry P., Louis H. Blair, Donald M. Fisk, John M. Greiner, John R. Hall Jr., and Philip S. Schaenman. *How Effective Are Your Community Services? Procedures for Measuring Their Quality,* 2d ed. Washington, D.C.: Urban Institute and ICMA, 1992.

Tigue, Patricia, and Dennis Strachota. *The Use of Performance Measures in City and County Budgets.* Chicago: Government Finance Officers Association, 1994.

9

Using Performance Standards

A local government official attempting to rate the performance of a particular department or operating unit may do so from any of several points of reference. A subjective assessment may be drawn from impressions, hearsay, the comments of the department's supervisor or the supervisors of interacting departments, the nature and volume of citizen compliments and complaints, or the official's own personal "feel" from occasional direct observation or from the individual experiences of family members and friends. Such assessments may be strongly held; they may also be incorrect.

A bit more objective are assessments based on expenditures and workload volume. Managers may contend, for example, that they have remained "within budget" for the last six or seven years in a row and are spreading more asphalt or processing more paperwork than ever before. Such assessments, however, may say little about the efficiency (unit costs) or effectiveness (quality or usefulness) of the service.

Officials best able to assess performance are those who can compare the efficiency and effectiveness of an operation with some meaningful benchmark. A jurisdiction with a good system of performance measures can compare its performance against that of other jurisdictions or simply against its own performance at an earlier point in time. As an alternative or supplement to such comparisons, it may compare actual performance to some target or pre-established standard. A target may be set to meet or exceed historical performance. A "standard" may be established using industrial engineering techniques or, in some cases, may be drawn from published sources. For example, standards are published for such functions as road maintenance, grounds maintenance, pest control, refuse collection, janitorial services, and vehicle repair.

SCENARIO: ARMADILLO, TEXAS

The city manager of Armadillo, Texas, has had his fill of bickering between the city's automotive garage and the various departments that operate vehicles repaired and maintained there. He long ago became weary of the charges and countercharges of the principal combatants: the vehicle-operating departments claiming that the mechanics were slow, inept, and poorly managed, and the garage staff countering that the departments were unreasonable and that operators abused the equipment. He had tried to address the problem from time to time, but for the most part only patches had been applied to this festering situation.

Today the battle of the city garage spilled past its normal limits. This morning the city manager found himself refereeing an argument between the police chief and the budget director over the chief's plan to have the department's squad cars repaired and maintained at a private garage. Like many other local governments, the city of Armadillo finances its garage through fees assessed to the user departments. The police chief considered the fees excessive and wanted to take his department's business elsewhere.

"The city garage's rates are too high, and their work is not that good," he snapped. "My plan will save the city money. I can get better service at a lower cost by having the cars repaired elsewhere."

"That won't save a dime! In fact, it will increase the city's expenditures," responded the budget director. "We will still have to pay all the mechanics' wages, and, without the police department's business, we'll have to raise everyone else's rates."

"Without the police department's business, you can cut costs by getting rid of some of those lazy mechanics," retorted the police chief.

It was clear to the city manager that this problem would not go away and would not be resolved by patchwork treatment. He asked the police chief to be patient for six months while he searched for a suitable long-term solution. The city manager told the budget director that he wanted a thorough investigation of the problem and a recommended remedy. "If we decide to continue operating a city garage," he said, "I want to have the facts that will show me it is operating efficiently."

WORK STANDARDS FOR MECHANICS

Some local government jobs have many routine elements that recur frequently enough to make the development of performance standards possible. Essentially, a performance standard answers the question: How long should it take a competent employee to perform this task? The budget director found that for mechanics in private garages this question was being answered by performance rates published in commercially produced manuals or on compact disks. They report, for example, that a complete tune-up on a 2000 model Ford Crown Victoria should take a competent mechanic 3.5 hours (see Table 9-1).

Upon further investigation, the budget director discovered that several local governments scattered across the country were applying in one form or another mechanics' standards based on the commercial manuals. He also learned that the adoption of such standards would probably not be a popular move with the city garage.[1]

The fundamental concept underlying the use of performance standards is that a city mechanic should be expected to perform at the same proficiency as a private garage mechanic. A job requiring 3.5 hours of a private mechanic's time should require approximately the same from a city mechanic.

---

[1] An account of union opposition to the use of work standards for mechanics in New York City is found in Frederick O. Hayes, *Productivity in Local Government* (Lexington, Mass.: Lexington Books, 1977), 231.

Table 9-1 Standard Times for Specified Maintenance of Full-Size Ford/Mercury Sedan (in hours)

Maintenance Task	Labor Hours
Compression Test	
1980–91	1.2
w/ AC add	0.3
1992–2000	1.6
Dynamometer Test	
1980–2000	0.4

Engine Tune Up (Electronic Ignition) includes: Test battery and clean connections. Tighten intake manifold mounting bolts. Check engine compression, clean and adjust or renew spark plugs. Test resistance of spark plug cables. Inspect distributor cap and rotor. Adjust air gap. Check vacuum advance operation. Check and adjust ignition timing. Adjust idle speed. If carburetor equipped, adjust idle mixture and inspect choke operation. Service air cleaner. Inspect crankcase ventilation system. Inspect and adjust drive belts. Check EGR valve operation.

1980–91	3.0
w/AC add	0.6
1992–2000	3.5
Perform EEC IV system test add	1.0

Source: MOTOR Labor Guide Manual: 1980 to 2000 (Troy, Mich.: Hearst Business Communications, Inc., 1999), 5.86. Excerpted by permission.
Note: Time based on servicing a full-size Ford/Mercury (for example, a Crown Victoria).

IMPLEMENTATION PLAN

The use of performance standards would allow the performance of city mechanics to be judged on the same basis as private garage mechanics. If city mechanics could meet or beat those standards, current criticisms would be considered groundless. Accordingly, the budget director proposed the following steps:

1. The superintendent of the city garage would secure copies of the two most commonly used rate manuals or CD-ROMs for mechanics.[2] City mechanics would be allowed to use as their standard the more lenient of the two publications for any particular repair work.

2. The garage superintendent would prepare a condensed rate manual drawn from the commercial manuals but tailored to the particular types of equipment in the

---

[2]Among the most popular of the rate manuals are the volumes known informally as the Mitchell Manual and the Alldata Manual, which are revised annually. See *Mechanical Labor Estimating Guide* (San Diego, Calif.: Mitchell International) and *MOTOR Labor Guide Manual* (Troy, Mich.: Hearst Business Communications, Inc.).

Table 9-2 Excerpt from City of Armadillo's Customized Standard Time Manual

Ford F-Series Pickup	
Maintenance Task	Standard Labor Hours
Basic Inspection and Road Test	
Ford F150, 1997–2000	0.9
Basic inspection includes checking the horn, ignition switch, lights, starter operation, transmission engagement and operation, speedometer, and gauges for temperature, fuel pressure, oil, etc. Inspector will also examine pedal pads, door catches and cushions, glass, mirrors, wipers, and tire condition.	
Engine Compartment Inspection and Adjustment	
Ford F150, 1997–2000	1.4
Scope engine and make any adjustments needed. Record compression for all cylinders. Clean and gap spark plugs. Adjust or replace points. Inspect distributor cap for cracks and carbon runs. Inspect ignition primary and secondary wiring. Check operation of the throttle and choke controls (with linkage). Set engine idling; check and set engine timing. Test battery and clean terminals. Inspect cooling system and service, as necessary.	
Chassis and Brake Inspection	
Ford F150, 1997–2000	1.7
Check king pins and bushings, drag link and toe in. Inspect master cylinder. Check power take-off shaft and bearings, hydraulic pump, etc. for wear and leaks. Inspect exhaust system. Check springs and shocks. Inspect drive line and U joints, operation of clutch and pedal clearance. Check brake operations. Remove wheels and drums. Repack bearings, replace seals, and inspect brake linings.	

   city fleet. The condensed manual would simplify administration of the new performance standard system (see Table 9-2).

3. The repair order form for garage work would be modified to include a column for standard times as well as actual time consumed by the work (see Figure 9-1).

4. The department's computerized management information system would be modified to allow entry of standard time and actual time to allow the garage to produce performance reports by mechanic (see Table 9-3), by shift, by the garage as a whole, by vehicle category, and by repair type (see Table 9-4).

5. Additional repair time required on vehicles improperly repaired initially would not be counted as a second repair job but instead would be added to the first job. A standard 2-hour repair job that consumed 1.5 hours initially and 2 more hours subsequently to do the job properly would be recorded as 3.5 hours—or 1.5 hours in excess of standard time.

Figure 9-1 Armadillo City Garage Equipment Work Order

Work Order No.					
Date	Repairs to Be Performed:	Standard Hours	Actual Hours	Date	Mechanic
Equip. license tag					
Equip. number					
Make					
Model					
Odometer					
Driver Complaint					
Name					
Dept.					
Phone					
Job completion notes:	Mechanic's notes:				
	Road test		YES	NO	
Total downtime days:					
Approved (by supervisor):					

Table 9-3 Excerpt from Performance Report, City Garage, September 5–11: Efficiency Ratings, by Mechanic

Mechanic	Date	Work Order	Repair Description	Standard Hours	Actual Hours	Efficiency Rating (%)
Bosquet, Buster	91101	34002	Exhaust	.8	1.1	72.7
	Total			29.4	30.2	97.4
Eberhart, Babe	90501	33807	Tune Up	3.1	2.5	124.0
		33812	Brakes	2.2	2.3	95.7
		33814	Emissions	.7	.7	100.0
		33816	Manifold	.9	.9	100.0
	90601	33820	Alternator	.9	.6	150.0
		33822	Emissions	.7	.7	100.0
		32116	Wheel Align	2.4	3.2	75.0
		33827	Rear Brakes	1.6	1.4	114.3
	90701	33830	Carburetor	1.6	1.8	88.9
		33832	Tune Up	3.1	3.1	100.0
		33833	Oil Change	.5	.5	100.0
		33835	Radiator/ Thermostat	1.4	1.2	116.7
	90801	33840	Emissions	.7	.7	100.0
		33842	Universal Joint	1.2	1.0	120.0
		33845	Struts	1.3	1.3	100.0
		33849	Ignition	.9	.8	112.5
		33853	Brakes	1.8	2.0	90.0
	90901	33856	Shocks	.4	.3	133.3
		33857	Hydraulics	2.2	2.8	78.6
	Total			27.6	27.8	99.3

6. Outstanding performance relative to standard rates would be recognized and rewarded.[3]

The city manager was delighted with the budget director's recommendation. Not only did the plan promote greater efficiency, it also provided a means of monitoring garage performance against a widely accepted standard.

RESULTS

Armadillo officials quickly discovered that the success of their new system depended upon competent and conscientious administration. Work orders had to be

---

[3]Most cities would have the option of rewarding a superior mechanic through performance evaluation and merit pay increase. Depending on state law and local ordinances, some would also have the option of special incentives, such as bonus payments or the grant of extra leave when requirements for a fair day's work have been met (for example, in some cities operating with a "task system," workers performing more than 80 "standard hours" of work in a two-week period are awarded extra vacation time for use during a subsequent period, even if the actual time worked is less than 80 hours).

Table 9-4 Excerpt from Performance Report, City Garage, September–November: Efficiency Ratings, by Repair Type

Mechanic	Date	Work Order	Repair Description	Standard Hours	Actual Hours	Efficiency Rating (%)
Bosquet, Buster	90101	32141	Tune Up	3.1	3.1	100.0
Bosquet, Buster	90901	32149	Tune Up	3.1	3.3	93.9
Bosquet, Buster	92901	32164	Tune Up	3.1	3.1	100.0
Bosquet, Buster	110101	32401	Tune Up	3.1	3.0	103.3
Corry, Cecil	101501	32248	Tune Up	3.1	3.6	86.1
Corry, Cecil	111401	32419	Tune Up	3.1	3.5	88.6
Corry, Cecil	112501	32581	Tune Up	3.1	3.0	103.3
Eberhart, Babe	90501	33807	Tune Up	3.1	2.5	124.0
Eberhart, Babe	90701	33832	Tune Up	3.1	3.1	100.0
Eberhart, Babe	102901	32247	Tune Up	3.1	2.9	106.9

prepared carefully and records maintained accurately. The most apparent initial cost of the new system was an increased administrative workload.

A second "cost" came in the form of employee dissension. Several mechanics, including some who had been with the city for many years, expressed displeasure with the new system. They complained that city management did not trust them to perform a fair day's work and insisted that city equipment was too specialized for private garage standards to apply. The dissension reached its peak shortly before implementation but began to subside as most mechanics discovered that they could attain the standards. Some even seemed to take pride in their performance compared to the standards and compared to the performance of their coworkers. Lingering opposition was confined primarily to those mechanics who had complained most vehemently at the outset and those whose performance inadequacies were revealed for the first time by the new system.

The benefits of the new performance measurement system far outweighed its cost. Gradually the city garage began to meet most of the standards and even to surpass some of them. The police chief still complained about garage performance, but the city manager could now refute many of the chief's claims of excessive repair time. He could also pinpoint problems when the claims were valid.

UTILITY OF PERFORMANCE STANDARDS

The development of performance standards from scratch can be tricky. Errors may have adverse consequences. Standards set too high may frustrate employees; standards set too low may be difficult to change. Poorly devised standards or inadequately monitored systems may even yield perverse responses. For example, sanitation workers judged only on the weight of garbage collected might be tempted to water down their loads before having them weighed, or police officers judged solely on number of arrests might become overzealous and thereby generate complaints of police harassment.

When standards derived from industrial engineering techniques already exist and have been published, many of the potential pitfalls can be minimized. Whether used for monitoring performance on a job-by-job basis or more generally for projecting, for budgetary purposes, the amount of work a group of employees should be able to perform in a year's time, published standards for common local government functions, such as automotive repair and maintenance, custodial services, street and grounds maintenance, and refuse collection, have considerable value.

Box 9-1 Other Applications of Performance Standards

The engineered standards for vehicle mechanics published regularly in flat rate manuals or on CDs provide a useful foundation for monitoring and evaluation systems focusing entirely on the performance of mechanics. Other standards relevant to garage operations are applicable when the focus extends beyond the maintenance and repair proficiency of mechanics.

In a study of the local motor pool and fleet administration, for example, the auditor's office in King County (Washington) compared local fleet costs not only with the benchmarks established by the National Association of Fleet Administrators but also with operating and maintenance costs reported in *Motor Trend* magazine.[1]

Exhibit 9A Comparison of Vehicle Costs: King County versus National Association of Fleet Administrators Benchmarks

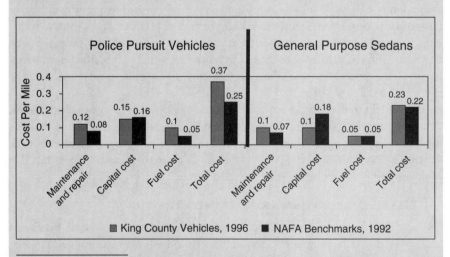

[1]King County Auditor's Office, *Special Study: Motor Pool* (Seattle, Wash.: County Auditor's Office, Metropolitan King County, 1997).
Source: King County Auditor's Office, *Special Study: Motor Pool* (Seattle, Wash.: County Auditor's Office, Metropolitan King County, 1997), 11–21.

(Box continues on next page)

Box 9-1 *(Continued)*

Exhibit 9B Comparison of Operating & Maintenance Costs Per Mile: King County versus *Motor Trend* Tests

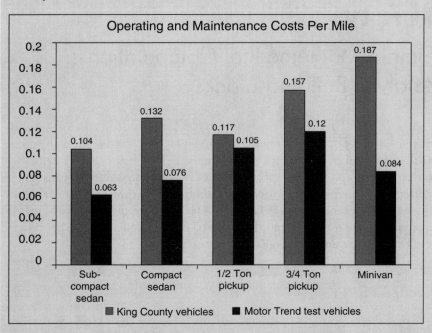

Source: King County Auditor's Office, *Special Study: Motor Pool* (Seattle, Wash.: County Auditor's Office, Metropolitan King County, 1997), 9–10.

Note: King County auditors report that *Motor Trend* test vehicles were new, while King County's figures include old and new vehicles. King County's figures also include overhead. Despite the absence of equivalency, the comparison "may provide a valuable perspective nonetheless."

SUGGESTED FOR FURTHER INFORMATION

Ammons, David N. *Municipal Benchmarks: Assessing Local Performance and Establishing Community Standards,* 2d ed.. Thousand Oaks, Calif.: Sage Publications, 2001.

Department of Defense. *Roads, Grounds, Pest Control & Refuse Collection Handbook: Engineered Performance Standards.* NAVFAC 0525-LP-156-0016. Washington, D.C.: U.S. Government Printing Office, 1984.

Department of the Navy. *Janitorial Handbook: Engineered Performance Standards.* NAVFAC 0525-LP-142-0061. Washington, D.C.: U.S. Government Printing Office, 1987.

Mitchell International. *Mechanical Labor Estimating Guide.* San Diego, Calif.: Mitchell International (updated annually).

MOTOR Labor Guide Manual. Troy, Mich.: Hearst Business Communications, Inc. (updated annually).

R. S. Means Company. *Means Site Work Cost Data.* Kingston, Mass.: R. S. Means Co. (updated annually).

Part IV
Simple Mathematical Computations: Analytic Building Blocks

How much will be paid—or saved—in interest by choosing one financing option rather than another? How much must be set aside each year at a projected rate of interest in order to accumulate the amount of resources needed for a desired capital project? How can the cost of major capital equipment be depicted in annual expenditure reports in a manner that reflects the use of that equipment not just in the year of acquisition but over an extended period of time? These questions can be answered readily with a few simple computations.

10

Basic Investment Calculations:
Figuring Interest Rates and Yields

Calculating interest rates and projecting investment yields are fundamental tasks that come up time and again—especially in the analysis of proposals having long-term financial ramifications for a local government. Getting it right is important.

SCENARIO: DENIA, OHIO

Manfred D. "Manny" Garber, budget analyst for the city of Denia, Ohio, shook his head as he reviewed the city's fleet inventory and recent vehicle replacement patterns. "This is crazy! Do you realize what we are doing? Each year we make our equipment replacement decisions mostly on the basis of how tight the budget is. The age and condition of our vehicles and other equipment is a relatively minor consideration. If we are short of cash, we expect our mechanics to perform miracles. We just keep the clunkers another year and ignore the fact that we probably are not saving a dime by trying to stretch the service life of some of these money-pits."

"Sure, it might be shortsighted compared to a rational equipment management strategy," replied Al Shorty, Denia's finance director, "but in the eleventh hour when we are trying to balance the budget I wouldn't want to be the one telling the city council that we cannot afford to hire a few additional police officers, that we need to trim the employee pay increase by a percentage point or two, or that we need to raise taxes because a lot of our fleet is pretty decrepit. When it comes to choices like these, it's a pretty easy call. Let's get out the bailing wire and patch Old Daisy up for another year of work."

"Even if it costs us more to keep Old Daisy running than we avoid in prorated replacement costs?"

This was the latest in a series of conversations on the topic of vehicle replacement strategies that had taken place intermittently in the city manager's office, the finance department, and fleet maintenance. Everyone was in agreement that it would be nice to have an equipment replacement fund, with annual contributions in the form of "rental" from vehicle users in amounts sufficient to allow timely replacement. With a fund dedicated to equipment replacement, the only haggling would be over whether a given vehicle was really worn out and whether the replacement specifications were appropriate—not whether equipment purchases would unbalance the budget. But getting *there* from *here* was the problem. How do you come up with the money to establish the fund in the first place? The last comment on the topic by the city manager was hardly reassuring: "The next time the city gets a revenue windfall, establishing an equipment replacement fund will be high on my list of priorities."

"Great," Manny remembers thinking, "and how long will that take?"

Patience was not one of Manny's strengths, but pragmatism was. "Can't we at least start building a fund rather than waiting for a windfall? Let's put a little something into the fund each year, draw interest, and let it grow until it reaches the point that we can begin operating from it. Getting where we want to be in five or ten years is better than not getting there at all."

"Put together a proposal," Al replied, "and we will see if it will fly."

INVESTMENT CALCULATIONS IOI

Analysts working with investments or attempting to evaluate alternate investment strategies would be wise to include four fundamental investment formulas in their toolkit of analytic techniques. These formulas will allow them to calculate:

1. yields based on simple interest
2. yields based on intrayear compound interest (for example, compounded quarterly)
3. the interest rate on an investment, knowing the initial investment, length of term, and yield
4. the yield from a series of even, annual cash investments (that is, annuities)

The fourth calculation will be especially pertinent to Manny's proposal for the city of Denia.

Calculating Yields Based on Simple Interest

$$FV_n = PV(1 + i)^n$$

where

FV_n = the future value of an investment following n periods
PV = amount of initial investment
i = interest rate per period
n = the number of interest periods

The entry $(1 + i)^n$ may be calculated by hand or may be found in a table of "Future Value Interest Factors" (see Appendix B).

Using this formula, an analyst could calculate the return from $10,000, invested three years at 7 percent annual interest.

$$FV_3 = \$10,000 \times 1.2250 = \$12,250$$

Calculating Yields Based on Intrayear Compound Interest

$$FV_n = PV\left(1 + \frac{i}{t}\right)^{tn}$$

where t is the number of times per year that interest is compounded.

Using this formula, an analyst could calculate the return from $10,000, invested two years at 8 percent interest compounded quarterly.

$$FV_2 = (\$10,000)\left(1 + \frac{.08}{4}\right)^{(4)(2)} = (\$10,000)(1 + .02)^8 = \$10,000 \times 1.1717 = \$11,717$$

Once again, the Future Value Interest Factors table (Appendix B) is consulted in this calculation, but this time the formula calls for the interest rate to be divided by the number of payments per year (8% divided by 4 = 2%) and the number of years to be multiplied by the number of payments per year (2 × 4 = 8). The cell entry for 2 percent and 8 periods is 1.1717. Comparing this result with the yield on simple interest demonstrates the impact of compounding.[1]

Calculating the Interest Rate on an Investment

If analysts know the amount of initial investment, length of term, and yield, they can calculate the interest rate using the following formula:

$$I = \frac{SP - PP}{PP} \times \frac{360}{D}$$

where

I	=	interest rate
SP	=	investment's value at sale or redemption (sale price)
PP	=	initial investment (purchase price)
D	=	number of days investment was held

Using this formula, an analyst could calculate the interest rate on a ninety-day U.S. Treasury bill, purchased for $9,850 and having a face value of $10,000, as

$$I = \frac{\$10,000 - 9,850}{\$9,850} \times \frac{360}{90} = 0.01523 \times 4 = 6.09\%$$

---

[1]The Future Value Interest Factor (FVIF) for this example was 1.1717, compared to a FVIF of 1.1664 for two years at 8 percent simple interest. On an investment of $10,000, that is a difference in yield of $53.

Calculating the Yield from a Series of Even, Annual Cash Investments

If a local government puts away equal annual sums (that is, annuities) in order to accumulate funds for some future use, an analyst wishing to compute the total of those funds at a future date may do so using the following formula:

$$SN = A(SAF_{i,n})$$

where

SN = sum of the annuity after N payments

A = amount deposited annually

$SAF_{i,n}$ = sum of annuity factor (see table in Appendix C)

Using this formula, an analyst would know that a city or county that plans to deposit $20,000 annually for 5 years at 7 percent interest will have a sum of $115,014 at the end of that period.[2]

$$SN = A(SAF_{i,n}) = \$20,000 \times 5.7507 = \$115,014$$

Alternatively, the analyst may calculate the annual payment amount necessary to accumulate a desired sum in a given timeframe using the following formula:

$$A = \frac{SN}{SAF_{i,n}}$$

BACK IN DENIA

Manny pored over the fleet management and purchasing records pertaining to the maintenance and acquisition of the city's vehicles. He had the advantage of hindsight in determining when vehicles *should have been replaced*. By calculating annual depreciation (see Chapter 11) and plotting the rise in maintenance costs as vehicles moved through their optimum service periods, he could identify the point at which replacement would have made the most sense.

Next, Manny devised a vehicle replacement schedule that prescribed replacement for vehicles in a given category based on miles or hours of service, but allowed exceptions for vehicles experiencing unusually high or low maintenance expenses. Applying this schedule to the current fleet, Manny found that systematic replacement could result in capital outlays as high as $850,000 in some years and as low as $380,000 in others. The average year appeared to require about $500,000 in capital expenditures for vehicles.

---

[2]Note that the SAF table in Appendix C assumes that annual payments are made *at the end* of each year. The SAF for every interest rate in period 1 is 1.0000, indicating that no interest is earned until the second period.

Box 10-1 Interest Calculations

Interest calculations can be tricky when done by hand because there are exponents and fractions to deal with. Microsoft Excel allows the user to eliminate these obstacles and simply plug numbers into a command that outputs the yield or interest rate.

To calculate **yields based on simple interest,** use the Future Value—**FV**—function. After the FV command, the user must enter several variables to complete the calculation. In the parentheses after the function, the user must enter the interest rate, the number of periods, the payments made during each period, the initial amount, and finally the type of payment made.

For the example used in this chapter, the initial investment was $10,000 with an interest rate of 7 percent over three years. To enter this example in the Excel command, the user would input "=FV(.07,3,0,10000,1)," and the output would be the future value of $12,250. Notice that because no payments are made over time, the third variable is "0." Also, the final variable "1" indicates that the payment was made at the beginning of the pay period. Users may find it especially helpful—and simpler—to use the Function option from the Insert menu, which includes the FV function, because the computer will offer prompts for the information needed in the parentheses.

Finding the **yield from intrayear compound interest** is a bit more complicated. Before using the FVSCHEDULE function, the user must create the schedule of interest rates to be compounded. By dividing the interest rate by the number of times compounded a year, the user can begin to create the schedule. If the interest rate is 8 percent and it is compounded quarterly, then the user should enter "=.08/4" in cell A1. The computer would output ".02." Because the investment encompasses a two-year period, the number of times it will be compounded is 8. Highlight cell A1, and move the mouse to the lower, right-hand corner of the cell. When the black cross appears, drag the mouse down to cell A8 or to the total number of times the investment will be compounded.

Now that the compounding schedule is created, it is time to use the FVSCHEDULE function. After the command, the variables entered in the parentheses by the user should indicate the initial investment and the cells that contain the schedule. In the example above, the user would enter "=FVSCHEDULE(10000,A1:A8)," and the computer would calculate the yield. (The future value in this case is $11,717.)

Excel also has a command that **computes the interest rate on an investment,** but instead of knowing the number of days the investment is held, the user must know the actual dates in order to use the command. To find an interest rate, use the INTRATE function. In the parentheses after the command, indicate the date the investment began, then the date the investment ended, then the initial investment, then the sale price, and finally the type of day count to use. If a U.S. Treasury bill was purchased on January, 1, 2001 for $9,850, had a face value of $10,000, and was held for 90 days, or until April 1, 2001, the interest rate may be calculated by entering "=INTRATE("1/1/2001", "4/1/2001", 9850, 10000, 2)". It is important to remember that quotation marks are needed around the dates. Also, the 2 appearing at the end of the sequence tells the computer to use a normal day count in which the number of days is divided by 360. (The interest rate in this case is 6.09 percent.)

Calculating the **yield from a series of even, annual cash investments** on Excel can be done with the same function used to calculate simple interest. Use the FV function (future value) and

(Box continues on next page)

Box 10-1 *(Continued)*

enter the same data variables in parentheses after the command: the interest rate, the number of periods, the payments made during each period, the initial amount, and when the payment is made. To find the total value for the example in this chapter, the user would enter "=FV(.07,5,20000,0,0)", and the computer would report the sum of the annuity after five payments—i.e., $115,014. Notice that the principle amount is zero and the type of payment is also zero, indicating the payments are not made in the beginning of the period.

To have a chance for his plan to succeed, Manny needed a strategy that would provide seed money for the proposed equipment replacement fund. For the time being, the city would continue to make equipment acquisition decisions as part of the annual budget deliberation, while setting aside a small appropriation each year that could draw interest and eventually grow into a fund large enough to do the job. He thought a fund of $550,000 would be adequate.

The formula for annuities required Manny to estimate an interest rate for the city's investments. He decided to estimate an interest rate of 8 percent and inserted it into the formula. After trying several combinations of payment amounts and payment periods, Manny found a combination he liked, one calling for seven years of payments:

$$A = \frac{SN}{SAF_{i,n}} = \frac{\$550,000}{8.9228} = \$61,640$$

Using this calculation, Manny decided to recommend seven annual appropriations of $61,640 into a newly established equipment replacement fund. At the end of seven years, the fund would have $550,000—more than the average annual equipment replacement requirement but not enough to cover a peak purchasing year. Beginning in the eighth year, "rental fees" for equipment use would be assessed to departments and equipment purchases from the fund would commence. These rental fees would cover annual maintenance expenses plus depreciation. In the eighth year, the special appropriations from the general fund would cease and purchases would be made from the equipment replacement fund, replenished annually by rental fees. Until then, the city would continue to make vehicle purchases from available funds through the annual budget process.

"I like this, Manny," Al said when he saw the proposal. "I think we have a decent chance to get approval of an appropriation this size. But what happens if that first year of purchases from the fund turns out to be one of the big years? It couldn't handle $850,000."

"That would be a problem, all right, but we are just as likely to get one of the lighter years. If it does turn out to be a peak purchase year, we have two things going for us. First, there is a little cushion built into the fund itself. Second, we will be drawing rental fees from the departments. That should give us a little flexibility, as long as we don't get two big years in a row. What do you think our chances would be for a special appropriation to the fund if it's a huge year for vehicle purchases?"

"I suppose that is a possibility, but I would say the smarter choice would be to manage our fleet between now and then to be sure that we do not hit a peak purchasing year just as the equipment replacement fund swings into action."

SUGGESTED FOR FURTHER INFORMATION

Adams, A. T., D. S. F. Bloomfield, P. M. Booth, and P. D. England. *Investment Mathematics and Statistics.* London: Graham & Trotman, 1993.

Coe, Charles K. *Public Financial Management.* Englewood Cliffs, N.J.: Prentice Hall, 1989.

Ross, Sheldon M. *An Introduction to Mathematical Finance: Options and Other Topics.* Cambridge, U.K.: Cambridge University Press, 1999.

Teall, John L. *Financial Market Analytics.* Westport, Conn.: Quorum Books, 1999.

Thomsett, Michael C. *The Mathematics of Investing: A Complete Reference.* New York: John Wiley & Sons, 1989.

11

Simple Options for Annualizing Costs of Capital Items:
Usage-Rate and Straight-Line Depreciation

Local government officials attempting to analyze program costs often are tempted to look only at the "bottom line" of a department's budget or expenditure record. Unfortunately, the bottom line sometimes provides an inaccurate reflection of annual expenses. Some relevant program costs may be reported elsewhere. Furthermore, the expenses shown may be influenced dramatically by the peaks and valleys of capital expenditures.

The cost of facility construction, equipment acquisition, and other capital items should be included when considering total program costs—but including capital costs in their entirety whenever they occur would distort an analysis. A more reasonable approach would be to depreciate capital items and include for each year a portion of the capital costs proportionate to the useful life of an item.

SCENARIO: HORACE AND JASPER, IOWA

Nat Kilgos had been on the job in the research and budget department of the city of Horace, Iowa, only a few days when he was given the assignment of comparing the animal control program in Horace with that of nearby Jasper. "See if we ought to make any changes to our system or if we should adopt Jasper's approach to animal control," the research and budget director had said.

Nat plunged eagerly into the task, diligently collecting program descriptions and budget documents, interviewing program supervisors of each operation, and pressing for performance measures and other indicators of the level of service and success of each program. He was determined to prove his worth as an administrative assistant.

The services provided by the animal control programs in the two communities were strikingly similar. The numbers of animals handled by each program annually were almost identical, and both programs boasted very favorable qualitative performance measures. The most apparent operating difference was that Horace's program was managed and staffed by city employees, while Jasper's was provided through a municipal contract with a local animal protection group. That group used the city-owned animal shelter and charged the city of Jasper a fixed annual fee to cover its expenses in running the program, which included the cost of full- and part-time employees, operation and maintenance of the shelter, utilities, supplies, vehicles, and other equipment.

Nat could see little difference in quality or scope of services to recommend one program over the other. Furthermore, his comparison of budget documents showed a difference of less than $8,000 between the two programs. The contractual program had the lesser expenditure, but there was no guarantee that a contractual system would work as well in Horace as it apparently did in Jasper. Should Horace give contracting for this service a try? Nat did not think so. All in all, an incentive of less than $8,000 seemed insufficient to justify the gamble and the program disruption that would be caused by such a substantial operating change.

Prior to finalizing the report for the research and budget director, Nat took his tabulation (see Table 11-1) to Chris Bogle, a senior budget analyst who had offered to review his work. "I just don't see that it would make sense to make the change for such a modest potential payoff," explained Nat.

"You might be right," replied Chris after spending a few minutes reviewing the tabulation and several supporting documents, "but I see a few holes in your analysis that you'll want to plug before presenting your report. Using budgets is handy for comparing expenditures, but you have to be careful to be sure that you're including everything."

"I did that," responded Nat. "The contract in Jasper includes everything except the animal shelter building and land, and that's not a cost factor in the Horace budget either, because it was paid for long ago. And the personnel costs for Horace include fringe benefits and everything. It looks like a fair comparison to me."[1]

"What about the cost of administering the contract?"

"It's negligible. I checked with the city manager. But I guess I should put a little something in there to reflect the fact that it's not absolutely cost free."

"What about our equipment costs? This year's budget shows nothing for equipment acquisition just because we replaced both trucks during the last two years and replaced the other major equipment three years ago. It wouldn't be fair to throw the full acquisition price into the annual cost comparison, but it's not fair to simply

---

[1]The administrative assistant is touching on a key point of relevance to comparisons such as this. If the purpose of the analysis is to determine which entity operates most efficiently, then all entities in a comparison should be examined on an equal basis (see Chapter 14). Including the fringe benefits or building depreciation for one and not the other would distort the comparison. In the case of Horace and Jasper, fringe benefits have been included for both programs. The animal shelter and associated land for both programs are city owned, so excluding depreciation or "facility rental" for both entities simplifies the analysis with little impact on results. However, if the Jasper animal shelter had been privately owned and provided as part of the contract, the Horace figure would have required adjustment to see which of the two is the more efficient operation (see Chapter 14). If, on the other hand, the purpose of the analysis is to consider contracting for a service, only the costs that would be eliminated with the shift of operations should be included in the Horace total (see Chapter 15).

Table 11-1 Animal Control Annual Budget Expenditures

Expenditure	City of Horace	City of Jasper
Salaries and benefits	$113,338	—
Supplies	8,500	—
Contractual/other services	10,000	$126,000
Maintenance	2,000	—
Capital	0	—
Total	$133,838	$126,000

ignore it just because we didn't buy anything this year. I'll bet the Jasper contract includes an amount being set aside by the contractor for equipment replacement. For a fair comparison, you ought to depreciate our capital equipment and show the annual depreciation in your analysis."

ANNUALIZING CAPITAL EXPENSES

Frequently the costs of a capital item are borne at one point in time, while the benefits are spread over several years. A truck purchased in 2002, for example, might still be providing benefits to its owner in 2007. Two of the simplest methods of allocating reasonable costs of a capital item over its useful life are allocations based on usage rate and allocations based on straight-line depreciation.

The rationale for allocating costs according to usage rate is tied to the premise that the deterioration of some capital items is caused more by the use of those items than by the passage of time. A machine that can be expected to last through 10,000 hours of operation—whether those hours occur in two years' time or ten years' time—is a good example. If the cost of such a machine is $10,500 and it is expected to have a salvage value of $500, it would be reasonable to assign annual costs for that equipment at the rate of $1 per hour of operation. The annual cost would be dependent on the anticipated or actual usage of the equipment per year. The formula for usage rate allocation of cost is:

$$a_i = \frac{u_i}{U}(C - S)$$

where

a_i = capital expense allocation for time period i
u_I = usage units consumed during time period i
U = total estimated usage units in the life of the asset
C = cost of the asset
S = salvage value after U usage units

An alternate method, more suitable for allocating annual cost for capital items whose deterioration is perhaps as much due to the passage of time as to actual usage, is straight-line depreciation. For example, although many buildings deteriorate more

From the Electronic Toolkit ●───────────────────────────────

Box 11-1 Finding Usage-Rate Allocation of Cost

Even without a specific Excel function for calculating usage rate allocation of cost, computers nevertheless can be programmed to perform the calculation of this or any of the other formulas mentioned in this book. After the formula is programmed into Excel once, the usage rate allocation can be determined again and again with different data.

First, enter the variable names or symbols—usage units consumed, total estimated usage units in the life of the asset, cost of the asset, and salvage value—in four consecutive cells in a given column. (For directions on opening Excel and entering data, see Box 2-1.) In the next column enter the numerical value for each variable in the cell adjacent to a given label or symbol. For example, you might enter "u(i)=" in cell A1 as a prompt for the numerical value of "2000" in cell B1. Then, in any cell, enter the formula for usage rate allocation of cost using the cell names as the variables. For example, if the numerical variables were entered in order from B1 through B4, enter the formula "=((B1/B2)*(B3–B4))", and after pressing "enter" the usage rate allocation of cost will appear. The calculation can be done for different sets of data by simply changing the data in cells B1 through B4.

quickly with heavy use, they nevertheless deteriorate with the passage of time even with fairly light use. Even when deterioration is directly related to usage, straight-line depreciation offers the advantage of minimizing guesswork in projecting annual costs (for example, How many hours will this item be used? How many visits will be made to this facility?).

The acquisition costs for most cars and trucks could be annualized using either usage-rate or straight-line depreciation. The life of an automobile could, for example, be estimated at 90,000 miles or, if it gets an average of 15,000 to 20,000 miles of use per year, at five years. For the sake of simplicity, straight-line depreciation might be chosen as the allocation technique, using the following formula:

$$a_i = \frac{C - S}{N}$$

where

a_i = capital expense allocation to each time period
C = cost of the asset
N = total number of time periods in the item's expected life
S = salvage value after N periods

MAKING APPROPRIATE ADJUSTMENTS

Two days later, the administrative assistant returned to the senior budget analyst with a revised set of figures. Following further inquiry into Jasper's cost for administering its contract, Nat was prepared to defend a cost estimate of $2,000 for contract

From the Electronic Toolkit

Box 11-2 Straight-Line Depreciation

Calculating straight-line depreciation using Excel is simple because of the SLN function. Click on the cell where you want the annual depreciation amount to appear. Then click on the Function key (**fx**) in the toolbar. Click the function category "All" in the pop-up menu, and the SLN function name. Following prompts, enter the initial cost, the salvage cost, and the total number of time periods in the item's expected life. For example, the straight-line depreciation of an item with the initial cost of $10,500, a salvage cost of $500, and an expected life of five years would be found by entering these amounts in the blanks. The outcome of $2,000 will appear in the designated cell.

administration. The program costs for Jasper's animal control program were adjusted upward by that amount.

The adjustment of Horace's numbers to account for capital costs on an annual basis was considerably greater (see Figure 11-1). The two pickup trucks used by the animal control program each cost $16,600 and, according to the superintendent of the city garage, had an expected life of three years and a salvage value of $700. All other capital equipment associated with the animal control program (for example, fiberglass beds with animal enclosures, mobile radios, nets, catch poles, and strobe lights) had been replaced in a package purchase three years ago at a total cost of $17,830. That equipment has a projected life of ten years and an anticipated salvage value of $300. The application of the straight-line depreciation technique indicates an annualized capital cost of $12,353 (Figure 11-1). Nat added that amount to Horace's program costs.

Figure 11-1 Animal Control Capital Equipment Straight-Line Depreciation

$$a_i = \frac{C - S}{N}$$

Pickup Trucks

$$\frac{\$16,600 - 700}{3} \;=\; \begin{array}{l} \$5,300 \quad \text{per year per truck} \\ \underline{\times\, 2} \quad\;\; \text{trucks} \\ \$10,600 \quad \text{per year} \end{array}$$

Other Equipment

$$\frac{\$17,830 - 300}{10} \;=\; \$1,753 \quad \text{per year}$$

Total
$10,600   trucks
+ 1,753   other
$12,353

Table 11-2 Animal Control: Revised Annual Costs

Expenditure	City of Horace	City of Jasper
Salaries and benefits	$113,338	—
Supplies	8,500	—
Contractual/other services	10,000	$126,000
Maintenance	2,000	—
Capital	12,353	—
Contract administration	0	2,000
Total	$146,191	$128,000

Adding $2,000 to Jasper's program costs and $12,353 to Horace's stretched the previous cost difference of $7,838 to a new estimated difference of $18,191 (see Table 11-2).

"I'm still not sure that the possibility of saving $18,000 or $19,000 is worth the risk of disrupting a good program," worried Nat. "I don't even know if we have an animal welfare group or other contractor willing to tackle the job for an amount similar to what Jasper pays."

"I share your concern," said Chris, "but with your latest revisions, the numbers are becoming a lot more tempting."

UTILITY OF TECHNIQUES FOR ANNUALIZING THE COST OF CAPITAL ITEMS

A persistent problem in the analysis of local government operations is the tendency to understate departmental or program expenditures. Sometimes this is caused by accounting or budgeting practices that fail to assign program costs precisely, perhaps allowing overhead costs to be absorbed elsewhere in the budget or reporting employee benefits in a separate account.

Box 11-3 Other Applications of Depreciation Calculations

Annualizing capital costs through usage-rate or straight-line depreciation is useful when comparing a local government's costs to those of other governments or to the bids of private vendors. The calculation of annualized capital costs is helpful in other instances as well—for example:

- when preparing to report unit costs for a given service
- when establishing fees intended to recover a specified portion of full costs for providing a given service
- when preparing a grant proposal or reporting annual costs for reimbursement purposes

Still another common cause of underreporting is failure to allocate capital costs properly. Many local governments include the entire costs for all capital acquisitions in the year in which they are purchased. This practice not only overstates the expenses of the program for the year in which a major capital outlay happens to occur, but it also understates the true costs of the program in the subsequent years when the costs for these items are disregarded. Annualized capital costs contribute to a much more reasonable statement of annual program costs.

SUGGESTED FOR FURTHER INFORMATION

Columbia University, Public Technology Inc., and the International City Management Association. *Evaluating Residential Refuse Collection Costs: A Workbook for Local Government.* Washington, D.C.: Public Technology Inc., 1978.

Hatry, Harry P., Sumner N. Clarren, Therese van Houten, Jane P. Woodward, and Pasqual A. DonVito. "Cost Estimation Issues." In *Efficiency Measurement for Local Government Services,* 175–204. Washington, D.C.: Urban Institute, 1979.

Kelley, Joseph T. *Costing Government Services: A Guide for Decision Making.* Washington, D.C.: Government Finance Officers Association, 1984.

Part V
Making Comparisons

Many of the multiyear and multijurisdictional comparisons that feed into local government decisions are misleading because they fail to include appropriate adjustments for inflation, reporting differences, and other extenuating circumstances that may give one year's performance or one jurisdiction a superficial advantage over another. A city government might spend more per mile for street striping than it did ten years ago, but that does not necessarily mean that it is less efficient than it was then. The effect of inflation on wages, equipment, and supplies might account for the full difference. Similarly, a simple comparison of the budgets of two or more local governments would be an unfair basis for judging relative efficiency if the scope and quality of services differ greatly or if different practices are followed in accounting for administrative overhead, fringe benefits, and capital expenditures.

In much the same way, recommendations regarding the optimum use of resources can be faulty when they fail to consider fully the ramifications of choosing one opportunity over another. Simple mathematical techniques can be used to make many of the adjustments needed for these and other types of relevant comparisons that local government decision makers may want to consider.

12

Adjusting for Inflation When Comparing Revenues or Expenditures

Comparing the amount of revenues received by a local government one year to the amount received in another year can be misleading. Although the more recent number may be larger, it might represent resources with less "buying power" than the smaller figure from an earlier year. Similarly, steadily increasing expenditures might be more attributable to inflation than to service expansion or loss of efficiency. Meaningful comparisons across years are possible only if the figures are adjusted to reflect "constant dollars."

SCENARIO: KEYSTONE, NEVADA

The city manager of Keystone, Nevada, was already worried about next year's budget, even though the budget hearings were still three months away. Years ago in college a professor had described what he called "rational-comprehensive decision making" and its application to the budget process, but very little seemed rational about the decision making taking place in Keystone these days.

Keystone had the third highest rate of population growth in the state, and the citizens were demanding improved services. With city council elections coming next spring, incumbents were already bracing for the onslaught of challengers grumbling about runaway expenditures. That morning a coalition of council members sent word through the mayor that it expected the city manager to hold the line on expenditures and would not, under any circumstances, consider a property tax increase for next year.

"Mayor, how can you and the others preempt me like this?" asked the city manager. "We're addressing important community needs, and we're managing our resources wisely. I had hoped to get a fair audience for what I am sure will be a solid budget proposal. Why the panic? Our increases haven't been extravagant."

"How can you say that?" responded the mayor. "Municipal expenditures are up 13 percent in two years' time. Don't think for a minute our opponents haven't pointed that out to potential supporters."

The mayor and the council members now banding together were clearly worried about their public image and the upcoming election. The mayor had been elected on a campaign that emphasized his business experience and his fiscally conservative philosophy. No wonder he felt stung by the 13 percent increase!

Soon after the mayor left, the city manager called the budget officer to his office. After describing the substance and tone of the mayor's message, the city manager said, "It won't be business-as-usual this year. There's no way that we'll be allowed to tap our resources the way we have in the past few years. The best we can hope for is a modest increase in expenditures funded by tax base expansion rather than a tax rate increase. But we won't even get that if we aren't prepared."

The city manager laid out a strategy for meeting the "runaway expenditures" charge head-on. He directed the budget officer to prepare a comparison of expenditures for this year and the previous two years using "constant dollars" rather than "current dollars."

"Start with our highest priority items, like police patrol. Let's see if we can get some information out that will help us—and the mayor and council—defend what we've been doing."

INFLATION INDEXES

When shoppers mutter, "A dollar doesn't go as far as it used to," they are right. An item that costs $1.10 today may have cost $1.00 only a few years ago. Inflation diminishes the value of money. Four quarters and a dime in that shopper's hand might look like $1.10 (and it is $1.10 in "current dollars"), but it is only $1.00 in "constant dollars" if these coins can buy no more than what $1.00 could buy in the base year.

Converting current dollars to constant dollars is a simple matter. Various price indexes are available for that purpose, the most popular one being the Consumer Price Index (CPI), compiled by the Bureau of Labor Statistics (see Table 12-1). The CPI measures changes in a variety of consumer products and is used frequently in labor negotiations and as a guide to various cost-of-living adjustments.[1] The index's rate of change from one year to another—for example, from 166.6 in 1999 to 172.2 in 2000, a rise of 3.36 percent—reflects inflation in consumer prices.

A second index—one more tailored to the needs of local government—is the implicit price deflator (IPD), which is compiled by the U.S. Department of Commerce's Bureau of Economic Analysis. The IPD is a better choice for most local government purposes because it reports an index based specifically on the kinds of goods and services that state and local governments purchase. Even so, the IPD, like all other indexes, is an imperfect gauge of inflation and users should be aware of that.[2]

Implicit price deflators are published throughout the year in the U.S. Department of Commerce's *Survey of Current Business*. A table from that publication, which shows

---

[1] For CPI information on-line, see the U.S. Bureau of Labor Statistics Web site at http://stats.bls.gov/cpihome.htm.

[2] For IPD information on-line, see the U.S. Bureau of Economic Analysis Web site at http://www.bea.doc.gov/bea/pub/1100cont.htm.

Table 12-1 Average Annual Consumer Price Index for All Urban Consumers, 1983–2000

Year	Average Annual CPI	Percentage Change from Previous Year
2000	172.2	3.36
1999	166.6	2.21
1998	163.0	1.56
1997	160.5	2.29
1996	156.9	2.95
1995	152.4	2.83
1994	148.2	2.56
1993	144.5	2.99
1992	140.3	3.01
1991	136.2	4.21
1990	130.7	5.40
1989	124.0	4.82
1988	118.3	4.14
1987	113.6	3.65
1986	109.6	1.86
1985	107.6	3.56
1984	103.9	4.32
1983	99.6	

Source: U.S. Department of Labor, Bureau of Labor Statistics, "Consumer Price Index," February 21, 2001 (ftp://ftp.bls.gov/pub/special.requests/cpi/cpiai.txt).

the IPD for state and local government consumption expenditures and gross investment, is provided in Table 12-2. Annual IPDs for state and local governments from 1995 through 1999 are shown in Table 12-3.

Converting current dollars to constant dollars involves simple mathematics. The formula for doing so is:

$$\text{current dollar revenue or expenditure} \times \frac{\text{base year IPD}}{\text{current IPD}} = \text{current revenues or expenditures in base year dollars}$$

First, a base year of the analyst's choosing is selected. Then, current dollars are multiplied by the ratio of the base-year IPD to the current IPD. The resulting figure will be the buying power of current dollars in base-year dollars. The term *current* is used for convenience; it may refer to this year or to any year other than the selected base year by simply saying "current dollars in 2001" or whatever year the analyst chooses.

Table 12-2 Implicit Price Deflators for Gross Domestic Product (Index Numbers, 1996 = 100)

| | 1998 | 1999 | Seasonally Adjusted | | | | | |
| | | | 1999 | | | 2000 | | |
			II	III	IV	I	II	III
Gross domestic product	103.22	104.77	104.65	104.89	105.24	106.10	106.73	107.26
Personal consumption expenditures	103.03	104.85	104.59	105.09	105.66	106.57	107.12	107.69
Durable goods	95.41	93.09	93.31	92.87	92.46	91.99	91.84	91.32
Nondurable goods	101.35	103.71	103.42	104.14	105.07	106.46	107.33	107.91
Services	105.50	107.99	107.65	108.26	108.87	109.88	110.43	111.27
Gross private domestic investment	98.92	98.83	99.06	98.71	98.41	98.99	99.44	99.93
Fixed investment	99.17	99.10	99.14	99.06	99.07	99.70	100.16	100.67
Nonresidential	97.13	95.84	96.00	95.62	95.42	95.84	96.23	96.69
Structures	107.71	110.19	109.65	110.44	111.43	112.73	113.75	114.64
Equipment and software	93.78	91.46	91.80	91.13	90.64	90.84	91.07	91.42
Residential	105.59	109.64	109.28	110.22	110.94	112.36	113.08	113.77
Exports of goods and services	96.26	95.86	95.61	95.87	96.50	96.97	97.42	97.65
Imports of goods and services	91.25	91.80	91.08	92.41	93.61	94.90	94.95	95.86
Government consumption expenditures and gross investment	103.67	106.40	105.99	106.81	107.61	109.28	110.01	111.02
Federal	102.60	105.27	104.93	105.43	106.00	108.00	108.17	108.92
National defense	102.20	104.75	104.39	104.90	105.51	107.34	107.55	108.34
Nondefense	103.37	106.27	105.96	106.44	106.94	109.24	109.34	110.02
State and local	104.28	107.05	106.60	107.59	108.51	110.02	111.04	112.20

Source: U.S. Department of Commerce, Economics and Statistics Administration, Bureau of Economic Analysis, *Survey of Current Business* 80, no. 11 (November 2000): D18. Accessed at http://www.bea.doc.gov/bea/pub/1100cont.htm.

Table 12-3 Implicit Price Deflators for State and Local Governments, 1995–1999 (Index numbers, 1996 = 100)

	Consumption Expenditures and Gross Investment	
Year	Implicit Price Deflator	Percentage Change from Previous Year
1999	107.05	2.66
1998	104.28	2.18
1997	102.06	2.06
1996	100.00	2.24
1995	97.81	

Source: Data drawn from "Quantity and Price Indexes for Gross Domestic Product," Table 7.1, in various issues of U.S. Department of Commerce, Economics and Statistics Administration, Bureau of Economic Analysis, *Survey of Current Business.*

SCENARIO: CONVERTING KEYSTONE'S POLICE PATROL EXPENDITURES TO "CONSTANT DOLLARS"

The budget officer in Keystone compiled a brief summary of police patrol positions and expenditures for the three most recent fiscal years (see Table 12-4). The increase in expenditures was slightly greater than the municipal average—14.4 percent, rather than 13.1 percent. The increase was in part attributable to adding two patrol officers and three public service officers during the last two years. Those increases, of course, had nothing to do with inflation. But what would the increase have been had it not been for inflation?

The budget officer converted each of the expenditure figures in Table 12-4 to constant dollars. Keystone's fiscal year begins July 1 of the calendar year and ends June 30 of the following year. Because these fiscal years do not coincide precisely with the calendar years listed in the IPD table, the budget officer had to make a reasonable choice that could be applied uniformly across his data. For example, the choice for a given fiscal year could be the IPD for the calendar year in which the fiscal year began, the year in which it ended, the first quarter IPD, or perhaps the midpoint between two annual IPDs. For the sake of simplicity, he decided to use the IPD for

From the Electronic Toolkit ●───────────────────────────────

Box 12-1 Access to Inflation Indexes

The latest Consumer Price Index information and an on-line "inflation calculator" are available at the Web site of the U.S. Bureau of Labor Statistics (http://stats.bls.gov/cpihome.htm). On-line access to Implicit Price Deflators is available through the U.S. Department of Commerce's Bureau of Economic Analysis (http://www.bea.doc.gov/bea/pub/1100cont.htm).

Table 12-4 Police Patrol: Positions and Expenditures, City of Keystone

	Fiscal Year 1997 Actual	Fiscal Year 1998 Actual	Fiscal Year 1999 Budget
Positions			
Sergeants	4	4	4
Patrol officers	26	27	28
Public service officers	2	4	5
Total	32	35	37
Expenditures			
Salaries and benefits	$1,157,380	$1,296,114	$1,406,058
Supplies	63,200	65,940	67,950
Other services	64,572	63,605	29,830
Maintenance	42,500	46,708	49,446
Capital	145,980	123,576	132,551
Total	$1,473,632	$1,595,943	$1,685,835

the year in which a given fiscal year ended. For example, fiscal year 1998–1999 (FY 1999) ended June 30, 1999, so for FY 1999 he used the 1999 IPD. The 1997 IPD of 102.06 was used as the base year, and the unadjusted FY 1997 expenditures were regarded as 1997 dollars. The calculations for converting total expenditures for FY 1998 and FY 1999 to 1997 constant dollars for the patrol activity of the Keystone cops are shown in Table 12-5. The full set of expenditures converted to 1997 dollars is shown in Table 12-6.

Table 12-5 Converting Keystone Police Patrol Expenditures for Fiscal Year 1998 and Fiscal Year 1999 to 1997 Constant Dollars

$$\text{current dollar revenue or expenditure} \times \frac{\text{base year IPD}}{\text{current IPD}} = \text{current revenues or expenditures in base year dollars}$$

Total Expenditures for FY 1998 Converted to 1997 Constant Dollars	**Total Expenditures for FY 1999 Converted to 1997 Constant Dollars**
$\$1,595,943 \times \dfrac{102.06}{104.28} = \$1,561,967$	$\$1,685,835 \times \dfrac{102.06}{107.05} = \$1,607,252$

Notes: For the FY 1998 calculation, $1,595,943 is the total FY 1998 expenditure reported in Table 12-4. The IPDs of 102.06 and 104.28 for 1997 and 1998, respectively, are reported in Table 12-3. For the FY 1999 calculation, $1,685,835 is the total FY 1999 expenditure reported in Table 12-4. The IPDs of 102.06 and 107.05 for 1997 and 1999, respectively, are reported in Table 12-3.

Table 12-6 Constant Dollar Comparison of Police Patrol Expenditures, City of Keystone, 1997–1999

Expenditures	FY 1997 Actual	FY 1998 Actual in 1997 Dollars	FY 1999 Budget in 1997 Dollars
Salaries and benefits	$1,157,380	$1,268,521	$1,340,516
Supplies	63,200	64,536	64,783
Other services	64,572	62,251	28,440
Maintenance	42,500	45,714	47,141
Capital	145,980	120,945	126,372
Total	$1,473,632	$1,561,967	$1,607,252

Note: All figures for fiscal years 1998 and 1999 have been converted to 1997 constant dollars using implicit price deflators for state and local government consumption expenditures and gross investment.

Box 12-2 Other Applications of Inflation Adjustments

Opportunities for the application of inflation indexes in local government are numerous. Such indexes are often used to peg cost-of-living increases in employee wages, annual adjustments in multiyear service contracts, and multiyear revenue and expenditure comparisons. Adjusting figures to constant dollars in such comparisons permits a more reasonable evaluation of fiscal trends.

"This will help, but we still have a lot of work to do," remarked the city manager when the budget officer showed him the constant dollar figures. "We're still up 9.1 percent in constant dollars in just two years' time, but that's a lot better than having to explain a 14.4 percent jump."

"We've increased the number of positions in that division by 16 percent to try to improve services and meet the demands of a growing population," commented the budget officer.

"That's true," responded the city manager. "Let's try to attack this thing on two fronts. See if you can come up with some performance indicators that would show improved service quality to help us defend expenditures in excess of inflation [see Chapter 8]. Also, let's adjust our expenditure figures to account for a growing population as well as inflation. Get the best population figures you can from the planning department and convert those constant dollar numbers to expenditures *per capita* reported in constant dollars. With the growth we've experienced in the last two years, I think the per capita figures will show a very modest increase. When we make those adjustments and compile our improved performance indicators, I'm confident we will present a very defendable record."

SUGGESTED FOR FURTHER INFORMATION

Leazes, Francis J., Jr., and Carol W. Lewis. "Now You See It, Now You Don't." In *Casebook in Public Budgeting and Financial Management*, edited by Carol W. Lewis and A. Grayson Walker III, 189–194. Englewood Cliffs, N.J.: Prentice-Hall, 1984.

13

The Time Value of Money:
Opportunity Costs, Discounting, Compounding, Future Value, and Present Value

A decision to spend financial resources eliminates the possibility of investing them for future use. A decision to use resources for one purpose eliminates the possibility of using those same resources for other purposes. Snap judgments on the wisdom of such a decision—choosing to spend rather than invest or to apply resources to one opportunity rather than another—are often subjective and typically reflect the biases of program proponents and opponents. Those who favor the expenditure are sure it will be money well spent; those opposed are just as convinced that it is wasteful. In many cases, a more objective assessment is possible.

The wisdom of a resource allocation decision can be assessed by placing the decision in context and by considering the time value of money. Was it a good decision compared to some other option—including the option of investing these funds? What opportunities did the local government forgo when it opted as it did?

A standard method of making such an assessment is to compare the "return" or benefit from a project to the return on a conservative investment of an equal amount of funds.[1] The fact that a good, conservative investment pays interest would seem to swing the analysis in favor of this option and against nonrevenue-generating alternatives, but the time value of money comes into play, too. A dollar in hand today is considered to be more valuable than a projected dollar to be received in the future for at least three reasons:

1. It is a sure thing—the risk of nonreceipt is eliminated.

---

[1]Stacking proposed uses up against possible investment returns is an analytic approach that is clearly relevant in cases where idle funds are available either for project expenditure or investment, but it is also relevant in cases where project funds would have to be raised through a special levy. If the voters reject the tax levy, the jurisdiction, of course, would not have the opportunity to invest these funds; however, taxpayers would have that opportunity themselves through individual, personal investments. In such instances, the question becomes: Would the citizens be better off allocating their resources to this project or investing the money elsewhere?

2. The possibility of consumption today rather than tomorrow is highly prized (if owners must wait before gaining access to their resources, compensation in the form of interest payment is expected in return for deferred gratification).
3. Inflation erodes the buying power of money.[2]

Put a dollar bill under your mattress tonight, then pull it out in four or five years and you will see the point clearly. Because your dollar has gained no interest under your mattress, it will not have kept pace with rising prices and will not buy as much as it would have if spent today. You would have to have something more than one dollar in four or five years in order to possess as much value as your dollar has today.

For purposes of analysis, equivalent values for the present and future need to be calculated—in other words, adjustments must be made for the time value of money. A "compounding" factor can be used to calculate the "future value" of a given quantity of current resources. Alternatively, a "discounting" factor can be used to calculate the "present value" of a given quantity of future resources to see how much buying power in today's dollars it will have at that point in the future. The compounding factor will be:

$$(1 + i)^n$$

where
i = interest rate
n = the number of interest periods

The formula for calculating the future value of a given quantity of current resources is:

$$F = P(1 + i)^n$$

where
F = future resources
P = present resources
i = interest rate
n = the number of interest periods

Alternatively, a given quantity of future resources may be discounted to reveal its present value by using the following formula:

$$P = F\left(\frac{1}{(1 + i)^n}\right)$$

where P would reflect the amount of current dollars possessing value equivalent to the specified amount of future dollars.

---

[2]A. John Vogt and Samuel H. Owen Jr., "Cost Calculations for Lease-Purchase Decisions: Methods," in *A Guide to Municipal Leasing*, ed. A. John Vogt and Lisa A. Cole (Chicago: Municipal Finance Officers Association, 1983), 116–117.

Table 13-1 Estimated Revenues and Costs for the Swimming Pool Proposal

Year	Revenues	Costs	Net Revenues
1	$ 0	$ 350,000	–$350,000
2	0	750,000	–750,000
3	110,000	110,000	0
4	135,000	110,000	25,000
5	155,000	110,000	45,000
6	175,000	120,000	55,000
7	195,000	125,000	70,000
8	210,000	130,000	80,000
9	230,000	135,000	95,000
10	250,000	140,000	110,000
11	260,000	145,000	115,000
12	260,000	150,000	110,000
13	265,000	160,000	105,000
14	265,000	170,000	95,000
15	270,000	180,000	90,000
16	270,000	190,000	80,000
17	275,000	200,000	75,000
Total	$3,325,000	$3,275,000	$ 50,000

SCENARIO: MAYBERRY, NORTH CAROLINA

Trey Dixon, the director of parks and recreation for the town of Mayberry, North Carolina, had hired two college interns, Larry Pendergrass and Emile Busby, to assist with various analytic projects. One of the interns was plainly bewildered.

"I guess I screwed up this analysis the director wanted," Larry confided. "I worked up some cost and revenue figures for the swimming pool proposal and showed him that we would break even on our investment in seventeen years and start to gain some net revenues at that point, but he wasn't impressed [see Table 13-1]. He kept talking about 'opportunity costs' and 'present value' and asked me to recalculate the numbers. I was too embarrassed to tell him that I didn't know what he was talking about. Do you have any idea what he meant?"

"I think so," Emile replied. "It all has to do with choices about the use of resources and the different benefits for each choice. When I pick one option, I lose the opportunity for the other benefits—hence the name, 'opportunity costs.' I seem to recall that most analysts calculate opportunity costs conservatively as the difference between the value of using the money now versus investing it, adjusted for the difference between what a dollar is worth today and what a dollar will be worth in a few years, since investment is one of the options I could pick."

"You've got to be kidding, Emile! You haven't invested a dime in your life. You are Mr. Immediate Gratification, himself."

"This is theoretical, Larry. Theoretically, I could invest a dollar and earn interest, or I could spend it and have the benefit of whatever I buy. The difference between the cumulative value of something I buy today and the cumulative value of a safe investment is the *opportunity cost*. You can figure the *present value* of a dollar available sometime in the future by *discounting* it for the effect of inflation between now and then. I really don't think it's too tough to do."

"What does all of that have to do with my projection of costs and revenues for a new outdoor swimming pool and superslide?"

"It's a multiyear projection, and the director doesn't want the changing value of money to distort the analysis."

DISCOUNT FACTOR

Calculating the present value of a future dollar is not particularly difficult, but it does require the analyst to exercise judgment. The calculation depends on an estimate of the rate of interest that could be earned on an investment by the local government over the period of time in question or by the jurisdiction's taxpayers if the money is left in their hands. That projected interest rate, of course, is related to the analyst's expectations regarding inflation.[3]

Once an interest rate is projected, a discount factor for each year of the analysis can be calculated using the formula noted previously:

$$\text{Discount factor} = \frac{1}{(1 + i)^n}$$

where i is the interest rate and n is the number of years. By multiplying a future dollar amount by the relevant discount factor, its present value may be determined.

PRESENT VALUE CALCULATIONS

Revising the swimming pool analysis proved to be surprisingly simple—and the results were surprising, as well. Larry projected an interest rate of 7 percent and applied discount factors based on that estimate to his earlier analysis (see Table 13-2).

The proposed pool would be equipped with a giant slide in hopes of drawing large enough crowds to produce sufficient operating revenues from admissions and concessions to more than offset operating costs and eventually recover capital costs. Property and design costs were estimated at $350,000. Projected costs of the pool, slide, and related facilities came to $750,000. Land acquisition and facility design would occur the first year; construction would occur the second. Annual operating costs of $110,000 were projected for years three through five, followed by a gradual escalation to $200,000 in year seventeen. Revenues from pool admissions and concessions would not begin until the pool opened the third year and were projected

---

[3]In choosing a particular rate of interest for this calculation, the analyst may wish to consider current interest rates and the forecasts of leading economists. At best, however, the choice will probably involve some guesswork. Ideally, the rate selected will prove accurate in the long run, but minimally it should be deemed reasonable at the time by most consumers of the analysis.

From the Electronic Toolkit

Box 13-1 Finding Present Value and the Discount Factor

There is no specific Excel function for present value and discount factor calculations, but users may find it beneficial to insert their own formula into the spreadsheet. After the equation is entered once, the spreadsheet can be saved and the calculation can be repeated for different data.

First, enter the variable names or symbols (for example, "future resources" or "F=") in consecutive cells of a given column. Then, enter the appropriate numerical values into cells adjacent to the labels or symbols in the next column. (For directions on opening Excel and entering data refer to Box 2-1.) To calculate present value, the variables that must be entered are future resources, interest rate, and the number of interest periods. After the data are entered, type the equation into any cell using the names of the cells in which the data appear rather than the symbols. For example, if future resources were entered in cell B1, the interest rate in cell B2, and the number of interest periods in cell B3, enter "=(B1*(1/((1+B2)^B3)))" to calculate present value. Notice the importance of the placement of parentheses.

To calculate the discount factor, simply enter the appropriate equation. If using the same data as in the present value calculation, enter "=(1/((1+B2)^B3))" to find the discount factor. It is important to remember to use an equal sign when entering an equation in the spreadsheet. If the equal sign is forgotten, the computer will read the equation as text and will not complete the calculation.

by Larry at a modest level in the beginning but growing fairly rapidly with the projected development of new residential subdivisions in the vicinity.

The new table prepared by Larry once again showed deficits the first two years, as costs exceed revenues. Not until the fourth year do net revenues begin to appear. Although the application of discount factors yields present value deficits less substantial than raw figures for the first two years, their application in later years has an even greater effect on net revenues. As a result, the total net revenue of $50,000 based on raw dollar tabulation is shown to have a present value that is actually a deficit of $429,272. The problem is that the high-cost years come at the beginning of the project and therefore are discounted very little, while the high-revenue years come late in the period of analysis when discounts are more substantial.

"I'm really disappointed," muttered Larry. "I never expected the pool to be enough of a money-maker to pay back the full capital expense in ten years' time, but I thought a seventeen-year project would not be too tough to sell. I still think we need that pool even with a net cost of almost a half million dollars, but this present-value analysis is a real eye-opener."

UTILITY OF OPPORTUNITY COST ANALYSIS

An articulate proponent can sometimes mesmerize public officials into believing that a favored program or facility costing $1 million to establish and generating $100,000 per year in revenues will pay for itself in ten years' time. The arithmetic is

Table 13-2 Present Value Analysis of the Swimming Pool Proposal

Year	Revenues	Costs	Net Revenues	Discount Factor[a] ($i = 7\%$)	Present Value of Net Revenues[b]
1	0	$ 350,000	–$350,000	0.9346	–$327,110
2	0	750,000	–750,000	0.8734	–655,050
3	110,000	110,000	0	0.8163	0
4	135,000	110,000	25,000	0.7629	19,073
5	155,000	110,000	45,000	0.7130	32,085
6	175,000	120,000	55,000	0.6663	36,647
7	195,000	125,000	70,000	0.6227	43,589
8	210,000	130,000	80,000	0.5820	46,560
9	230,000	135,000	95,000	0.5439	51,671
10	250,000	140,000	110,000	0.5083	55,913
11	260,000	145,000	115,000	0.4751	54,637
12	260,000	150,000	110,000	0.4440	48,840
13	265,000	160,000	105,000	0.4150	43,575
14	265,000	170,000	95,000	0.3878	36,841
15	270,000	180,000	90,000	0.3624	32,616
16	270,000	190,000	80,000	0.3387	27,096
17	275,000	200,000	75,000	0.3166	23,745
Total	$3,325,000	$3,275,000	$ 50,000		–$429,272

[a]Discount factor = $1/(1+i)^n$ where i is the interest rate (7 percent in this case) and n is the number of years. In this example, for instance, the discount factor for the fifth year is $1/(1.07)^5$ or 0.7130.
[b]The present value is calculated by multiplying net revenue by the discount factor.

simple; unfortunately, its logic is simplistic. The calculation of opportunity costs would reveal a substantial deficit even after the tenth year. The project could still be a good idea, but public officials should make their decision with full awareness that it would not have paid for itself in the declared time period.

Box 13-2 Other Applications of Present Value Analysis

Present value analysis is likely to produce revealing insights in many local government situations, including the following:

- when a proposal requires a major up-front expenditure that proponents promise "will pay for itself" over a period of several years
- when user fees projected for a multiyear period are established to recover major capital costs incurred at the outset of the fee period
- when a grant provides start-up costs but requires the local government to continue the program into the future

SUGGESTED FOR FURTHER INFORMATION

Malan, Roland M., James R. Fountain Jr., Donald S. Arrowsmith, and Robert L. Lockridge II. "Analysis." In *Performance Auditing in Local Government,* 139–167. Chicago: Government Finance Officers Association, 1984.

McKenna, Christopher K. "Cost-Benefit Analysis." In *Quantitative Methods for Public Decision Making,* 127–163. New York: McGraw-Hill, 1980.

Thomas, Henry B., and Jeffrey I. Chapman. "Cost-Benefit Analysis: Theory and Use." In *Managing Public Systems: Analytic Techniques for Public Administration,* edited by Michael J. White, Ross Clayton, Robert Myrtle, Gilbert Siegel, and Aaron Rose, 291–318. Lanham, Md.: University Press of America, 1985.

Vogt, A. John, and Samuel H. Owen Jr. "Cost Calculations for Lease-Purchase Decisions: Methods," In *A Guide to Municipal Leasing,* edited by A. John Vogt and Lisa A. Cole, 115–145. Chicago: Municipal Finance Officers Association, 1983.

14

Identifying Full Costs of a Program

Local governments tend to understate the cost of individual programs or activities in much the same manner that most people would underestimate, say, the annual cost of operating their own automobiles.[1] In these estimates, car owners would probably include the cost of gasoline and oil; they might also include their monthly payments or some appropriate component of the initial purchase price if they bought the car outright. But unless very careful, most people would slip up somewhere. They might forget to distribute the down payment over the life of the car or neglect to include interest charges. They might forget to include insurance premiums, the charge for the extended warranty, maintenance and repair charges, the cost of tires, the new paint job, the tag fee, the charge for an operator's license, parking fees, or fines for occasional speeding tickets. Each of these costs is directly associated with the operation of a vehicle; omitting any would understate expenses. Other related expenses, such as the cost of a garage and driveway, in the case of homeowners, might not be eliminated by a decision to sell the car and use public transit; but in a full accounting of related expenses, these expenses should be included on a pro rata basis as well.

Understating the cost of a program or activity in local government is rarely the product of deliberate deceit. More often it is simply the result of overlooking expenses that are related to a program but budgeted elsewhere or allocated in a previous fiscal year.

Unless all expenses associated with a program are identified, the cost of that program will be understated and comparisons with similar programs offered by other entities, or even comparisons over time in a single jurisdiction, will be inaccurate and misleading. Incomplete estimates of program costs are especially troublesome when a local government's decision makers are considering major program changes or service delivery alternatives.

SCENARIO: BARROW, MAINE

The city council of Barrow, Maine, had just adopted the budget for the upcoming year, and the budget director and her assistant were relaxing in her office, cele-

---

[1]E.S. Savas compared actual costs for various services with budget figures in sixty-eight jurisdictions and discovered actual costs 30 percent greater than the figures shown on budget pages. See E. S. Savas, "How Much Do Government Services Really Cost?" *Urban Affairs Quarterly* 15 (September 1979): 23–42.

brating the high points and commiserating over the low points of the previous months. Suddenly, the budget director interrupted the conversation with what seemed a strange question.

"What kind of a budget would you say we have?"

"A program budget," the budget analyst responded.

"A program budget?"

"Yes. Sure. We call them 'activities,' but each page describes a program and reports all of its costs."

"All of its costs?"

"Yeah. I think so."

The budget director shook her head. "Three years ago, the city council adopted a policy calling for full-cost recovery by the various internal service funds and for all services having user fees. Departmental charges for equipment maintenance, information services, the print shop, and all the other internal services are supposed to cover all their costs. So are the user fees for fee-supported outside services, such as the team fees for softball."

"We do that, don't we?"

"I don't think so. We cover the amount shown on the program's budget page, but I think we're underreporting our costs. And, if I'm correct, then our fees are falling short of full-cost recovery."

"What costs do you think we're missing?" asked the budget analyst.

"Well, I'm not sure we're including all the costs of employee benefits with each program, for one thing. We're not allocating costs for administrative overhead, for another. Some of the costs of the finance department, the personnel department, and other administrators here at city hall should be allocated to the various programs that benefit from the services they provide. I'll bet that we also badly understate various overhead costs associated with our facilities. We don't even charge building rental."

"Building rental? The city owns these buildings. Why should a department have a rental charge?"

"The building wasn't free. Some form of rental or depreciation for all capital items would more accurately reflect the costs of providing a particular program."

DETERMINING FULL COSTS

The budget director and budget analyst continued to discuss various costs that might be missed in the current budget format and service fee analyses. By the end of their conversation, the list was rather long, and the budget analyst had offered to explore the matter more systematically.

A review of available reference materials led the budget analyst to the discovery of two alternate paths for assigning full costs:

- *Activity-Based Costing (ABC)*—a rigorous costing method that typically relies on the logging of work activities, work sampling, or other means to achieve a high degree of precision in assigning direct and indirect costs to a work activity as part of a detailed accounting system.

- *Program Costing through Estimates and General Allocation Formulas (traditional cost accounting)*—a less rigorous method of assigning direct and indirect costs to activities or clusters of activities (that is, "programs") based on allocation formulas deemed "reasonable."

The greater precision possible through ABC was appealing, but after learning a few details the analyst recognized that the data collection requirements of ABC would impose a heavy burden not only on the finance department but also on the operating departments. "Maybe someday we will be ready for activity-based costing," the

Box 14-1 Activity-Based Costing

Developed in the private sector and designed especially to meet the needs of manufacturing industries, activity-based costing (ABC) offers managers a higher degree of precision than traditional cost-accounting systems in accounting for all costs of a given product or service. This can be particularly valuable to managers as they set out to emphasize profitable product lines, deemphasize less profitable lines, control overhead and production costs, make outsourcing decisions, and assign prices to their products. In a true ABC system, costs are assigned to a given activity (typically a distinct function within a program), based on that activity's consumption of resources. All costs associated with the activity, whether direct (for example, materials and labor directly involved in production) or indirect (for example, administrative support within and beyond the department, as well as other overhead costs), are recorded either as they occur or by a method far more precise than general allocation formulas typical of traditional cost accounting systems.

Some proponents of ABC draw a particularly sharp contrast with traditional cost accounting systems.

> Traditional cost accounting arbitrarily allocates nondirect overhead costs, a method that corrupts cost integrity. To ABC . . . , allocation is a dirty word. ABC . . . resolves misallocations by using resource and activity drivers that reflect unique consumption patterns and link cause and effect to the cost-assignment process.[1]

In earlier eras, overhead costs often were minor portions of total product costs. General approximations of overhead imposed only minor inaccuracies in the bottom line. In today's economy, overhead commands a bigger share of the total cost of products and services. Apportioning overhead on a pro rata basis according to employee counts, budget appropriations, or other arbitrary methods may introduce substantial inaccuracies. Labor-intensive services might not require any greater overhead service than others, for example, but if overhead is assigned based on proportions of full-time equivalent employees, full-cost figures are inappropriately inflated. ABC offers an appealing level of precision that overcomes such inaccuracies, but the system imposes a heavy data collection burden that, so far, has limited its adoption in the public sector.

[1]Gary Cokins, Alan Stratton, and Jack Helbling, *An ABC Manager's Primer: Straight Talk on Activity-Based Costing* (Montvale, N.J.: Institute of Management Accountants, 1993), 11.

Box 14-1 *(Continued)*

CONVERTING A TRADITIONAL COST ACCOUNTING SYSTEM TO ABC

A city or county with a traditional cost accounting system might divide its recreation program to capture separate costs for its swimming pools, community center, and other recreation programs.[2] Each would include direct costs for wages, supplies, and so forth, plus a share of the costs from the local government's "overhead pools" (for example, buildings and maintenance, engineering, law, finance, and administration). Costs from the first two of these pools—buildings and maintenance, engineering—might be divided among operating programs based on a given program's share of total fixed assets; costs from the third and fourth overhead pools—law, finance—might be allocated based on a given program's budget as a percentage of all nonoverhead budgets; and costs from the fifth pool—administration—assigned based on a given program's share of all nonoverhead employees.

Although each allocation formula is tied to a generally plausible rationale, none reflects a cause-and-effect relationship precisely. The time and effort of the director of administration and the costs incurred for printing, copying, and liability insurance—all included in the overhead pool for administration—are only roughly proportional to a program's share of local government employees. Controversial programs will require disproportionate amounts of administrative time; programs with high risk exposure will require disproportionate liability insurance; and swimming pools will require fewer printing and copying services than other recreation programs.

To convert this traditional cost accounting system to ABC, each of the three program categories would be subdivided to establish more precise activities within each program. Furthermore, each of the five overhead pools would be divided into activities so that overhead costs assigned to a program activity would be based not on an allocation formula but instead on the performance of an overhead activity that directly benefits the program.

A WORD OF CAUTION

Organizations often overstate their use of techniques deemed to be "progressive" or "advanced." Over the years, for example, many have claimed the use of zero-based budgeting, cost-benefit analysis, and benchmarking on the strength of practices that only faintly resembled the actual technique. It is likely that some organizations adopting a formula-based allocation approach to full-cost accounting, commendable as that step may be, will nevertheless overstate their accomplishment by calling it ABC. Other local governments following their lead should understand that, although they may have substantially upgraded their cost accounting system and done so in a most pragmatic way, their revised system may still not constitute true activity-based costing.

---

[2]This example is based on an assessment of the advisability of upgrading the cost accounting system of the city of Wooster, Ohio, as reported in Richard E. Brown, Mark J. Myring, and Cadillac G. Gard, "Activity-Based Costing in Government: Possibilities and Pitfalls," *Public Budgeting and Finance* (Summer 1999): 3–21.

analyst thought, "but right now, even the less ambitious approach will be a big step forward—and will be a lot more practical to do."

Although he felt a little guilty for passing up the chance to promote something as "cutting edge" as ABC, the analyst decided it would be more prudent, given current staff resources, to propose a less ambitious step forward in cost accounting. He would recommend that the city more conscientiously track direct costs by program whenever possible and use allocation formulas for assigning less easily tracked direct costs as well as overhead costs to get a more complete picture of full costs (traditional cost accounting). Accordingly, he set out to develop five worksheets for identifying the costs of a selected local government program or activity.

WORKSHEETS

Personal services—salaries, wages, and fringe benefits—are a major expense in most local government programs. By compiling information that more accurately identifies employee time devoted to a given program and excludes time directed elsewhere, a better picture of program costs begins to emerge. Worksheet 14-1 calls for

1. identification of all positions directly engaged in the selected program or activity
2. staffing of each such position in full-time equivalents (FTEs; for example, if the employee works twenty hours per week year round, the FTE is 0.5; if the position is filled by a seasonal employee working forty hours per week for three months, the FTE is 0.25)
3. estimation of the percentage of each employee's time on the job *spent on the selected program* (for example, a full-time employee devoting twenty hours per week to the program would have 0.5 recorded in this column, as would a twenty-hour per week employee devoting ten hours to the program)
4. notation of annual salary or wages for each position on a full-time basis (or the average, if several employees engaged in the program have the same title)
5. computation of the product of columns 2, 3, and 4 (the sum of column 5 plus total overtime payments for the program captures the salaries and wages of personnel directly engaged in the program)

Worksheet 14-2 addresses fringe benefit costs. The person-years devoted to the program and covered by specified benefits are multiplied by the cost per person-year for those benefits to derive total fringe benefit costs.

Worksheet 14-3 addresses other operating expenses. Common expenses such as supplies, building expenses, vehicles, equipment, insurance, and contractual services are identified on the form, but many programs have unusual expense items that should also be identified and included in the total.

Capital items and internal services deserve special attention in calculating program expenses. The costs of acquiring and maintaining buildings and vehicles, for example, often are not reflected in the budget of the program that benefits from their use. The building may have been constructed years ago with resources from the sale of bonds, the debt service for which is budgeted in another activity. Automobiles

Worksheet 14-1 Salaries and Wages of Personnel for a Selected Program/Activity

Titles of Positions Directly Engaged in Selected Program/Activity[a] (1)	No. of Employees (in full-time equivalents) (2)	Fraction of Time on the Job Spent on Selected Program/Activity (3)	Annual Expenditure per Person-Year ($) (4)	Total (2) × (3) × (4) (5)
			$	$

Total overtime payment for selected program/activity[b]: $ _____

Total salary and wage costs: $ _____

Source: Adapted from Columbia University, Public Technology, Inc., and the International City Management Association, Evaluating Residential Refuse Collection Costs: A Workbook for Local Government and Worksheet Supplement (Washington, D.C.: Public Technology, Inc., 1978).

a Include supervisory and support personnel (for example, secretaries, clerks, custodians) from the same department.

b For overtime figure, see budget or financial records.

Box 14-2 Making Cost Worksheets

Some administrators will find that assembling cost worksheets can be simplified using techniques similar to those used for preparing work-distribution charts (see Box 7-1). To make a cost worksheet, enter the column labels and the data that correspond to the labels. (For directions on opening Excel and entering data refer to Box 2-1.)

After the data are entered, Excel can do various calculations. In Worksheet 14-1 the figures in the right-hand column indicate the products of the data in each row. For this worksheet the product for each row of data in columns B through D needs to be found and these products must appear in column E. In cell E2 enter "=B2*C2*D2" in order to multiply the data from the previous columns. The product will appear in cell E2.

Another method for multiplying data is to use the PRODUCT function. Simply enter the command and the range of data being multiplied. In this example, enter "=PRODUCT(B2:D2)." (An alternative to typing this instruction would be to use the Function choice (fx) from the Insert menu. The fx symbol also appears on the toolbar.)

To copy either formula for the other cells in the column, the calculation may be entered manually by retyping the commands and changing the names of the multipliers. For example, in cell E3 enter "=B3*C3*D3" or "=PRODUCT(B3:D3)." But there is a quicker method for entering these formulas. After entering the formula in cell E2, highlight that cell and move the cursor to the lower, right-hand corner of the cell. Wait for a thin, black cross to appear. Then click and hold the mouse down and drag it down through the number of cells that need the same formula. Release the mouse and the products will be displayed.

Other functions that may be useful in worksheets like these are SUM and QUOTIENT. These commands are used in exactly the same manner as described for the "product" function. Simply enter the command and then enter the range of the affected data. For example, Worksheet 14-1 calls for a grand total of the entries in the right-hand column (the fifth column, alternatively called column E). To find the total of column E, enter "=SUM(E2:E13)." By using these functions in cost worksheets, calculations may be performed more easily and more reliably.

assigned to the program may have been purchased last year, with this year's budget showing no acquisition costs whatsoever. The expense of maintaining buildings and vehicles may be reflected only in the budgets of the internal service departments responsible for those maintenance activities. In such cases, program expenses are understated, making the program appear less costly than it actually is.

A more accurate statement of program expenses would assign proportionate capital and maintenance expenses to the programs that derive benefits from those facilities and equipment. Various options exist for determining reasonable assessments. Annual costs for building "rental," for example, may be the program's proportionate share (based on square footage) of an annualized capital assessment tied to the building's acquisition or replacement cost. Alternatively, they may be based on the annual debt service requirements—principal and interest—to retire the bonds

Worksheet 14-2 Fringe Benefit Costs for a Selected Program/Activity

Benefit (1)	Person-Years Devoted to Program/Activity That Are Covered by Specified Benefit[a] (2)	Expenditure per Person-Year ($) (3)	Total (2) × (3) (4)
FICA/Social Security	_____	$ _____	$ _____
Insurance			
A. Hospital/medical	_____	_____	_____
B. Dental	_____	_____	_____
C. Life	_____	_____	_____
D. Disability	_____	_____	_____
E. Workers' compensation	_____	_____	_____
F. Unemployment compensation	_____	_____	_____
Retirement contribution	_____	_____	_____
Supplemental retirement payments	_____	_____	_____
Deferred compensation/401(k)[b]	_____	_____	_____
Uniforms and cleaning	_____	_____	_____
Safety equipment (for example, gloves, shoes)	_____	_____	_____
Longevity or bonus pay	_____	_____	_____
Other	_____	_____	_____
		Total fringe benefits	$ _____

Source: Adapted from Columbia University, Public Technology, Inc., and the International City Management Association, *Evaluating Residential Refuse Collection Costs: A Workbook for Local Government* and *Worksheet Supplement* (Washington, D.C.: Public Technology, Inc., 1978) and William C. Rivenbark, ed., *A Guide to the North Carolina Local Government Performance Measurement Project* (Chapel Hill: University of North Carolina Institute of Government, 2001).

[a] Full-time equivalent of employees who are engaged at least partially in the selected program and who are entitled to benefit coverage multiplied by the fraction of their time spent on that program.

[b] Include here only if not charged to salaries/wages (see Worksheet 14-1).

Worksheet 14-3 Other Operating Expenses for a Selected Program/Activity

Category (1)	Total Annual Expenses (2)	% Applicable to Selected Program (3)	Total (2) × (3) (4)
Supplies			
_____	$_____	_____	$_____
_____	_____	_____	_____
Others	_____	_____	_____
Building expenses	_____	_____	_____
telephone	_____	_____	_____
utilities	_____	_____	_____
rent[a]	_____	_____	_____
maintenance	_____	_____	_____
_____	_____	_____	_____
other	_____	_____	_____
Vehicles			
rent[a]	_____	_____	_____
operation[b]	_____	_____	_____
maintenance[b]	_____	_____	_____
Other equipment			
maintenance and repair	_____	_____	_____
_____	_____	_____	_____
_____	_____	_____	_____
Purchases for resale	_____	_____	_____
Training and travel	_____	_____	_____
Fees and licenses	_____	_____	_____
Advertising	_____	_____	_____
Uniform purchase or rental	_____	_____	_____
Dues/memberships/subscriptions	_____	_____	_____
MIS/Data Processing/IT/GIS	_____	_____	_____
Insurance	_____	_____	_____
_____	_____	_____	_____
_____	_____	_____	_____
Contractual services			
_____	_____	_____	_____
_____	_____	_____	_____

Worksheet 14-3 *(Continued)*

Category (1)	Total Annual Expenses (2)	% Applicable to Selected Program (3)	Total (2) × (3) (4)
Contract administration			
Other operating expenses			
		Total[c]	$

Source: Adapted from Columbia University, Public Technology, Inc., and the International City Management Association, *Evaluating Residential Refuse Collection Costs: A Workbook for Local Government* and *Worksheet Supplement* (Washington, D.C.: Public Technology, Inc., 1978) and William C. Rivenbark, ed., *Guide to the North Carolina Local Government Performance Measurement Project* (Chapel Hill: University of North Carolina Institute of Government, 2001).

[a]If the local government is renting office space and vehicles for this program, those amounts should be entered here. If the local government possesses its own program facilities and vehicles, it is still appropriate to enter "rental" of some kind (perhaps based on annual allocations for replacement, on a depreciation schedule, on debt service, or on market rates) rather than to imply that they are "free."

[b]Fuel, parts, and maintenance expenses should be recorded here, except when such expenses would duplicate previous entries (for example, if repair personnel are listed on Worksheet 14-1, labor charges should not be repeated here).

[c]"Cost recovery" is excluded from the tabulation of operating expenses in this worksheet. Fairness of comparison among multiple programs or options will demand uniform treatment of program receipts, sometimes labeled "cost recovery" and reported in the budget as an expenditure reduction and sometimes labeled "general revenue" and having no such effect on reported program expenditures. Uniformity is achieved here by treating all receipts as revenues to be considered elsewhere, rather than as a reduction of operating expenses.

sold to finance construction of the building. Vehicle "rental" may be based on a depreciation schedule (see Chapter 11) or annual contributions to a vehicle replacement fund in amounts sufficient to have enough money available to purchase a replacement vehicle when the current vehicle is no longer serviceable. An alternate approach for annualizing selected capital costs, based on simple rules of thumb, is shown in Table 14-1. Vehicle maintenance assessments should be based on actual costs or a proportionate share of general maintenance expenses.

Worksheet 14-4 addresses the tabulation of overhead costs—a program's proportionate share of the expense of various administrative and support services provided by other departments of the local government. The city manager's time, for example, is divided among the various programs of the local government. Similarly, the personnel department provides services on an organizationwide basis. Each program derives benefits from these services and is spared the trouble and expense of performing various functions itself. It is only proper that a proportionate share of the costs of overhead agencies be borne by the various programs of the local govern-

Table 14-1 Rule of Thumb Alternatives for Annualizing Capital Costs

Costs to be Annualized	Rule of Thumb Options
Furniture and office equipment	10 percent of acquisition cost
Maintenance/construction equipment	12 percent of acquisition cost
Automobiles and light equipment	30 percent of acquisition cost
Medium/heavy motor equipment	16 percent of acquisition cost
Data processing equipment	20 percent of acquisition cost
Light/miscellaneous equipment	10 percent of acquisition cost
Other equipment	based on judgment of useful life
Rental equipment	report rental payments
Buildings	2 percent of the original construction cost plus capitalized renovations
Rental space	report rental payments

Source: William C. Rivenbark and K. Lee Carter, "Benchmarking and Cost Accounting: The North Carolina Approach," *Journal of Public Budgeting, Accounting and Financial Management* 12 (Spring 2000): 132.
Note: These rules of thumb are used to simplify and standardize cost accounting procedures among the cities and counties participating in the North Carolina Local Government Performance Measurement Project. A local government attempting to identify the full costs of an activity should also consider annual debt service for capital items secured through debt financing. Alternatively, annual capital costs for an activity could be derived more precisely using depreciation calculations described in Chapter 11.

ment on some proportionate basis. The basis used in Worksheet 14-4 varies from one overhead item to another, although most frequently it is the program's number of full-time equivalent employees as a percentage of the entire local government workforce. The assumption—an imperfect one, at best—is that a program that includes 10 percent of the local government's workforce probably also receives about 10 percent of the benefit of the city manager's office, the finance department, the city clerk's office, and other overhead agencies. Other bases of allocation are used for some overhead items on Worksheet 14-4, with still other options noted in Table 14-2.

Worksheet 14-5 combines the figures from the other four worksheets to arrive at a cost summary for the program. That total may differ substantially from the amount listed for the activity in the local government's annual budget. It provides a much improved basis for calculating efficiency measures (for example, unit costs), for comparing program costs with those of other jurisdictions (assuming similar cost-accounting methods), for documenting program costs in grant applications, and for developing service fees.

UTILITY OF FULL-COST IDENTIFICATION

A true program budget reports all the costs associated with a given program. A basic premise of such a system is that full-cost reports will help policy makers in their deliberations regarding needs, priorities, and options. Systems that presume to report full costs but fail to do so are deceptive and may contribute to ill-advised decisions.

Worksheet 14-4 Overhead Costs for Selected Program/Activity

Overhead Agency	Total Expenditures of Overhead Agency	Basis of Allocation to Selected Program/Activity[a]	Overhead Agency Expenditures Allocated to Selected Program/Activity
Executive/mayor/manager	$	Program's FTEs as percentage of total FTEs[b]	$
Governing body/council		Program's FTEs as percentage of total FTEs[b]	
Finance, comptroller, budget, treasurer		Program's FTEs as percentage of total FTEs[b]	
Billing and collections		Percentage of expenditures attributable to program/activity	
Clerk		Program's FTEs as percentage of total FTEs[b]	
Attorney/legal		Program's FTEs as percentage of total FTEs[b]	
Central support services (for example, stockroom, mail services, printing)		Percentage of stock requisitions, postage charges, copies attributable to program activity	
General services		Program's FTEs as percentage of total FTEs[b]	
MIS/data processing/IT/GIS[c]		Program's FTEs as percentage of total FTEs[b,c]	
Purchasing		Program's number of purchase orders as percentage of total	
Human resources/personnel		Program's FTEs as percentage of total FTEs[b]	
Risk management		Program's FTEs as percentage of total FTEs[b]	
Liability insurance		Program's FTEs as percentage of total FTEs[b]	
Property insurance		Program's square footage as percentage of total	
Insurance on equipment and vehicles		Program's vehicles/equipment as percentage of total	
		Total Overhead Costs:	$

Source: Adapted from Columbia University; Public Technology, Inc., and the International City Management Association, *Evaluating Residential Refuse Collection Costs: A Workbook for Local Government* and *Worksheet Supplement* (Washington, D.C.: Public Technology, Inc., 1978) and William C. Rivenbark, ed., *A Guide to the North Carolina Local Government Performance Measurement Project* (Chapel Hill: University of North Carolina Institute of Government, 2001).

Note: FTE = full-time equivalent employee. MIS = management information services. IT = information technology. GIS = geographic information system.

[a] An alternate basis of allocation may be chosen that provides a more reasonable representation of actual expenditures attributable to the support of the selected program. See Table 14-2.

[b] Alternatively, the selected program/activity's salaries and wages as a percentage of the local government's salary and wage total.

[c] Include here only if not included as a direct charge on Worksheet 14-3.

Table 14-2 Possible Allocation Bases for Various Indirect (Overhead) Cost Assignments

Costs	Allocation Base
Accounting	Number of invoices attributable to a given activity, as a percentage of all invoices
Building maintenance	Fixed assets of the activity, as a percentage of all fixed assets
Custodial service	Square feet of space assigned to the activity, as a percentage of total square feet maintained by custodial service
Data processing	Percentage of central processing unit time devoted to the activity
Engineering	Fixed assets of the activity, as a percentage of all fixed assets
Finance	Budgeted expenses of the activity, as a percentage of the local government's entire budget, or number of accounting transactions attributable to the activity, as a percentage of all transactions
General administration	Number of full-time equivalent (FTE) employees assigned to the activity, as a percentage of the entire workforce
Insurance	Number of FTEs assigned to the activity, as a percentage of the entire workforce
Law department	Budgeted expenses of the activity, as a percentage of the local government's entire budget
Mayor/Manager's office	Number of FTEs assigned to the activity, as a percentage of the entire workforce
Payroll preparation	Number of FTEs assigned to the activity, as a percentage of the entire workforce
Personnel/Human Resources	Number of FTEs assigned to the activity, as a percentage of the entire workforce
Purchasing	Number of purchase orders attributable to the activity, as a percentage of all purchase orders
Rent	Square feet of space assigned to the activity, as a percentage of total square feet
Telephone	Number of phones assigned to the activity, as a percentage of all telephones
Treasurer	Number of checks attributable to the activity, as a percentage of all checks
Utilities	Square feet of space assigned to the activity, as a percentage of total square feet
Vehicles	Number of miles driven on tasks associated with the activity, as a percentage of all miles driven[a]

Sources: Adapted from Mark D. Abrahams and Mary Noss Reavely, "Activity-Based Costing: Illustrations from the State of Iowa," *Government Finance Review* 14 (April 1998): 16; Richard E. Brown, Mark J. Myring, and Cadillac G. Gard, "Activity-Based Costing in Government: Possibilities and Pitfalls," *Public Budgeting and Finance* 19 (Summer 1999): 3–21; and William C. Rivenbark and K. Lee Carter, "Benchmarking and Cost Accounting: The North Carolina Approach," *Journal of Public Budgeting, Accounting and Financial Management* 12 (Spring 2000): 130.

[a]Alternatively, vehicle costs for the activity could be derived from actual maintenance and repair costs incurred for the upkeep of the activity's vehicles, plus annual capital costs based on depreciation (see Chapter 11).

Worksheet 14-5 Cost Summary for Selected Program/Activity

Total personnel salaries and wages from Worksheet 14-1 $ _____

Total fringe benefits from Worksheet 14-2   _____

Other operating costs from Worksheet 14-3   _____

Total overhead costs from Worksheet 14-4   _____

Total cost $ _____

Source: Adapted from Columbia University, Public Technology, Inc., and the International City Management Association, *Evaluating Residential Refuse Collection Costs: A Workbook for Local Government* and *Worksheet Supplement* (Washington, D.C.: Public Technology, Inc., 1978).

Unless they have identified the full costs of a program, officials are unable to answer some very basic questions: How much are we paying for this service? What is the cost per unit of service? How does our cost compare with that of other jurisdictions? How does the cost of this service compare with the costs of various other services offered by our city or county government? How much of the cost is being recovered by current service fees?

Box 14-3 Uniform Cost Accounting for
Comparative Performance Measurement Projects

Several projects undertaken in the past decade have been carefully designed to permit reliable comparison of cost and performance data among participating local governments. Examples include a large-scale project sponsored by the International City/County Management Association; separate projects in North Carolina, South Carolina, and Tennessee; and substate regional projects involving local governments in the vicinity of Kansas City, Missouri, and Syracuse, New York. To achieve their objective of cost comparability, each project had to secure agreement among participants on a set of uniform cost accounting rules. Otherwise, costs assigned to a given program by one jurisdiction might be counted differently or even excluded from the program costs reported by a counterpart, thereby distorting the comparison.

Individual local governments that attempt to compare their own performance and cost data with data collected independently from other units face a formidable task. Measures of service quality often can be compared with relatively few compatibility problems. Similarly, measures of efficiency that relate units of service to units of employee time (for example, staff-hours per application processed, curb-miles swept per operator-hour) are easily compared in most cases. In contrast, cost data or measures of efficiency that rely on cost accounting systems (for example, unit costs for a given service) are less easily compared because of wide variation in cost accounting practices from one local government to another. The desire to resolve this incompatibility is a major reason for establishing a cooperative performance measurement project.

Box 14-4 Other Applications of Cost Accounting

Cost accounting systems that identify the full costs associated with a given service or activity facilitate analysis and bolster accountability. Among the uses of such systems are:

- efficiency measurement, when combined with output data, for performance reports and operations reviews
- analysis of expenditure trends for a given service, including changes in unit costs over time
- the establishment of user fees to recover all or a specified portion of service expenses
- reconsideration of resource allocations in light of citizen priorities, service demands, and more precise cost information

SUGGESTED FOR FURTHER INFORMATION

Abrahams, Mark D., and Mary Noss Reavely. "Activity-Based Costing: Illustrations from the State of Iowa." *Government Finance Review* 14 (April 1998): 15–20.

Anderson, Bridget M. "Using Activity-Based Costing for Efficiency and Quality." *Government Finance Review* (June 1993): 7–9.

Brimson, James A., and John Antos. *Activity-Based Management for Service Industries, Government Entities, and Nonprofit Organizations.* New York: John Wiley & Sons, 1994.

Brown, Richard E., Mark J. Myring, and Cadillac G. Gard. "Activity-Based Costing in Government: Possibilities and Pitfalls." *Public Budgeting and Finance* 19 (Summer 1999): 3–21.

Cokins, Gary, Alan Stratton, and Jack Helbling. *An ABC Manager's Primer: Straight Talk on Activity-Based Costing.* Montvale, N.J.: Institute of Management Accountants, 1993.

Columbia University, Public Technology, Inc., and the International City Management Association. *Evaluating Residential Refuse Collection Costs: A Workbook for Local Government and Worksheet Supplement.* Washington, D.C.: Public Technology, 1978.

Friedman, Marvin. "Calculating Compensation Costs." In *Budget Management: A Reader in Local Government Financial Management,* edited by Jack Rabin, W. Bartley Hildreth, and Gerald J. Miller, 116–127. Athens, Ga.: Carl Vinson Institute of Government, University of Georgia, 1983. Reprinted from *The Use of Economic Data in Collective Bargaining* by Marvin Friedman. Washington, D.C.: U.S. Department of Labor, 1978.

Goldsmith, Stephen. "The ABCs of Competitive Government: The Indianapolis Experience." *Government Finance Review* 15, no. 5 (October 1999): 7–9.

Kehoe, Joseph, William Dodson, Robert Reeve, and Gustav Plato. *Activity-Based Management in Government.* Washington, D.C.: Coopers & Lybrand, 1995.

Kelley, Joseph T. *Costing Government Services: A Guide for Decision Making.* Washington, D.C.: Government Finance Officers Association, 1984.

Rivenbark, William C., ed. *A Guide to the North Carolina Local Government Performance Measurement Project.* Chapel Hill: University of North Carolina Institute of Government, 2001.

Rivenbark, William C., and K. Lee Carter. "Benchmarking and Cost Accounting: The North Carolina Approach." *Journal of Public Budgeting, Accounting and Financial Management* 12 (Spring 2000): 125–137.

Walters, Jonathan. "Government by the Numbers." *Governing* (April 2000): 30–32.

Weiss, Barbara. *Activity-Based Costing and Management: Issues and Practices in Local Government.* Chicago: Government Finance Officers Association, 1997.

15

Calculating Go-Away Costs for Privatization Decisions

Calculating the full costs of a program, including indirect and capital costs (see Chapter 14), strengthens the ability of local government officials to gauge program efficiency and assess the adequacy of fees for services. However, using the *full costs* of an in-house operation as the basis for a decision to contract for that service from an outside entity could lead the local government to a major mistake.

Several local governments at the forefront of efforts to apply the privatization tool wisely—including the cities of Phoenix, Indianapolis, and Charlotte—refrain from using full costs in such deliberations, opting instead for what they call "go-away costs" as the basis for their decisions. They recognize that in preparing for a privatization decision, two categories of local government costs must be identified: (1) *contract administration costs,* which include the costs of administering the contract and monitoring performance; and (2) *go-away costs,* which include only that portion of full costs of an in-house program or service that will actually *go away* when the service is produced by an outside entity.

The sum of contract administration costs and the bid price of an outside entity may be compared to go-away costs to assess the net gain or loss from a decision to contract. This procedure excludes from consideration all costs that will continue to be incurred by the local government following initiation of the contract. For example, a full-cost calculation for a given program probably includes portions of the salaries of the city or county manager, finance director, human resource director, and other management officials. It also includes annualized costs for capital equipment and facilities. In the event that the local government decides to contract for a given service, it is doubtful that the salaries of any of the key officials listed above will be reduced. Their costs will be redistributed among continuing programs, but they will not *go away.* On the other hand, if the contracted program is large, it is possible that the staff of payroll clerks in the finance department or personnel specialists in the human resources department might be reduced as a result. If previously shared capital equipment will now be retained by the other department and if vacated space will be filled by other in-house programs without any net reduction in local government expenditures, then these costs, although appropriately included in an accounting of full costs, should be excluded from go-away costs.

SCENARIO: BUCKAROO, WYOMING

"How could this happen?" wondered Herb Jada, budget officer for the city of Buckaroo. "This is going to be embarrassing."

Herb was already dreading the thought of trying to explain the budgeting fiasco that followed Buckaroo's heralded foray into privatization. Last fall the city had solicited bids from vendors for residential refuse collection services, fleet maintenance, and custodial services.

The city had attempted to be thorough in its analysis of the contracting option and, at the urging of vendors, had carefully calculated the full costs of the in-house refuse collection and fleet maintenance programs, including costs of facilities, capital equipment, and overhead. After all, the vendors had reminded the city that contractor costs for these items would be included in their bids, so full cost accounting by the city would simply ensure "a level playing field."

When bids were received and the cost comparison showed an advantage for privatization (see Table 15-1), Herb and others had eagerly recommended entering all three contracts. But now, putting the numbers for next year's budget together six months later, something is wrong. In frustration, Herb called a former classmate who was now on the budget staff of a city that had been involved in privatization for several years.

"I'm at a loss, Bob, and, unfortunately, so is our budget," Herb began. "We were planning our budget around an anticipated $300,000 in increased expenditures in the upcoming fiscal year, but that was supposed to be partially offset by almost $160,000 in savings from decisions to contract-out three formerly in-house services. I was anticipating the need for about $140,000 in new revenues, but the numbers come out to be more like $240,000 in needed revenue expansion. I cannot figure out where $100,000 of our contract savings went!"

After asking a few questions, Herb's friend spotted the problem. "You used full costs in your analysis rather than go-away costs," Bob said. "Look at the things you included as overhead costs—shares of the expenses of the manager's office, the finance department, things like that. Were the expenditures of any of those departments reduced following initiation of the contracts?"

"No, they weren't," Herb replied. "I see what you mean. We included them in the figures for in-house services in order to show our full costs, but most of those costs stayed in the organization even when the decision was made to contract-out these three services. No one asked the city manager and finance director to take a cut in pay just because a portion of their salaries had been in the overhead for a service that is no longer performed by a city department."

"Did the fleet maintenance contractor move into the city garage?" Bob inquired.

"No, they have their own facility."

"If you included facility costs in your full costing, did they go away with the decision to contract?"

Table 15-1 Full Cost of In-House Operation Compared to Low Bids

	In-House Full Costs	Contract Costs	Difference
Custodial Services			
Salaries/wages	$ 72,340		
Fringe benefits	16,638		
Other operating costs	18,500		
Overhead	18,364		
Low bid		$ 113,800	
Contract administration		4,000	
Total	$ 125,842	$ 117,800	$ 8,042
Fleet Maintenance			
Salaries/wages	$ 101,418		
Fringe benefits	22,343		
Other operating costs	23,727		
Overhead	25,201		
Low bid		$ 115,850	
Contract administration		10,000	
Total	$ 172,689	$ 125,850	$ 46,839
Residential Refuse Collection			
Salaries/wages	$ 191,430		
Fringe benefits	47,278		
Other operating costs	745,268		
Overhead	168,128		
Low bid		$1,037,000	
Contract administration		10,000	
Total	$1,152,104	$1,047,000	$105,104
		TOTAL	$159,985

"No, we still have the garage. The public works department is moving some of its offices and equipment in there. Those costs aren't going away either."

"You might also check to see if some transitional costs are affecting your budget," Bob suggested. "It's usually a good idea to handle staff reductions associated with privatization through attrition and reassignment, if you can, but sometimes that means carrying some extra personnel costs for a while. You might find some of the expenses there."

"It's a mess, isn't it, Bob?"

"Maybe, but you'll probably find that contracting for these services was a good idea—just not as beneficial as originally thought. This won't be a message that will be fun to deliver, but it is better that *you* discovered it rather than an elected official or a local critic."

"Thanks, Bob."

Table 15-2 Go Away Costs Compared to Contract Costs

| | In-House | | | |
	Full Costs	Go-Away Costs	Contract Costs	Savings via Contracting[a]
Custodial Services				
Salaries/wages	$ 72,340	$ 72,340		
Fringe benefits	16,638	16,638		
Other operating costs	18,500	18,300		
Overhead	18,364	0		
Low bid			$ 113,800	
Contract administration			4,000[b]	
Total	$ 125,842	$ 107,278	$ 117,800	−$10,522
Fleet Maintenance				
Salaries/wages	$ 101,418	$ 101,418		
Fringe benefits	22,343	22,343		
Other operating costs	23,727	23,727		
Overhead	25,201	8,500		
Low bid			$ 115,850	
Contract administration			10,000[b]	
Total	$ 172,689	$ 155,988	$ 125,850	$30,138
Residential Refuse Collection				
Salaries/wages	$ 191,430	$ 191,430		
Fringe benefits	47,278	47,278		
Other operating costs	745,268	745,268		
Overhead	168,128	103,250		
Low bid			$1,037,000	
Contract administration			10,000[b]	
Total	$1,152,104	$1,087,226	$1,047,000	$40,226
			TOTAL	$59,842

[a]Savings are the difference between go away costs and contract costs.
[b]The contract administration costs estimated by Buckaroo officials are minimal. Some authorities suggest 10 percent of the contract amount as a rule of thumb.

REANALYSIS IN BUCKAROO

Herb reanalyzed the contracting decisions, this time using go-away costs rather than full costs (Table 15-2).[1] The new numbers showed that Bob's prediction had been two-thirds correct: contracting-out the services had been the proper choice in two of the three services. Herb was now convinced, however, that Buckaroo should

[1]Distinguishing costs that will go away from those that will stay is less a matter of accounting than a process involving analysis of operations and negotiation with departmental officials who may try to preserve resources by keeping them out of the go-away category.

Box 15-1 Other Applications of Go-Away Costs Analysis

The usefulness of go-away costs is limited only by the range of possible contracting options in local government, which is to say the potential use of this technique is broad indeed. Although vendors will argue for full-cost comparisons (see Chapter 14), prudent cities and counties will make all their contracting decisions based on go-away costs instead.

have retained custodial services in-house. Luckily, that was the smallest of the three contracted operations. The new numbers also solved the mystery of the missing $100,000 in anticipated savings. Actual savings would be about $60,000 rather than $160,000.

Gathering his tables and his courage, Herb began walking down the hall to tell the city manager about his discovery. "This has been a valuable lesson," he thought. "I just wish I had learned it some easier way."

SUGGESTIONS FOR FURTHER READING

Martin, Lawrence L. "Evaluating Service Contracting." In *Management Information Service Report*, 25, no. 3, 1–14. Washington, D.C.: International City/County Management Association, March 1993.

16

Cost-Effectiveness Analysis:
A Truncated Version of Cost-Benefit Analysis

All managers would like to believe that the benefits derived from their programs exceed the costs. Furthermore, conscientious managers want to believe that the approach they have adopted to deliver a particular program provides a more favorable return relative to costs than would any other approach. Only rarely, however, are the costs and benefits associated with program alternatives—even the most obvious and most direct ones—identified and analyzed in a systematic fashion. This chapter introduces cost-effectiveness analysis, a truncated version of cost-benefit analysis that offers a practical decision-making tool applicable to cases where either of two conditions exists: (1) the costs of all alternatives are equal, or (2) the benefits of all alternatives are equal—or may be presumed to be equal.

Cases that do not meet these conditions—that is, cases in which one policy or program option carries costs and benefits that are complex and differ from the costs and benefits of other options—require the more complicated analytic technique of cost-benefit analysis.

COST-BENEFIT AND COST-EFFECTIVENESS ANALYSES

Although the focus here is on the simpler technique of cost-effectiveness analysis, a few of the fundamentals of cost-benefit analysis will be explored first. Cost-benefit analysis in its most sophisticated form can be quite complex. It is a technique designed to weigh all of an action's costs against all of its benefits to assist decision makers in their choices.

Part of the technique's complexity lies in the difficulty of identifying all costs and benefits associated with a given program or decision. Part lies in the difficulty of quantifying costs and benefits in comparable units of measurement (for example, dollars). Most easily recognized are the costs and benefits that are both tangible and direct (for example, labor, equipment, and energy costs associated with a given program and the value of a particular product). More difficult to identify and measure are intangible direct costs and benefits, indirect costs and benefits, and pecuniary costs and benefits. Indirect costs and benefits, often referred to as *spillover effects* or, in the jargon of cost-benefit analysis, as *externalities,* are often unanticipated and are especially difficult to identify.

Comprehensive cost-benefit analysis addresses each of these elements and provides decision makers with a method of assessing the return on a particular investment or comparing the relative advantages of a variety of options. Program options may be judged, for example, on net benefit (the difference between benefits and costs) or benefit-to-cost ratios.

Many administrative reports in local government are incorrectly portrayed by their authors as "cost-benefit analysis," when actually they fall short of the rigor required by this technique. Analysts conducting true cost-benefit analysis must sort out and quantify tangible costs and benefits to the local government, service recipients, and the broader society for each alternative; intangible costs and benefits; and net social benefits. Relevant considerations may include elasticity of demand and supply, pecuniary effects, shadow pricing, and redistribution effects. Readers confronting cases where neither the costs nor the benefits of a set of options are equal are encouraged to consult any of the more extensive texts on the subject of cost-benefit analysis for more thorough instruction. For the purposes here, however, the focus is on the analysis of options with (a) equivalent price tags, where the analyst seeks the alternative that will produce greatest benefits, or (b) equivalent benefits, where the search is for lowest cost. In either of these cases, the related, though simpler technique of cost-effectiveness analysis is appropriate.

SCENARIO: SURF CITY, FLORIDA

Surf City is a small Florida town of 12,000 people. Residents enjoy a broad range of municipal services, including refuse collection.

Christopher Hogan, the sanitation director of Surf City, has long taken pride in his small operation. For several years he has provided both residential and commercial refuse collection services, as well as special brush pickups, with a department consisting of only nine refuse collectors. Two three-person crews handle most of the residential collections, and the other three collectors provide commercial dumpster service, brush collection, and residential backup, as needed. Hogan used to think that he had a pretty lean staff, but recently he has begun to question that assumption. Over the last year and a half a parade of vendors has marched through his office singing the praises of different equipment options and reduced crew sizes.

"I've always been skeptical of the claims of salesmen," Hogan confided to his secretary following yet another vendor's spiel, "but several cities in the region have gone to two-person and even one-person crews, apparently with good results. Most of the salesmen have been downplaying the cost of their equipment and emphasizing reduced labor costs. I'm going to try to sort out all the major costs and benefits for various crew sizes and equipment types and see what makes the most sense."

DIRECT COSTS AND BENEFITS OF REFUSE
COLLECTION OPTIONS

Chris Hogan identified four equipment and employee configurations that he considered to be practical for residential refuse collection based on his own experience, the claims of various equipment vendors, and reports from sanitation directors in other communities. Although the costs varied from one option to another, all four would deliver comparable services or benefits—making cost-effectiveness analysis an appropriate technique for this case. The four alternatives were:

- three-person crews using rear-loading trucks (Option A, the current system)
- two-person crews using rear-loading trucks (Option B)
- two-person crews using side-loading trucks (Option C)
- one-person crews using side-loading trucks (Option D)

Each option addressed only basic residential refuse collection. Additional arrangements would have to be made for servicing businesses and for collecting brush and other yard waste.

The first alternative for residential refuse collection stood as the baseline against which the other alternatives could be compared. Currently, two three-person crews use rear loaders to cover all residential routes in Surf City. Three other drivers handle commercial service and brush collection, as well as provide backup coverage for the residential crews. Because this is the system now in place, its feasibility has been well established (see Table 16-1).

The premise of the second alternative is that two workers should be able to do the work that previously required three, with little, if any, modification of equipment. The basis for such a premise is normally that workers have been underutilized either because they have been required to exert less than a full day's effort or because of deployment problems, such as imbalanced routes. Hogan had his doubts about this alternative (Option B), but decided to include it anyway.

The third alternative (Option C) also offers crew-reduction advantages, but does so by means of revised equipment configurations offering labor-saving features. Side-loader trucks equipped with right-side steering from a curbside compartment make it more practical for the driver to help load the truck. This option accommodates the smaller crew size by reducing the length of the routes and adding a third residential refuse collection crew.

The fourth option (Option D) takes the third alternative one step further. The driver-collector becomes solely responsible for the collection of the refuse route. In such instances the side-loader vehicle is equipped with a hydraulic lift to partially or fully mechanize the system and make one-person operation feasible. Option D restores the backup crew availability that is eliminated in Option C.

After perusing a few books and articles on the use of cost-benefit analysis and a few others on cost-effectiveness analysis, Hogan was satisfied that he could apply the simpler of the two techniques to the analysis of his options. Because the benefits

Table 16-1 Equipment and Crew Requirements of Four Refuse Collection Options

	Option A	Option B	Option C	Option D
Crew 1	Residential Route *rear loader* 1 equipment operator 2 laborers	Residential Route *rear loader* 1 equipment operator 1 laborer	Residential Route *side loader* 1 equipment operator 1 laborer	Residential Route *side loader* 1 equipment operator
Crew 2	Residential Route *rear loader* 1 equipment operator 2 laborers	Residential Route *rear loader* 1 equipment operator 1 laborer	Residential Route *side loader* 1 equipment operator 1 laborer	Residential Route *side loader* 1 equipment operator
Crew 3	Commercial Route, Brush, and Residential Backup *front loader* 1 equipment operator	Commercial Route *front loader* 1 equipment operator	Residential Route *side loader* 1 equipment operator 1 laborer	Residential Route *side loader* 1 equipment operator
Crew 4	Commercial Route, Brush, and Residential Backup *front loader* 1 equipment operator	Commercial Route *front loader* 1 equipment operator	Commercial Route *front loader* 1 equipment operator	Commercial Route *front loader* 1 equipment operator
Crew 5	Commercial Route, Brush, and Residential Backup *rear loader* 1 equipment operator	Brush Collection and Residential Backup *rear loader* 1 equipment operator	Commercial Route *front loader* 1 equipment operator	Commercial Route *front loader* 1 equipment operator
Crew 6	None	None	Brush Collection *rear loader* staffed part-time by commercial route crews	Brush Collection and Residential Backup *rear loader* 1 equipment operator
Total	**Equipment** 3 rear loaders 2 front loaders 0 side loaders **Personnel** 5 equipment operators 4 laborers	**Equipment** 3 rear loaders 2 front loaders 0 side loaders **Personnel** 5 equipment operators 2 laborers	**Equipment** 1 rear loader 2 front loaders 3 side loaders **Personnel** 5 equipment operators 3 laborers	**Equipment** 1 rear loader 2 front loaders 3 side loaders **Personnel** 6 equipment operators 0 laborers

of the four options were virtually equal, this case qualified for cost-effectiveness analysis. Using cost-effectiveness analysis, he could concentrate on differences in cost.

Although Hogan understood the potential significance of indirect costs, intangible costs, and even pecuniary costs, he decided as a matter of expedience that he would keep in mind the possible existence of such factors, try to identify the most important ones, and attempt to take them into account in deciding a close call between two alternatives. He would not, however, try to quantify such factors. He would focus instead on identifying and quantifying major direct costs. The results of his effort to tabulate direct costs are shown in Table 16-2.

Major costs associated with all four options center on employees, equipment, and landfill fees. Each option requires a different number of employees, thereby affecting the budget for wages, benefits, and uniforms. Each requires at least five equipment operators, while the number of laborers ranges from none to four. In recognition of the greater individual responsibility associated with one-person operations, Hogan included a 15 percent wage increase for equipment operators assigned that duty.

Operating expenses for equipment include maintenance, fuel, and associated supplies. Annualized capital costs for equipment, based on costs for different types of vehicles, a six-year projected life, and 5 percent salvage value, are shown in Table 16-3. (See Chapter 11 for a description of straight-line depreciation.)

Projected landfill fees do not vary from one option to another. The total tonnage of solid waste collected and disposed will not be affected by the choice of one option over another.

Viewed on a communitywide basis, the benefits of each of the alternatives would include the value of refuse collection services to service recipients individually (removal of their garbage) and collectively (community appearance and public health). This analysis assumes that these benefits would be secured equally from each of the four options. If the benefits, like the costs, had varied from one option to another, Hogan would not have been able to apply cost-effectiveness analysis to this problem. With cost-effectiveness analysis, one or the other—either costs or benefits—must be stable across all options, allowing the analysis to focus on the one that varies. If both costs *and* benefits had varied from one option to another, the more sophisticated cost-benefit analysis would have been required.

The residents and businesses of Surf City pay refuse collection fees totaling $810,000. For his analysis, Hogan used this amount to approximate the value—or benefit—of the refuse collection service.

The results of the analysis indicated advantages for two of the three alternatives when compared to the current three-person rear-loading system, attributable primarily to reduced crew sizes (see Table 16-4). Although Option B showed the greatest potential gain, Hogan remained skeptical about whether two-person crews could actually complete their work on schedule with current equipment and route lengths. As he promised himself, Hogan attempted to consider some of the indirect and intangible costs and benefits, although without trying to quantify them precisely. On this score, he had further doubts about Option B. Side-loading trucks are designed

Table 16-2 Projected Annual Direct Costs of Four Refuse Collection Options

	Option A	Option B	Option C	Option D
Standard mode of operation for residential collection	rear loader with 3-person crew	rear loader with 2-person crew	side loader with 2-person crew	side loader with 1-person crew
Personnel for residential, commercial, and special solid waste collection	9: two 3-person residential crews; 3 persons for commercial, brush, and backup	7: two 2-person residential crews; 3 persons for commercial, brush, and backup	8: three 2-person residential crews; 2 persons for commercial and brush; no backup	6: three 1-person residential crews; 3 persons for commercial, brush, and backup
COSTS				
Wages[a]				
equipment operators	$147,500	$147,500	$147,500	$190,275[a]
laborers	96,800	48,400	72,600	0
Overtime	2,500	2,500	2,500	2,500
FICA[b]	18,757	15,078	16,918	14,651
Insurance[c]	24,430	19,590	22,010	19,028
Retirement contribution[d]	19,744	15,872	17,808	15,422
Uniforms[e]	5,400	4,200	4,800	3,600
Supplies	6,000	6,000	6,000	6,000
Equipment annualized capital cost[f]				
rear loaders	69,351	69,351	23,117	23,117
side loaders	0	0	78,375	78,375
front loaders	43,700	43,700	43,700	43,700
operation and maintenance	59,000	62,000	65,000	65,000
Landfill fees	310,000	310,000	310,000	310,000
Total	$803,182	$744,191	$810,328	$771,668

[a]Based on annual wages of $29,500 for an equipment operator on a 2- or 3-person crew, $33,925 for an equipment operator on a one-person residential route crew, and $24,200 for a laborer.
[b]Budgeted at 7.6 percent of wages and overtime.
[c]Estimated at 10 percent of wages.
[d]Budgeted at 8 percent of wages and overtime.
[e]Budgeted at $600 per employee.
[f]See Table 16-3.

Table 16-3 Annualized Capital Costs for Refuse Collection Vehicles

Vehicle	Purchase Price	Anticipated Useful Life	Projected Salvage Value[a]	Annualized Capital Cost[b]
Rear loader (for residential service)	$146,000	6 years	$7,300	$23,117
Side loader (for residential service)	$165,000	6 years	$8,250	$26,125
Front loader (for commercial dumpster service)	$138,000	6 years	$6,900	$21,850

[a]Assumes 5 percent salvage value at the end of 6 years.
[b]Based on straight-line depreciation (see Chapter 11).

for driver involvement in the loading process; rear loaders are not. Without a side-loading truck, would a driver moving to the rear of the vehicle and climbing into and out of the cab be more accident-prone? Would the two-member crew be more injury-prone than the current three-member crew or even a one-person crew relying on a hydraulic lift? Would a two-person crew on a route previously handled by a three-member crew be forced to cut corners to keep pace, resulting in more spillage, more complaints, and a host of negative externalities?

If it were time for the current system to give way to a new approach, Hogan would prefer Option D. By shifting to one-person side loaders for the residential routes, Hogan figured he could reduce route length, add a truck to the current configuration, retain backup services, probably reduce back injuries, and save more than $38,000 per year.

POSTSCRIPT

The techniques associated with cost-benefit and cost-effectiveness analysis provide a useful basis for sorting out difficult choices. These techniques may be especially revealing when applied rigorously and on a comprehensive basis—and somewhat less useful when applied less rigorously or less comprehensively.

Public managers conducting cost-effectiveness analysis—and especially those conducting the more rigorous cost-benefit analysis—must be realistic not only about the time required and the complexity of this process but also about their expectations regarding the impact of analysis. They must also recognize their obligation to disclose the assumptions embedded in their analysis, as well as the possible weaknesses introduced by any procedural shortcuts.

A realistic expectation for cost-effectiveness or cost-benefit analysis in public decision making is that it can help to objectively inform a process that is, and will continue to be, largely political in nature. Greater thoroughness often strengthens the

Table 16-4 Projected Annual Direct Costs of Four Refuse Collection Options

	Option A	Option B	Option C	Option D
Standard Mode of Operation for Residential Collection	Rear Loader with Three-Person Crew	Rear Loader with Two-Person Crew	Side Loader with Two-Person Crew	Side Loader with One-Person Crew
Benefits	$810,000	$810,000	$810,000	$810,000
Costs	$803,182	$744,191	$810,328	$771,668
Net benefits[a]	$6,818	$65,809	−$328	$38,332
Benefit-to-cost ratio[b]	1.0085	1.0884	0.9996	1.0497

[a]Net benefit is the difference between benefits and costs. This is the "return on investment" in actual dollars rather than as a ratio or "rate of return."
[b]The benefit-to-cost ratio is calculated by dividing benefits by costs. The result shows the "return on investment" as a ratio that may be converted easily to "rate of return" or percentage gain or loss. In this example, the benefits of Option D are projected to exceed costs by approximately 5 percent.

influence of an analytic effort, but even the most comprehensive and sophisticated analysis might not have the final word.

In the case of Surf City, several assumptions included in the calculations or omitted from explicit consideration in that analysis should be mentioned by the sanitation director in his presentation to decision makers. For example, he chose a life expectancy of six years for all trucks and a 15 percent pay differential for the operators of one-person vehicles. Higher or lower figures could influence the results of the analysis.[1]

Decision makers should also be informed about any important indirect or intangible factors relevant to the refuse collection considerations. For example, after conferring with the streets superintendent, Sanitation Director Hogan confidently projects a reduction in curb damage if the city switches to one-person side loaders with smaller wheelbases than the current equipment. Furthermore, Hogan anticipates a reduction in employee injuries, especially in instances where the trucks are equipped with hydraulic lifts. Of extreme importance with regard to successful implementation is anticipated employee morale. That factor, which in part prompted the proposed wage adjustment for one-person collection crews, should be addressed in the deliberations.

---

[1]Performing the computations a few additional times using different numbers for vehicle depreciation or pay levels or substituting slightly different figures for other key assumptions (a process known as *sensitivity analysis*) reveals how sensitive the analysis is to such decisions or to possible errors in various assumptions. Analysts are wise to take that additional step.

Box 16-1 Other Applications of Cost-Effectiveness Analysis

Many local government projects, services, and strategies are suitable subjects for cost-effective-ness analysis, with its relative deemphasis of externalities when compared to *classic* cost-benefit analysis. A local government, for example, might analyze the impacts and costs associated with a new tax levy and the services thereby funded, perhaps taking three different perspectives: the government itself, a citizen with average income, and a citizen with low income. A city might use cost-effectiveness analysis to examine its plan for converting its current twice-a-week back-door refuse collection service to once-a-week curbside pickup. The range of potential subjects suitable for cost-effectiveness analysis is almost endless.

In 1992 the city of Milwaukee, Wisconsin, decided to contract out the citation processing and cash management function in its police department. The city anticipated that contract costs could be offset by the elimination of 13 clerical positions and that 10 police officers could be reassigned from cashier duties to district patrol functions. Five years later, the city subjected the privatization decision to a cost-effectiveness analysis to see if the system was living up to its ear-lier promises.[1] Analysts confirmed that privatization had indeed freed 10 police officers for law enforcement activities and allowed the elimination of 13 clerical positions. Additionally, privatization had yielded better management information, improved scheduling of court hear-ings and attorney conferences, and greater flexibility in adjusting to periodic fluctuations in cita-tion volume. The analysis showed, however, that contract costs exceeded the projected costs of continuing in-house operations (see Table A).

Table A Citation Processing Costs for the City of Milwaukee

	1991	1993	1995
Police department salaries	$ 847,003	$ 69,459	$ 70,176
Charges	222,825	111,207	76,040
Contract coordinator		70,247	70,614
Contract processing fees		1,687,091	1,687,739
Contract collection fees		422,248	417,341
Registration hold fees	521,860	268,650	322,125
Lockbox fees	69,115		
Municipal court data entry			22,000
Miscellaneous	122,090	135,480	150,535
Conversion		60,000	60,000
Total Citation Processing Cost	$1,782,893	$2,824,382	$2,876,570
Privatized cost	NA	$2,824,382	$2,876,570
Estimated city cost under old system	$1,782,893	2,063,354	2,212,999
Increased cost via privatization	—	$ 761,028	$ 663,571

Source: City of Milwaukee Citation Processing and Cash Management Costs and Benefits Audit (Milwaukee, Wis.: City Comptroller, City of Milwaukee, June 1997), 17.

---

[1] *City of Milwaukee Citation Processing and Cash Management Costs and Benefits Audit* (Milwaukee, Wis.: City Comptroller, City of Milwaukee, June 1997).

Box 16-1 *(Continued)*

A search for reasons for the disparity between anticipated and actual costs revealed that the excess costs were due to rapid increases in citation volume and a contract that tied fees to volume. A processing fee, adjusted each year by a Consumer Price Index factor, was charged for each citation entered into the system. Although a review of citation volume, collection rates, and collection revenues showed an increase in revenues far greater than the unanticipated processing fees (see Table B), the analysts concluded that only 10 percent of the revenue increase was attributable to greater collection rates achieved through privatization. Accordingly, they recommended that future contracts include a declining scale of citation processing fees tied to specified volume ranges (for example, 1 to 700,000 citations; 700,001 to 900,000; 900,001 or greater) in order to benefit from economies of scale.

Table B Citation Revenues for the City of Milwaukee

	Milwaukee Police Department 1991	Contractor 1995
Citations issued	657,392	802,040
Collection rate	68.82%	71.56%
Dollars collected	$6,756,440	$9,791,997

Source: City of Milwaukee Citation Processing and Cash Management Costs and Benefits Audit (Milwaukee, Wis.: City Comptroller, City of Milwaukee, June 1997), 16.

Finally, feasibility issues—technical and political—associated with each alternative should be considered. Are the projected advantages of a one-person operation realistic? Will such an operation work in Surf City? Is too much on-street parking permitted to allow the side loader to maneuver close enough to the curb to collect garbage with its mechanical arm? Will new policies affecting residents, such as the required use of special roll-out containers or plastic bags or restricted on-street parking, be necessary? Will residents accept such policies or resist them by political means? Will employee groups support the alternatives to secure better wages or oppose them because they reduce employment? Would strong employee resistance destroy the viability of an alternative? A variety of specific factors influence the organizational and political environment of a jurisdiction. Although many will be difficult to quantify, they should nevertheless be considered in some fashion along with their more easily quantified counterparts.

SUGGESTED FOR FURTHER INFORMATION

Downs, George W., and Patrick D. Larkey. "Better Performance through Better Analysis: Nothing but the Facts." In *The Search for Government Efficiency: From Hubris to Helplessness,* 95–144. New York: Random House, 1986.

Freeman, Therese A., Ernest G. Niemi, and Peter M. Wilson. "Evaluating Public Expenditures: A Guide for Local Officials." In *Budget Management: A Reader in Local Government Financial Management,* edited by Jack Rabin, W. Bartley Hildreth, and Gerald J. Miller, 92–105. Athens: Carl Vinson Institute of Government, University of Georgia, 1983.

Gianakis, Gerasimos A., and Clifford P. McCue. *Local Government Budgeting: A Managerial Approach.* Westport, Conn.: Quorum Books, 1999. See Chapter 5, "Analytical Techniques," 81–99.

Gramlich, Edward M. *Benefit-Cost Analysis of Government Programs.* Englewood Cliffs, N.J.: Prentice Hall, 1981.

Gupta, Dipak K. *Decisions by the Numbers: An Introduction to Quantitative Techniques for Public Policy Analysis and Management.* Englewood Cliffs, N.J.: Prentice Hall, 1994. See, especially, pp. 325–359.

Kee, James E. "Benefit-Cost Analysis in Program Evaluation." In *Handbook of Practical Program Evaluation,* edited by Joseph S. Wholey, Harry P. Hatry, and Kathryn E. Newcomer, 456–488. San Francisco: Jossey-Bass, 1994.

McGowan, Robert P., and Dennis P. Wittmer. "Five Great Issues in Decision Making." In *Handbook of Public Administration,* 2d ed., edited by Jack Rabin, W. Bartley Hildreth, and Gerald J. Miller, 293–319. New York: Marcel Dekker, 1998.

McKenna, Christopher K. "Cost-Benefit Analysis." In *Quantitative Methods for Public Decision Making,* 127–163. New York: McGraw-Hill, 1980.

Thomas, Henry B., and Jeffrey I. Chapman. "Cost-Benefit Analysis: Theory and Use." In *Managing Public Systems: Analytic Techniques for Public Administration,* edited by Michael J. White, Ross Clayton, Robert Myrtle, Gilbert Siegel, and Aaron Rose, 291–318. Lanham, Md.: University Press of America, 1985.

Weimer, David L., and Aidan R. Vining. *Policy Analysis: Concepts and Practice,* 2d ed. Englewood Cliffs, N.J.: Prentice Hall, 1992. See, especially, pp. 218–222, 259–311, 357–381.

17

Life-Cycle Costing

Local governments are consumers and, like individual consumers, frequently purchase the cheapest of several similar items performing the same function, believing that the lowest-priced item is the "best buy." Sadly, however, this is not always true because the cost of owning an item includes more than its purchase price.

Life-cycle costing is a technique increasingly used in business and government to determine the total cost of owning an item, including costs associated with the item's acquisition, operation, and maintenance. The technique accounts not only for the purchase price of the item but also identifies hidden costs of ownership. This chapter describes the life-cycle approach to costing, suggests when the use of this technique is most appropriate, and offers a simple formula for calculating the lifetime cost of owning an item.

WHEN TO APPLY THE TECHNIQUE OF LIFE-CYCLE COSTING

Life-cycle costing can be applied to many local government purchases but is most frequently used to determine the lifetime costs of moderately expensive, energy-consuming equipment, including motor vehicles, climate-control systems, data processing equipment, and lighting systems. Table 17-1 illustrates how considering energy costs can affect a potential purchaser's assessment of two 15-horsepower electric motors. Based solely on the purchase price, the motor offered by vendor A seems less expensive than the motor offered by vendor B. However, motor A has a higher rate of energy consumption (14.40 kilowatts/hour) than motor B (12.58 kilowatts/hour)—a very important factor in this decision because the purchasing local government plans to run the motor ten hours a day, five days a week (that is, 2,600 hours per year). As shown in Table 17-1, motor A will actually cost $6,119 more than motor B over their lifetimes, assuming equal maintenance costs.

The underlying concepts of life-cycle costing may also be used to strengthen performance standards in bid specifications. The specifications should call for the bidders to provide all the technical information necessary to project life-cycle costs. While it may be helpful to give a reference brand name to act as a guideline to poten-

---

The original version of this chapter was written by Roderick C. Lee and appeared in this volume's first edition.

Table 17-1 Supplementing Purchase Price with Lifetime Energy Costs

Life-Cycle Cost	Motor from Vendor A	Motor from Vendor B
Horsepower	15	15
RPM	3,450	1,160
Bid price	$1,956	$2,935
Duty cycle	2,600 hours per year	2,600 hours per year
Life	15 years	15 years
Efficiency rating	78.2%	86%
Energy consumption (kilowatts per hour)	14.40	12.58
Energy costs (kilowatt hour consumption rate × $.10/kilowatt hour × 39,000 hours)	$56,160	$49,062
Life-cycle cost (bid cost + energy cost)	$58,116	$51,997

Life-cycle cost difference
($58,116 − $51,997) = $6,119

tial bidders, care should be taken to avoid preempting the competitive process. In the bid invitation, the manager or local government purchasing agent should require each potential supplier to submit documentation regarding an item's expected energy consumption rate and the anticipated useful life of the item, assuming a given duty cycle (how much use it is expected to get over a one-year period).

PREPARING A LIFE-CYCLE COST ANALYSIS

Three cost factors—acquisition cost, lifetime maintenance costs, and energy costs—and salvage value are core elements of a life-cycle cost analysis. The acquisition cost of an item includes its purchase price and transportation and installation costs. The acquisition cost should also reflect discounts in the purchase price and credit for trade-in equipment. An item's projected lifetime maintenance and energy costs are the anticipated costs for keeping the item in operable condition and for energy consumed in operating the item. Salvage value is also fundamental to the analysis. How much can the local government recoup by selling the item at the end of its projected life? Adding the three cost factors and subtracting the salvage value provides a simplified version of the life-cycle cost of an item (see Figure 17-1).

Calculating life-cycle costs based solely on acquisition costs, maintenance and energy costs, and salvage value may be sufficient for most analyses. However, for especially large or otherwise significant purchases, managers may find it useful to examine, when applicable, seven other costs associated with ownership:

- *failure costs,* including downtime, production losses, and rental costs
- *training costs* for personnel training in equipment usage, including tuition, time away from job, meals, transportation, and lodging
- *consumable supply costs* arising from an item's use

- *storage costs* for the item or for repair parts
- *secondary costs* for disposal of by-products associated with the item's use (such costs may be positive or negative—for example, waste heat can be used to reduce energy consumption in colder months, reducing overall costs)
- *labor costs* or the wages and benefits for employees engaged in the operation of an item
- *money costs,* including interest paid for a loan to purchase the item or interest forgone on money that could be invested elsewhere if not tied up in equipment purchases

The following example demonstrates the use of a life-cycle costing formula that considers acquisition cost, maintenance and energy consumption costs, salvage value, and one other cost factor—failure cost.

SCENARIO: LINDSEY, VIRGINIA

City officials in Lindsey, Virginia, plan to purchase a new 1.13 cubic yard hydraulic crawler/track excavator for the water and sewer department. The machine is expected to operate 2,000 hours a year for eight years.

Figure 17-1 Formula for Life-Cycle Costing

The basic life-cycle cost formula is **Life-cycle costs**	**= acquisition cost + lifetime maintenance costs** **+ lifetime energy costs – salvage value**
Where Acquisition costs	= purchase price + transportation cost + installation cost – trade-ins and discounts
Lifetime maintenance costs	= anticipated costs of keeping the item in operable condition
Lifetime energy costs	= energy consumption rate × cost of energy × duty cycle × life of the item
Salvage value	= anticipated worth at the end of the item's projected life
The components of the lifetime energy costs are	
Energy consumption rate	= the rate at which energy is consumed (kilowatts per hour)
Cost of energy	= dollars per energy unit (cents per kilowatt hour)
Duty cycle	= annual number of hours item is used (number of hours in use per day × number of days in use)
Life	= length of time until item is replaced (number of years in use based on the duty cycle)

Source: Adapted from League of California Cities, *A Guide to Life Cycle Costing: A Purchasing Technique That Saves Money* (Sacramento: League of California Cities, December 1983), 3–4. Adapted by permission of the League of California Cities.

Table 17-2 Applying Life-Cycle Costing

	Bid A	Bid B	Bid C
Purchase price (bid)	$150,000	$158,000	$164,000
Less trade-in on present unit	8,000	7,800	9,200
Acquisition cost	142,000	150,200	154,800
Energy cost[a]	76,800	64,000	51,200
Maintenance cost[b]	40,000	32,000	32,000
Failure cost[c]	8,000	6,400	6,400
Less expected resale value[d]	21,000	23,000	26,000
Life-cycle cost	$245,800	$229,600	$218,400

[a]The energy costs for all bids were calculated using a diesel fuel cost of $1.60 per gallon. The machine in Bid A was estimated to consume 48,000 gallons over the eight-year period. The machines in Bid B and Bid C were estimated to consume 40,000 and 32,000 gallons, respectively, over the period.
[b]Maintenance costs for all bids were based on cost records for similar machines secured from state and local governments by the city of Lindsey.
[c]Anytime the machine is not available for work, renting back-up equipment is necessary. Records indicate rental equipment is 20 percent of each machine's maintenance cost.
[d]Resale values were based on average sale prices as a percent of original price at used equipment auctions for eight-year-old crawler/track excavators of the proposed makes.

Competitive bids were received from three vendors, proposing equipment with purchase prices ranging from $150,000 to $164,000 (see Table 17-2). Despite the purchase price advantage of equipment offered by vendor A, the city's purchasing agent and director of water and sewer are recommending that the city accept bid C. While bid C's acquisition price is the highest of the three bids, the life-cycle cost of the crawler/track excavator offered in bid C is $27,400 lower than that of bid A and $11,200 lower than that of bid B.

From the Electronic Toolkit ●━━━━━━━━━━━━━━━━━━━━━━━━━━━━━━━━━━━

Box 17-1 Calculating Life-Cycle Costs

Some administrators may decide to use Excel to calculate life-cycle costs by programming the equation into a spreadsheet. First, enter the variable names or symbols (that is, acquisition cost, lifetime maintenance costs, lifetime energy costs, and salvage value) into consecutive cells of a given column. Then, enter the appropriate numerical values into cells in the adjacent column. (For directions on opening Excel and entering data refer to Box 2-1.)

After the data are entered, type the equation for the life-cycle cost using normal mathematical notations and the cell names of the data instead of symbols for the variables. For example, if the acquisition cost was entered in cell B1, lifetime maintenance costs in cell B2, lifetime energy costs in cell B3, and salvage value in cell B4, enter "=B1+B2+B3−B4" to calculate life-cycle costs. Similar equations can be entered into Excel for each variable.

VARIABILITY OF RELEVANT FACTORS

This example illustrates the variety of characteristics of significance to the life-cycle costs of a particular piece of equipment. For other items, a different set of cost factors may be more significant. For example, a life-cycle cost analysis for microfiche readers for county libraries and court systems might be especially concerned with the useful life of the readers, the duty cycle, and energy costs. The local administrator will also want to know about failure rates and service costs, the availability of parts and prompt service in the event of a breakdown, and the degree of specialized training needed to service the readers.

Requiring the use of a carefully designed bid worksheet approved by the local government can assure that all information needed for calculating life-cycle costs will be uniformly secured from all bidders. Comprehensiveness and uniformity of information will permit a more direct and complete comparison of bids.

LIMITATIONS OF LIFE-CYCLE COSTING

While life-cycle costing can be a useful tool for local governments, it has its limitations. The technique requires local government managers to accumulate detailed information about the various costs associated with a potential purchase. The manufacturers and sellers of equipment may supply some of that information, including energy consumption and other product performance data. Local government managers should attempt to get complete documentation from manufacturers and sellers regarding all claims made for their products. The remedies available to governments that have been deceived by false vendor claims depend on the conditions specified in the purchase contract and whether the information was presented in a deliberately misleading or inaccurate manner.

Local government managers attempting to use life-cycle costing will find that their projections can be much more accurate if they are maintaining good performance records for their own equipment. Much of the cost information related to maintenance, downtime, rental and storage charges, and other pertinent expenses may be based, in part, on the government's previous experience with those cost factors for identical or similar equipment or on the experience of other local governments that have used the particular model in question. As such, the adequacy of the technique is linked in most cases to the availability of useful information.

Life-cycle costing can be applied to many types of local government purchases. However, the information requirements and analytic effort associated with this technique may make its application impractical in some cases. Local government managers may wish to prioritize the items that are candidates for life-cycle costing.

Finally, a frequent problem in applying life-cycle costing in local governments is the question of legal authority for basing purchasing decisions on life-cycle costs rather than simply on purchase price. While several local governments, such as Baltimore, Maryland, have adopted life-cycle costing as a major component of the decision-making process for purchasing equipment, many others assume, often incor-

Box 17-2 Other Applications of Life-Cycle Costing

Life-cycle costing is applicable to any purchase, but it is most practical and beneficial for large purchases, especially those involving energy-consuming equipment. In local governments this is likely to include computer equipment, heating and air conditioning equipment, vehicles, public works equipment, and equipment associated with water and sewer treatment, among others.

rectly, that they have no choice other than awarding the bid to the vendor with the lowest purchase price. In reality, many regulations specify that awards should go to the "lowest and best bid," language that appears to leave the door open for consideration of factors other than price tag. Life-cycle costing does not eliminate the lowest bid concept; rather, it applies the concept to a greater range of costs. Local government managers who wish to use life-cycle costing should make themselves aware of applicable legal requirements in their particular community.

SUGGESTED FOR FURTHER INFORMATION

Brown, Robert J., and Rudolph R. Yanuck. *Life Cycle Costing.* Atlanta: Fairmont Press, 1980.
Coe, Charles K. *Public Financial Management.* Englewood Cliffs, N.J.: Prentice Hall, 1989. See, especially, pp. 95–97.
Gecoma, Richard M., Arthur B. Mohor, and Michael G. Jackson. *Energy Efficient Purchasing for Local Governments.* Athens: Carl Vinson Institute of Government, University of Georgia, 1980.
League of California Cities. *A Guide to Life Cycle Costing: A Purchasing Technique That Saves Money.* Sacramento: League of California Cities, December 1983. Reprinted as "Life Cycle Costing," in *Practical Financial Management: New Techniques for Local Government,* edited by John Matzer Jr. Washington, D.C.: International City Management Association, 1984.
"Life Cycle Costing Saves Money for Albuquerque." *Public Works* 115 (June 1984): 100.
Malan, Roland M., James R. Fountain Jr., Donald S. Arrowsmith, and Robert L. Lockridge II. "Analysis." In *Performance Auditing in Local Government,* 139–167. Chicago: Government Finance Officers Association, 1984.
Winslow, R., B. Morrow, R. Carbone, and E. Cross. *Life-Cycle Costing for Procurement of Small Buses.* Washington, D.C.: U.S. Department of Transportation, 1980.
Wubbenhorst, Klaus L. "Life Cycle Costing for Construction Projects." *Long Range Planning* 19 (August 1986): 87–97.
Zemansky, Stanley D. "Life-Cycle Cost Procurement." In *Costing Government Services: A Guide for Decision Making,* edited by Joseph T. Kelley, 115–139. Washington, D.C.: Government Finance Officers Association, 1984.

18

Lease or Buy?

A wide variety of equipment is needed to perform the full array of local government functions. Traditionally, much of that equipment, such as trucks, sedans, and office furniture, has been purchased by local governments; however, other types of equipment, such as computers and copy machines, often have been leased.

Increasingly, consideration is being given to the relative advantages of buying versus leasing equipment. This chapter describes a technique for performing such analysis.

SCENARIO: ALLEGHENY COUNTY, WEST VIRGINIA

Allegheny County, West Virginia, has been leasing two brand-new office copiers for the past four months.[1] The first, a large capacity, high-speed copier for the sheriff's office, is leased by the county for $686 a month including maintenance. The second, a slower-speed copier for the inspection and permit office, leases for $389 a month including maintenance. The vendor has recently offered to sell both copiers to the county. The sale price for the copier used by the sheriff's office is $18,000, plus $121 per month for maintenance; the copier in the inspection and permit office is $8,600, plus $121 per month for maintenance.

Should the county continue to lease the copiers or should it buy them? To answer this question, decision makers must compare the series of monthly payments required to lease the copiers with the one-time purchase prices and monthly maintenance fees to purchase the copiers.

EQUIVALENT ANNUAL WORTH

A comparison such as the one needed by Allegheny County can be developed using the *equivalent annual worth* method, an analytic technique for converting the

The original version of this chapter was written by Roderick C. Lee and appeared in this volume's first edition.

[1]The scenario presented here is modeled on a Winston-Salem, North Carolina, case study reported in A. John Vogt and Samuel H. Owen Jr., "Cost Calculation for Lease-Purchase Decisions," in *A Guide to Municipal Leasing*, ed. A. John Vogt and Lisa A. Cole (Chicago: Municipal Finance Officers Association, 1983), 148–152.

up-front purchase price of an item into a stream of uniform annual costs over the item's useful life. This stream of uniform costs can then be compared with the costs associated with leasing the item over the same period of time.

Using the equivalent annual worth method to compare the costs of leasing with the costs of purchasing is a three-step process. First, analysts must make several assumptions regarding the item they are considering for lease or purchase. Second, based on these assumptions, they apply the formula for calculating equivalent annual worth to the known cost information. Finally, they review the analysis to determine how "sensitive" the lease-or-buy analysis is to changes in the choices and assumptions. The following discussion uses Allegheny County's lease-or-buy dilemma to illustrate this three-step process.

Making Assumptions

As a preliminary step in applying the equivalent annual worth method, the county's administrators or analysts must make some assumptions about the copiers and the costs associated with owning and operating them. First, an assumption must be made about the expected useful life of each copier. Vendors can provide helpful information in that regard. Also, employees in the sheriff's office and the inspection and permit office can provide insights into how long copiers have routinely remained in service in their offices in the past. Based on information from these sources, administrators in Allegheny County assume that the copiers will continue in use for at least five more years.

Second, administrators must make assumptions regarding the salvage value of the copiers at the end of five years. As with determining the length of service, information gathered from vendors and from county employees can be used to estimate salvage value. An extremely conservative assumption would be that the copiers will have no salvage value. This assumption reflects the greater risk faced by Allegheny County in buying the copiers rather than leasing them. Buying the copiers also represents a commitment to the current technology of the copiers. If new technology makes the county's copiers obsolete, their salvage value will decline sharply. On the other hand, if the county continues to lease the copiers, it can cancel the leases at the end of the term and lease newer, state-of-the-art models. For this analysis, the county assumes the copiers will have no salvage value, an assumption creating a modest bias toward leasing.

Third, an assumption has to be made regarding the length of term of leasing and maintenance payments. To simplify this analysis, it is assumed that all periodic payments are annual. This means that the sixty monthly maintenance fees under the purchasing alternative and the sixty monthly lease payments under the leasing alternative are converted to five annual payments. This, too, creates a slight distortion in the analysis that favors leasing the copiers.

The fourth assumption involves projected inflation. The advisability of a particular lease-or-buy decision may be influenced by projected inflation if a substantial portion of the annual cost is vulnerable to fluctuation—for example, if the purchase price is small relative to ongoing maintenance expenses or if annual lease payments are not fixed for a multiyear period but, instead, are adjusted annually in accordance with an inflation index such as the consumer price index.[2] In the case of Allegheny County, a five-year, fixed-rate lease is being offered. Accordingly, the inflation factor may be disregarded with little effect on the analysis.

Finally, an interest rate must be selected to convert payments at different points in time to a comparable basis of value. There have been lengthy and conflicting discussions regarding the optimal interest rates governments should use in considering lease-or-buy alternatives.[3] One recommendation is that the interest rate used in government applications of annual worth analyses should be the rate that the government would earn from an investment over the term of the agreement.[4] In this analysis, Allegheny County administrators assume a 6 percent annual interest rate.

Calculating the Equivalent Annual Worth

Based on these assumptions, the county can compare its lease-or-buy alternatives using the formula for the equivalent annual worth method. The formula is as follows:

$$A = P \times USCRF \text{ (for interest rate } i \text{ and } n \text{ years or periods),}$$

where

A = an annual or periodic amount in a uniform series of such amounts in the future

P = a single purchase price at the present time

$USCRF$ = uniform series capital recovery factor

i = the interest rate for each future interest period over n periods

n = the number of interest periods or like intervals in the future

The uniform series capital recovery factor is an interest factor based on a formula used to convert a single amount at the beginning of a period (for example, the present) into an equivalent series of equal payments made or received during the period.[5] In the Allegheny County analysis, the one-time purchase prices for the copiers are

---

[2]Inflation is typically disregarded in simple annual worth analyses, as in the Allegheny County example. The assumption in doing so is that inflation will have roughly the same effect on each financing alternative. For a discussion of when and how to incorporate the effects of inflation into an annual worth analysis, see Robert E. Pritchard and Thomas J. Hindelang, *The Lease/Buy Decision* (New York: AMACOM, 1980), 60–67.

[3]A. John Vogt and Samuel H. Owen Jr., "Cost Calculations for Lease-Purchase Decisions: Methods," in *A Guide to Municipal Leasing*, ed. A. John Vogt and Lisa A. Cole (Chicago: Municipal Finance Officers Association, 1983), 139–44. Vogt and Owen outline the major schools of thought regarding the most appropriate interest rate to use in lease-or-buy decisions.

[4]Edward A. Dyl and Michael D. Joehnk, "Leasing as a Municipal Finance Alternative," *Public Administration Review* 38 (November/December 1978): 561–562.

[5]Vogt and Owen, "Cost Calculations," 124–125.

Table 18-1 Interest Factors for Compounding Uniform Series Capital Recovery Factors

Interest Periods	Capital Recovery Factors at Selected Rates of Interest				
n	4 percent	5 percent	6 percent	10 percent	15 percent
1	1.0400	1.0500	1.0600	1.1000	1.1500
2	0.5302	0.5378	0.5454	0.5762	0.6151
3	0.3603	0.3672	0.3741	0.4021	0.4380
4	0.2755	0.2820	0.2886	0.3155	0.3503
5	0.2246	0.2310	0.2374	0.2638	0.2983
6	0.1908	0.1970	0.2034	0.2296	0.2642
7	0.1666	0.1728	0.1791	0.2054	0.2404
8	0.1485	0.1547	0.1610	0.1874	0.2229
9	0.1345	0.1407	0.1470	0.1736	0.2096
10	0.1233	0.1295	0.1359	0.1627	0.1993
15	0.0899	0.0963	0.1030	0.1315	0.1710
20	0.0736	0.0802	0.0872	0.1175	0.1598
25	0.0640	0.0710	0.0782	0.1102	0.1547

Source: Excerpted from "Appendix 1: Interest Factors for Compounding and Discounting," in *A Guide to Municipal Leasing*, ed. A. John Vogt and Lisa A. Cole (Chicago: Municipal Finance Officers Association, 1983), 171–198. Used by permission of the Government Finance Officers Association.

converted to annualized purchase prices using the USCRF for 6 percent interest over a five-year period. The USCRF can be calculated using the following formula:

$$USCRF = \frac{i(1+i)^n}{(1+i)^n -}$$

where

  i = interest rate

  n = number of years or interest periods[6]

Because Allegheny County officials assumed 6 percent interest and a five-year period, their USCRF calculation was as follows:

$$USCRF_{(6\%,5 \text{ years})} = \frac{.06(1+.06)^5}{(1+.06)^5 - 1} = \frac{.06 \times 1.3382}{1.3382 - 1} = \frac{0.0803}{0.3382} = 0.2374$$

Alternatively, the analyst may simply consult a USCRF table, if one is available (Table 18-1 is a limited example).

Table 18-2 illustrates the application of the equivalent annual worth method to the copier in the sheriff's office. The analysis reveals that the county would expect

---

[6]Vogt and Owen, "Cost Calculations," 124–125.

Table 18-2 Equivalent Annual Worth Analysis of the Sheriff's Office Copier

Annual cost to lease ($686 × 12 months)	$8,232
Annual cost to purchase	
maintenance ($121 × 12 months)	$1,452
annualized purchase price:	
($18,000) × (USCRF for 6 percent interest and	
5 years in service) = ($18,000) × (.2374)	$4,273
Subtotal, annual cost to purchase	$5,725
Expected annual savings by purchasing	$2,507

Source: Adapted from A. John Vogt and Samuel H. Owen Jr., "Cost Calculation for Lease-Purchase Decisions," in *A Guide to Municipal Leasing,* ed. A. John Vogt and Lisa A. Cole (Chicago: Municipal Finance Officers Association, 1983), 150. Adapted by permission of the Government Finance Officers Association.

to realize annual savings of $2,507 by purchasing the copier rather than continuing to lease it. As illustrated in Table 18-3, the application of the equivalent annual worth method to the copier decision in the inspection and permit office reveals an expected annual savings of $1,174 by purchasing rather than leasing.

Testing the Sensitivity of the Results

The two analyses produce results that clearly favor the purchase of the copiers. Because the results are based in part on a set of assumptions, it is important to consider how changes in these assumptions would affect the results of the analyses. In essence, how "sensitive" are the results to the assumptions?

One assumption that easily can be tested for its impact is the interest rate. What if county administrators had used a 10 percent interest rate rather than the assumed

Table 18-3 Equivalent Annual Worth Analysis of the Inspection and Permit Office Copier

Annual cost to lease ($389 × 12 months)	$4,668
Annual cost to purchase	
maintenance ($121 × 12 months)	$1,452
annualized purchase price:	
($8,600) × (USCRF for 6 percent interest and	
5 years in service) = ($8,600) × (.2374)	$2,042
Subtotal, annual cost to purchase	$3,494
Expected annual savings by purchasing	$1,174

Source: Adapted from A. John Vogt and Samuel H. Owen Jr., "Cost Calculation for Lease-Purchase Decisions," in *A Guide to Municipal Leasing,* ed. A. John Vogt and Lisa A. Cole (Chicago: Municipal Finance Officers Association, 1983), 151. Adapted by permission of the Government Finance Officers Association.

From the Electronic Toolkit ●

Box 18-1 Finding the Uniform Series Capital Recovery Factor

By entering the equation for the USCR into an Excel spreadsheet, tricky calculations can be simplified and done repeatedly for different sets of data.

Begin by entering names or symbols (that is, interest rate and interest periods) into consecutive cells of a given column. Then, enter the appropriate numerical values in the cells in the next column. (For directions on opening Excel and entering data refer to Box 2-1.)

To find the USCRF, enter the equation using the cell names of the data instead of letter variables. Be careful about the placement of parentheses. If the interest rate is in cell B1 and the number of years or interest periods is in cell B2, type "=((B1*((1+B1)^B2))/(((1+B1)^B2)-1))" to calculate USCRF.

To calculate the equivalent annual worth, enter the purchase price into a cell, and in a separate cell of your choice specify an equation that multiplies the cell with the purchase price by the cell with the USCRF. For example if the USCRF was in cell A3 and the purchase price in cell A4, enter "=A3*A4." After saving the spreadsheet, the calculations can be made again with different data.

6 percent? With the higher interest rate, the equivalent annual worth of the copier used in the sheriff's office over five years would be \$4,748 (\$18,000 × 0.2638). At the 10 percent interest rate, the equivalent annual worth of the inspection and permit office's copier would be \$2,269 (\$8,600 × 0.2638). While the higher interest rate makes the purchasing alternative less attractive, purchasing still would produce expected annual savings in both cases, as illustrated in Table 18-4.

Another assumption that could be easily tested for its impact is the anticipated useful life of the copiers. For example, how much would the results of the analysis change if the in-service periods for the copiers were reduced from five years to three? The shorter service life would tend to favor the leasing alternative because the purchase price would be annualized over a shorter period of time. As illustrated in Table 18-5, the three-year period almost eliminates the advantage of purchasing the copier for the sheriff's office and completely eliminates the purchasing advantage in the case of the inspection and permit office.

If assumption factors in a lease-or-buy analysis are weighted slightly in favor of one option (for example, lease) and still the analysis consistently favors the other option (for example, purchase), the result may be taken as a clear endorsement of the second option. More ambiguous results are less easily interpreted. In addition, less quantifiable factors, such as losing the opportunity to lease updated state-of-the-art equipment, must be weighed against projected savings to reach a satisfactory decision.

Table 18-4 Testing the Sensitivity of Interest Rates for Equivalent Annual Worth Analysis

	Sheriff's Office Copier	Inspection and Permit Office Copier
Annual cost to lease	$8,232	$4,668
At 6 percent interest rate		
maintenance	1,452	1,452
annualized purchase price[a]	4,273	2,042
annual cost to purchase	5,725	3,494
expected annual savings by purchasing	2,507	1,174
At 10 percent interest rate		
maintenance	1,452	1,452
annualized purchase price[a]	4,748	2,269
annual cost to purchase	6,200	3,721
expected annual savings by purchasing	$2,032	$ 947

Source: Adapted from A. John Vogt and Samuel H. Owen Jr., "Cost Calculation for Lease-Purchase Decisions," in *A Guide to Municipal Leasing*, ed. A. John Vogt and Lisa A. Cole (Chicago: Municipal Finance Officers Association, 1983), 150–151. Adapted by permission of the Government Finance Officers Association.
[a]For five-year in-service period.

Table 18-5 Testing the Sensitivity of In-Service Periods for Equivalent Annual Worth Analysis

	Sheriff's Office Copier	Inspection and Permit Office Copier
Annual cost to lease	$8,232	$4,668
At five-year in-service period		
maintenance	$1,452	$1,452
annualized purchase price[a]	4,273	2,042
annual cost to purchase	$5,725	$3,494
expected annual savings by purchasing	$2,507	$1,174
At three-year in-service period		
maintenance	$1,452	$1,452
annualized purchase price[a]	6,734	3,217
annual cost to purchase	$8,186	$4,669
expected annual savings (loss) by purchasing	$ 46	$ (1)

Source: Adapted from A. John Vogt and Samuel H. Owen Jr., "Cost Calculation for Lease-Purchase Decisions," in *A Guide to Municipal Leasing*, ed. A. John Vogt and Lisa A. Cole (Chicago: Municipal Finance Officers Association, 1983), 150–151. Adapted by permission of the Government Finance Officers Association.
[a]With 6 percent interest.

Box 18-2 Other Applications of Lease-Buy Analysis

Lease-buy analysis has broad potential applicability for local government decision making. Cities and counties sometimes make mode-of-acquisition decisions almost out of habit for items ranging from heavy-duty road maintenance equipment to office furnishings. For example, most local governments purchase their police and motor pool fleets without seriously considering the leasing option, and most make office building and other facility decisions without fully considering the alternatives. Better informed choices could be made by incorporating lease-buy analysis into the process.

In the case of Allegheny County, the analysis was most sensitive to assumptions regarding the useful life of the equipment. Local officials would be well advised to reassess their confidence in a five-year lifespan for copiers before committing to their purchase.

SUGGESTED FOR FURTHER INFORMATION

Canada, John R., and John A. White. *Capital Investment Decision Analysis for Management and Engineering.* Englewood Cliffs, N.J.: Prentice-Hall, 1980.

Coe, Charles K. *Public Financial Management.* Englewood Cliffs, N.J.: Prentice Hall, 1989. See, especially, pp. 95–98.

Isom, Terry A., Shawn D. Halladay, Sudhir P. Amembal, R. Douglas Leininger, and Jonathan M. Ruga. *The Handbook of Equipment Leasing.* Salt Lake City: Amembal and Isom, 1988.

Pritchard, Robert E., and Thomas J. Hindelang. *The Lease/Buy Decision.* New York: AMACOM, 1980.

Vogt, A. John, and Samuel H. Owen Jr. "Cost Calculations for Lease-Purchase Decisions: Methods" and "Cost Calculations for Lease-Purchase Decisions: Five Case Studies." In *A Guide to Municipal Leasing,* edited by A. John Vogt and Lisa A. Cole, 115–145, 147–170. Chicago: Municipal Finance Officers Association, 1983.

Part VI
Selected Applications of Analytic Techniques in Local Government

Each of the techniques included in this volume was selected for its ease of use and practical applicability to the analysis of common local government problems. Seven more applications are presented in this section. The analytic processes highlighted in the following seven chapters range from the simple calculation of floating averages to more complex techniques introducing statistical correlation and regression.

19

Smoothing Data Trends by Using Floating Averages

Standing too close to a data trend line can sometimes lead an analyst to a hasty recommendation or a department head or manager to a hasty decision. Sometimes it is better to step back and take a broader view rather than overreacting to what might be an anomalous spike or trough in the data. When the occurrence of a single favorable or unfavorable event can seriously distort or misrepresent a department's performance or a community's condition, analysts and managers might find it easier to take a broader view by examining and reporting data as "floating averages" rather than analyzing data solely by individual time periods.

SCENARIO: ZORNIG, MINNESOTA

Keri Kelly was dutifully working on the fire department's performance measurement section for the upcoming budget. "This looks awful!" she thought, as she filled in the column labeled "Last Year's Actual." Chief Harold Behr, known to his friends as "Smoky," had submitted a figure for last year's fire loss that stood out like a sore thumb. "This can't be right," muttered Keri. "I'd better go see the chief."

Occasionally, departments are a little careless in completing their budget sheets. A column here or there does not add up; a subtotal is not calculated correctly; or a pair of digits in a performance measure are transposed. Budget analysts moan when they discover errors of that type, but privately they delight in discovering them.

"Good morning, Chief," said Keri as she strode into the fire department's administrative office. After exchanging a few pleasantries, she got down to business. "Let me ask you about last year's fire losses."

Fully anticipating that she had discovered a typo in the department's material and that the chief would be puzzled by her inquiry, she was startled by his response. "It looks terrible, doesn't it?" Chief Behr replied. "Do you remember the warehouse fire at the beginning of the year? It destroyed the structure and all its contents."

"Yeah, I do, now that you mention it. I had forgotten about that."

"We take pride in our fire suppression effectiveness," the chief continued, "but that one was out of hand before we were even contacted. The building was totally engulfed when we arrived. We responded quickly, but we had no chance of saving that structure."

"So what do you want to do about this?" asked Keri.

"Well, we are pushing for tougher regulations regarding sprinkler systems. . . ," the Chief began, as Keri cut him off.

"No, I mean what do you want to do about the performance measurement section of your budget page?"

"What I would *really like to do* is drop that fire loss statistic out of the table," replied Chief Behr, "but I guess we shouldn't do that. It is unfortunate that one bad incident can so distort our record. This community has a better fire department than last year's fire loss figure suggests."

"We will need to report it," said Keri, "but, like you, I am concerned that this will leave an inaccurate perception regarding the quality of fire services that the citizens of Zornig receive from the city. At the very least, we will want to add an explanatory note to the table of performance measures, but let me give this some thought. I will get back to you soon."

FLOATING AVERAGES

In circumstances like the one facing the Zornig Fire Department, a truer depiction of reality may be achieved by examining performance or conditions over a broader slice of time than what normally is reported. Rather than reporting annual statistics year by year, the department might consider reporting the average annual fire loss for a three-year or five-year period. Using the average over a longer span of time has the effect of smoothing the data and blunting the impact of an unusually bad or unusually good year. The degree of shock that Chief Behr and Budget Analyst Kelly expected to witness on the faces of startled members of the city council when they gazed at last year's fire loss figure would appear only if a recurring pattern of fire losses developed—that is, only if the community experienced two or three bad years in a row. The effect of an anomaly would be muted.

Floating averages (also known as *moving averages*) may be calculated by simply adding together the figures for the desired span of periods (for example, three annual totals for a three-year floating annual average; six monthly totals for a six-month floating monthly average, and so forth) and dividing the total by the number of periods (for example, three for a three-year floating annual average; six for a six-month floating monthly average).

The formula for calculating a floating average is:

$$\text{Floating average} = \frac{x_1 + x_2 + \ldots x_n}{n}$$

where

x = the total for a single period

n = the number of periods included in the floating average

Table 19-1 Fire Losses in Zornig, by Fiscal Year

	Fiscal Year				
	1997–1998	1998–1999	1999–2000	2000–2001	2001–2002
Fire loss	$210,500	$262,300	$212,387	$338,258	$1,088,600
Fire loss as a percentage of value of properties involved	5%	7%	5%	2%	30%

Zornig's raw fire loss statistics for the last five fiscal years are reported in Table 19-1. Only three columns of performance measures are reported in the budget. Table 19-2 shows how these columns would appear as single-year statistics and as floating averages. The floating average is not as sensitive to data fluctuations in a single period, but it has some advantages in more appropriately depicting performance or conditions "over the long haul."

POSTSCRIPT

When Keri returned to Chief Behr with a suggestion that he consider using a floating average to report fire loss statistics, the chief's deliberation took only three seconds. "Let's do it!" he quickly responded. "There's some luck as well as skill in having a good year or a bad year on fire losses. We might not be quite as good as we look in a lucky year, and *I know we are not as bad as we looked last year.* Taking a larger slice of time seems to remove some of the luck factor from the equation."

Table 19-2 Depicting Zornig's Fire Loss Statistics

	Fiscal Year		
	1999–2000	2000–2001	2001–2002
Single-Period Format			
Fire loss	$212,387	$338,258	$1,088,600
Fire loss as a percentage of value of properties involved	5%	2%	30%
	1998–2000	1999–2001	2000–2002
Three-Year Floating Annual Averages			
Fire loss, three-year annual average	$228,396	$270,982	$546,415
Fire loss as a percentage of value of properties involved, three-year annual average (unweighted)	5.7%	4.7%	12.3%

From the Electronic Toolkit ●

Box 19-1 Floating Averages

Calculating floating averages using Excel is simple. First, enter the data that are being averaged. (For directions on opening Excel and entering data refer to Box 2-1.) In the case of the town of Zornig, Keri Kelly would enter the year-by-year statistics for fire losses in a row (or column) of the spreadsheet. Then, she would calculate the three-year averages by using the AVERAGE function and grouping the data by threes.

Suppose, for example, that the fire loss statistics for FY 1998 through FY 2002 were entered from cell A1 to E1. Then to calculate the first three-year floating average (FY 1998 through FY 2000), Kelly would enter "=AVERAGE(A1:C1)" in whichever cell she wishes to have that result appear. (An alternative to typing this instruction would be to use the Function choice (**fx**) from the Insert menu. The symbol for this choice—**fx**—also appears on the toolbar.) The three-year floating average for the FY 1999 through FY 2001 period is calculated by entering "=AVERAGE(B1:D1)" in the cell of her choice.

It is easy to alter the time period covered by a floating average using Excel because changes in the amount of data averaged can be made simply with the click of a mouse. To make alterations in the average formulas, simply highlight the cell with the formula in it and then move the mouse to the formula bar at the top of the screen. Click anywhere in the formula bar and type any changes that are needed using the arrow keys and the regular keypad.

Box 19-2 Other Applications of Floating Averages

Like their hypothetical counterpart of Zornig, Minnesota, several real cities also use floating averages to report performance, especially when performance is susceptible to sharp fluctuations that can be influenced only partially by local government action. In Massachusetts, the city of Boston uses a floating average to demonstrate trends in community-oriented policing by comparing current rates of serious crime in specified districts to three-year averages in the same districts.[1] In Wisconsin the city of Milwaukee uses a floating five-year average to report the local infant mortality rate.[2] The city of Greensboro, North Carolina, reports floating averages among its local fire statistics, noting a rolling civilian five-year fire death rate and, like Zornig, using a floating average to calculate its five-year average annual fire loss figure.[3]

Floating averages can also be useful in forecasting revenues. The effects of an especially strong or a particularly weak year for a given revenue source are muted in trend-based projections using this technique.

---

[1]City of Boston, Massachusetts, *Mayor's Management Report: FY 1996*, 57.
[2]City of Milwaukee, Wisconsin, *1999 Plan and Budget Summary* (Milwaukee: Department of Administration, Budget and Management Division), 121.
[3]City of Greensboro, North Carolina, *Fire Department Work Plan: Fiscal Year 2000–2001.*

SUGGESTED FOR FURTHER INFORMATION

Hatry, Harry P. *Performance Measurement: Getting Results.* Washington, D.C.: Urban Institute Press, 1999. See, especially, p. 133.

20

Staffing Factor Calculation
Projections for Extended-Hour or Uninterruptible Services

Local government departments providing extended-hour services or performing functions that cannot tolerate even temporary operational lapses present staffing demands that differ from the more typical 40-hour-a-week office operations. The recreation center and swimming pool may be open 70 hours a week. While the number of recreation supervisors on duty can fluctuate with absences, the lifeguard stand at the pool must never be unoccupied. The police and fire departments are around-the-clock operations that sometimes can tolerate a little—but only a little—deviation from authorized strength, but the chair of the public safety dispatcher must always be filled.

Staffing decisions are complicated by the fact that many local government departments operate more hours each week than are included in the standard workweek of their employees. The recreation department, for instance, might operate 70 hours per week using employees who work 40. The police department is open for business all 168 hours of every week, but the standard workweek per employee is 40 hours. Additionally, allowance must be made for vacations, holidays, sick days, and other forms of absence.

CALCULATING THE STAFFING FACTOR

A simple technique for determining the number of employees needed to provide an extended-hour or uninterruptible government service requires the calculation of the *staffing factor,* which is the number of employees needed to provide full coverage of an employee station or post. The analyst may choose to calculate employees needed for one shift or for multiple shifts, such as around-the-clock coverage. The first step of the two-step calculation is as follows:

$$E = P - A$$

where

E = the number of effective hours per employee per year or hours actually worked by the average employee

P = the number of paid hours per employee per year
A = the average number of hours of paid absences per employee per year (such as vacation and sick leave)

Typical employees may be paid for 2,080 hours per year (40 hours a week × 52 weeks a year), but actually work only 1,936 hours if they take a two-week vacation (2 weeks × 40 hours a week = 80 hours of vacation leave) and use 8 days of sick leave (8 days × 8 hours per day = 64 hours of sick leave). In this example, paid hours (P) are 2,080; paid absences (A) total 144 hours (80 hours of vacation leave and 64 hours of sick leave); and effective hours (E) are the difference between the two (2,080 − 144 = 1,936).

The second step uses effective hours per employee (E) to calculate the staffing factor:

$$\frac{\text{Staffing}}{\text{Factor}} = \frac{\text{Hours per year of operation}}{E}$$

If, for example, the operation functions 8 hours a day, 7 days a week year-round (8 hours × 365 days = 2,920 hours) and a review of employee benefits or absenteeism records indicates that effective hours per employee-year is 1,936, then the staffing factor would be 1.51 (2,920 divided by 1,936). In other words, one full-time and one half-time employee—or an equivalent combination of part-time employees—would be needed to provide uninterrupted coverage of the post. The following case further illustrates the calculation of the staffing factor.

SCENARIO: WHITE DUNES COUNTY, SOUTH CAROLINA

For thirteen weeks every summer, the 28,000 permanent residents of White Dunes County, South Carolina, welcome nearly 175,000 tourists a week to their oceanside communities. In past years the county's police department has responded to the seasonal need for increased traffic control and crowd management by allowing patrol officers to work as many as 8 hours per week of overtime. However, it has become increasingly apparent to the county administrator and chief of police that the county's fifteen patrol officers are severely overworked during the peak tourist season. Therefore, they are interested in hiring supplemental, parapolice officers to provide one additional traffic control officer to each of the two busiest 8-hour shifts 7 days a week for the 91-day season. There seems to be an abundant supply of qualified persons to hold the seasonal positions. But how many additional officers are needed to provide 16-hour supplemental coverage for 91 days?

Applying the Staffing Factor to White Dunes County

The first step in answering this question (and in calculating the staffing factor) is to determine the number of effective hours that could be provided by each supple-

From the Electronic Toolkit ●────────────────────────────

Box 20-1 Calculating the Staffing Factor

Although there is no Excel function dedicated to staffing factor calculations, readers may find it helpful to enter the staffing factor formula into a spreadsheet and allow Excel to perform the calculations. Once the proper equation is entered into Excel, the program can repeatedly process this calculation or any other calculation with different sets of data.

To set up the spreadsheet, reserve column A for data labels or symbols (for example, paid hours—P) and column B for data (for example, 2080). Enter the labels and data for number of paid hours per employee per year, the average number of hours of paid absences per employee per year, and the hours per year of operation. (For directions on opening Excel and entering data refer to Box 2-1.) After the data are entered, type the formula for the staffing factor into any cell using typical mathematical signs and cell addresses as the variables. If the numerical value for P was entered in cell B1, the numerical value for A in cell B2, and the hours of operation in cell B3, enter the formula "=(B3/(B1–B2))." Notice that the placement of the parentheses indicates which mathematical calculation to carry out first. Without the parentheses around B1–B2, the computer would first calculate B3/B1 and then subtract B2. Be careful to use the parentheses correctly. Once the staffing factor has been entered, the spreadsheet can be saved and the calculation can be done for other operations with different total hours or different rates of absenteeism.

mental employee per year, confined in this instance to a 91-day period. If each employee is scheduled and paid for 40 hours a week for 13 weeks, the number of paid hours (P) is 520. Full-time, year-round employees of White Dunes County are granted paid holidays, vacation time, sick days, and other forms of paid leave, but the benefits of seasonal employees are much more limited. After consulting with police departments in neighboring counties that already use seasonal police personnel, the White Dunes County police chief recommended that each parapolice officer hired for the summer receive up to 3 compensated days off—2 allowable sick days and 1 paid holiday. Projecting that all 3 days of paid absences would be taken (A = 3 days × 8 hours = 24 hours), the chief calculated effective hours per employee (E) as follows:

$$E = P - A$$
$$= 520 - 24$$
$$= 496$$

The calculation of the staffing factor could address a single shift or both shifts simultaneously. A single-shift staffing factor is as follows:

$$\begin{aligned} \text{Staffing} \ \text{Factor} \quad &= \quad \frac{\text{hours per year of operation}}{E} \\[1.2em] &= \quad \frac{8 \text{ hours per day} \times 91 \text{ days}}{496} \\[1.2em] &= \quad \frac{728}{496} \\[1.2em] &= \quad 1.47 \end{aligned}$$

One full-time and one half-time employee, or an equivalent combination of part-time employees, should be sufficient to provide uninterrupted coverage of the post. A consolidated staffing factor for 16-hour per day coverage could be derived by doubling the single-shift staffing factor or by inserting a comprehensive figure for hours of operation into the calculation:

$$\begin{aligned} \text{Staffing} \ \text{Factor} \quad &= \quad \frac{\text{hours per year of operation}}{E} \\[1.2em] &= \quad \frac{16 \text{ hours per day} \times 91 \text{ days}}{496} \\[1.2em] &= \quad \frac{1456}{496} \\[1.2em] &= \quad 2.94 \end{aligned}$$

Three full-time employees, or an equivalent combination of full- and part-time employees, should be sufficient to provide uninterrupted coverage of the post.

Using the Information

Determining the staffing factor of a service is a major element in calculating the costs of adding personnel, but other elements are also important. The costs of employee benefits as well as additional equipment, supplies, work space, or other facilities must also be considered. In the White Dunes County case, for example, known costs related to wages, uniforms, insurance, and other expenses should provide a reasonable estimate of the costs for the three parapolice officers needed to cover the extra positions. If desired, the estimate for supplemental staffing on one or both shifts can be compared with other staffing alternatives (such as continuing to allow full-time, year-round patrol officers to work overtime or contracting out for addi-

Box 20-2 Other Applications of Staffing Factor Calculations

Staffing factor calculations are relevant to any local government operation that is open for business substantially more than 40 hours a week. For example, a library or animal shelter that features weekend hours in addition to weekday operations would join various public safety and recreation units in this category.

tional police or security officers) to determine which approach to providing seasonal police protection for the county will cost the least.

UTILITY OF THE STAFFING FACTOR

Calculating a staffing factor can quickly enlighten a debate over the need for and cost of putting another police officer or fire fighter on duty around the clock. Too often advocates of such a move naively assume that the cost is roughly equivalent to one annual salary. A well-prepared public official can quickly project a more realistic estimate of the cost of such a proposal.

SUGGESTED FOR FURTHER INFORMATION

Kelley, Joseph T. "Applications in Practice." In *Costing Government Services: A Guide for Decision Making*, 55–72. Washington, D.C.: Government Finance Officers Association, 1984.

21

Potential Gains Through Timely Invoicing

Conscientious program officials sometimes discover that they have more ideas for operational improvements than time to explore those ideas. Choosing one improvement opportunity usually means deferring another. Simple analytic techniques that permit a program manager or analyst to estimate the magnitude of a problem and the likely payoff from correcting it can assist officials in assigning priorities. Such techniques can help them direct their resources wisely, assigning greatest and earliest analytic and implementation efforts to those opportunities likely to yield the most beneficial results.

This chapter describes a technique that permits program officials to examine inefficiencies in a jurisdiction's invoicing procedures and to estimate the resource benefits from correcting those inefficiencies.

SCENARIO: DRY GULCH, KANSAS

Fred Faust, the finance director of Dry Gulch, Kansas, got approval to hire a summer intern by assuring the mayor that capable students could more than earn their keep even on a short-term basis. Faust had in mind several analytical projects focusing on suspected operational deficiencies. If his suspicions were correct, revised operations would generate a substantial return on the analytic investment.

Most of Dry Gulch's municipal services are supported by taxes and provided to the public with no additional charges. Several services, however, are provided to individual "customers" upon request, and those service recipients are billed accordingly. For example, the fire department is occasionally asked to fill a swimming pool from a fire hydrant or to hose down a commercial parking lot; those service recipients are then billed for the water and labor involved. Developers frequently request, receive, and pay for special services from the public works department as they open new subdivisions.

Dry Gulch had not been particularly diligent in promptly billing service recipients—or so it seemed to the finance director. When asked about lax billing procedures, the employees in accounts receivable passed the buck. They said that they get the invoices out "pretty quickly," once they finally receive the paperwork from the other departments involved. "The major delay," they contended, "is out there."

Table 21-1 Prescribed Sample Size

Total Number of Invoices	Recommended Invoice Sample Size
Less than 1,000	300
1,000–1,999	335
2,000–2,999	350
3,000–9,999	385
10,000–49,999	400

Source: Charles K. Coe, *Maximizing Revenue, Minimizing Expenditure for Local Governments* (Athens: Institute of Government, University of Georgia, 1981), 20–21.

The first assignment for the new intern was to analyze the invoicing practices of the city, focusing on the delay or lag time from service delivery to billing, the cost of such delay, and the identification of responsibility for that delay.

Because Dry Gulch issues more than a thousand invoices annually, Faust knew that it would not be practical for the intern to review the delays associated with every invoice. Although a comprehensive assessment would be desirable and practical in smaller operations, in this case the intern was instructed to examine a random sample of the invoices and use the average dollar amount and period of unnecessary delay found in the sample to estimate figures for the entire operation. (See Chapter 2 for a description of a procedure for drawing a random sample.) She was instructed to use the prescription in Table 21-1 to decide on the size of the sample she would need.

ESTIMATING REVENUE LOSSES

Unnecessary delays in collecting payments result in lost revenues. Uncollected receivables are not available for investment by the local government, thereby diminishing interest income.

Estimating the losses attributable to a slow collection system requires judgment as well as simple arithmetic skills. Judgment comes into play not only in determining the amount of unnecessary delay in the processing of invoices but also in estimating a reasonable rate of return on investments. These, along with the total value of invoices affected, are the essential elements in projecting revenue losses.

To estimate the extent of avoidable delays in the billing process, the analyst must compare the time required by the current process to the time that would be required by an efficient billing system. The first step, then, is to design a streamlined procedure for reporting services rendered and for issuing invoices. The time required under that procedure provides a baseline for expected processing time. Any difference between that expectation and the actual time consumed is considered avoidable delay.

The second element in the calculation is the estimated rate of return on investments. The value of investments may be projected conservatively using average earn-

Worksheet 21-1 Projecting Revenue Losses from Late Invoices

Dollar amount of invoices[a]	$ _____
× average time lag (that is, avoidable delay) in number of days	× _____
÷ number of days in year	÷ 365
× prevailing interest rate (or borrowing rate)	× _____%
= Total lost revenues	= _____

Source: Adapted from Charles K. Coe, *Maximizing Revenue, Minimizing Expenditure for Local Governments* (Athens: Institute of Government, University of Georgia, 1981), 20–21.
[a]If the actual total for all invoices is unavailable, an estimate may be calculated from the sample as follows:

$$\begin{array}{ccccc} \text{estimated dollar} \\ \text{amount of all} & = & \text{dollar amount} \\ \text{invoices} & & \text{of sample} \\ & & \text{invoices} \end{array} \times \dfrac{\begin{array}{c}\text{total number}\\\text{of all invoices}\end{array}}{\begin{array}{c}\text{number of}\\\text{sample invoices}\end{array}}$$

ings for the jurisdiction's current investments or existing rates for certificates of deposit or U.S. treasury bills.[1]

Estimating lost revenues is simply a matter of applying the estimated interest rate to the amount of money affected and the duration of all delays. The figures for invoice amounts and avoidable delays may be based on a sample of invoices, with findings projected from the sample to the "population" of all invoices issued by the jurisdiction.[2] Formulas for making this projection and performing the revenue-loss calculation are provided in Worksheet 21-1.

DRY GULCH'S FINDINGS

Finance director Faust asked the intern to try to complete her analysis quickly—within two weeks, if possible. He had other projects waiting for her.

A visit with the accounts receivable staff revealed that 1,550 invoices (invoices numbered G24857 through G26406) had been issued during the previous twelve months, convincing the intern that Faust's advice that she base her analysis on a sample of the invoices rather than the full set was wise. She drew a random sample of 335

---

[1]An on-line source of recent U.S. Treasury bill rates is http://www.publicdebt.treas.gov/servlet/OFBills/.
[2]A similar procedure could be used to estimate losses to a local government that retains large amounts of idle, or uninvested, cash. The analyst would first decide on a reasonable level of idle cash and then estimate lost investment opportunities based on excess daily balances and projected interest rates.

invoices (as prescribed in Table 21-1) and sorted them into nine piles according to department of origin.

The intern visited all nine of the departments that had performed work for billable customers to discuss procedures and paper flow. She found two departments to be especially efficient and prompt in routing documentation to the accounts receivable staff. Four other departments were somewhat erratic in their procedures—sometimes forwarding paperwork promptly and sometimes not. The other three departments were astonishingly slow. One considered the billing process such a low priority that it sometimes neglected to follow through for months and, on more than one occasion, had been prompted to begin processing its paperwork only after the accounts receivable staff had received calls of inquiry from service recipients waiting for their bills! Another department considered its slow billing practice a point of pride: it always waited to be sure there were no complaints on its work before routing the paperwork for a bill.

In addition to delays in initiating the routing of paperwork, the intern also found unnecessary steps in the routing process and modest delays in the processing by the accounts receivable staff. Each of the originating departments routed its paperwork through its department head and through finance director Faust on its way to the accounts receivable staff. The delay at Faust's desk was usually 1 day but had been as much as 14 days in a few instances. If he was out of town, the paperwork stopped until he returned. In no instance was there any indication that Faust's perusal of the paperwork had resulted in any substantive change. Delays at other department heads' desks were less predictable: paperwork was sometimes handled promptly; at other times it apparently sat in in-boxes for weeks at a time.

The intern documented current practices on process flow charts (see Chapter 6) and developed a proposed procedure for handling invoices that would move the paperwork more quickly through appropriate channels. The proposed procedure also eliminated some steps from the existing paper flow to expedite the process. For example, routing the paperwork past the finance director would no longer be a routine intermediate step between the department of origin and the accounts receivable staff. The finance director would become involved in the process only when (1) an invoice exceeded $3,000, (2) the bill was for an unusual service, or (3) the invoice was judged to be out-of-the-ordinary by the accounts receivable staff.

Application of the streamlined procedures would trim away a great deal of time. When the analyst examined the sample of invoices in light of the time required under the new procedure, she discovered an average avoidable delay of 20 days.

Assuming an average time tag of 20 days for the city's 1,550 invoices (totaling $392,650) and a prevailing interest rate of 7 percent, the intern estimated lost revenues from late invoices at $1,506 over the previous 12 months (see Table 21-2).

"This projection is only as good as the estimates I've made on a couple of factors," the intern warned as she showed the figures to the finance director. "I'm sure that the dollar amount of invoices is accurate. Our accounting system allowed me to simply run a total of all 1,550 invoices, so I didn't have to project an estimated total from

Table 21-2 Intern's Projections of Revenue Losses from Late Invoices

Dollar amount of invoices	$392,650
× average time lag (that is, avoidable delay) in number of days	× 20
÷ number of days in a year	÷ 365
× prevailing interest rate	× 7%
= Total lost revenues	= $ 1,506

my sample. The average time tag and prevailing interest rate projections are more a matter of judgment. If my judgments are correct, a revised procedure would have saved about $1,500."

Faust was a little surprised at the results. He anticipated the major delays that the intern would find but expected greater savings from resolving those problems. The two-week period that the intern had committed to this project was time well spent. Even by detecting opportunities for only modest savings, she had fulfilled Faust's promises to the mayor that she would more than earn her modest salary. Still, Faust was a little surprised to discover that without a larger volume of accounts receivable or a much higher interest rate, fairly large time lags—four- or five-day delays that offended his sense of efficiency and professionalism—would not result in what could be considered major losses.

Box 21-1 Other Applications of Revenue-Loss Analysis

The technique described in this chapter can be applied easily by local governments interested in examining the efficiency of their invoicing procedures. With only a few modifications, a similar technique could be used to project opportunities for increased revenue through improved cash-management and the reduction of uninvested idle funds. A major advantage of preliminary analysis, such as that undertaken in the Dry Gulch case, is that it permits projections of the potential benefits from improvements in current practices. Program managers can then make informed decisions regarding the nature and magnitude of administrative resources they are willing to commit to the task of designing and implementing procedural improvements.

SUGGESTED FOR FURTHER INFORMATION

Coe, Charles K. *Maximizing Revenue, Minimizing Expenditure for Local Governments.* Athens: Institute of Government, University of Georgia, 1981.

22

Making Choices Systematically— From Audit Targets to Capital Projects

Critics of government are quick to point out inefficiencies, inconsistencies, and seemingly irrational decisions emanating from city halls and county courthouses, as well as state and national capitols. Often they argue that government should be more "businesslike," a plea frequently echoed by candidates for public office.

Government is not a business, as successful candidates soon learn. Goals often are more ambiguous than those of a private corporation. The objectives of one program sometimes conflict with those of another. Politics—rather than business models, market shares, or profit margins—plays a decisive role in charting the course of government, as it should. Critics are unlikely ever to see a day when government is run as a business. However, if they look carefully, even the critics can find systems in place in many local governments that are designed to clarify community priorities and to help align decisions with local goals and operating objectives. These systems are not intended to supplant the political process, but rather to ensure that political as well as administrative choices are made with relevant analytic information at hand. If this is what the critics mean by more businesslike, then that day has already arrived in many communities.

SCENARIO: HENDRON, MICHIGAN

"We need to start making smarter choices when it comes to directing our audit resources," declared Seth Pearson. "We've got to do a better job of focusing our efforts on targets with greater potential results."

Pearson, who was appointed chief auditor in Hendron two years ago, has become increasingly disenchanted with the haphazard manner in which audit projects are selected. "Two years ago, the benefits from our projects far outweighed our personnel costs for conducting them. This year, I'm not so sure. We are taking on some pretty marginal stuff and giving more promising targets a pass."

"We take pride in being responsive," protested Lee Revell, one of four auditors on Pearson's staff. "When the mayor, city council, or city manager wants an office audited, we move it to the head of our list."

"I want us to continue to be responsive," Pearson said, "but we need to be more assertive in developing our list of upcoming operations audits. The mayor, council, and manager should see that we have a good rationale for the targets we select. Then, if they still want to interject other projects, we will make adjustments."

"I want us to come up with a rating system," Pearson continued, "that would give a high priority to potential projects that are most likely to generate significant audit recommendations and ultimately improved operations. I'd like for you to see if you can come up with a rating system like that. You might begin by checking to see if anyone is already doing anything along these lines."

RATING SYSTEMS

Rating systems are designed to help *rationalize* choices based on specific criteria. Goals and objectives relevant to a particular decision are identified along with other criteria deemed to be significant. Each of these factors is weighted according to its importance.[1] Potential choices, then, are assessed on each factor.

Some city and county governments, for example, have established rating systems for prioritizing capital improvement projects. The system used by the city of Reno, Nevada, considers factors ranging from availability of funding to impacts on future operating budgets and the environment. Each project earns a score that assigns it to a category of greater or lesser priority. The ratings in Reno and other communities using systematic rating systems typically are influential, but rarely are they considered inviolate. Elected officials are free to debate and adjust the priorities assigned to various projects.

RATING SYSTEM FOR POTENTIAL AUDITEES IN HENDRON

"I think I have a rating system that will help us prioritize our audit opportunities," said Lee Revell, handing a copy to Seth Pearson (see Table 22-1). "My proposal is based on a system already being used in another city, with just a few modifications I have made here and there."

Revell explained that the system addressed various factors presumed to make a given office or department a more or less promising target for an operations audit. An office that was the subject of rumors of improprieties, handled a lot of cash, and had not been recently audited, for example, would receive a hefty score and be considered a high priority for audit on this scale.

"This is just the sort of thing I was hoping to get," responded Pearson, as he quickly scanned the chart. "Give copies to the other auditors. Then let's get together to see if we need to make any further modifications. I want to be sure that all the

---

[1]The weights assigned to various factors can dramatically affect the results. Entries with low point totals in an unweighted system can be catapulted to high-point status in a weighted system if they are distinctive on a few high-priority, heavily weighted factors. Assigned weights are likely to differ from community to community, as factors deemed especially important in one place are considered less significant elsewhere, and from one time to another even within a single community as conditions and priorities change. Governments choosing to adopt either of the rating systems described in this chapter, for instance, might decide to alter the weights (that is, the multiplier in the capital project rating system and the point scales in the audit-potential rating system) to reflect local priorities.

Box 22-1 Capital Planning in Reno, Nevada

Capital planners in the city of Reno use a systematic rating scale to assist in ranking proposed capital projects (see table, below). The scale addresses thirteen criteria for establishing priorities among the projects, ranging from the availability of dedicated funding to the projected frequency of facility use. Each proposal is scored based on its categorization for each factor. The scoring of each criterion is weighted according to its importance, with the scores of criteria deemed most important multiplied by three.

Three of the thirteen criteria include special "override" categories. These categories indicate conditions so urgent that a project receiving an "override" designation is moved automatically to a high priority status. These projects, along with others scoring 100 points or more, are deemed "essential" and are moved ahead of less essential projects in the city's capital planning process.

Rating Criteria and Scoring of Proposed Capital Projects: City of Reno

Criteria	Points	Weighting (multiplier)	Range of Possible Scores[a]
Funding			
Ongoing funding from already identified source	Override		
Existing funds available now	4	3	3 to
Potential funds now available	2		Override
Potential funds to be sought	2		
No identified funds available	1		
Legal Mandates			
Court decision requirement	Override		
Regulatory requirement	Override	3	0 to
Pending legal action	4		Override
Potential legal action	3		
Normal project liability	0		
Public Health and Safety			
Existing hazard (severe)	Override		
Existing hazard (minor)	3	3	0 to
Potential hazard (severe)	3		Override
Potential hazard (minor)	1		
No health or safety issue	0		
Preservation of Facility			
Loss of facility eminent if project not done	5		
Additional damage likely if project not done	4	3	0 to 15
Project constitutes normal major maintenance	3		
Project constitutes normal minor maintenance	1		
New facility or none of the above	0		
Project Life			
Greater than twenty years with no extraordinary maintenance	5		
Greater than twenty years with extraordinary maintenance	4	2	2 to 10
Greater than ten years with no extraordinary maintenance	3		
Greater than ten years with extraordinary maintenance	2		
Less than ten years	1		

Rating Criteria and Scoring of Proposed Capital Projects: City of Reno—*(Continued)*

Criteria	Points	Weighting (multiplier)	Range of Possible Scores[a]
Conformance to City Plans or Goals			
In the city's master plan	5		
In neighborhood plans	4	2	2 to 10
Under consideration for master plan	3		
Recommended by board/commission	2		
Recommended by citizen action	1		
Conformance to Department Plans or Goals			
Critical item to accomplish established goals/plans	5		
Desirable item to accomplish goals/plans	4	3	3 to 15
Will assist in accomplishing established goals/plans	3		
Will not hinder accomplishment of goals/plans	2		
Necessary for one department, but may have adverse impact on another	1		
Operating Budget Impact			
Decreases operating/maintenance costs	5		
No impact on operating/maintenance costs	3	2	0 to 10
Increases operating/maintenance costs $5,000–14,999	2		
Increases operating/maintenance costs $15,000–24,999	1		
Increases operating/maintenance costs $25,000+	0		
Cost Effectiveness			
Most cost effective alternative	5		
Cost effective compared to doing nothing	4	2	0 to 10
Same as cost of other alternatives	2		
Not cost effective	0		
Environmental or Pollution Impact			
Enhances environment/reduces pollution	5		
Benefits environment/slightly reduces pollution	3	1	0 to 5
No environmental change/no effect on pollution	2		
Minor negative environmental impact/slight pollution production	1		
Diminishes environment/creates pollution	0		
Percentage of City Population Benefiting			
50 percent or more	5		
35 to 49 percent	4	2	2 to 10
25 to 34 percent	3		
10 to 24 percent	2		
Less than 10 percent	1		
Recreation/Cultural/Aesthetic Value			
Major value	5		
Moderate value	3	1	0 to 5
No value	1		
Slightly detrimental value	0		
Frequency of Use			
Used seven days a week	5		
Used five days a week	4	1	1 to 5
Used two to five days a week	2		
Used once a week or less	1		

Source: City of Reno (Nevada), *Capital Improvement Project Checklist* (October 1997).
Note: Projects with scores of 100 or greater and projects with override designation are considered "essential" and are moved ahead of all others in the Capital Improvement Plan. Projects scoring 80–99 are deemed "desirable," 60–79 "acceptable," and 40–59 "deferrable."
[a]Override designation moves a project automatically into highest priority status.

Table 22-1 Audit-Potential Rating System

Category	Points	Maximum Possible Score
Outside Allegations		50
Existence of specific allegations of impropriety	50	
Some vague allegations	30	
No allegations	0	
Time Since Most Recent Audit		45
Last audited three or more years ago	45	
Audited within three years, but not last year	27	
Amount of Revenues/Cash Handled		40
Greater than $2 million per year	40	
$200,000 to $2 million	32	
$50,000 to $199,999	24	
Cash handled regularly, but less than $50,000	16	
Cash handled only occasionally	8	
Amount of Discretionary Funds		35
Budgeted funds in discretionary categories		
greater than $500,000	35	
$200,000 to $500,000	28	
$100,000 to $199,999	21	
$50,000 to $99,999	14	
less than $50,000	7	
Management Dispersion		30
Number of shifts and/or locations to be supervised:		
more than three shifts/locations	30	
three shifts/locations	18	
less than three shifts/locations	6	
Auditor's Impression of Internal Controls		25
Pre-audit impression:		
Unacceptable controls	25	
Controls not followed completely	15	
Acceptable controls	0	
Types of Commodities Purchased		20
Most readily convertible for personal use or resale	20	
Some convertible for personal use or resale	12	
Insufficient quantity for personal use or resale	0	
Staff Size/Turnover Rate (add applicable subcategories)		15
More than 100 employees	9	
25 to 100 employees	6	
Less than 25 employees	3	
Turnover rate greater than 25 percent a year	6	
Turnover rate of 10–25 percent a year	3	

Table 22-1 *(Continued)*

Category	Points	Maximum Possible Score
Rate of Growth (add applicable subcategories)		10
Change in discretionary funds during prior 24 months:		
10 percent growth or greater	8	
5 percent to 9.9 percent growth	6	
increase of less than 5 percent	4	
static level or loss of discretionary funds	2	
Increased personnel during prior year	2	
Autonomy		5
Financial review by:		
neither internal department nor outside agency	5	
internal department or outside agency	3	
both	1	
Maximum Possible Score		275

Source: Adapted from City of Savannah (Georgia), *Operations Audit Review Program* (Savannah, Ga.: City of Savannah, Internal Audit Program, Reference 1512, December 2, 1991).

most important factors are included and that they are given appropriate weights in the points system."

POSTSCRIPT

The audit staff discussed several possible modifications but ultimately decided to adopt the rating system proposed by Revell. To test the value of the system, projects from the past two years were scored retroactively. (Recall that the projects two years ago produced recommendations and benefits valued far in excess of audit costs, while last year's projects did not.) The test confirmed Pearson's suspicions regarding some poor choices of audit targets last year. The group of projects two years ago earned a much higher score. Had the system been in place at the time, it would have designated the earlier group of projects to be a higher priority set than last year's projects and would have predicted a greater return on the investment of audit time and resources.

"If we had been using this system last year," Pearson remarked, "we probably could have elevated the mix of projects we tackled. Not only would we have taken the initiative to propose a more promising set of projects, but we probably also would have defended our proposed work plan more effectively. This system would have enabled us to clarify the tradeoff when someone was urging us to pick up a lower priority audit."

Box 22-2 Other Applications of Rating Systems

Rating systems are designed to increase the likelihood that decisions reflect pre-established priorities. Their potential applicability is broad. In addition to the uses noted in this chapter, rating systems may also be developed for such diverse purposes as rating job applicants, new program proposals, grant applications, product bids, and alternate sites for landfills, treatment plants, public housing, and airports.

SUGGESTED FOR FURTHER INFORMATION

City of Savannah (Georgia), *Operations Audit Review Program.* Savannah, Ga.: City of Savannah, Internal Audit Program, Reference 1512, December 2, 1991.

Vogt, A. John. *A Manager's Guide to Local Government Capital Budgeting.* Washington, D.C.: International City/County Management Association, forthcoming.

23

Analyzing Survey Data: Revealing Graphics and Simple Statistics

Sometimes the best way to find out how people feel about a particular service or issue is the most direct way—just ask them. If the service is received by a relatively small number of persons, ask them all. If the number is large, then asking a representative sample often is a more practical way of gauging the sentiment of service recipients.[1]

Conducting a survey sounds easy enough, but getting it right is more complicated than it may seem at first blush. Proper randomization (see Chapter 2) is one issue. The sample is supposed to represent accurately the population as a whole.[2] Biased selection of the sample—even inadvertent bias—would damage representativeness.

Sample size is another issue. Large samples are better than small ones, but sample size quickly reaches a point of diminishing returns (see Table 2-3).[3] Once basic sample size needs are met, adding more and more respondents brings less and less additional value to the survey. Relatively few communitywide surveys, even in large cities, include more than 700 respondents. In fact, a survey of approximately 400 to 500 persons, if drawn and conducted properly, will suffice in most cases.

Questionnaire design and survey mode are also important issues. Topics addressed in the questionnaire should be suitable for the survey format and appropriate for the array of people being questioned. Asking general citizens if they are satisfied with their water services or if they have noticed any odor lately in their tap water would be appropriate; asking them if they consider the city's water testing program to be adequate or its infrastructure financing strategy to be wise would not be. It would be reasonable to assume knowledge about the former, but less reasonable to expect

---

[1] Even if the number of service recipients is not particularly large, local officials might still choose to draw a sample from the community's population as a whole—either because they have no registry identifying service recipients or because they also want to hear from nonrecipients to learn why they choose not to receive the service.

[2] In some cases, the surveyors may devise sampling strategies to intentionally overrepresent some small segments of the population in order to have enough respondents from these segments to be able to perform the statistical analyses they have in mind.

[3] Mathematical computations based on the desired confidence levels for the survey can be used in lieu of Table 2-3 to prescribe a recommended sample size.

insights among the general populace regarding the latter. Furthermore, questions must be worded and posed appropriately, so as not to influence the respondents' answers.

By including a few semipersonal questions in the survey—for instance, asking respondents to identify their neighborhood, age category, and perhaps their race and broad income category—analysts later attempting to interpret survey results will be able to detect any important differences in perceptions of service adequacy that may exist from one neighborhood to another or among other relevant characteristics of respondents. But be careful. Questions that are perceived by respondents as too personal may result in refusal to participate and a low response rate for the survey.

Survey modes continue to expand. Added to the standard triumvirate of survey modes—mail questionnaires, face-to-face interviews, and telephone interviews—are newer techniques utilizing personal computers. Each mode has its advantages and disadvantages. Mail questionnaires are inexpensive, but they often yield poor response rates that can jeopardize confidence that the results are representative. Face-to-face interviews are expensive to conduct, but they typically yield better response rates and allow interviewers to probe responses in greater depth. Telephone interviews have been widely accepted as a generally suitable compromise, providing better response rates than many mail surveys at a lower cost than face-to-face interviews. But even the telephone survey option is not problem free.

Among the drawbacks to telephone surveys are a pair of problems—one perceptual and the other technical. At a time when telemarketers seem to be waging a relentless assault on every community's residents, some local governments are reluctant to engage in an activity that contributes to the assault. Options may be limited by this perception.

From a technical standpoint, the representativeness of survey respondents assumes that all citizens are equally accessible by telephone, an assumption that is challenged by the discovery of households with no phones or with multiple telephone lines—and, hence, less or more likelihood of being contacted. Similar concerns regarding representativeness challenge the usefulness or appropriateness of surveys conducted via personal computers, unless the population of interest is known to be accessible by this medium.

Local governments that desire the valuable feedback surveys can provide would be wise to secure expert assistance or to consult some of the excellent references published on this topic, some of which are listed at the end of this chapter. Careful attention to details and to the rules and nuances of sample selection, questionnaire design, and survey administration can be the difference between survey results that are meaningful and those that are not.

Once the data from a carefully designed and administered survey are collected, the focus moves to the analysis of findings and the reporting of results. What options does the manager or analyst have in this regard?

SCENARIO: TILLERY, COLORADO

The budget staff in Tillery, Colorado, meets each week, mostly to discuss budget procedures, problems, and forecasts. Occasionally the conversation shifts to budgetary maneuvering by various departments or to predicted council stances on tax increases in the upcoming year. Today's discussion departed from the usual set of topics.

"We've been conducting citizen surveys in Tillery for a long, long time, and I am proud of that," said Eve Bauer, the city's budget director. "Because we've been doing them so long, the city of Tillery has gained a reputation as a leader in citizen surveying. That's flattering, but, to be honest, I think I could be criticized for how little we use the information. We don't go as far as we should in the analysis of our survey data."

Nick Wilson and Maria Pickwick, the two budget analysts who had worked most closely with the survey data in the past, responded quickly and a bit defensively. "We report the results for each item," Wilson said, "so we know whether most folks are satisfied with a given service or not."

"And we always include tables that show whether the percentages are more or less favorable than in previous years," added Pickwick. "Departments know whether public regard for their programs is moving in the right direction."

"That's absolutely correct," replied Bauer. "I'm not saying we are doing a bad job of conducting the survey or a bad job of reporting the most fundamental results. I am simply saying that we can step up to the next level of analysis without a great deal of effort. We might learn something more from the data if we do so."

Wilson and Pickwick agreed to explore options for enhancing the analysis of the citizen survey. Bauer encouraged the analysts to investigate what other local governments were doing in the analysis of survey data and urged them to focus primarily on the use of more revealing graphics and simple statistics that could be explained easily to department heads, council members, and other readers of the survey report. "I am looking for tools that will help us understand and explain to others what the citizens are telling us. The simpler the better, as long as it does the job well."

MORE REVEALING GRAPHICS

Summary graphs and statistics can mask a lot of important details. Knowing, for example, that 60 percent of all Tillerians feel "safe" or "very safe" walking alone in their neighborhoods at night makes Tillery seem like a pretty secure place. But what if that 60 percent figure is based on an 85 percent affirmative response from males and only 35 percent from females? If barely more than one-third of Tillery's women feel safe walking alone in their neighborhoods at night, would this discovery prompt new programs to reduce their vulnerability or their level of anxiety? What if the overall 60 percent security level hides remarkable variation among neighborhoods, some reaching as high as 90 percent and others as low as 30 percent? Would this discovery lead to more focused police efforts and higher visibility in targeted areas?

Often, survey results such as the ones noted in the preceding paragraph are depicted in tables called "cross-tabulations" or simply "cross-tabs." One set of variables is displayed in the rows and another set in the columns. For example, a two-by-two cross-tab for the case presented above would contain four cells, with separate cells showing the number of males feeling safe, males feeling unsafe, females feeling safe, and females feeling unsafe walking alone in their neighborhood at night.[4]

By producing tables and graphs that depict key distinctions in the responses of different groups of citizens, an analyst might spur important new strategies in a community at a time when changes are needed. In contrast, by producing only a summary graph that camouflages these differences an analyst could inadvertently and inappropriately rationalize continuation of the status quo.

When the responses of different groups of respondents almost mirror one another, and therefore differ little from the overall average, a single summary graph or table will suffice. In fact, a single graph in such cases is preferable to multiple graphs that shed no new light on the topic. However, when responses vary sharply from one group of respondents to another, the absence of tabular or graphic displays depicting these differences would be a serious breach of thoroughness in staff work. An analyst performing thorough staff work will alert the audience to such significant differences.

PERTINENT STATISTICS

The most common statistics reported with local government surveys are *descriptive statistics,* such as proportions and measures of central tendency (especially the mean or median—see Chapter 2). These are extremely simple statistics to calculate and explain to the audience of the survey report. Unfortunately, they do not always reveal as much as the analyst needs to show.

While descriptive statistics present clear evidence about the characteristics or views of a *sample of respondents,* they often can leave the analyst and audience wondering whether the differences evident among groups in the sample reflect similar differences in the general population. When the sample is large and the results are lopsided, most people are comfortable making an intuitive inference. For instance, if 90 percent of the 500 male respondents to a survey and only 20 percent of the 500 female respondents said they would support the establishment of a rugby league in the city's recreation program, the analyst would probably be confident in reporting a clear gender split on this topic. Intuitively, the analyst knows that a split so stark in a sample this large is likely to reflect a similar division in the population as a whole. But what if the split were less pronounced, with perhaps a support level of 60 percent among men and 50 percent among women? While it would be accurate to declare that men *in this sample* were more supportive than women *in the sample,* would the analyst be foolish to declare that men *in the community* are more supportive than women of a new rugby league, when the division of responses is so narrow? This

[4]For an example of a cross-tabulation, see Table 23-3.

Table 23-1 Support for Proposed Rugby League among Sample of Citizens

Gender of Respondent	Favor	Oppose	Total
Female			50
Male			50
Total	60	40	100

is a common occurrence in the analysis of survey data and a problem that simple statistics can help to solve.

Chi-square is a statistic used in the analysis of categorical or nominal data (for example, data that may be categorized as men or women, recipients of a particular service or nonrecipients, city residents or visitors, satisfied with the service or dissatisfied, and so on). The chi-square statistic helps the analyst learn whether respondents in one category (for example, men) are significantly different in a statistical sense from those in another category (for example, women) with regard to another set of nominal data (for example, satisfied or dissatisfied with a given service). The chi-square (depicted symbolically as X^2) is calculated using the following formula:

$$X^2 = \sum \frac{(f_o - f_e)^2}{f_e}$$

where f_o and f_e refer respectively to the observed and expected frequencies for each cell in a table presenting one set of nominal data as rows and another set as columns.

Suppose 50 men and 50 women were interviewed, with 60 respondents favoring a new rugby league and 40 opposing it. Because half of the respondents are men, it might be *expected* that half of the proponents (that is, 30) and half of the opponents (that is, 20) would be men. These expected frequencies can be calculated by constructing a table for the variables (see Table 23-1), focusing only on the totals for the rows and columns (known as "marginals"), and applying the proportions for rows to the totals for columns to calculate an expected frequency for each cell.[5] If the proportion of women is 50 out of 100 respondents (50/100) and that proportion is applied to the "favor" column, the result is an expected frequency of 30 in the female-favor cell (50/100 $\times$ 60 = 30) (see Table 23-2).

Now, suppose that the observed frequencies (the actual responses, as shown in Table 23-3) differ from the expected frequencies. The chi-square statistic can be used to determine if the findings are statistically significant—that is, if they are sufficiently different from expected frequencies to conclude that differences in one variable in the population as a whole are likely to be related to differences in the other (that is, gender). In the case of the rugby survey, the calculations of the various elements in the formula yield a chi-square of 8.166 (see Table 23-4). The value of chi-square is

---

[5]Alternatively, the proportions for columns could be applied to the totals for rows to get the same results.

Table 23-2 Calculating the Expected Frequency of Cells from Knowledge of the Marginals

Gender of Respondent	Favor	Oppose	Total
Female	$f_e = 30$	$f_e = 20$	50
Male	$f_e = 30$	$f_e = 20$	50
Total	60	40	100

Note: f_e is the expected frequency for a given cell based on the proportions found in the marginals. Calculation for a given cell is:
$$f_e = (\text{row marginal}/N) \times \text{column marginal}.$$
For example,
$$f_e \text{ for upper left cell} = (50/100) \times 60 = 30.$$

Table 23-3 Actual Support ("Observed Frequencies") for Proposed Rugby League among a Sample of Citizens

Gender of Respondent	Favor	Oppose	Total
Female	23	27	50
Male	37	13	50
Total	60	40	100

said to be "statistically significant" only if it exceeds the relevant value shown in a chi-square table (see Appendix D).

Calculating the chi-square yields one of the three things needed in order to use the chi-square table. The second task is to decide how rigorous the test should be—in other words, how small the probability (p) of a mistaken verdict should be (for example, a p of 0.01 imposes a more stringent test than a p of 0.05). A p of 0.02 will be used here.

Finally, the *degrees of freedom* in the table of survey results must be determined. Degrees of freedom (df) can be calculated using the following formula:

$$df = (r - 1)(c - 1)$$

where r is the number of rows in the table and c is the number of columns. In the example, the table has two rows (favor and oppose) and two columns (male and female), which yields only 1 degree of freedom.[6]

---

[6]If the marginals (row and column totals) and enough of the cell entries are known in a given table, the values for all the remaining cells in that table can be filled in. *Degrees of freedom* indicate how many cells have to be known in a given table, along with the marginals, in order to be able to fill out the rest of that table. In the case of a table with two rows and two columns, knowing just one cell value ($df = 1$) along with the row and column totals is all the information needed to complete the table.

Table 23-4 Calculations for Chi-Square

Cell	f_o	f_e	$f_o - f_e$	$(f_o - f_e)^2$	$(f_o - f_e)^2 / f_e$
a	23	30	−7	49	1.633
b	27	20	7	49	2.450
c	37	30	7	49	1.633
d	13	20	−7	49	2.450
Total	100	100			8.166

Armed with these three pieces of information ($x^2 = 8.166$, $p = 0.02$, and $df = 1$), the chi-square table can be used to determine that the results are statistically significant at the .02 level only if the chi-square is greater than or equal to 5.412. Because the value in the example ($x^2 = 8.166$) exceeds that level, it can confidently be asserted that males in this community are more favorably inclined toward a community rugby league than are females. The odds are great that these two sets of variables (that is, gender and support for a rugby league) are related to each other and that the survey results did not simply occur by chance. The odds that the data distribution in this table could have occurred simply by chance, rather than because of a relationship between variables, are less than 2 percent ($p < .02$).

Chi-square can be a valuable analytic tool for exploring relationships between variables that are nominal or categorical in nature as long as the sample categories are large enough for this statistic to be applicable (that is, an expected frequency in each cell of 6 or greater). Other easy-to-apply statistics that are often useful in the analysis of citizen surveys are rank-order correlations, which are applicable when respondents are asked to rank preferences or the relative performance of different departments, and t-tests, which allow the analyst to assess whether differences in the average response of two groups are statistically significant. Neither of these statistics will be detailed here, but both may be found in any basic statistics textbook.

BACK IN TILLERY

Analysts Nick Wilson and Maria Pickwick explored how other local governments were analyzing survey data and using graphs to depict important findings. They also brushed up on chi-square and a few other basic statistics and began to look at their own survey reports in a new light. "I used to think our analysis was more thorough and our reports more impressive and useful than I do now," Wilson confessed. "In fact, I thought Eve was off base when she asked us to look into this. But not anymore."

"I know what you mean," replied Pickwick. "My feeling now is that we can do a lot more with the great data we get from the survey. I think our next report can be much better than the last one, even by incorporating some of the simple techniques we've picked up in the last few days."

Box 23-1 Testing for Statistical Significance

The Excel spreadsheet will test for statistical significance and report probabilities based on chi-square tests of data distributions. Unfortunately, however, Excel does not report the chi-square value itself.

   To use this significance-testing function, enter the sets of data for the actual frequencies and the expected frequencies for a cross-tabulation into the spreadsheet. (For directions on opening Excel and entering data refer to Box 2-1.) The intern from the example in the book would enter the expected frequency of men and women that were opposed to or in favor of a rugby league as well as the actual support for the league from the sample observations. After the data are entered, type CHITEST and enter the cell names of the actual range and the expected range of frequencies in parentheses after the command. For example, if the expected data were entered in chart form in cells B2 through C3 and the actual data were entered in cells B6 through C7, then the intern would enter "=CHITEST(B2:C3,B6:C7)" in any cell. An alternative to typing this instruction would be to use the Function choice (**fx**) from the Insert menu. The symbol for this choice (**fx**) also appears on the toolbar. The output indicates the probability—in this case, .004267—that the results occurred by chance. It does not show the actual chi-square statistic that would be found if using a statistics package rather than a spreadsheet or if doing the calculations by hand. Excel does, however, report the probability that the user would otherwise have to search for on a chart. Because the probability reported in this example (.004267) is very small and, more important, is less than the specified .02 probability mark, the result is said to be statistically significant. There is little likelihood that the relationship depicted in this cross-tabulation (see Table 23-3) could have happened by chance.

Before meeting again with Budget Director Bauer to share the results of their investigation, the analysts decided to develop a prototype for the next survey report by using their new tools on a small portion of last year's survey results. In most cases, they pursued a four-part strategy:

1. Examine results overall and also by relevant categories of respondents.
2. Develop cross-tabulations that compare results by relevant categories, and check to see whether the differences are statistically significant.
3. Do not commit *information overload* by including all of these cross-tabulations in the report. If none of the cross-tabulations produce statistically significant results, then report only the overall results for each major topic or issue.
4. If significant relationships are detected, report them in a manner that commands the attention they deserve.

The prototype report they prepared included a dozen graphs and tables, including those shown here as Figures 23-1 and 23-2. The budget director was pleased. "This is just the sort of analysis I had in mind," Bauer said. "Not only does it give

Figure 23-1 Perceived Housing Availability for Various Household Income Ranges in Tillery (in percentages)

us a more informative report, but I predict that some of these breakdowns by neighborhood will actually influence some operating strategies. Then we can see whether these strategies begin to improve the effectiveness and equity of our services. In my book, we are finally beginning to see the *real value* of citizen surveys."

Figure 23-2 Perceived Magnitude of Speeding Problem, by Neighborhood in Tillery (in percentages)

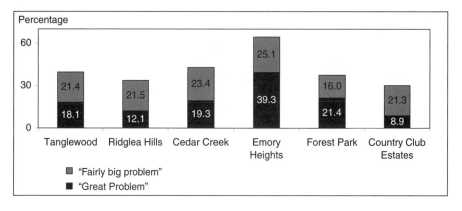

Box 23-2 Other Applications of the Chi-Square Statistic

In addition to its usefulness in detecting and reporting statistically significant survey results, the chi-square statistic can perform the same service for other types of nominal data collected by means other than surveys. Consider, for instance, the debate in a given community over the qualifications for new police officers or the effectiveness of a tuition reimbursement program as a retention device for employees in general. Is the evidence that rookie officers with college degrees are more likely to complete probation and less likely to be the target of citizen complaints statistically significant? Are employees who participate in the tuition reimbursement program more likely than nonparticipants to remain with the local government at least five years? Because these questions involve nominal (categorical) variables—that is, college degreed versus nondegreed candidates, completion versus noncompletion of probation, recipient versus nonrecipient of citizen complaints, tuition program participant versus nonparticipant, employment of five years or more versus employment of a shorter duration—each can be analyzed with cross-tabulations of data that are probably on hand and answered with the chi-square statistic. The same applies to questions involving nominal data and other local government issues.

SUGGESTED FOR FURTHER INFORMATION

Blalock, Hubert M., Jr. *Social Statistics.* New York: McGraw-Hill, 1979.

Cronk, Brian C. *How to Use SPSS: A Step-by-Step Guide to Analysis and Interpretation.* Los Angeles: Pyrczak Publishing, 1999.

Fink, Arlene, and Jacqueline Kosecoff. *How to Conduct Surveys: A Step-By-Step Guide,* 2d ed. Thousand Oaks, Calif.: Sage Publications, 1998.

Folz, David H. *Survey Research for Public Administration.* Thousand Oaks, Calif.: Sage Publications, 1996.

Gupta, Dipak K. *Decisions by the Numbers: An Introduction to Quantitative Techniques for Public Policy Analysis and Management.* Englewood Cliffs, N.J.: Prentice-Hall, 1994.

Hatry, Harry P., John E. Marcotte, Therese van Houten, and Carol H. Weiss. *Customer Surveys for Agency Managers: What Managers Need to Know.* Washington, D.C.: Urban Institute Press, 1998.

Miller, Thomas I. "Designing and Conducting Surveys." In *Handbook of Practical Program Evaluation,* edited by Joseph S. Wholey, Harry P. Hatry, and Kathryn E. Newcomer, 271–292. San Francisco: Jossey-Bass, 1994.

Renner, Tari. *Statistics Unraveled: A Practical Guide to Using Data in Decision Making.* Washington, D.C.: International City Management Association, 1988.

Sapsford, R. *Data Collection and Analysis.* Thousand Oaks, Calif.: Sage Publications, 1996.

Wallgren, A., B. Wallgren, R. Persson, U. Jorner, and J. A. Haaland. *Graphing Statistics and Data.* Thousand Oaks, Calif.: Sage Publications, 1996.

Webb, Kenneth, and Harry P. Hatry. *Obtaining Citizen Feedback: The Application of Citizen Surveys to Local Governments.* Washington, D.C.: Urban Institute Press, 1973.

Weisberg, H. F., J. A. Krosnick, and B. D. Brown. *An Introduction to Survey Research, Polling and Data Analysis.* Thousand Oaks, Calif.: Sage Publications, 1996.

24

Correlation Coefficients and Advanced Demand Analysis

How closely do staffing patterns and other resource allocation strategies match the demand for services? The graphic technique described in Chapter 3 provides a "rough cut" demand analysis that in many cases is sufficient for detecting a demand-to-resource mismatch and devising a practical solution. But what about cases that require a finer analytic instrument to supplement the demand graphs? Local governments that want greater precision might consider calculating the correlation between the pattern of demand for a service and their pattern of resource allocation.

SCENARIO: SATTERFIELD, ALABAMA

Chet Warren was polite to the caller but was noticeably agitated when he hung up the telephone. A chief of police is supposed to be calm, collected, and under control—not to mention thick-skinned—and by all accounts Warren is an excellent chief, but this call got to him.

"Sometimes people say things because they think it is fashionable or funny to say them," he muttered. "But say it enough and people start believing it's true!"

Chief Warren turned to Lester Scott, an administrative assistant in the police department who was pulling some material from the file cabinet in the corner of the chief's office. "I know it's just a cliché to most folks, but I am getting pretty tired of hearing, 'There's never a police officer around when you need one.' The woman on the phone just now made some serious allegations and concluded her comments with that little declaration. I heard the same thing yesterday in a half-joking manner, I think, at the Lion's Club. I wish I had a better response."

"We can't put an officer on every street corner," said Lester. "What do they expect?"

"They expect us to deploy our officers wisely," responded the chief. "If we do, we ought to be able to document the soundness of our scheduling and assignment patterns. And if we don't, I need to get the situation corrected."

"What do you have in mind?"

"Run some correlations. Look at the pattern of calls for service—by day of the week, time of day, and neighborhood or assignment zone. See how well that pattern correlates with the number of patrol officers on duty at those times and locations. Let's get the facts and go from there."

PERTINENT STATISTICS

To determine the extent to which one variable (for example, officers on duty) increases or decreases in relation to changes in another variable (for example, calls for service), a *measure of association* must be obtained. The choice in this case is the correlation coefficient *r*, which was introduced by Karl Pearson and often is called the Pearson product-moment correlation. This coefficient ranges from +1.0 to −1.0, depending on the nature and strength of the relationship between the two variables.

If Satterfield's deployment strategies match the call-for-service demand patterns precisely, then the correlation coefficient will be +1.0 or very close to that level. This would be a strong positive correlation, meaning that as the number of calls for service increases, so does the number of police officers on duty. In contrast, if the correlation coefficient approaches −1.0, then there is a strong negative correlation, meaning that Satterfield's on-duty strength tends to drop just when there is the greatest demand for service. If this turns out to be the case, then the local critics would be proven correct. If the correlation coefficient falls somewhere in the mid-range near 0.0, this would signify a weak or nonexistent relationship between the two variables. As calls for service increase, the number of on-duty officers either is unaffected or it varies in an unpredictable pattern, sometimes increasing and sometimes declining. Chief Warren is hoping to find a strong, positive correlation between calls for service and officers on duty.

Calculation of the correlation coefficient by hand is not especially difficult, but it is a bit time consuming and tedious. The wide availability of computer software that includes capability for calculating correlation coefficients—even from spreadsheets—makes hand calculation an increasingly less popular choice.[1] Still, it is simple, as shown below.

The formula for the correlation coefficient *r* is as follows:

$$r = \frac{N\sum XY - \left(\sum X\right)\left(\sum Y\right)}{\sqrt{\left[N\sum X^2 - \left(\sum X\right)^2\right]\left[N\sum Y^2 - \left(\sum Y\right)^2\right]}}$$

where
  X is one of the two variables (for example, calls for service)
  Y is the other variable (for example, officers on duty)
  N is the number of sets of variables
  Σ signifies the summation (that is, addition) of the indicated variables

---

[1]See, for example, Brian C. Cronk, *How to Use SPSS: A Step-by-Step Guide to Analysis and Interpretation* (Los Angeles: Pyrczak Publishing, 1999). Even some popular spreadsheet programs, such as Microsoft Excel, possess the capability of calculating correlation coefficients. The coefficients displayed in Table 24-3 were calculated using Excel.

Table 24-1 Service Calls and Officers on Duty, Satterfield Police Department, Sunday, February 2

Zone/Shift		Calls for Service (X)	Officers on Duty (Y)
I.	A	2	1
	B	4	2
	C	2	1
II.	A	3	1
	B	5	2
	C	2	1
III.	A	3	1
	B	7	2
	C	2	1
Total		30	12

When Lester began compiling information, he started with data for a recent Sunday, February 2. He separated information on calls for service and officer assignments according to the police department's three response zones and further subdivided this information by the three daily work shifts. When he was through, Lester had nine pairs of data ($N = 9$), showing calls for service (variable X) and officers on duty (variable Y) for each zone and shift combination (see Table 24-1).

To calculate the correlation coefficient using the computational formula, Lester had to figure products and averages; he had to square some of the numbers and calculate square roots for others; and he had to do a good bit of adding and subtracting. But without too much trouble, he found the correlation coefficient for the two sets of variables to be +0.87 (see Table 24-2). He would be able to report to the chief that for Sunday, February 2, at least, there had been a strong, positive correlation between the patterns of service demand and officer deployment.

GETTING A MORE COMPLETE PICTURE

Lester, of course, needed more than one day's worth of statistics in order to tell whether the department's patrol resources were being deployed wisely. He decided to gather information on calls for service and officers on duty, by response zone and duty shift, for a two-week period. He could then examine correlations across zones and shifts for a given day, correlations across days for a given zone and shift, and the overall correlation across all zones, shifts, and days. Lester wanted to find if officers were being deployed imprudently in any zone or shift, or if the department was overstaffing a particular day.

Table 24-2 Calculating the Correlation Coefficient for Service Calls and Officers on Duty, Satterfield Police Department, Sunday, February 2

Zone/Shift	Calls for Service (X)	Officers on Duty (Y)	XY
I. A	2	1	2
B	4	2	8
C	2	1	2
II. A	3	1	3
B	5	2	10
C	2	1	2
III. A	3	1	3
B	7	2	14
C	2	1	2
Total	30	12	46

$\Sigma X = 30 \qquad \Sigma Y = 12$

$\bar{X} = 3.33 \qquad \bar{Y} = 1.33$

$$r = \frac{N\sum XY - \left(\sum X\right)\left(\sum Y\right)}{\sqrt{\left[N\sum X^2 - \left(\sum X\right)^2\right]\left[N\sum Y^2 - \left(\sum Y\right)^2\right]}}$$

$$= \frac{(9 \times 46) - (30 \times 12)}{\sqrt{\left[(9 \times 124) - 900\right]\left[(9 \times 18) - 144\right]}} = \frac{414 - 360}{\sqrt{(1,116 - 900)(162 - 144)}}$$

$$= \frac{54}{\sqrt{(216 \times 18)}} = \frac{54}{\sqrt{3,888}} = \frac{54}{62.354} = 0.87$$

Lester found an overall correlation coefficient of +0.81 for the two-week period (see Table 24-3). To the extent that any demand-to-deployment mismatches existed, they tended to be on weekdays, when calls for service and on-duty staffing are usually lightest. In most poor correlation cases, an extra officer had been assigned on a weekday to a shift or zone that had little need for reinforcement. On February 10, for example, an extra officer was assigned not to Zone III's B shift, typically the heaviest duty assignment, but instead to the midnight shift in Zone I. Lester gathered his materials and headed to the chief's office, hoping to catch him before his next appointment.

Box 24-1 Correlation, Not Causation!

Just because a correlation coefficient for a pair of variables is large, an analyst should not jump to the conclusion that one of the variables is causing the other. The correlation statistic establishes only that the two variables are related to each other. Perhaps one is causing increases or decreases in the other, or perhaps yet another variable is influencing changes in one or both of the variables being examined. In this chapter's example, calls for service and officers on duty in a hypothetical community are shown to be related to each other, but neither directly *caused* the other. Declarations of causation—that is, that changes in one variable caused changes in another—based on simple correlation statistics are a common error of beginning analysts.

CHIEF WARREN'S RESPONSE

Lester was in luck. The chief's 1:00 p.m. meeting ended earlier than anticipated, so they had twenty minutes to review Lester's table of correlation statistics before his 3:00 p.m. appointment.

Chief Warren looked over the statistics on demand-and-deployment patterns and was delighted with what he saw. "This is terrific, Lester. I can't say that I am happy with how we are handling everything, but overall it looks pretty good," he said. "And where we have a few problems, I think we can develop some solutions."

"So you like this report okay, huh, Chief?" Lester asked, knowing already that he did, but hoping to get another compliment.

"You bet, I do, Lester," the chief responded. "In fact, I want one of these tables to be produced every two weeks. I want to receive a copy and I want other copies to go to everyone having responsibility for scheduling work shifts. We are going to make this part of our management information around here."

Later, Chief Warren met with his management team—the department "brass," as they were called. He described the correlation statistic as a tool for alerting them whenever they experienced a mismatch between workload and personnel. He distributed copies of Lester's table and allowed Lester to explain the details.

Lester loved the limelight. After ten minutes, he was still going strong, when Chief Warren gracefully regained control of the meeting.

"I want us to manage our resources wisely," the chief said. "That means getting good results, while holding down costs. To do that, we've got to put our officers on duty when and where they are needed most. Get used to this table, because you are going to be seeing one like it every two weeks. I want us to consistently keep our overall correlation coefficient above 0.80, even if some dips on a given day or shift are inevitable."

"If what you're getting at, Chief, is good planning," interjected a sergeant, "how about using 'officers assigned' instead of 'officers on duty.' We know what the demand

Table 24-3 Officer Deployment-to-Demand Correlations, Satterfield Police Department, February 2–15

Date		Zone I			Zone II			Zone III			Total	Correlation
		A	B	C	A	B	C	A	B	C		
2/2 Su	Calls for service	2	4	2	3	5	2	3	7	2	30	0.87
	Officers on duty	1	2	1	1	2	1	1	2	1	12	
2/3 M	Calls for service	3	4	2	2	2	3	3	5	3	27	0.85
	Officers on duty	1	2	1	1	1	1	1	2	1	11	
2/4 Tu	Calls for service	2	2	2	3	3	2	0	2	3	19	-0.04
	Officers on duty	1	1	2	1	1	1	1	1	1	10	
2/5 W	Calls for service	2	3	3	2	3	1	3	5	1	23	0.74
	Officers on duty	1	1	1	1	1	1	1	2	1	10	
2/6 Th	Calls for service	0	3	1	2	5	1	1	4	2	19	0.67
	Officers on duty	1	1	1	1	2	1	1	1	1	10	
2/7 F	Calls for service	4	6	2	3	6	5	5	9	5	45	0.84
	Officers on duty	2	2	1	1	2	2	1	3	2	16	
2/8 Sa	Calls for service	2	6	5	2	6	3	4	8	4	40	0.92
	Officers on duty	1	2	2	1	2	1	2	3	2	16	
2/9 Su	Calls for service	2	3	2	2	3	1	2	5	1	21	0.82
	Officers on duty	1	1	1	1	1	1	1	2	1	10	
2/10 M	Calls for service	1	3	2	2	3	2	1	3	2	19	-0.05
	Officers on duty	1	1	2	1	1	1	1	1	1	10	
2/11 Tu	Calls for service	2	3	2	1	3	1	2	4	0	18	0.31
	Officers on duty	1	1	1	1	2	1	1	1	1	10	
2/12 W	Calls for service	1	4	3	1	1	0	2	6	3	21	0.73
	Officers on duty	1	1	1	1	1	1	1	2	1	10	
2/13 Th	Calls for service	1	4	1	2	3	1	2	3	2	19	0.48
	Officers on duty	1	2	1	2	1	1	1	1	1	11	
2/14 F	Calls for service	5	5	3	1	7	2	3	9	5	40	0.88
	Officers on duty	2	1	1	1	2	1	1	3	2	14	
2/15 Sa	Calls for service	4	5	2	3	7	6	4	8	7	46	0.85
	Officers on duty	2	2	1	1	2	2	1	3	2	16	
Correlation		0.84	0.67	0.39	-0.03	0.82	0.86	0.32	0.95	0.84		0.81

Notes: (1) Duty shifts in Satterfield are A, 7 A.M. to 3 P.M.; B, 3 P.M. to 11 P.M.; and C, 11 P.M. to 7 A.M. (2) Correlations in the right-hand column reflect the department's sensitivity to differences in call-for-service patterns by time of day (that is, from one shift to another) and by location (that is, from one zone to another). (3) Correlations in the bottom row reflect the department's sensitivity to differences in call-for-service patterns by day of the week.

From the Electronic Toolkit ●────────────────────────

Box 24-2 Finding the Correlation Coefficient

Calculating the correlation coefficient by hand can be a long process and leaves plenty of opportunities for careless mistakes that may affect the results. Excel offers a quick and reliable alternative to calculation by hand—the CORREL function. First, enter the two sets of data. (For directions on opening Excel and entering data refer to Box 2-1.) Then, in any cell, enter the CORREL command followed by the cell names in parentheses for the two ranges of data. For example, if Lester entered the calls for service from Table 24-2 in cell A1 through cell A9 and the number of officers on duty in cell B1 through B9, then he would enter the formula "=CORREL(A1:A9,B1:B9)" to determine the correlation of .866 between the two sets of data. (An alternative to typing this instruction would be to use the Function choice (**fx**) from the Insert menu. The symbol for this choice (**fx**) also appears on the toolbar.)

patterns are and we can draw up good duty rosters, but if someone is out on vacation or if someone is sick. . . ."

"No," the chief interrupted, "what I am getting at is *good management.* That includes good planning, but it also means making adjustments when necessary. Shifting assignments, redeploying from light call zones to heavy call zones, occa-

Box 24-3 Other Applications of the Correlation Statistic

Good management often requires the development of strategies of resource deployment that result in resource allocation patterns that coincide approximately with the peaks and valleys of service demand—by time, location, or both. A swimming pool needs more lifeguards on duty when conditions are crowded. A utilities office needs more clerks available for counter duty during hours when lines are most apt to form. Sometimes a simple graph showing patterns of service demand and staff on duty will be sufficient to convince the manager or analyst either that current strategies are adequate or that modifications are needed. Simply reviewing the graphs might be enough. In other cases, however, a single statistic might be preferred.

In Kansas City, Missouri, the city auditor used ambulance system data to construct a pair of graphs depicting patterns of ambulance calls and ambulance availability by time of day during a seven-month period in 1999 (see below).[1] The similarity of the peaks and valleys in the two graphs was sufficient to satisfy the audit team that staffing strategies were adequate. If greater precision had been desired, the auditor could have reported the correlation of ambulance calls and ambulance availability hour by hour throughout the period. Calculating the correlation coefficient using only the hourly averages depicted as data points in the graphs below rather than more precise hour-by-hour figures, the result suggests an extremely high correlation of approximately +0.96.

---

[1]City of Kansas City Auditor's Office, *Performance Audit: Emergency Medical Services System* (Kansas City, Mo.: City Auditor's Office, City of Kansas City, January 2000), 30.

(Box continues on next page)

Box 24-3 *(Continued)*

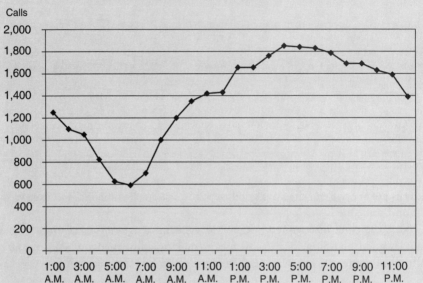

Ambulance Calls Received in Kansas City by Hour of Day

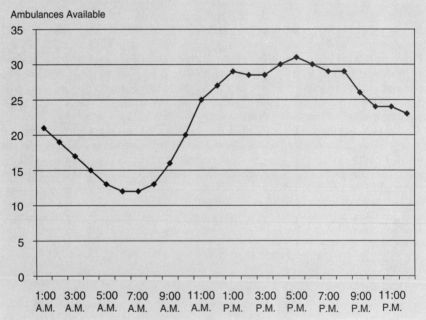

Ambulance Deployment in Kansas City by Hour of Day

sionally calling in off-duty officers for overtime—these are things I want you, as managers, to consider, keeping performance and cost in mind, of course."

"The next time someone says 'There's never a police officer around when you need one,' " the chief continued, "I want to be able to prove them wrong. These correlation coefficients plus some good response time statistics should do the trick. If we are deploying officers wisely and they still think they don't see enough officers around, then it probably means we are understaffed, given their expectations—not that our staff resources are being managed poorly—and we will be happy to accept their help in getting more police officers."

SUGGESTED FOR FURTHER INFORMATION

Blalock, Hubert M., Jr. *Social Statistics*. New York: McGraw-Hill, 1979.

Cronk, Brian C. *How to Use SPSS: A Step-by-Step Guide to Analysis and Interpretation*. Los Angeles: Pyrczak Publishing, 1999.

Renner, Tari. *Statistics Unraveled: A Practical Guide to Using Data in Decision Making*. Washington, D.C.: International City Management Association, 1988.

25

Analysis of Operations Via Benchmarking

In the corporate world, the term *benchmarking* refers to a performance improvement process with well-defined steps and a distinct lingo. The technique, popular since the 1980s, is meticulously analytic and focuses not on an entire corporation, department, or program but instead on a single key process—for instance, the acquisition of raw materials, product assembly, or product warehousing and distribution.

Rather than starting with a blank slate in the design of improvements, organizations engaged in benchmarking seek out top performers of the selected process—that is, other organizations considered to be "best in class" or "world class" in that particular activity—in hopes of gaining their cooperation as the benchmarking organization attempts to identify factors that account for superior performance. The superior results achieved by "best in class" performers are their *benchmarks*; cooperating organizations are *benchmarking partners*; and the analytic endeavor is designed to identify *best practices* that can be adopted or, more likely, adapted for use by the benchmarking organization to improve its performance. A simple graphic depiction of the technique is shown in Figure 25-1.

A somewhat more detailed description of the steps, developed for the application of corporate-style benchmarking in the public sector, follows:

- decide what to benchmark
- study the processes in your own organization
- identify benchmarking partners
- gather information
- analyze
- implement for effect
- monitor results and take further action as needed[1]

This type of benchmarking has been used successfully by some local governments,[2] but corporate-style benchmarking is only one of three versions of bench-

---

[1]Southern Growth Policies Board and Southern Consortium of University Public Service Organizations, "Benchmarking Best Practices," Module 2 of *Results-Oriented Government*. (Research Triangle Park, N.C.: Southern Growth Policies Board, 1997), 5. Reprinted by permission.

[2]See, for example, Patricia Keehley, Steven Medlin, Sue MacBride, and Laura Longmire, *Benchmarking for Best Practices in the Public Sector* (San Francisco: Jossey-Bass, 1997); City of Arlington (Texas) Parks and Recreation Department, *Program Division Benchmarking Projects* (August 1993).

Figure 25-1 A Five-Stage Benchmarking Process

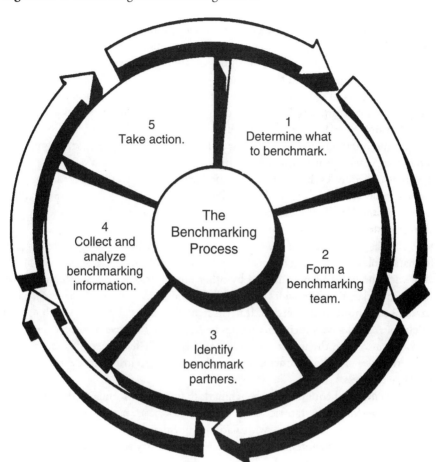

Source: Reprinted from *The Benchmarking Book,* by Michael J. Spendolini. Copyright © 1992 AMA-COM. Used by permission of the publisher, AMACOM.

marking in the public sector. Public sector examples can be found for each of the following types of benchmarking:

- corporate-style benchmarking
- "visioning" initiatives using benchmarks
- comparison of performance statistics as benchmarks

The most widely publicized of all public sector benchmarking efforts have been those that may be categorized as "visioning" initiatives—the second form of public sector benchmarking.[3] These initiatives have engaged private sector entities, civic organizations, the philanthropic community, and citizens, as well as government offi-

---

[3]Jonathan Walters, "The Benchmarking Craze," *Governing,* April 7, 1994, 33–37.

cials, in establishing a vision for the future of a given state or community, and they have established benchmarks to track progress toward that vision. Examples at the state level have included the Oregon Benchmarks, Florida Benchmarks, and Minnesota Milestones.[4] Similar initiatives at the community level have appeared in Jacksonville, Florida, and Seattle, Washington, among others.

Although less publicized than popular visioning initiatives, the most common form of benchmarking in local government is the comparison of local performance statistics with relevant standards or the comparison of performance statistics among organizations—the third form of public sector benchmarking. Interjurisdictional comparison offers a broader context for judging local performance, something that internal or year-to-year comparisons cannot provide.

Cities and counties that measure their performance in even the most rudimentary fashion know whether their workload is increasing or declining from year to year. If their set of measures includes more than mere indicators of workload or output, they also know whether the quality and efficiency of their services are improving (see Chapter 8). What they *do not and cannot know* from year-to-year, single-organization performance analysis is whether the quality and efficiency of their services compare favorably with the levels being achieved by other organizations. A city or county that wishes to declare that it provides high-quality services needs more than internal comparisons to confirm that assertion. It needs reputable external pegs on which to base its claim. A local government that wishes to emphasize improvement of a given service and move it to the upper echelon of quality or efficiency needs to know what top performers elsewhere are achieving, as a benchmark to inspire its own efforts and to gauge progress.

Many cities and counties that benchmark their own performance through comparison of performance statistics do so on an ad hoc basis, perhaps comparing their library's performance statistics with national norms in one study, comparing the record of their fleet maintenance mechanics with industry standards in another, and surveying a group of respected cities or counties to gather road maintenance statistics for still another comparative study. Some cities and counties have joined cooperative performance measurement or benchmarking projects to gain such information and to increase the reliability of performance and cost data through uniform collection and compilation across jurisdictions.[5]

Local governments that assemble a set of comparative performance statistics for a given function can place their own statistics in the mix and see where they stand in volume of activity and, more important, in quality, efficiency, and effectiveness

---

[4]See, for example, Oregon Progress Board, *Achieving the Oregon Shines Vision: The 1999 Benchmark Performance Report* (Salem: Oregon Progress Board, 1999).

[5]Cooperative projects have been sponsored at the national level by the International City/County Management Association (www.icma.org/performance) and at the state level by the Institute of Government at the University of North Carolina (http://ioginfo.iog.unc.edu/programs/perfmeas/index.html) and the Institute of Public Affairs at the University of South Carolina (www.iopa.sc.edu/cfg/Benchmarking/Index.htm), among others.

of service. This is valuable information. In some cases, this information alone may prompt service improvements. But can the analyst take these data and gain additional insights using simple analytic techniques? That is the question facing a young management analyst in the fictional city of Eliza, California.

ELIZA, CALIFORNIA

Lisa Bootmaker was looking for some bucks she could squeeze out of the budget. *Better, faster, cheaper* had long been the mantra among the team of management analysts who occupied the cubicles on the south wing of city hall's fourth floor, but this year *better* and *faster* were taking a back seat to *cheaper*. The city government was facing a budget crisis, and the analysts were desperately seeking options that could save big bucks without ravaging services. Lisa had turned her attention to the sanitation department, where the hefty budget for residential refuse collection offered a tempting target.

Lisa and fellow analyst Lindy Hall liked to share stories and bounce ideas off one another. They found the practice entertaining, spiced as most of these conversations were with amusing anecdotes from the field. Lindy often said that truth was stranger than fiction, but Lisa wondered how much fiction worked its way into the hilarious "truths" Lindy sometimes told. Offering more than just entertainment value, these conversations also gave the analysts a chance to air their thinking on important projects and secure feedback from a colleague who would not pull any punches when their reasoning was off base. On several occasions, each had been spared future embarrassment when an ill-conceived conclusion had been exposed in one of these conversations and revised before it went any further.

"I am leaning more and more toward recommending that we experiment with 'managed competition' for residential refuse services," Lisa said, "but it is tough to guess how much we can squeeze from the budget. I'm afraid it won't be the wad of cash I thought originally."

"By managed competition, you mean the approach where the sanitation department would compete to provide the service?" asked Lindy. "The department would submit a bid along with outside companies that are interested in the job?"

"That's right."

"Why mess with that? You want to know how to save money in refuse collection?" Lindy asked, not waiting for a response. "Cut services to once a week or contract it out. Or do both. Simple."

"I don't think it's quite that simple, Lindy," Lisa replied. "It's true that reducing the service from twice a week to once a week would save money by eliminating one round through the entire city every week, but the remaining round would be that much heavier in terms of tonnage collected and therefore much slower. It would result in a sizable savings, but it wouldn't be as much as you might think. Besides, the city manager said he wants us to solve this problem with as little adverse effect on services as possible. A proposal to reduce collection frequency would be a powder keg in this community."

"Okay, then let's just contract the service. I have seen plenty of reports that say contracting for refuse services is cheaper."

"I have seen those studies, too, and they say contracting *tends* to be cheaper. It's no guarantee. A well-managed in-house operation still beats an average or weak contractor."

"Is that what we have, Lisa—a well-managed in-house operation?"

"I'm not sure it couldn't be," replied Lisa, "with proper conditions and the right incentives. That's why I am leaning toward managed competition. Give them a chance to tighten their operation. Then, if they are the best choice, keep the work in-house. But if they cannot compete, turn part or all of the business over to outside companies."

"Do you have facts and figures to support this recommendation?" Lindy asked.

"I think I do."

SCATTERPLOTS AND REGRESSION LINES

Lisa stepped back to her own cubicle and retrieved several charts. For the past several years the city of Eliza has cooperated with twenty-nine other cities in a comparative performance measurement project. The project is designed to produce reliable, uniformly collected performance and cost information pertaining to a variety of local government services. Lisa has used the refuse collection data from this project in her analysis.

The first chart Lisa showed Lindy was a scatterplot (also called a scattergram or scatter diagram) showing the number of refuse accounts (that is, households) and the expenditures per account in Eliza and nine other cities (see Figure 25-2).[6] Eliza, for example, served 201,650 accounts at an expenditure rate of $95.62 per account, placing it near the center of the scatterplot.

"I thought there were 30 cities in that project," Lindy interjected. "Why are there only 10 in the scatterplot."

"These are the ones with twice a week service," Lisa responded. "Including the others would distort the analysis. I'm looking for expenditure differences attributable to economies of scale or operating strategies rather than lower service levels."

The second chart showed the scatterplot again, but this time it had a line running through it (see Figure 25-3). Lisa explained that this is a regression line drawn by the computer to depict the relationship between the two variables (number of accounts and expenditure per account) insofar as the evidence from these ten cities is concerned. It reveals—by the line and by an accompanying equation—how the scale of the operation (that is, number of accounts) tends to influence expenditures per account.

---

[6]Performance data for the city of Eliza are hypothetical. Statistics for the other nine cities are based on data from International City/County Management Association, *Comparative Performance Measurement: FY 1997 Data Report* (Washington, D.C.: ICMA, 1999).

Figure 25-2 Residential Refuse Accounts and Expenditures per Residential Refuse Account for Ten Cities

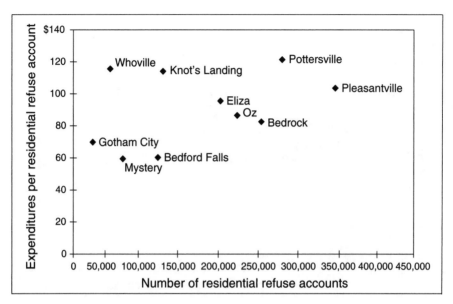

"This isn't perfect and it isn't especially sophisticated," Lisa explained, "but it is informative and it's easy to do. I prepared these charts using the regression tool in Excel. [See Appendix E for a description of the procedure for doing so.] For purposes of analysis, I consider the line to be the *expected value* of the expenditure per account for a given number of refuse accounts. A city can identify its expected expenditure per account simply by knowing how many accounts it is serving. Using that information, a city can pinpoint its spot on the horizontal line at the base of the figure. A vertical line from that point will intersect the regression line at its expected expenditure level. When a city's actual point lies above the regression line, meaning higher than expected expenditure, it can be considered to be less efficient than average—judging strictly from the size of the operation and ignoring all other factors. When a city's actual point is below the regression line, it is doing something right. It is more efficient than average."

Lisa went on to explain that the analysis to this point does two things for her. First, it reassures her about citing the research literature on economies of scale in refuse collection. Previous studies indicated that refuse services enjoy economies of scale only until they reach a customer base of about 50,000 population.[7] After that, costs tend

---

[7]E. S. Savas, *The Organization and Efficiency of Solid Waste Collection* (Lexington, Mass.: Lexington Books, 1977).

Figure 25-3 Relationship Between Number of Residential Refuse Accounts and Expenditures per Residential Refuse Account *(Correlation: 0.39)*

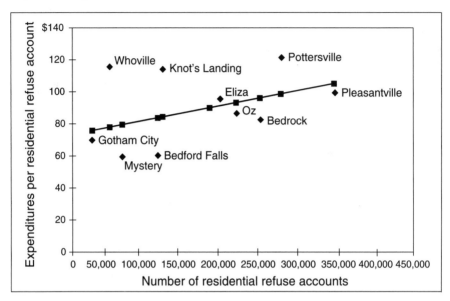

to level out. All the cities in Lisa's analysis have populations far in excess of 50,000. The smallest city serves 28,740 households (that is, accounts) and has a population of 110,950. The expenditure pattern in her cities suggests *diseconomies of scale,* with greater expenditures per account as the number of accounts increases. This not only strengthens her confidence in the earlier studies and in her own figures, it also supports her managed competition recommendation. If managed competition results in splitting Eliza into two or more refuse collection territories served by different service producers, city officials need not be overly concerned that the split will result in the loss of economies of scale.

Second, her analysis tells Lisa that the city of Eliza's refuse service costs are well within the normal range for its customer base. In fact, Eliza's point almost hugs the regression line for expected cost. Unlike a city with excessive in-house expenditures for a given service, Eliza is unlikely to reap a huge windfall in cost savings by shifting to contract service. Still, there is room for improvement, as evidenced by other cities with lower than expected expenditures. Managed competition is a strategy to secure these improvements either by streamlining in-house operations or by contracting with a more efficient outside provider.

"This is pretty cool," Lindy remarked. "So the most efficient city is the one that is farthest below the regression line, right?"

Lisa explained that for her analysis, she was using the *percentage* difference above or below the line rather than the raw difference. She further explained that the dis-

Box 25-1 Scatterplot Patterns

In a scatterplot, a set of data points exhibiting a positive relationship between two variables presents a pattern that moves upward from left to right—that is, away from the horizontal base (see Figure A). As one variable increases, the other variable tends to increase, too.

A set of data points exhibiting neither a positive nor negative relationship between the variables is depicted by a horizontal regression line (see Figure B).

A set of data points exhibiting a negative relationship between the variables presents a pattern that moves downward from left to right (see Figure C). As one variable increases, the other tends to decrease.

Figure A Positive Relationship

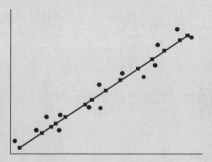

Figure B No Relationship

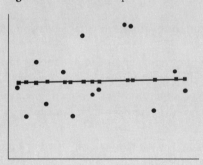

Figure C Negative Relationship

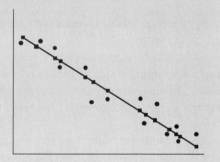

tance between the point and the line is called the *residual* and that she was looking at the residual as a percentage of the expected expenditure. So if a city is $10 below an expected expenditure of $80, which is 12.5 percent below the expected value, it is considered to be more efficient than a city with an expenditure $10 below an expected $100 per account, or 10 percent below. "But before we get too carried away with declaring this city or that one to be the most efficient, let's remember that we are only looking at two variables here. We would undoubtedly get a more precise line

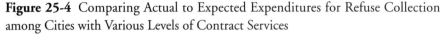

Figure 25-4 Comparing Actual to Expected Expenditures for Refuse Collection among Cities with Various Levels of Contract Services

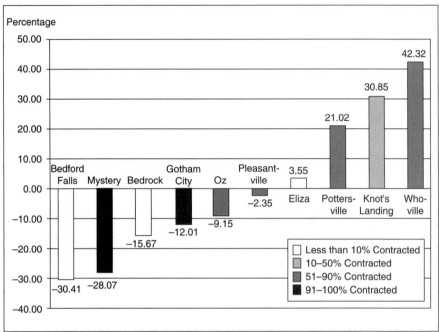

with more variables using multiple regression, but I think this simple version will do the job for me."

Although the scatterplot and regression line were helpful components of Lisa's analysis, stopping at this point would have fallen short of what Lisa *really wanted to know.* "If I am going to recommend managed competition—or contracting, for that matter—I would like to have some reassurance that there is a high probability of a favorable result."

Lisa presented another chart (see Figure 25-4). Each residual, expressed as a positive or negative percentage from the expected expenditure, was shown in a bar graph. The bars depicting unfavorable results (that is, positive residuals) appear above the horizontal line. The bars depicting favorable results (that is, greater efficiency reflected by negative residuals) appear below the horizontal line.

Among the data collected in the comparative performance measurement project was information on the extent of contracting for refuse services—specifically, the percentage of all refuse accounts served by contract. Each of the bars in Figure 25-4 is coded to reflect the extent of residential refuse collection contracting in that city. Only Eliza among the ten cities handles all collection using city employees. Two cities handle everything by contract. The other seven cities operate with split systems— part in-house and part by contract.

Box 25-2 Key Statistics Related to Regression

The basic regression formula is:

$$Y = a + bX$$

where
> Y is the dependent variable
> X is the independent variable
> a is the Y intercept (where the regression line passes through the Y axis)
> b is the slope of the line

Once the analyst knows the regression coefficients (the values for a and b), the value of Y can be predicted simply by plugging a given value of X into the formula.

The correlation coefficient, r, ranges from +1.0 to −1.0 and tells the analyst the direction (positive or negative) and strength of the relationship between variables. Squaring the correlation coefficient produces the *coefficient of determination*, R^2, which reveals the amount (percentage) of the variation in Y that can be explained by knowing X.

Statistical *significance* tells the analyst how likely it is that the apparent relationship between variables simply happened by chance, based on a given set of observations or data points. In most cases the analyst will be looking for a significance figure of 0.05 or less (sometimes settling for 0.10 or less) before declaring the relationship to be statistically significant.

Analysts using the regression technique would be wise to consult a basic statistics textbook for more complete information on the use of regression and the interpretation of regression results and statistics.

"I was hoping this chart would give me a clearer answer regarding 'best practice,' " Lisa said. "Still, it is helpful. Most of all, it cautions me not to expect contracting to be a magic potion. Sure, the two cities that contract their refuse collection entirely have favorable residuals (lower than expected expenditures), but another city that contracts almost everything has much higher than expected expenditures. And two cities that operate mostly in-house have great results!"

POSTSCRIPT

Lisa prepared a report recommending that the city proceed toward managed competition for refuse services. She incorporated her charts into the report and noted with some pleasure the city manager's surprise at the absence of economies of scale among large service providers and the surprise of two business executives on the city council at the absence of clearer evidence in support of contracting for services. Four others joined these two in a 6–3 vote to move gradually toward managed competition, beginning with a single quadrant of the city. One council member, who previously had been considered proprivatization, said he was now convinced that competition, rather than privatization, is the key to good performance and that he hoped the sanitation department could develop the winning bid. Funds were appropriated

Box 25-3 Other Applications of Benchmarking and Regression

Any local government operation could probably benefit from careful benchmarking. An animal control unit, for example, might discover that its pet adoption rates are far lower than those of some of its counterparts, thus leading to a series of conversations that reveal the other unit's secrets to success. A sanitation department might discover that the tonnage of refuse collected by its average worker is much less than the comparable figure for its benchmarking partners, with further analysis revealing that its equipment is outmoded or its collection routes poorly designed.

The usefulness of regression analysis extends well beyond benchmarking projects. Regression is applicable as well to many other projects in which an analyst is attempting to sort out or project the impact of one or more variables on another variable. For example, what are the relative impacts of a community's age profile and the local economy on the demand for golf and swimming facilities or tot lots? How much of the golf course or swimming pool's failure to meet its cost-recovery targets can be attributed to unusual weather patterns last year? What factors have the greatest influence on general fund revenue variations? Given certain assumptions regarding these factors, how much revenue may we project?

to assist the sanitation department in reviewing its operation, evaluating equipment and deployment practices, and preparing its bid.

Projected savings from managed competition in refuse collection were pegged at a modest level. The search for major budget savings continued elsewhere.

Lisa's management analyst colleague Lindy was persuaded by the charts and statistics that sorting out the promises and benefits of contracting is a lot more complicated than he thought originally. He backed away from his blind advocacy of that option.

SUGGESTED FOR FURTHER INFORMATION

Ammons, David N. *Municipal Benchmarks: Assessing Local Performance and Establishing Community Standards,* 2d ed. Thousand Oaks, Calif.: Sage Publications, 2001.

Andersen, Bjorn, and Per-Gaute Pettersen. *The Benchmarking Handbook.* London: Chapman & Hall, 1996.

Camp, Robert C. *Benchmarking: The Search for Industry Best Practices that Lead to Superior Performance.* Milwaukee, Wis.: Quality Press, 1989.

City of Arlington (Texas) Parks and Recreation Department. *Program Division Benchmarking Projects.* Arlington, Tex.: Author, 1993.

Cronk, Brian C. *How to Use SPSS: A Step-by-Step Guide to Analysis and Interpretation.* Los Angeles: Pyrczak Publishing, 1999.

Gupta, Dipak K. *Decisions by the Numbers: An Introduction to Quantitative Techniques for Public Policy Analysis and Management.* Englewood Cliffs, N.J.: Prentice-Hall, 1994.

Keehley, Patricia, Steven Medlin, Sue MacBride, and Laura Longmire. *Benchmarking for Best Practices in the Public Sector.* San Francisco: Jossey-Bass, 1997.

Oregon Progress Board. *Achieving the Oregon Shines Vision: The 1999 Benchmark Performance Report.* Salem: Oregon Progress Board, 1999.

Poister, Theodore H. *Benchmarking the City of Atlanta's Performance in Selected Areas of Service Delivery.* Atlanta: Research Atlanta, Inc., and Georgia State University, School of Policy Studies, 1998.

Renner, Tari. *Statistics Unraveled: A Practical Guide to Using Data in Decision Making.* Washington, D.C.: International City Management Association, 1988.

Savas, E. S. *The Organization and Efficiency of Solid Waste Collection.* Lexington, Mass.: Lexington Books, 1977.

Southern Growth Policies Board and Southern Consortium of University Public Service Organizations. "Benchmarking Best Practices," Module 2 of *Results-Oriented Government.* Research Triangle Park, N.C.: Southern Growth Policies Board, 1997.

Spendolini, Michael J. *The Benchmarking Book,* 2d ed. New York: AMACOM, 2000.

Taylor, Bernard W., III. *Introduction to Management Science,* 6th ed. Upper Saddle River, N.J.: Prentice-Hall, 1999.

Walters, Jonathan. "The Benchmarking Craze," *Governing,* April 7, 1994, 33–37.

Part VII

Wrap Up

Carefully conducted analyses can contribute to well-informed decisions in local government. Such analyses often can help a government seize an opportunity or avoid a serious misstep. Nevertheless, other factors sometimes carry the day, leading decision makers to deviate from analytically based recommendations.

Analysts who are committed to their craft and determined to bring analysis to bear on local government decisions do not simply give up in the wake of occasional disappointments, frustrated that their recommendations were not followed. Instead, dedicated analysts enjoy their successes, accept their disappointments, learn from both kinds of experience, and look forward to the next opportunity to apply their analytic skills.

26

The Role of Analysis in a Political Environment

If analysts or analytically oriented managers expect facts, figures, and logic always to prevail in the decision-making process, they have many surprises awaiting. Local governments are not businesses; their decisions are not made under the influence of a single "bottom-line" objective.

Local government decision makers must contend with multiple and often conflicting objectives. Efficiency, for example, normally is presumed to be one of the objectives, but rarely the only objective. Political objectives, as well as concerns for responsiveness, equity, and effectiveness, may override the influence of efficiency.

Careful analysis geared toward identifying the most efficient method of performing a particular function may produce recommendations short on political sensitivity, with little chance of approval. For example, the most efficient methods of dealing with delinquent taxpayers, speeding motorists, stray dogs, uncooperative developers, and belligerent service recipients may not be politically acceptable. Similarly, the most logical decisions regarding the fate of a dilapidated building, the signalization of a street intersection, or the siting of an airport or landfill may not be politically acceptable.

DISAPPOINTMENT, YES; DISCOURAGEMENT, NO

Analysts who have devoted hundreds of hours to a project only to see their recommendations rejected are sure to feel disappointment. Allowing that disappointment to be transformed into discouragement, however, could deprive the decision-making process of an important element.

Astute analysts and savvy managers understand that any of a variety of factors affecting the decision-making process can influence the eventual decision. Personal views or biases, loyalties, political allegiances, or emotion can be as potent as analytical insights in swaying individual or collective choices. And sometimes, analytically based arguments do not deserve to win! Sometimes, analysis is poorly performed or otherwise produces faulty recommendations—for quantitative analysis is not infallible.

Even the product of carefully conducted, thorough analysis will not convince every audience or carry every decision, but *sometimes it can be influential.* Sometimes it will prevail. A discouraged manager who on the heels of a rejection of sound analytical advice vows never again to expend the personal and staff resources to conduct elaborate analysis would, if faithful to that vow, deprive the decision-making process of ever again having a chance for that influence.

Thoughtful analysis normally elevates the quality of debate on an issue. Important aspects of a decision and its likely ramifications become more apparent. Sometimes the analysis is so compelling that its recommendations are adopted in full; sometimes recommendations are modified to be more politically acceptable, but are nevertheless adopted with most characteristics intact. Even when its recommendations are rejected, careful analysis permits decision makers to proceed with eyes wide open, fully aware of the likely consequences of a particular decision.

Occasional rejections of recommendations from analytic efforts should be neither surprising nor discouraging. That other elements influence local government decisions is simply a fact of life. The wise analyst, however, will not simply dismiss rejections as "their problem," scoffing at the shortsightedness of decision makers. Analysts who hope to learn from their experiences—bad and good—will challenge their own analyses:

- Did I use appropriate methods of analysis?
- Were the assumptions underlying the analysis reasonable?
- Were my recommendations logical, given my findings?
- Did I explain my analysis—including methods, findings, and recommendations—clearly?
- Did I anticipate the factors that were most influential to the ultimate decision? Did I offer alternative recommendations that accommodated most of those factors?
- Were my recommendations reasonable and feasible?
- Was my work completed in a timely fashion?
- Whether my recommendations were approved or not, how could the analysis, interpretation, recommendations, report, and presentation have been improved?

Analysts committed to improving their product with each new opportunity can expect to achieve a respectable batting average for approvals. Still, they will strike out on occasion, and it will do no good to throw their bat when they do. It may ease the frustration of an analyst still smarting from a recent rejection to recall that no one with several turns at the plate has ever completed a career still hitting 1.000.

Appendix A
Table of Random Digits

The random digits table is reproduced by permission of the RAND Corporation, *A Million Random Digits with 100,000 Normal Deviates* (Glencoe, Ill.: Free Press, 1955).

10097	32533	76520	13586	34673	54876	80959	09117	39292	74945
37542	04805	64894	74296	24805	24037	20636	10402	00822	91665
08422	68953	19645	09303	23209	02560	15953	34764	35080	33606
99019	02529	09376	70715	38311	31165	88676	74397	04436	27659
12807	99970	80157	36147	64032	36653	98951	16877	12171	76833
66065	74717	34072	76850	36697	36170	65813	39885	11199	29170
31060	10805	45571	82406	35303	42614	86799	07439	23403	09732
85269	77602	02051	65692	68665	74818	73053	85247	18623	88579
63573	32135	05325	47048	90553	57548	28468	28709	83491	25624
73796	45753	03529	64778	35808	34282	60935	20344	35273	88435
98520	17767	14905	68607	22109	40558	60970	93433	50500	73998
11805	05431	39808	27732	50725	68248	29405	24201	52775	67851
83452	99634	06288	98083	13746	70078	18475	40610	68711	77817
88685	40200	86507	58401	36766	67951	90364	76493	29609	11062
99594	67348	87517	64969	91826	08928	93785	61368	23478	34113
65481	17674	17468	50950	58047	76974	73039	57186	40218	16544
80124	35635	17727	08015	45318	22374	21115	78253	14385	53763
74350	99817	77402	77214	43236	00210	45521	64237	96286	02655
69916	26803	66252	29148	36936	87203	76621	13990	94400	56418
09893	20505	14225	68514	46427	56788	96297	78822	54382	14598
91499	14523	68479	27686	46162	83554	94750	89923	37089	20048
80336	94598	26940	36858	70297	34135	53140	33340	42050	82341
44104	81949	85157	47954	32979	26575	57600	40881	22222	06413
12550	73742	11100	02040	12860	74697	96644	89439	28707	25815
63606	49329	16505	34484	40219	52563	43651	77082	07207	31790
61196	90446	26457	47774	51924	33729	65394	59593	42582	60527
15474	45266	95270	79953	59367	83848	82396	10118	33211	59466
94557	28573	67897	54387	54622	44431	91190	42592	92927	45973
42481	16213	97344	08721	16868	48767	03071	12059	25701	46670
23523	78317	73208	89837	68935	91416	26252	29663	05522	82562

04493	52494	75246	33824	45862	51025	61962	79335	65337	12472
00549	97654	64051	88159	96119	63896	54692	82391	23287	29529
35963	15307	26898	09354	33351	35462	77974	50024	90103	39333
59808	08391	45427	26842	83609	49700	13021	24892	78565	20106
46058	85236	01390	92286	77281	44077	93910	83647	70617	42941
32179	00597	87379	25241	05567	07007	86743	17157	85394	11838
69234	61406	20117	45204	15956	60000	18743	92423	97118	96338
19565	41430	01758	75379	40419	21585	66674	36806	84962	85207
45155	14938	19476	07246	43667	94543	59047	90033	20826	69541
94864	31994	36168	10851	34888	81553	01540	35456	05014	51176
98086	24826	45240	28404	44999	08896	39094	73407	35441	31880
33185	16232	41941	50949	89435	48581	88695	41994	37548	73043
80951	00406	96382	70774	20151	23387	25016	25298	94624	61171
79752	49140	71961	28296	69861	02591	74852	20539	00387	59579
18633	32537	98145	06571	31010	24674	05455	61427	77938	91936
74029	43902	77557	32270	97790	17119	52527	58021	80814	51748
54178	45611	80993	37143	05335	12969	56127	19255	36040	90324
11664	49883	52079	84827	59381	71539	09973	33440	88461	23356
48324	77928	31249	64710	02295	36870	32307	57546	15020	09994
69074	94138	87637	91976	35584	04401	10518	21615	01848	76938
09188	20097	32825	39527	04220	86304	83389	87374	64278	58044
90045	85497	51981	50654	94938	81997	91870	76150	68476	64659
73189	50207	47677	26269	62290	64464	27124	67018	41361	82760
75768	76490	20971	87749	90429	12272	95375	05871	93823	43178
54016	44056	66281	31003	00682	27398	20714	53295	07706	17813
08358	69910	78542	42785	13661	58873	04618	97553	31223	08420
28306	03264	81333	10591	40510	07893	32604	60475	94119	01840
53840	86233	81594	13628	51215	90290	28466	68795	77762	20791
91757	53741	61613	62269	50263	90212	55781	76514	83483	47055
89415	92694	00397	58391	12607	17646	48949	72306	94541	37408
77513	03820	86864	29901	68414	82774	51908	13980	72893	55507
19502	37174	69979	20288	55210	29773	74287	75251	65344	67415
21818	59313	93278	81757	05686	73156	07082	85046	31853	38452
51474	66499	68107	23621	94049	91345	42836	09191	08007	45449
99559	68331	62535	24170	69777	12830	74819	78142	43860	72834
33713	48007	93584	72869	51926	64721	58303	29822	93174	93972
85274	86893	11303	22970	28834	34137	73515	90400	71148	43643
84133	89640	44035	52166	73852	70091	61222	60561	62327	18423
56732	16234	17395	96131	10123	91622	85496	57560	81604	18880
65138	56806	87648	85261	34313	65861	45875	21069	85644	47277

38001 02176	81719 11711	71602 92937	74219 64049	65584 49698
37402 96397	01304 77586	56271 10086	47324 62605	40030 37438
97125 40348	87083 31417	21815 39250	75237 62047	15501 29578
21826 41134	47143 34072	64638 85902	49139 06441	03856 54552
73135 42742	95719 09035	85794 74296	08789 88156	64691 19202
07638 77929	03061 18072	96207 44156	23821 99538	04713 66994
60528 83441	07954 19814	59175 20695	05533 52139	61212 06455
83596 35655	06958 92983	05128 09719	77433 53783	92301 50498
10850 62746	99599 10507	13499 06319	53075 71839	06410 19362
39820 98952	43622 63147	64421 80814	43800 09351	31024 73167
59580 06478	75569 78800	88835 54486	23768 06156	04111 08408
38508 07341	23793 48763	90822 97022	17719 04207	95954 49953
30692 70668	94688 16127	56196 80091	82067 63400	05462 69200
65443 95659	18288 27437	49632 24041	08337 65676	96299 90836
27267 50264	13192 72294	07477 44606	17985 48911	97341 30358
91307 06991	19072 24210	36699 53728	28825 35793	28976 66252
68434 94688	84473 13622	62126 98408	12843 82590	09815 93146
48908 15877	54745 24591	35700 04754	83824 52692	54130 55160
06913 45197	42672 78601	11883 09528	63011 98901	14974 40344
10455 16019	14210 33712	91342 37821	88325 80851	43667 70883
12883 97343	65027 61184	04285 01392	17974 15077	90712 26769
21778 30976	38807 36961	31649 42096	63281 02023	08816 47449
19523 59515	65122 59659	86283 68258	69572 13798	16435 91529
67245 52670	35583 16563	79246 86686	76463 34222	26655 90802
60584 47377	07500 37992	45134 26529	26760 83637	41326 44344
53853 41377	36066 94850	58838 73859	49364 73331	96240 43642
24637 38736	74384 89342	52623 07992	12369 18601	03742 83873
83080 12451	38992 22815	07759 51777	97377 27585	51972 37867
16444 24334	36151 99073	27493 70939	85130 32552	54846 54759
60790 18157	57178 65762	11161 78576	45819 52979	65130 04860
03991 10461	93716 16894	66083 24653	84609 58232	88618 19161
38555 95554	32886 59780	08355 60860	29735 47762	71299 23853
17546 73704	92052 46215	55121 29281	59076 07936	27954 58909
32643 52861	95819 06831	00911 98936	76355 93779	80863 00514
69572 68777	39510 35905	14060 40619	29549 69616	33564 60780
24122 66591	27699 06494	14845 46672	61958 77100	90899 75754
61196 30231	92962 61773	41839 55382	17267 70943	78038 70267
30532 21704	10274 12202	39685 23309	10061 68829	55986 66485
03788 97599	75867 20717	74416 53166	35208 33374	87539 08823
48228 63379	85783 47619	53152 67433	35663 52972	16818 60311

60365 94653	35075 33949	42614 29297	01918 28316	98953 73231
83799 42402	56623 34442	34994 41374	70071 14736	09958 18065
32960 07405	36409 83232	99385 41600	11133 07586	15917 06253
19322 53845	57620 52606	66497 68646	78138 66559	19640 99413
11220 94747	07399 37408	48509 23929	27482 45476	85244 35159
31751 57260	68980 05339	15470 48355	88651 22596	03152 19121
88492 99382	14454 04504	20094 98977	74843 93413	22109 78508
30934 47744	07481 83828	73788 06533	28597 20405	94205 20380
22888 48893	27499 98748	60530 45128	74022 84617	82037 10268
78212 16993	35902 91386	44372 15486	65741 14014	87481 37220
41849 84547	46850 52326	34677 58300	74910 64345	19325 81549
46352 33049	69248 93460	45305 07521	61318 31855	14413 70951
11087 96294	14013 31792	59747 67277	76503 34513	39663 77544
52701 08337	56303 87315	16520 69676	11654 99893	02181 68161
57275 36898	81304 48585	68652 27376	92852 55866	88448 03584
20857 73156	70284 24326	79375 95220	01159 63267	10622 48391
15633 84924	90415 93614	33521 26665	55823 47641	86225 31704
92694 48297	39904 02115	59589 49067	66821 41575	49767 04037
77613 19019	88152 00080	20554 91409	96277 48257	50816 97616
38688 32486	45134 63545	59404 72059	43947 51680	43852 59693
25163 01889	70014 15021	41290 67312	71857 15957	68971 11403
65251 07629	37239 33295	05870 01119	92784 26340	18477 65622
36815 43625	18637 37509	82444 99005	04921 73701	14707 93997
64397 11692	05327 82162	20247 81759	45197 25332	83745 22567
04515 25624	95096 67946	48460 85558	15191 18782	16930 33361
83761 60873	43253 84145	60833 25983	01291 41349	20368 07126
14387 06345	80854 09279	43529 06318	38384 74761	41196 37480
51321 92246	80088 77074	88722 56736	66164 49431	66919 31678
72472 00008	80890 18002	94813 31900	54155 83436	35352 54131
05466 55306	93128 18464	74457 90561	72848 11834	79982 68416
39528 72484	82474 25593	48545 35247	18619 13674	18611 19241
81616 18711	53342 44276	75122 11724	74627 73707	58319 15997
07586 16120	82641 22820	92904 13141	32392 19763	61199 67940
90767 04235	13574 17200	69902 63742	78464 22501	18627 90872
40188 28193	29593 88627	94972 11598	62095 36787	00441 58997
34414 82157	86887 55087	19152 00023	12302 80783	32624 68691
63439 75363	44989 16822	36024 00867	76378 41605	65961 73488
67049 09070	93399 45547	94458 74284	05041 49807	20288 34060
79495 04146	52162 90286	54158 34243	46978 35482	59362 95938
91704 30552	04737 21031	75051 93029	47665 64382	99782 93478

94015	46874	32444	48277	59820	96163	64654	25843	41145	42820
74108	88222	88570	74015	25704	91035	01755	14750	48968	38603
62880	87873	95160	59221	22304	90314	72877	17334	39283	04149
11748	12102	80580	41867	17710	59621	06554	07850	73950	79552
17944	05600	60478	03343	25852	58905	57216	39618	49856	99326
66067	42792	95043	52680	46780	56487	09971	59481	37006	22186
54244	91030	45547	70818	59849	96169	61459	21647	87417	17198
30945	57589	31732	57260	47670	07654	46376	25366	94746	49580
69170	37403	86995	90307	94304	71803	26825	05511	12459	91314
08345	88975	35841	85771	08105	59987	87112	21476	14713	71181
27767	43584	85301	88977	29490	69714	73035	41207	74699	09310
13025	14338	54066	15243	47724	66733	47431	43905	31048	56699
80217	36292	98525	24335	24432	24896	43277	58874	11466	16082
10875	62004	90391	61105	57411	06368	53856	30743	08670	84741
54127	57326	26629	19087	24472	88779	30540	27886	61732	75454
60311	42824	37301	42678	45990	43242	17374	52003	70707	70214
49739	71484	92003	98086	76668	73209	59202	11973	02902	33250
78626	51594	16453	94614	39014	97066	83012	09832	25571	77628
66692	13986	99837	00582	81232	44987	09504	96412	90193	79568
44071	28091	07362	97703	76447	42537	98524	97831	65704	09514
41468	85149	49554	17994	14924	39650	95294	00556	70481	06905
94559	37559	49678	53119	70312	05682	66986	34099	74474	20740
41615	70360	64114	58660	90850	64618	80620	51790	11436	38072
50273	93113	41794	86861	24781	89683	55411	85667	77535	99892
41396	80504	90670	08289	40902	05069	95083	06783	28102	57816
25807	24260	71529	78920	72682	07385	90726	57166	98884	08583
06170	97965	88302	98041	21443	41808	68984	83620	89747	98882
60808	54444	74412	81105	01176	28838	36421	16489	18059	51061
80940	44893	10408	36222	80582	71944	92638	40333	67054	16067
19516	90120	46759	71643	13177	55292	21036	82808	77501	97427
49386	54480	23604	23554	21785	41101	91178	10174	29420	90438
06312	88940	15995	69321	47458	64809	98189	81851	29651	84215
60942	00307	11897	92674	40405	68032	96717	54244	10701	41393
92329	98932	78284	46347	71209	92061	39448	93136	25722	08564
77936	63574	31384	51924	85561	29671	58137	17820	22751	36518
38101	77756	11657	13897	95889	57067	47648	13885	70669	93406
39641	69457	91339	22502	92613	89719	11947	56203	19324	20504
84054	40455	99396	63680	67667	60631	69181	96845	38525	11600
47468	03577	57649	63266	24700	71594	14004	23153	69249	05747
43321	31370	28977	23896	76479	68562	62342	07589	08899	05985

64281	61826	18555	64937	13173	33365	78851	16499	87064	13075
66847	70495	32350	02985	86716	38746	26313	77463	55387	72681
72461	33230	21529	53424	92581	02262	78438	66276	18396	73538
21032	91050	13058	16218	12470	56500	15292	76139	59526	52113
95362	67011	06651	16136	01016	00857	55018	56374	35824	71708
49712	97380	10404	55452	34030	60726	75211	10271	36633	68424
58275	61764	97586	54716	50259	46345	87195	46092	26787	60939
89514	11788	68224	23417	73959	76145	30342	40277	11049	72049
15472	50669	48139	36732	46874	37088	73465	09819	58869	35220
12120	86124	51247	44302	60883	52109	21437	36786	49226	77837
19612	78430	11661	94770	77603	65669	86868	12665	30012	75989
39141	77400	28000	64238	73258	71794	31340	26256	66453	37016
64756	80457	08747	12836	03469	50678	03274	43423	66677	82556
92901	51878	56441	22998	29718	38447	06453	25311	07565	53771
03551	90070	09483	94050	45938	18135	36908	43321	11073	51803
98884	66209	06830	53656	14663	56346	71430	04909	19818	05707
27369	86882	53473	07541	53633	70863	03748	12822	19360	49088
59066	75974	63335	20483	43514	37481	58278	26967	49325	43951
91647	93783	64169	49022	98588	09495	49829	59068	38831	04838
83605	92419	39542	07772	71568	75673	35185	89759	44901	74291
24895	88530	70774	35439	46758	70472	70207	92675	91623	61275
35720	26556	95596	20094	73750	85788	34264	01703	46833	65248
14141	53410	38649	06343	57256	61342	72709	75318	90379	37562
27416	75670	92176	72535	93119	56077	06886	18244	92344	31374
82071	07429	81007	47749	40744	56974	23336	88821	53841	10536
21445	82793	24831	93241	14199	76268	70883	68002	03829	17443
72513	76400	52225	92348	62308	98481	29744	33165	33141	61020
71479	45027	76160	57411	13780	13632	52308	77762	88874	33697
83210	51466	09088	50395	26743	05306	21706	70001	99439	80767
68749	95148	94897	78636	96750	09024	94538	91143	96693	61886
05184	75763	47075	88158	05313	53439	14908	08830	60096	21551
13651	62546	96892	25240	47511	58483	87342	78818	07855	39269
00566	21220	00292	24069	25072	29519	52548	54091	21282	21296
50958	17695	58072	68990	60329	95955	71586	63417	35947	67807
57621	64547	46850	37981	38527	09037	64756	03324	04986	83666
09282	25844	79139	78435	35428	43561	69799	63314	12991	93516
23394	94206	93432	37836	94919	26846	02555	74410	94915	48199
05280	37470	93622	04345	15092	19510	18094	16613	78234	50001
95491	97976	38306	32192	82639	54624	72434	92606	23191	74693
78521	00104	18248	75583	90326	50785	54034	66251	35774	14692

96345 44579	85932 44053	75704 20840	86583 83944	52456 73766
77963 31151	32364 91691	47357 40338	23435 24065	08458 95366
07520 11294	23238 01748	41690 67328	54814 37777	10057 42332
38423 02309	70703 85736	46148 14258	29236 12152	05088 65825
02463 65533	21199 60555	33928 01817	07396 89215	30722 22102
15880 92261	17292 88190	61781 48898	92525 21283	88581 60098
71926 00819	59144 00224	30570 90194	18329 06999	26857 19238
64425 28108	16554 16016	00042 83229	10333 36168	65617 94834
79782 23924	49440 30432	81077 31543	95216 64865	13658 51081
35337 74538	44553 64672	90960 41849	93865 44608	93176 34851
05249 29329	19715 94082	14738 86667	43708 66354	93692 25527
56463 99380	38793 85774	19056 13939	46062 27647	66146 63210
96296 33121	54196 34108	75814 85986	71171 15102	28992 63165
98380 36269	60014 07201	62448 46385	42175 88350	46182 49126
52567 64350	16315 53969	80395 81134	54358 64578	47269 15747
78498 90830	25955 99236	43286 91064	99969 95144	64424 77377
49553 24241	08150 89535	08703 91041	77323 81079	45127 93686
32151 07075	83155 10252	73100 88618	23891 87418	45417 20268
11314 50363	26860 27799	49416 83534	19187 08059	76677 02110
12364 71210	87052 50241	90785 97889	81399 58130	64439 05614
59467 58309	87834 57213	37510 33689	01259 62486	56320 46265
73452 17619	56421 40725	23439 41701	93223 41682	45026 47505
27635 56293	91700 04391	67317 89604	73020 69853	61517 51207
86040 02596	01655 09918	45161 00222	54577 74821	47335 08582
52403 94255	26351 46527	68224 90183	85057 72310	34963 83462
49465 46581	61499 04844	94626 02963	41482 83879	44942 63915
94365 92560	12363 30246	02086 75036	88620 91088	67691 67762
34261 08769	91830 23313	18256 28850	37639 92748	57791 71328
37110 66538	39318 15626	44324 82827	08782 65960	58167 01305
83950 45424	72453 19444	68219 64733	94088 62006	89985 36936
61630 97966	76537 46467	30942 07479	67971 14558	22458 35148
01929 17165	12037 74558	16250 71750	55546 29693	94984 37782
41659 39098	23982 29899	71594 77979	54477 13764	17315 72893
32031 39608	75992 73445	01317 50525	87313 45191	30214 19769
90043 93478	58044 06949	31176 88370	50274 83987	45316 38551
79418 14322	91065 07841	36130 86602	10659 40859	00964 71577
85447 61079	96910 72906	07361 84338	34114 52096	66715 51091
86219 81115	49625 48799	89485 24855	13684 68433	70595 70102
71712 88559	92476 32903	68009 58417	87962 11787	16644 72964
29776 63075	13270 84758	49560 10317	28778 23006	31036 84906

Appendix B
Future Value Interest Factors (FVIF)

PERIODS, n	\multicolumn{15}{c}{Interest Rate, i, %}

PERIODS, n	1	2	3	4	5	6	7	8	9	10	11	12	13	14	15
1	1.0100	1.0200	1.0300	1.0400	1.0500	1.0600	1.0700	1.0800	1.0900	1.1000	1.1100	1.1200	1.1300	1.1400	1.1500
2	1.0201	1.0404	1.0609	1.0816	1.1025	1.1236	1.1449	1.1664	1.1881	1.2100	1.2321	1.2544	1.2769	1.2996	1.3225
3	1.0303	1.0612	1.0927	1.1249	1.1576	1.1910	1.2250	1.2597	1.2950	1.3310	1.3676	1.4049	1.4429	1.4815	1.5209
4	1.0406	1.0824	1.1255	1.1699	1.2155	1.2625	1.3108	1.3605	1.4116	1.4641	1.5181	1.5735	1.6305	1.6890	1.7490
5	1.0510	1.1041	1.1593	1.2167	1.2763	1.3382	1.4026	1.4693	1.5386	1.6105	1.6851	1.7623	1.8424	1.9254	2.0114
6	1.0615	1.1262	1.1941	1.2653	1.3401	1.4185	1.5007	1.5869	1.6771	1.7716	1.8704	1.9738	2.0820	2.1950	2.3131
7	1.0721	1.1487	1.2299	1.3159	1.4071	1.5036	1.6058	1.7138	1.8280	1.9487	2.0762	2.2107	2.3526	2.5023	2.6600
8	1.0829	1.1717	1.2668	1.3686	1.4775	1.5938	1.7182	1.8509	1.9926	2.1436	2.3045	2.4760	2.6584	2.8526	3.0590
9	1.0937	1.1951	1.3048	1.4233	1.5513	1.6895	1.8385	1.9990	2.1719	2.3579	2.5580	2.7731	3.0040	3.2519	3.5179
10	1.1046	1.2190	1.3439	1.4802	1.6289	1.7908	1.9672	2.1589	2.3674	2.5937	2.8394	3.1058	3.3946	3.7072	4.0456
11	1.1157	1.2434	1.3842	1.5395	1.7103	1.8983	2.1049	2.3316	2.5804	2.8531	3.1518	3.4785	3.8359	4.2262	4.6524
12	1.1268	1.2682	1.4258	1.6010	1.7959	2.0122	2.2522	2.5182	2.8127	3.1384	3.4985	3.8960	4.3345	4.8179	5.3502
13	1.1381	1.2936	1.4685	1.6651	1.8856	2.1329	2.4098	2.7196	3.0658	3.4523	3.8833	4.3635	4.8980	5.4924	6.1528
14	1.1495	1.3195	1.5126	1.7317	1.9799	2.2609	2.5785	2.9372	3.3417	3.7975	4.3104	4.8871	5.5348	6.2613	7.0757
15	1.1610	1.3459	1.5580	1.8009	2.0789	2.3966	2.7590	3.1722	3.6425	4.1772	4.7846	5.4736	6.2543	7.1379	8.1371
16	1.1726	1.3728	1.6047	1.8730	2.1829	2.5404	2.9522	3.4259	3.9703	4.5950	5.3109	6.1304	7.0673	8.1372	9.3576
17	1.1843	1.4002	1.6528	1.9479	2.2920	2.6928	3.1588	3.7000	4.3276	5.0545	5.8951	6.8660	7.9861	9.2765	10.7613
18	1.1961	1.4282	1.7024	2.0258	2.4066	2.8543	3.3799	3.9960	4.7171	5.5599	6.5436	7.6900	9.0243	10.5752	12.3755
19	1.2081	1.4568	1.7535	2.1068	2.5269	3.0256	3.6165	4.3157	5.1417	6.1159	7.2633	8.6128	10.1974	12.0557	14.2318
20	1.2202	1.4859	1.8061	2.1911	2.6533	3.2071	3.8697	4.6610	5.6044	6.7275	8.0623	9.6463	11.5231	13.7435	16.3665

21	1.2324	1.5157	1.8603	2.2788	2.7860	3.3996	4.1406	5.0338	6.1088	7.4002	8.9492	10.8038	13.0211	15.6676	18.8215
22	1.2447	1.5460	1.9161	2.3699	2.9253	3.6035	4.4304	5.4365	6.6586	8.1403	9.9336	12.1003	14.7138	17.8810	21.8447
23	1.2572	1.5769	1.9736	2.4647	3.0715	3.8197	4.7405	5.8715	7.2579	8.9543	11.0263	13.5523	16.6266	20.3616	24.8914
24	1.2697	1.6084	2.0328	2.5633	3.2251	4.0489	5.0724	6.3412	7.9111	9.8497	12.2392	15.1786	18.7881	23.2122	28.6252
25	1.2824	1.6406	2.0938	2.6658	3.3864	4.2919	5.4274	6.8485	8.6231	10.6347	13.5855	17.0001	21.2305	26.4619	32.9189
26	1.2953	1.6734	2.1566	2.7725	3.5557	4.5494	5.8074	7.3964	9.3992	11.9182	15.0799	19.0401	23.9905	30.1666	37.8568
27	1.3082	1.7069	2.2213	2.8834	3.7335	4.8223	6.2139	7.9881	10.2451	13.1100	16.7366	21.3249	27.1093	34.3899	43.5353
28	1.3213	1.7410	2.2879	2.9987	3.9201	5.1117	6.6488	8.6271	11.1671	14.4210	18.5799	23.8839	30.6335	39.2045	50.0656
29	1.3345	1.7758	2.3566	3.1187	4.1161	5.4184	7.1143	9.3173	12.1722	15.8631	20.6237	26.7499	34.6158	44.6931	57.5754
30	1.3478	1.8114	2.4273	3.2434	4.3219	5.7435	7.6123	10.0627	13.2677	17.4494	22.8923	29.9599	39.1159	50.9501	66.2118
31	1.3613	1.8476	2.5001	3.3731	4.5380	6.0881	8.1451	10.8677	14.4618	19.1943	25.4104	33.5551	44.2010	58.0832	76.1435
32	1.3749	1.8845	2.5751	3.5081	4.7649	6.4534	8.7153	11.7371	15.7633	21.1138	28.2056	37.5817	49.9471	66.2148	87.5651
33	1.3887	1.9222	2.6523	3.6484	5.0032	6.8406	9.3253	12.6760	17.1820	23.2251	31.3082	42.0915	56.4402	75.4849	100.6998
34	1.4026	1.9607	2.7319	3.7943	5.2533	7.2510	9.9781	13.6901	18.7284	25.5477	34.7521	47.1425	63.7774	86.0528	115.8048
35	1.4166	1.9999	2.8139	3.9461	5.5160	7.6861	10.6766	14.7853	20.4140	28.1024	38.5748	52.7996	72.0685	98.1002	133.1755

Source: Charles K. Coe, Public Financial Management (Englewood Cliffs, N.J.: Prentice-Hall, 1989), 240.

Appendix C
Sum of Annuity Factor (SAF)

PERIODS, n	Interest Rate, i, %														
	1	2	3	4	5	6	7	8	9	10	11	12	13	14	15
1	1.0000	1.0000	1.0000	1.0000	1.0000	1.0000	1.0000	1.0000	1.0000	1.0000	1.0000	1.0000	1.0000	1.0000	1.0000
2	2.0100	2.0200	2.0300	2.0400	2.0500	2.0600	2.0700	2.0800	2.0900	2.1000	2.1100	2.1200	2.1300	2.1400	2.1500
3	3.0301	3.0604	3.0909	3.1216	3.1525	3.1836	3.2149	3.2464	3.2781	3.3100	3.3421	3.3744	3.4069	3.4396	3.4725
4	4.0604	4.1216	4.1836	4.2465	4.3101	4.3746	4.4399	4.5061	4.5731	4.6410	4.7097	4.7793	4.8498	4.9211	4.9934
5	5.1010	5.2040	5.3091	5.4163	5.5256	5.6371	5.7507	5.8666	5.9847	6.1051	6.2278	6.3528	6.4803	6.6101	6.7424
6	6.1520	6.3081	6.4684	6.6330	6.8019	6.9753	7.1533	7.3359	7.5233	7.7156	7.9129	8.1152	8.3227	8.5355	8.7537
7	7.2135	7.4343	7.6625	7.8983	8.1420	8.3938	8.6540	8.9228	9.2004	9.4872	9.7833	10.0690	10.4047	10.7305	11.0668
8	8.2857	8.5830	8.8923	9.2142	9.5491	9.8975	10.2598	10.6366	11.0265	11.4359	11.8594	12.2997	12.7573	13.2328	13.7268
9	9.3685	9.7546	10.1591	10.5828	11.0266	11.4913	11.9780	12.4876	13.0210	13.5795	14.1640	14.7757	15.4157	16.0853	16.7858
10	10.4622	10.9497	11.4639	12.0061	12.5779	13.1808	13.8164	14.4866	15.1929	15.9374	16.7220	17.5487	18.4197	19.3373	20.3037
11	11.5668	12.1687	12.8078	13.4864	14.2068	14.9716	15.7836	16.6455	17.5603	18.5312	19.5614	20.6546	21.8143	23.0445	24.3493
12	12.6825	13.4121	14.1920	15.0258	15.9171	16.8699	17.8884	18.9771	20.1407	21.3843	22.7132	24.1331	25.6502	27.2707	29.0017
13	13.8093	14.6803	15.6178	16.6268	17.7130	18.8821	20.1406	21.4953	22.9534	24.5227	26.2116	28.0291	29.9847	32.0888	34.3519
14	14.9474	15.9739	17.0863	18.2919	19.5986	21.0151	22.5505	24.2149	26.0192	27.9750	30.0949	32.3926	34.8827	37.5811	40.5047
15	16.0969	17.2934	18.5989	20.0236	21.5766	23.2760	25.1290	27.1521	29.3609	31.7725	34.4053	37.2797	40.4174	43.8424	47.5804
16	17.2579	18.6393	20.1569	21.8245	23.6575	25.6725	27.8880	30.3243	33.0034	35.9497	39.1899	42.7533	46.6717	50.9803	55.7175
17	18.4304	20.0121	21.7616	23.6975	25.8404	28.2129	30.8402	33.7502	36.9737	40.5447	44.5008	48.8837	53.7391	59.1176	65.0751
18	19.6147	21.4123	23.4144	25.6454	28.1324	30.9056	33.9990	37.4502	41.3013	45.5992	50.3959	55.7497	61.7251	68.3941	75.8363
19	20.6109	22.8405	25.1169	27.6712	30.5390	33.7600	37.3790	41.4463	48.0184	51.1591	56.9395	63.4397	70.7494	76.9692	88.2118
20	22.0190	24.2974	26.8704	29.7781	33.0659	36.7856	40.9955	45.7620	51.1601	57.2750	64.2028	72.0524	80.9468	91.0249	102.4436

21	23.2392	25.7833	28.6765	31.9692	35.7192	39.9927	44.8652	50.4229	56.7645	64.0025	72.2651	81.6987	92.4699	104.7684	118.8101
22	24.4716	27.2990	30.5368	34.2480	38.5052	43.3923	49.0057	55.4567	62.8733	71.4027	81.2143	92.5026	105.4910	120.4360	137.6316
23	25.7163	28.8450	32.4529	36.6179	41.4305	46.9958	53.4361	60.8933	69.5319	79.5430	91.1479	104.8029	120.2048	138.2970	159.2764
24	26.9734	30.4219	34.4265	39.0826	44.5020	50.8158	58.1767	66.7648	76.7898	88.4973	102.1741	118.1552	136.8315	158.6586	184.1676
25	28.2432	32.0303	36.4593	41.6459	47.7271	54.8645	63.2490	73.1059	84.7009	98.3470	114.4133	133.3339	155.6196	161.8706	212.7930
26	29.5256	33.6709	38.5530	44.3117	51.1134	59.1564	68.6765	79.9544	93.3240	109.1818	127.9988	150.3339	176.8501	208.3327	245.7120
27	30.8209	35.3443	40.7096	47.0842	54.6691	63.7058	74.4838	87.3508	102.7231	121.0999	143.0766	169.3740	200.8406	238.4993	283.5686
28	32.1291	37.0512	42.9309	49.9676	58.4026	68.5281	80.6977	95.3388	112.9682	134.2099	159.8173	190.6869	227.9499	272.8892	327.1040
29	33.4504	38.7922	45.2188	52.9663	62.3227	73.6398	87.3465	103.9659	124.1353	148.6309	178.3972	214.5827	258.5833	312.0935	377.1897
30	34.7849	40.5681	47.5754	56.0849	66.4388	79.0582	94.4808	113.2832	136.3075	164.4940	199.0209	241.3327	293.1990	356.7866	434.7451
31	36.1327	42.3794	50.0027	59.3283	70.7608	84.8017	102.0730	123.3459	149.5752	181.9434	221.9132	271.2925	332.3149	407.7368	500.9568
32	37.4941	44.2270	52.5027	62.7015	75.2968	90.8898	110.2181	134.2135	164.0370	201.1378	247.3236	304.6477	376.5159	465.8201	577.1003
33	38.8690	46.1116	55.0778	66.2095	80.0638	97.3432	118.9334	145.9506	179.8003	222.2515	275.5291	342.4294	426.4631	532.0349	664.6653
34	40.2577	48.0338	57.7302	69.8579	85.0670	104.1837	128.2588	158.6267	196.9823	245.4767	306.8374	384.5208	482.9033	607.5198	765.3852
35	41.6603	49.9945	60.4621	73.6522	90.3203	111.4348	138.2369	172.3168	215.7106	271.0242	341.5894	431.6633	546.6807	693.5725	881.1699

Source: Charles K. Coe, *Public Financial Management* (Englewood Cliffs, N.J.: Prentice-Hall, 1989), 242.

Appendix D
Distribution of Chi-Square

df	.99	.98	.95	.90	.80	.70	.50	.30	.20	.10	.05	.02	.01	.001
1	$.0^3157$	$.0^3628$	.00393	.0158	.0642	.148	.455	1.074	1.642	2.706	3.841	5.412	6.635	10.827
2	.0201	.0404	.103	.211	.446	.713	1.386	2.408	3.219	4.605	5.991	7.824	9.210	13.815
3	.115	.185	.352	.584	1.005	1.424	2.366	3.665	4.642	6.251	7.815	9.837	11.345	16.266
4	.297	.429	.711	1.064	1.649	2.195	3.357	4.878	5.989	7.779	9.488	11.668	13.277	18.467
5	.554	.752	1.145	1.610	2.343	3.000	4.351	6.064	7.289	9.236	11.070	13.388	15.086	20.515
6	.872	1.134	1.635	2.204	3.070	3.828	5.348	7.231	8.558	10.645	12.592	15.033	16.812	22.457
7	1.239	1.564	2.167	2.833	3.822	4.671	6.346	8.383	9.803	12.017	14.067	16.622	18.475	24.322
8	1.646	2.032	2.733	3.490	4.594	5.527	7.344	9.524	11.030	13.362	15.507	18.168	20.090	26.125
9	2.088	2.532	3.325	4.168	5.380	6.393	8.343	10.656	12.242	14.684	16.919	19.679	21.666	27.877
10	2.558	3.059	3.940	4.865	6.179	7.267	9.342	11.781	13.442	15.987	18.307	21.161	23.209	29.588
11	3.053	3.609	4.575	5.578	6.989	8.148	10.341	12.899	14.631	17.275	19.675	22.618	24.725	31.264
12	3.571	4.178	5.226	6.304	7.807	9.034	11.340	14.011	15.812	18.549	21.026	24.054	26.217	32.909
13	4.107	4.765	5.892	7.042	8.634	9.926	12.340	15.119	16.985	19.812	22.362	25.472	27.688	34.528
14	4.660	5.368	6.571	7.790	9.467	10.821	13.339	16.222	18.151	21.064	23.685	26.873	29.141	36.123
15	5.229	5.985	7.261	8.547	10.307	11.721	14.339	17.322	19.311	22.307	24.996	28.259	30.578	37.697

Probability

df													
16	5.812	6.614	7.962	9.312	11.152	12.624	15.338	18.418	20.465	23.542	26.296	29.633	32.000	39.252
17	6.408	7.255	8.672	10.085	12.002	13.531	16.338	19.511	21.615	24.769	27.587	30.995	33.409	40.790
18	7.015	7.906	9.390	10.865	12.857	14.440	17.338	20.601	22.760	25.989	28.869	32.346	34.805	42.312
19	7.633	8.567	10.117	11.651	13.716	15.352	18.338	21.689	23.900	27.204	30.144	33.687	36.191	43.820
20	8.260	9.237	10.851	12.443	14.578	16.266	19.337	22.775	25.038	28.412	31.410	35.020	37.566	45.315
21	8.897	9.915	11.591	13.240	15.445	17.182	20.337	23.858	26.171	29.615	32.671	36.343	38.932	46.797
22	9.542	10.600	12.338	14.041	16.314	18.101	21.337	24.939	27.301	30.813	33.924	37.659	40.289	48.268
23	10.196	11.293	13.091	14.848	17.187	19.021	22.337	26.018	28.429	32.007	35.172	38.968	41.638	49.728
24	10.856	11.992	13.848	15.659	18.062	19.943	23.337	27.096	29.553	33.196	36.415	40.270	42.980	51.179
25	11.524	12.697	14.611	16.473	18.940	20.867	24.337	28.172	30.675	34.382	37.652	41.566	44.314	52.620
26	12.198	13.409	15.379	17.292	19.820	21.792	25.336	29.246	31.795	35.563	38.885	42.856	45.642	54.052
27	12.879	14.125	16.151	18.114	20.703	22.719	26.336	30.319	32.912	36.741	40.113	44.140	46.963	55.476
28	13.565	14.847	16.928	18.939	21.588	23.647	27.336	31.391	34.027	37.916	41.337	45.419	48.278	56.893
29	14.256	15.574	17.708	19.768	22.475	24.577	28.336	32.461	35.139	39.087	42.557	46.693	49.588	58.302
30	14.953	16.306	18.493	20.599	23.364	25.508	29.336	33.530	36.250	40.256	43.773	47.962	50.892	59.703

Source: Appendix D is reprinted from Table IV of R. A. Fisher and F. Yates, *Statistical Tables for Biological, Agricultural, and Medical Research* 6th edition © R.A. Fisher and F. Yates 1963. Reprinted by permission of Pearson Education Limited.

Note: For larger values of df, the expression $\sqrt{2x^2} - \sqrt{2df-1}$ may be used as a normal deviate with unit variance, remembering that the probability for χ^2 corresponds with that of a single tail of the normal curve.

Appendix E
Instructions for Performing Regression
Using Microsoft Excel

Open the Microsoft Excel program and enter the data to be analyzed in column format. (For directions on opening Excel and entering data refer to Box 2-1.)

EXAMPLE

Officials of the city of Prairie View, Wyoming, know that calls for police service are influenced by a variety of factors. Unemployment rates, youth population, and even the success of the local visitors' bureau in attracting tourists can influence demand for police service. City officials want to know how much of the demand is based on population growth alone. They wish to examine the correlation between Prairie View's calls for police service from fiscal year 1996 to fiscal year 2000 and total annual resident population.

The question officials wish to answer is: In what manner and to what extent does population directly affect police workload? To answer this question using Excel, key in the calls-for-service and population figures in the following column format:

Fiscal Year	Calls for Police Service	Prairie View Population
1999–2000	79,800	158,000
1998–1999	63,900	142,000
1997–1998	67,430	130,000
1996–1997	49,500	99,000
1995–1996	44,150	86,000

Once the data have been entered, go to the "Tools" option of Excel and select "Data Analysis." Once "Data Analysis" has been located, select "Regression" from the list of "Analysis Tools" and click "OK."

This appendix was prepared by Carla Pizzarella and Stacey Teachey.

If your system does not have a Data Analysis Option, it may be installed in the following manner:

On the "Tools" menu, click "Add-Ins."

If "Analysis ToolPak" is not listed in the "Add-Ins" dialog box, click "Browse" and locate the drive, folder name, and file name for the "Analysis ToolPak" add-in, Analys32.xll. This is usually located in the "Library/Analysis" folder—or it may be accessed through the "Setup" program if it is not installed.

Select the "Analysis ToolPak" check box.

The first step is to identify the input ranges for the data. The Y variable is the dependent variable. (The analysis focuses on determining whether the X variable influences or is related to Y.)

EXAMPLE

In the Prairie View example, the analysis is to determine if population has a direct effect on calls for police service.

Y variable = Column B, Calls for Police Service
X variable = Column C, Prairie View Population

In Excel, click in the "Input Y Range" box. Highlight the figures appearing in the Calls for Police Service column of the chart. The range of Y variables should appear within the "Input Y Range" box. Now, click in the "Input X Range" box.

Highlight the figures appearing in the population column of the chart. The range of X variables should appear within the "Input X Range" box.

Once these items are entered, look for the section of the "Regression" box titled "Residuals" (it should be two boxes below the input ranges.) Click on the box for "Residuals." A ☑ should appear. Click on the box for "Line Fit Plot." A ☑ should appear. Click on the "OK" button.

A new worksheet will be added to the workbook. The sheet will contain records of all the statistical data computed and analyzed by Excel when producing the regression chart. The regression chart should appear to the right of all the data tables.

To expand the chart, click on the bottom right corner of the chart. Black boxes should appear around the perimeter of the chart. Hold the left-mouse button down while positioned on the right bottom-corner black box. A double-sided arrow will appear. Pull the arrow down and to the right to enlarge the graph.

Note the legend appearing on the chart.

Dark Purple Diamonds = Y variable (Calls for Police Service)
Fuchsia Diamonds = the Predicted Y variable

The Predicted Y variable is the computer's prediction of Y values for various corresponding X values, given the relationship between actual Xs and Ys in this data set.

At this point, the chart can be "cleaned up" by taking a few extra steps:

- Change font size of all captions, so they will appear clearly on the chart.
- Change the "Y" label on the legend and chart, so they will reflect what has been designated as "Y." In the Prairie View example, "Y" would be changed to "Calls for Police Service."
- Change the "X Variable 1" so that it reflects what has been designated as "X." In the Prairie View example, "X" would be changed to "Prairie View Population."
- Change the title of the chart from "X Variable 1 Line Fit Plot" to better reflect what is being studied. In the Prairie View example, the chart title might be "Relationship Between Prairie View's Population and Calls for Police Service: FY 96 to FY 00."
- Using a text box, add a note under the legend that defines "Y." In the Prairie View example, the note might be, "Y = Calls for Police Service."
- Double-click on the fuchsia dots. The Format Data Series Window will pop up. Click on the tab for "Patterns." Go to the drop-down window for "Weight," and select the type of line wanted. This line will provide a "trend line" and make it easier to note the path of the Predicted Y.
- To change the minimum and maximum values appearing on the X and Y axes (for example, to display only the 40,000–160,000 range), double-click on the numbers that appear on a given axis. The "Format Axis" window will pop up. Adjust Maximum, Major Unit, and Minor Unit to the desired numbers. Click "OK." Perform the same process on the other axis.

At this point, the regression chart is complete. It is now time to analyze what has been produced.

Bibliography

Abrahams, Mark D., and Mary Noss Reavely. "Activity-Based Costing: Illustrations from the State of Iowa." *Government Finance Review* 14 (April 1998): 15–20.

Adams, A. T., D. S. F. Bloomfield, P. M. Booth, and P. D. England. *Investment Mathematics and Statistics*. London: Graham and Trotman, 1993.

Aft, Lawrence S. *Work Measurement and Methods Improvement*. New York: John Wiley and Sons, 2000.

Ammons, David N. *Municipal Benchmarks: Assessing Local Performance and Establishing Community Standards*, 2d ed. Thousand Oaks, Calif.: Sage Publications, 2001.

Ammons, David N., ed. *Accountability for Performance: Measurement and Monitoring in Local Government*. Washington, D.C.: International City/County Management Association, 1995.

Andersen, Bjorn, and Per-Gaute Pettersen. *The Benchmarking Handbook*. London: Chapman and Hall, 1996.

Anderson, Bridget M. "Using Activity-Based Costing for Efficiency and Quality." *Government Finance Review* (June 1993): 7–9.

Barnes, Ralph M. *Motion and Time Study: Design and Measurement of Work*. New York: John Wiley and Sons, 1980.

Berman, Evan M. *Productivity in Public and Nonprofit Organizations: Strategies and Techniques*. Thousand Oaks, Calif.: Sage Publications, 1998.

Bingham, Richard D., and Marcus E. Ethridge, eds. *Reaching Decisions in Public Policy and Administration: Methods and Applications*. New York: Longman, 1982.

Blalock, Hubert M., Jr. *Social Statistics*. New York: McGraw-Hill, 1979.

Brimson, James A., and John Antos. *Activity-Based Management for Service Industries, Government Entities, and Nonprofit Organizations*. New York: John Wiley and Sons, 1994.

Broom, Cheryle, Marilyn Jackson, Vera Vogelsang Coombs, and Jody Harris. *Performance Measurement: Concepts and Techniques*. Washington, D.C.: American Society for Public Administration, 1998.

Brown, Richard E., Mark J. Myring, and Cadillac G. Gard. "Activity-Based Costing in Government: Possibilities and Pitfalls." *Public Budgeting and Finance* 19 (summer 1999): 3–21.

Brown, Robert J., and Rudolph R. Yanuck. *Life Cycle Costing*. Atlanta, Ga.: Fairmont Press, 1980.

Camp, Robert C. *Benchmarking: The Search for Industry Best Practices That Lead to Superior Performance*. Milwaukee, Wis.: Quality Press, 1989.

Canada, John R., and John A. White. *Capital Investment Decision Analysis for Management and Engineering*. Englewood Cliffs, N.J.: Prentice-Hall, 1980.

City of Arlington (Texas) Parks and Recreation Department. *Program Division Benchmarking Projects*. Arlington, Tex.: Author, 1993.

City of Bellevue (Washington). "1998 Performance Measures." Bellevue, Washington: Author, 1998.

City of Kansas City Auditor's Office. *Kansas City, Missouri, Police Department Patrol Deployment: Blackout Analysis*. Kansas City, Mo.: Author, 1998.

———. *Performance Audit: Emergency Medical Services System*. Kansas City, Mo.: Author, 2000.

City of Milwaukee City Comptroller. *City of Milwaukee Citation Processing and Cash Management Costs and Benefits Audit*. Milwaukee, Wis., 1997.

City of Savannah (Georgia). *Operations Audit Review Program.* Savannah, Ga.: City of Savannah, Internal Audit Program, Reference 1512, December 2, 1991.

Clayton, Ross. "Techniques of Network Analysis for Managers." In *Managing Public Systems: Analytic Techniques for Public Administration,* ed. Michael J. White, Ross Clayton, Robert Myrtle, Gilbert Siegel, and Aaron Rose, 86–107. Lanham, Md.: University Press of America, 1985.

Coe, Charles K. *Maximizing Revenue, Minimizing Expenditure for Local Governments.* Athens: Institute of Government, University of Georgia, 1981.

———. *Public Financial Management.* Englewood Cliffs, N.J.: Prentice-Hall, 1989.

Cokins, Gary, Alan Stratton, and Jack Helbling. *An ABC Manager's Primer: Straight Talk on Activity-Based Costing.* Montvale, N.J.: Institute of Management Accountants, 1993.

Columbia University, Public Technology, Inc., and the International City Management Association. *Evaluating Residential Refuse Collection Costs: A Workbook for Local Government* and *Worksheet Supplement.* Washington, D.C.: Public Technology, Inc., 1978.

Cronk, Brian C. *How to Use SPSS: A Step-by-Step Guide to Analysis and Interpretation.* Los Angeles: Pyrczak Publishing, 1999.

Department of Defense. *Roads, Grounds, Pest Control and Refuse Collection Handbook: Engineered Performance Standards.* NAVFAC 0525-LP-156-0016. Washington, D.C.: U.S. Government Printing Office, 1984.

Department of the Navy. *Janitorial Handbook: Engineered Performance Standards.* NAVFAC 0525-LP-142-0061. Washington, D.C.: U.S. Government Printing Office, 1987.

Downs, George W., and Patrick D. Larkey. "Better Performance through Better Analysis: Nothing but the Facts." In *The Search for Government Efficiency: From Hubris to Helplessness,* 95–144. New York: Random House, 1986.

Eppen, G. D., F. J. Gould, C. P. Schmidt, Jeffrey H. Moore, and Larry R. Weatherford. *Introductory Management Science,* 5th ed. Upper Saddle River, N.J.: Prentice-Hall, 1998.

Fink, Arlene, and Jacqueline Kosecoff. *How to Conduct Surveys: A Step-by-Step Guide.* Thousand Oaks, Calif.: Sage Publications, 1998.

Folz, David H. *Survey Research for Public Administration.* Thousand Oaks, Calif.: Sage Publications, 1996.

Franke, Richard H., and James D. Kaul. "The Hawthorne Experiments: First Statistical Interpretation." *American Sociological Review* 43, 5 (October 1978): 623–643.

Freeman, Therese A., Ernest G. Niemi, and Peter M. Wilson. "Evaluating Public Expenditures: A Guide for Local Officials." In *Budget Management: A Reader in Local Government Financial Management,* ed. Jack Rabin, W. Bartley Hildreth, and Gerald J. Miller, 92–105. Athens, Ga.: Carl Vinson Institute of Government, University of Georgia, 1983.

Friedman, Marvin. "Calculating Compensation Costs." In *Budget Management: A Reader in Local Government Financial Management,* ed. Jack Rabin, W. Bartley Hildreth, and Gerald J. Miller, 116–127. Athens, Ga.: Carl Vinson Institute of Government, University of Georgia, 1983. Reprinted from *The Use of Economic Data in Collective Bargaining.* Washington, D.C.: U.S. Department of Labor, 1978.

Gecoma, Richard M., Arthur B. Mohor, and Michael G. Jackson. *Energy Efficient Purchasing for Local Governments.* Athens: Institute of Government, University of Georgia, 1980.

Gianakis, Gerasimos A., and Clifford P. McCue. In "Analytical Techniques." *Local Government Budgeting: A Managerial Approach,* 81–99. Westport, Conn.: Quorum Books, 1999.

Goldsmith, Stephen. "The ABCs of Competitive Government: The Indianapolis Experience." *Government Finance Review* 15, 5 (October 1999): 7–9.

Gramlich, Edward M. *Benefit-Cost Analysis of Government Programs.* Englewood Cliffs, N.J.: Prentice-Hall, 1981.

Groebner, David F., and Patrick W. Shannon. *Management Science.* New York: Macmillan/Dellen, 1992.

Groves, Sanford M., and Maureen Godsey Valente. *Evaluating Financial Condition: A Handbook for Local Government,* 2d ed. Washington, D.C.: International City/County Management Association, 1994.

Gupta, Dipak K. *Decisions by the Numbers: An Introduction to Quantitative Techniques for Public Policy Analysis and Management.* Englewood Cliffs, N.J.: Prentice-Hall, 1994.

Hatry, Harry P. *Performance Measurement: Getting Results.* Washington, D.C.: Urban Institute Press, 1999.

Hatry, Harry P., Louis H. Blair, Donald M. Fisk, John M. Greiner, John R. Hall Jr., and Philip S. Schaenman. *How Effective Are Your Community Services? Procedures for Measuring Their Quality,* 2d ed. Washington, D.C.: Urban Institute and International City/County Management Association, 1992.

Hatry, Harry P., Sumner N. Clarren, Therese van Houten, Jane P. Woodward, and Pasqual A. DonVito. "Cost Estimation Issues." In *Efficiency Measurement for Local Government Services,* 175–204. Washington, D.C.: Urban Institute, 1979.

Hatry, Harry P., John E. Marcotte, Therese van Houten, and Carol H. Weiss. *Customer Surveys for Agency Managers: What Managers Need to Know.* Washington, D.C.: Urban Institute Press, 1998.

Haynes, Patricia. "Industrial Engineering Techniques." In *Productivity Improvement Handbook for State and Local Government,* ed. George J. Washnis, 204–236. New York: John Wiley and Sons, 1980.

Hicks, Philip E. "Production Systems Design." In *Introduction to Industrial Engineering and Management Science,* 61–104. New York: McGraw-Hill, 1977.

Isom, Terry A., Shawn D. Halladay, Sudhir P. Amembal, R. Douglas Leininger, and Jonathan M. Ruga. *The Handbook of Equipment Leasing.* Salt Lake City, Utah: Amembal and Isom, 1988.

Kee, James E. "Benefit-Cost Analysis in Program Evaluation." In *Handbook of Practical Program Evaluation,* ed. Joseph S. Wholey, Harry P. Hatry, and Kathryn E. Newcomer, 456–488. San Francisco: Jossey-Bass, 1994.

Keehley, Patricia, Steven Medlin, Sue MacBride, and Laura Longmire. *Benchmarking for Best Practices in the Public Sector.* San Francisco: Jossey-Bass, 1997.

Kehoe, Joseph, William Dodson, Robert Reeve, and Gustav Plato. *Activity-Based Management in Government.* Washington, D.C.: Coopers and Lybrand, 1995.

Kelley, Joseph T. *Costing Government Services: A Guide for Decision Making.* Washington, D.C.: Government Finance Officers Association. 1984.

King County Auditor's Office. *Special Study: Motor Pool.* Seattle, Wash.: County Auditor's Office, Metropolitan King County, 1997.

Koehler, Jerry W., and Joseph M. Pankowski. *Continual Improvement in Government: Tools and Methods.* Delray Beach, Fla.: St. Lucie Press, 1996.

League of California Cities. *A Guide to Life Cycle Costing: A Purchasing Technique That Saves Money.* Sacramento: Author, December 1983. Reprinted as "Life Cycle Costing." In *Practical Financial Management: New Techniques for Local Government,* ed. John Matzer Jr. Washington, D.C.: International City Management Association, 1984.

Leazes, Francis J., Jr., and Carol W. Lewis. "Now You See It, Now You Don't." In *Casebook in Public Budgeting and Financial Management,* ed. Carol W. Lewis and A. Grayson Walker III, 189–194. Englewood Cliffs, N.J.: Prentice-Hall, 1984.

"Life Cycle Costing Saves Money for Albuquerque." *Public Works* 115 (June 1984): 100.

Lock, Dennis. *Project Management,* 6th ed. Brookfield, Vt.: Gower, 1996.

Malan, Roland M., James R. Fountain Jr., Donald S. Arrowsmith, and Robert L. Lockridge II. *Performance Auditing in Local Government.* Chicago: Government Finance Officers Association, 1984.

Manion, Patrick. "Work Measurement in Local Governments." *Management Information Service Report,* vol. 6, no. 10. Washington, D.C.: International City Management Association, 1974.

McGowan, Robert P., and Dennis P. Wittmer. "Five Great Issues in Decision Making." In *Handbook of Public Administration,* 2d ed., ed. Jack Rabin, W. Bartley Hildreth, and Gerald J. Miller, 293–319. New York: Marcel Dekker, 1998.

McKenna, Christopher K. *Quantitative Methods for Public Decision Making.* New York: McGraw-Hill, 1980.

Meier, Kenneth J., and Jeffrey L. Brudney. *Applied Statistics for Public Administration,* 4th ed. Fort Worth, Texas: Harcourt Brace, 1997.

Miller, Thomas I. "Designing and Conducting Surveys." In *Handbook of Practical Program Evaluation,* ed. Joseph S. Wholey, Harry P. Hatry, and Kathryn E. Newcomer, 271–292. San Francisco: Jossey-Bass, 1994.

Mitchell International. *Mechanical Labor Estimating Guide.* San Diego, Calif.: Mitchell International. (Updated annually.)

Morley, Elaine. *A Practitioner's Guide to Public Sector Productivity Improvement.* New York: Van Nostrand Reinhold Co., 1986.

MOTOR Labor Guide Manual. Troy, Mich.: Hearst Business Communications, Inc. (Updated annually.)

Mundel, Marvin E. *Motion and Time Study: Improving Productivity.* Englewood Cliffs, N.J.: Prentice-Hall, 1985.

Nyhan, Ronald C., and Lawrence L. Martin. "Assessing the Performance of Municipal Police Services Using Data Envelopment Analysis: An Exploratory Study." *State and Local Government Review* 31, 1 (winter 1999): 18–30.

Nyhan, Ronald C., and Lawrence L. Martin. "Comparative Performance Measurement: A Primer on Data Envelopment Analysis." *Public Productivity and Management Review* 22, 3 (March 1999): 348–364.

O'Sullivan, Elizabethann, and Gary R. Rassel. *Research Methods for Public Administrators,* 3d ed. New York: Longman, 1999.

Oregon Progress Board. *Achieving the Oregon Shines Vision: The 1999 Benchmark Performance Report.* Salem: Author, 1999.

Parsons, H. M. "What Caused the Hawthorne Effect?" *Administration and Society* 10 (November 1978): 259–283.

Poister, Theodore H. *Benchmarking the City of Atlanta's Performance in Selected Areas of Service Delivery.* Atlanta: Research Atlanta, Inc., and Georgia State University, School of Policy Studies, 1998.

Pritchard, Robert E., and Thomas J. Hindelang. *The Lease/Buy Decision.* New York: AMACOM, 1980.

R. S. Means Company. *Means Site Work Cost Data.* Kingston, Mass.: Author. (Updated annually.)

Renner, Tari. *Statistics Unraveled: A Practical Guide to Using Data in Decision Making.* Washington, D.C.: International City Management Association, 1988.

Rivenbark, William C., ed. *A Guide to the North Carolina Local Government Performance Measurement Project.* Chapel Hill: University of North Carolina Institute of Government, 2001.

Rivenbark, William C., and K. Lee Carter. "Benchmarking and Cost Accounting: The North Carolina Approach." *Journal of Public Budgeting, Accounting and Financial Management* 12 (spring 2000): 125–137.

Roethlisberger, F. J. *Management and Morale.* Cambridge, Mass.: Harvard University Press, 1941.

Ross, Sheldon M. *An Introduction to Mathematical Finance: Options and Other Topics.* Cambridge, U.K.: Cambridge University Press, 1999.

Sapsford, R. *Data Collection and Analysis.* Thousand Oaks, Calif.: Sage Publications, 1996.

Savas, E. S. *The Organization and Efficiency of Solid Waste Collection.* Lexington, Mass.: Lexington Books, 1977.

Schachter, Hindy Lauer. *Frederick Taylor and the Public Administration Community: A Reevaluation.* Albany: State University of New York Press, 1989.

Siegel, Gilbert B. "Seeing the Problem Systematically: Flowcharting." In *Managing Public Systems: Analytic Techniques for Public Administration,* ed. Michael J. White, Ross Clayton, Robert Myrtle, Gilbert Siegel, and Aaron Rose, 47–85. Lanham, Md.: University Press of America, 1985.

Siu, Stanley Y. "Performance Chart Increases Crew Productivity." *Journal of the American Water Works Association* 84, 2 (1992): 53–56.

Southern Growth Policies Board and Southern Consortium of University Public Service Organizations. "Benchmarking Best Practices." Module 2 of *Results-Oriented Government.* Research Triangle Park, N.C.: Southern Growth Policies Board, 1997.

Spendolini, Michael J. *The Benchmarking Book,* 2d ed. New York: AMACOM, 2000.

Starling, Grover. "Implementation and Evaluation." In *Managing the Public Sector,* 240–294. Chicago: Dorsey Press, 1986.

Summers, Michael R. *Analyzing Operations in Business: Issues, Tools, and Techniques.* Westport, Conn.: Quorum Books, 1998.

Taylor, Bernard W., III. *Introduction to Management Science,* 6th ed. Upper Saddle River, N.J.: Prentice-Hall, 1999.

Taylor, James. *A Survival Guide for Project Managers.* New York: AMACOM, 1998.

Teall, John L. *Financial Market Analytics.* Westport, Conn.: Quorum Books, 1999.

Thomas, Henry B., and Jeffrey I. Chapman. "Cost-Benefit Analysis: Theory and Use." In *Managing Public Systems: Analytic Techniques for Public Administration,* ed. Michael J. White, Ross Clayton, Robert Myrtle, Gilbert Siegel, and Aaron Rose, 291–318. Lanham, Md.: University Press of America, 1985.

Thomas, John S. "Operations Management: Planning, Scheduling, and Control." In *Productivity Improvement Handbook for State and Local Government,* ed. George J. Washnis, 171–203. New York: John Wiley and Sons, 1980.

Thomsett, Michael C. *The Mathematics of Investing: A Complete Reference.* New York: John Wiley and Sons, 1989.

Tigue, Patricia, and Dennis Strachota. *The Use of Performance Measures in City and County Budgets.* Chicago: Government Finance Officers Association, 1994.

Vogt, A. John. *A Manager's Guide to Local Government Capital Budgeting.* Washington, D.C.: International City/County Management Association, forthcoming.

Vogt, A. John, and Lisa A. Cole. *A Guide to Municipal Leasing.* Chicago: Municipal Finance Officers Association, 1983.

Vogt, A. John, and Samuel H. Owen Jr. "Cost Calculations for Lease-Purchase Decisions: Methods," 115–145, and "Cost Calculations for Lease-Purchase Decisions: Five Case Studies," 147–170. In *A Guide to Municipal Leasing,* ed. A. John Vogt and Lisa A. Cole. Chicago: Municipal Finance Officers Association, 1983.

Wallgren, A., B. Wallgren, R. Persson, U. Jorner, and J. A. Haaland. *Graphing Statistics and Data.* Thousand Oaks, Calif.: Sage Publications, 1996.

Walters, Jonathan. "The Benchmarking Craze." *Governing,* April 7, 1994, 33–37.

———. "Government by the Numbers." *Governing,* April 2000, 30–32.

Webb, Kenneth, and Harry P. Hatry. *Obtaining Citizen Feedback: The Application of Citizen Surveys to Local Governments.* Washington, D.C.: Urban Institute, 1973.

Weimer, David L., and Aidan R. Vining. *Policy Analysis: Concepts and Practice,* 2d ed. Englewood Cliffs, N.J.: Prentice-Hall, 1992.

Weisberg, H. F., J. A. Krosnick, and B. D. Brown. *An Introduction to Survey Research, Polling and Data Analysis.* Thousand Oaks, Calif.: Sage Publications, 1996.

Weiss, Barbara. *Activity-Based Costing and Management: Issues and Practices in Local Government.* Chicago: Government Finance Officers Association, 1997.

Welch, Susan, and John Comer. *Quantitative Methods for Public Administration: Techniques and Applications.* Chicago: Dorsey, 1988.

White, Michael J., Ross Clayton, Robert Myrtle, Gilbert Siegel, and Aaron Rose. *Managing Public Systems: Analytic Techniques for Public Administration.* Lanham, Md.: University Press of America, 1985.

Wholey, Joseph S., Harry P. Hatry, and Kathryn E. Newcomer, eds. *Handbook of Practical Program Evaluation.* San Francisco: Jossey-Bass, 1994.

Winslow, R., B. Morrow, R. Carbone, and E. Cross. *Life-Cycle Costing for Procurement of Small Buses.* Washington, D.C.: U.S. Department of Transportation, 1980.

Wubbenhorst, Klaus L. "Life Cycle Costing for Construction Projects." *Long Range Planning* 19 (August 1986): 87–97.

Zemansky, Stanley D. "Life-Cycle Cost Procurement." In Joseph T. Kelley, *Costing Government Services: A Guide for Decision Making,* 115–139. Washington, D.C.: Government Finance Officers Association, 1984.

Index